1991

LEADING CASES IN THE
COMMON LAW

Leading Cases in the Common Law

A. W. BRIAN SIMPSON

CLARENDON PRESS · OXFORD
1995

Oxford University Press, Walton Street, Oxford OX2 6DP
Oxford New York
Athens Auckland Bangkok Bombay
Calcutta Cape Town Dar es Salaam Delhi
Florence Hong Kong Istanbul Karachi
Kuala Lumpur Madras Madrid Melbourne
Mexico City Nairobi Paris Singapore
Taipei Tokyo Toronto
and associated companies in
Berlin Ibadan

Oxford is a trade mark of Oxford University Press

Published in the United States
by Oxford University Press Inc., New York

British Library Cataloguing in Publication Data
Data available

Library of Congress Cataloging in Publication Data
Simpson, A. W. B. (Alfred William Brian)
Leading cases in the common law / A. W. Brian Simpson.
p. cm.
Includes bibliographical references and index.
1. Common law—Great Britain—Cases. 2. Common law—United
States—Cases. I. Title.
KD671.A7S56 1995
340.57′0941—dc20 95–5089
ISBN 0–19–825852–6

1 3 5 7 9 10 8 6 4 2

Typeset by Graphicraft Typesetters Ltd., Hong Kong
Printed in Great Britain
on acid-free paper by
Biddles Ltd., Guildford and King's Lynn

For Timothy, Zoë, and Jane

Preface

THIS book contains studies of a number of leading cases, written, I hope, in a style which will make them acceptable both to readers who are expert in the branch of law to which they belong, and to those who are not. They do not follow any uniform scheme, but in all of them I have tried to recreate the original historical context of the litigation, in so far as the sources make this possible. I have also tried to address more general questions about the cases which I have selected, and to give an account of their subsequent life in the history of law and legal thought. Was *Shelley's Case* (1581) really a product of the doctrines of property law, or was it perhaps a political decision? Is it possible to tell? How does an antique quarrel about the capture of wild ducks, *Keeble* v. *Hickeringill* (1707), retain an educational and doctrinal significance nearly three centuries later? Was the very absurdity of *Jee* v. *Audley* (1787) perhaps its guarantee of immortality? Whatever happened about accidents at work before *Priestley* v. *Fowler* (1837), and what induced the victim's father in that case to take the unprecedented step of suing his employer for damages in tort law? Why did the case of *Raffles* v. *Wichelhaus and Busch* (1864) ever come to court, and why did a case which includes no judicial opinion whatsoever become a focus of academic interest, principally fuelled by ignorance? What light does a historical analysis of *Tipping* v. *St Helen's Smelting Company* (1865) throw upon economic theories as to how nuisance cases arising out of conflicting land uses ought to be decided? Was the decision in *Rylands* v. *Fletcher* (1868) really about Mr Ryland's unprepossessing and still defective reservoir? What has the case of *R.* v. *Keyn* (1876) to tell us about the value and the possibility of the ideal of the rule of law? What is the relationship between quack medicine, *Carlill* v. *Carbolic Smoke Ball Company* (1893), and the dogmatics of contract law?

Underlying these and other questions which I ask in this book lies a philosophical interest in the casuistic processes of the common law, and a belief that the understanding of judicial decisions is little furthered by the elaboration of imaginative abstract theories, which have little connection with anything but themselves.

So this book, like two others I have written, offers at one level a criticism of the deeply anti-empirical tradition of the world of academic law and legal theory. At a less solemn level I hope it may show that we can obtain greater enjoyment and instruction from the study of cases if we discover more about them than is provided by law reports.

Three of the chapters in this book are based upon articles which have previously appeared in legal journals. I have made some modifications to enhance readability. These include reducing the bulk of footnotes; those who need fuller documentation can use the original versions. Chapter 6 is based upon 'Contracts for Cotton to Arrive: The Case of the Two Ships *Peerless*', which appeared in the *Cardozo Law Review* in 1989, and is published with the permission of that journal.[1] Chapter 8 is based upon 'Legal Liability for Bursting Reservoirs: The Historical Context of *Rylands* v. *Fletcher*', which appeared in the *Journal of Legal Studies* in 1984.[2] Chapter 10 is based upon 'Quackery and Contract Law: The Case of the Carbolic Smoke Ball', which appeared in the same journal in 1985.[3] These two chapters are here published with the permission of the University of Chicago Press. Chapter 5 is based upon an inaugural lecture delivered in the University of Cambridge, and Chapter 9 began life as a Selden Society lecture.

The research for this book has been supported by the University of Michigan Law School, and earlier by the Nuffield Trust. A large number of individuals have also helped; I should particularly mention Mr Christopher Aggs, Dean Douglas G. Baird, Professor John H. Baker, Professor Mary E. Becker, Mr A. M. Berrett, Mrs Anil T. Blundell, Mrs Paula Bryars, Mr L. W. Capes, Miss Elizabeth Carlill, Mr Peter D. R. Carlill, the Revd J. H. C. Davies, Professor Charles Donahue, Professor Richard A. Epstein, Dr D. A. Farnie, Mrs G. Foyle, Mr G. M. Binnie, Professor Richard H. Helmholz, Mr S. Geoffrey Holland, Professor Dennis Hutchinson, Dr David Ibbetson, Mr C. P. C. Johnson, Mr R. C. B. Jones, Mrs Vivienne Jones, Mr H. Kent, Professor John H. Langbein, Mrs Hilda Lawn, Dr Geoffrey Marston, Mr G. Mast, Dr Boye Meyer-Friese, Dr Eric Poole, Miss Ruth Tinley, Mrs Victoria M. Tipping, Dr R. F. Van der Sluis, and Mr Alan Watson. I am also grateful as ever to Margaret Leary, Director of the University of Michigan Law Library, and to all those who work in that remarkable institution, in particular Barbara Vaccaro and the research librarians, and to the staff of the Public Record Office, the House of Lords Records Office, and the Essex, Lincolnshire, Northamptonshire, Shropshire, Staffordshire, and West Sussex Record Offices.

Finally I am most grateful to John Whelan, my editor, and to Hilary Walford and Kate Elliott for converting an untidy manuscript into a book.

Illustrations number 1 and 3 are reproduced by permission of the National Monuments Record, illustration number 2 by permission of the British Library, illustration number 6 by permission of the National Maritime Museum, and illustration number 8 by permission of the Manchester Public Libraries.

Crown copyright material in the Public Record Office is reproduced by permission of the controller of Her Majesty's Stationery Office.

A. W. B. S.

---

[1] 11: 287.   [2] 13: 209, copyright 1984 University of Chicago.
[3] 14: 345, copyright 1989 University of Chicago.

Contents

List of Illustrations

Abbreviations

APC	Acts of the Privy Council
ASSI	Assize Records (in PRO)
B	Bankruptcy (in PRO)
BL	British Library
BLSH	*Boston, Louth and Spalding Herald*
BPP	British Parliamentary Papers
BT	Board of Trade (in PRO)
BT	Bishop's Transcripts
C	Chancery (in PRO)
CA	Court of Appeal
CAR	Calendar of Assize Records
CCC	Cox's Criminal Cases
CCCR	Court of Crown Cases Reserved
CLJ	*Cambridge Law Journal*
Cmnd.	Command Paper
CO	Colonial Office (in PRO)
CPR	Calendar of Patent Rolls
CUL	Cambridge University Library
DPP	Director of Public Prosecutions (in PRO)
DRO	Diocescan Record Office
E	Exchequer (in PRO)
EC	Exchequer Chamber
ER	English Reports
EC	Exchequer Chamber
ERO	Essex Record Office
FO	Foreign Office (in PRO)
GLR	*Georgia Law Review*
HMC	Historical Manuscripts Commission
HO	Home Office (in PRO)
IGI	International Genealogical Index
ILN	*Illustrated London News*
IND	Index (in PRO)
IPM	Inquisition *post mortem*
IUP	Irish Universities Press
J	Supreme Court of Judicature (in PRO)
JLE	*Journal of Law and Economics*
JLS	*Journal of Legal Studies*
JRH	*Journal of Recusant History*

LBGNG	*Lincoln, Boston, Gainsborough Newark Gazette*
LBNG	*Lincoln Boston and Newark Gazette*
LBNTG	*Lincoln, Boston and Newark Tuesday's Gazette*
LCC	Lincoln Consistory Court
LCGA	*Lincoln Chronicle and General Advertiser*
LJRO	Lichfield Joint Record Office
LQR	*Law Quarterly Review*
LRO	Lincoln Record Office
LRSM	*Lincoln Rutland and Stamford Mercury*
MH	Ministry of Health (in PRO)
MLR	*Modern Law Review*
MR	Master of the Rolls
MT	Ministry of Transport (in PRO)
NRO	Northamptonshire Record Office
NP	Nisi prius
OBSP	Old Bailey Sessions Papers
OED	*Oxford English Dictionary*
OJLS	*Oxford Journal of Legal Studies*
OS	Ordnance Survey
PCC	Prerogative Court of Canterbury
PP	Parliamentary Papers
PRO	Public Record Office
PROB	Probate (in PRO)
RCNV	Royal Commission on Noxious Vapours
RG	Record Group (in PRO)
SAC	Sussex Archaeological Society
SCNV	Select Committee on Noxious Vapours
SHRO	Shropshire Record Office
SOED	*Shorter Oxford English Dictionary*
SP	State Papers (in PRO)
SRS	Sussex Record Society
SS	Selden Society
STAC	Star Chamber (in PRO)
UCINLR	*University of Cincinnati Law Review*
UCL	University College London
UCLR	*University of Chicago Law Review*
VCH	*Victoria County History*
WSRO	West Sussex Record Society
YLJ	*Yale Law Journal*

I

The Study of Cases

Records and Law Reports

When Chaucer, in the *Prologue* to his *Canterbury Tales*, set out to give a convincing picture of the Serjeant at Law, the only hardware, as we might now call it, which he described him as possessing was a set of law reports:

> In bookes had he cas and doomes alle,
> That from the time of King Willyam had yfalle.

The serjeant also needed ready access to statutory texts, but these he had off by heart. Today, and indeed for many centuries, the common law system has been the product of a prolonged exercise in casuistry, an activity more generally associated with moral reasoning.[1] The judges, by deciding particular cases presented to them in litigation, respecting the claims, often conflicting, of consistency and rationality, have provided the raw materials from which has been built up a system of law. This system, the common law, evolved out of the traditional practices followed in the Royal Courts in resolving disputes. One way in which we can view the common law, conceived as a complex body of abstract doctrine, is as a way of thinking about, of conceptualizing, or rationalizing what has traditionally been done. Courts decide those few disputes which cannot otherwise be settled, and the notion of a decision is everywhere problematic. Anyone who has worked, for example, in a large organization will be familiar with the problem of discovering who actually takes the decisions, and why, and when, and where, and with the fact that they themselves never seem to be involved. It is hardly surprising that the relationship between judicial decisions, free will, and abstract legal doctrine, has long been a subject of a theoretical dispute which shows no sign of ending.

High theory has never caused much anxiety to practical lawyers, and since Chaucer's time, and indeed long before, the study of cases has been the principal mechanism whereby a person came to rank as a truly learned lawyer, and to understand, or perhaps we should say become indoctrinated in, the artificial reason of the law. Cases, apart from being simply remembered, are preserved in two different legal forms. One is on the formal record of the court. Originally the only record of the decision might be the memory of the judges and court

---

[1] See on the history E. Leites (ed.), *Conscience and Casuistry in Early Modern Europe* (Cambridge, 1988); A. R. Jonsen and S. Toulmin, *The Abuse of Casuistry: A History of Moral Reasoning* (Cambridge, 1988).

officials. But from a very early period the Royal Courts adopted the practice of keeping a written record, in Latin, of the formal stages in the litigation and its outcome, if there was one. The record was kept on sheepskin, which is extraordinarily long-lasting. Tons of court records survive in the Public Record Office, the contribution to legal history of an untold multitude of deceased sheep. But the story provided by the record is very artificially restricted, a product of the elaborate procedural rules which governed litigation. The record tells you what was decided, but little of why the decision went the way it did.

So far as the profession was concerned there was another difficulty. The record was retained by the courts, and although court lawyers could obtain access to them, or select extracts, there was no possibility of the record becoming a published text. The sheer volume of litigation ruled that out. In any event much of what was recorded was of a routine nature, and of no particular general interest or value.

Hence it came about that during the second half of the thirteenth century a different form of text evolved, hand in hand with the evolution of the learned legal profession which it helped to make possible. This was the law report, which principally records things which were said by judges and counsel in the course of court proceedings. Incidentally reports often give so much of the story of the case and the formal steps taken as seems necessary to enable the reader to understand the conversations and exchanges which are the principal subject matter of the report. Little is known about the provenance of early law reports; some may have been produced as teaching instruments, some by lawyers for personal self-improvement, some may have been in the nature of legal diaries— all sorts of miscellaneous information and gossip is to be found in them. Though many have survived, the vast majority have perished, and with them the chance of fully understanding the way in which they were produced.

The Function of Law Reports

Over the course of the centuries the form and character of law reports have changed considerably. But their basic function and relationship to the court record have not significantly varied. This, as Sir William Blackstone said in his *Commentaries on the Laws of England*, was to *explain* the decisions preserved in the record of the court. He indeed neatly described the whole system:

And thus much for the first ground and chief corner stone of the laws of England, which is, general immemorial custom or common law, from time to time declared in the decisions of the courts of justice; *which decisions are preserved among our public records, explained in our reports, and digested for general use in the authoritative writings of the venerable sages of the law.*[2]

---

[2] Blackstone, *Commentaries on the Laws of England* (London, 1765–9), i. 73.

The record told you what was done, the law report helped you to understand why. This explanatory function is related to a dogmatic theory of the nature of court decisions. The theory starts from the assumption that any dispute which comes before a court must involve either a dispute about the facts of the matter, as to what actually happened, or a dispute as to the law which is applicable to those facts. Courts apply law to facts. With factual disputes, typically determined by juries, and earlier by God, lawyers, as such, had no particular interest or concern. Only when lawyers became advocates was this to change. The professional expertise of a lawyer lay in his knowledge and understanding of the law, which provides the correct solution of any legal dispute. The point of studying cases through reading law reports was to achieve knowledge and understanding of the law, and skill in applying it to the myriad circumstances of life, an activity exemplified in reported cases. It was this knowledge, understanding, and skill which constituted the common learning of the legal profession—'the established wisdom of the little intellectual world of Westminster Hall'.[3]

The further dogmatic assumption was made that, except in cases where errors occur—for the judges, though oracles of the law, were human and fallible—cases actually were decided in conformity with the common law. By reading the exchanges between expert judges and counsel, understood in the context of the facts of particular cases, readers of law reports could both understand why the case was decided in the way it was and, by intelligent imitation, learn to apply the law correctly themselves. Thus they could in time become learned lawyers.

The volume of cases was so large that there was no way in which a lawyer could study them all. Law reporting has of necessity always been selective; the cases which are reported are those which raise novel questions, 'cases of first impression', or particularly tricky points, or those in which professional opinion is divided, 'borderline' cases, 'arguable' cases. In modern times R. M. Dworkin has, somewhat oddly, popularized the expression 'hard case', which used to mean a case in which the application of the law caused hardship.[4] But even with selection, the volume of reported cases became very large, and the profession adjusted to the groaning shelves of the law library in a variety of ways. One was to produce systematically arranged abridgements of cases, works such as Anthony Fitzherbert's *Grand Abridgement* (1514–16), or Charles Viner's twenty-three volume *General Abridgement of Law and Equity* (1741–53). Another was for the venerable sages of the law to summarize the learning to be found in the cases in systematic legal treatises, a practice which largely dates from the late eighteenth century.[5] In the nineteenth century a new solution to the problem became fashionable. This claimed that the right way to acquire a mastery of legal principles

---

[3] See J. H. Baker, *An Introduction to English Legal History*, 226.
[4] Hence 'hard cases make bad law'—hard cases provoke sympathy which distorts the law.
[5] Explored in my 'The Rise and Fall of the Legal Treatise: Legal Principles and the Forms of Legal Literature' (1981) 48 *UCLR*, 632, reprinted in *Legal Theory and Legal History. Essays on the Common Law* (London, 1987), Ch. 12.

was not to read large numbers of cases, but rather to concentrate attention upon the limited number of 'leading' cases which provided the best illustrations of their application, or those in which a principle was first clearly expounded. In much the same way one might master a language by concentrating upon its best writers. All the cases studied in this book rank in legal pedagogy as leading cases.

The Invention of Leading Cases

In the nineteenth century, both in England and the United States, it was usual for common lawyers to believe, as they had believed in the past, that the law consisted in principles, whose application in specific circumstances was exemplified in law reports. It became common to apply the term 'science' to the knowledge and understanding of these principles. Versions of the theory of legal science are by no means extinct. Indeed as I write this book I hold the Goodhart Chair of Legal Science in the University of Cambridge, endowed by a noted American legal scholar, the late Arthur Lehman Goodhart (1891–1978), so it would hardly be appropriate for me to suggest that legal science is dead. Indeed a flamboyant modern version of the theory, law as integrity, has been fairly recently published in R. M. Dworkin's very successful *Law's Empire* (1986), which has, as it were, reassured many lawyers that what they have always believed was true after all. Theories of legal science could be developed in various ways, but the central idea was that the law which the courts—if we really believe in the rule of law—apply in the resolution of disputes is derivative of certain basic or fundamental legal principles, and the expertise of the professional lawyer consists in his knowledge and understanding of these principles, and his skill in working out how they should properly be applied to the complexities of life. These principles underlie the practice of the courts in much the same way as the principles of language underlie the process of human communication, and only experts can identify and formulate them correctly. The theory provided a clear programme for legal education, set out in lyrical prose in 1892 by Professor the Honourable Edward J. Phelps of the Yale Law School, now a somewhat forgotten figure, but in his day by no means negligible:

The very first and indispensable requisite in legal education ... is the acquisition of a clear and accurate perception, a complete knowledge, a strong and tenacious grasp of those unchangeable principles of the common law which underlie and permeate its whole structure, and which control all its details, its consequences, its applications to human affairs.[6]

One source wherein which these principles could be sought was reported cases, but it was conceded that the task was not a simple one. As M. Dawes, a barrister of the Inner Temple, explained in his *Epitome of the Law of Landed Property*,

---

[6] (1892) 1 *YLJ* 139 at 140.

a beginners' work published in 1818: 'the first principles of the science are obscured by their bulk . . . Every science has its rudiments; and the law, like a river which never runs back to its source, expands and deepens in its current, and grows more and more arduous to fathom.' Versions of the theory of legal science underpinned the nineteenth-century flowering of the practice of writing legal treatises, which claimed to set out, explain, illustrate, and systematize the basic principles of different branches of the law, and, if possible, enunciate clearly the rules of law which could be derived from them.[7] In the reports of cases extending back into the Middle Ages could be found both authority and illustration of the principles and rules of law, as well as examples of situations in which the judges, who were human and fallible, had made occasional mistakes in the task of refinement and application.

A version of legal science became associated with the Harvard Law School where, in the 1870s, Christopher Columbus Langdell, who had become Dane Professor on 6 January 1870, and Dean in the following September, pioneered the case system of instruction, which came to dominate legal education in American law schools. Langdell believed that:

the number of fundamental legal doctrines is much less than is commonly supposed; the many different guises in which the same doctrine is constantly making its appearance, and the great extent to which legal treatises are a repetition of each other, being the cause of much misapprehension.[8]

He thought that law students, if given a selection of leading cases to study in class under the supervision of a professor, could be trained to become legal scientists themselves, learning how to tease out the principles from the cases, and how to apply them to the complex disputes which were presented to courts in litigation.

Langdell did not however invent the idea of publishing collections of 'leading cases'. It was suggested by Samuel Warren, best known for his novel *Ten Thousand a Year*. He also published *A Popular and Practical Introduction to Law Studies* (1835), a work designed 'to smooth the rugged access to legal science'.[9] In it, as he later wrote, he had extolled the value to the law student and practitioner 'of early mastery, as so many nuclei of future legal acquisitions, a few of the "leading cases" in the Law Reports'.[10] He assured his student

---

[7] See n. 5 above and 'Legal Iconoclasts and Legal Ideals', 58 *UCINLR* V 819.

[8] C. Langdell, *A Selection of Cases on the Law of Contracts* (Boston, Mass., 1871), vi–vii.

[9] At vi (1807–67); special pleader, 1831–7, barrister on the northern circuit, master in lunacy 1859–77. See *DNB*.

[10] S. Warren's *Memorial of John William Smith of the Inner Temple*, from *Blackwood's Magazine*, in S. Warren, *Miscellaneous Critical, Imaginative, and Juridical Contributions to Blackwood's Magazine*. Although the expression 'leading case' did not become common until the nineteenth century it can be found much earlier in the sense of a decision which would lead other cases to follow it. See *Golding* v. *Griffin* (1612–13) C 33/123 at fo. 413. I am indebted through Professor J. H. Baker to Mr Neil Jones for this reference; Professor Baker has seen an earlier instance but has mislaid the reference.

readers: 'Fifty or sixty leading cases, thoroughly understood and distinctly rec-ollected, will be found of incalculable value in practice—serving as so many landmarks upon the trackless wilds of the law.'[11] He was a friend of John W. Smith.[12] His depiction of him, and of his deathbed (Smith's last thought was on the forms of action), sometimes suggests that with such a friend Smith had no need for enemies:

His personal appearance was, it must be candidly owned, certainly insignificant and unprepossessing. He was of slight make, a trifle under middle height, his hair was rather light, and his complexion pale. He wore spectacles, being excessively near-sighted, and had a slight cast in his eyes, which were rather full and prominent. The expression of his features, at all events in repose, was neither intellectual nor engaging, but improved when he was animated or excited in his conversation . . . When he shook hands with you he placed his cold hand into yours, like a dead man's hand—even with his most intimate friends.[13]

But Smith, whose retreating forehead some, Warren conceded, thought intellec-tual, had established a reputation through his *Compendium of Mercantile Law* (1834), and he took up Warren's idea, publishing between 1835 and 1840 his two-volume *Leading Cases in Various Branches of the Law*. This was praised by many English judges and by the great American Justice Story, who wrote to congratulate him. The work went through many editions, thirteen in England, the last in 1929, and nine in America, the last in 1888. It was imitated by other writers, as by J. I. Clark Hare and H. B. Wallace, editors of the English edition, in their *American Leading Cases* (1847), which had by 1871 reached its fifth edition, and by Frederick T. White and Owen D. Tudor with their *A Selection of Leading Cases in Equity* (1847).

Hare and Wallace waxed eloquent on the merits of Smith's system, which they viewed as the answer to the ever increasing numbers of reported cases: 'Where then, and how, is relief to be found in this never-ending still-beginning projection of new cases. Nohow and nowhere, manifestly, but in the system which the evil has suggested . . . the system of LEADING CASES.' They were 'the great "lighthouses of the law", which never fail, are never dimmed, and are most visible in those times when the need for guide is mostly felt'. So it was that the notion of a leading case became part of legal culture.

Christopher Columbus Langdell's achievement was to marry the idea of a leading case to an educational technique, the case system of instruction. He chose contract law as the vehicle for this experiment in legal education. In the hands of Langdell, who, to judge from his portrait, was by no means as un-prepossessing as Smith, the theory of legal science, dinned into the students

---

[11] 1835 ed. at 434.   [12] 1809–45.

[13] 1845, written after Smith's death from consumption; reprinted in S. Warren, *Miscellaneous Critical, Imaginative and Juridical Contributions to Blackwood's Magazine* (London, 1855), i. 116. Smith was also an indifferent poet.

through his and other classes, was coupled to the idea that, although it was easy to make mistakes, there was, at least in principle, a correct answer to every legal problem. Since Langdell's students apparently found some difficulty in extracting the principles correctly from the cases, he soon provided them with a handy guide, a summary of the law of contract, which was appended to the second edition of his case book.[14] To this day the case class system only works in the American law schools because students make use of various commercially produced summaries of the law, 'nutshells', 'Gilberts', and the like, which serve to redress the disorderly confusion of the case book from which it is pretended that they learn the law.

Iconoclastic Theories of Legal Decision

The belief in legal science, in the deep principles of the common law, which underlies the conception of the leading case remains, as I have said, very influential today. There has long, however, existed an iconoclastic tradition which either wholly or partially rejects the theory of legal science.[15] Rival theories have arisen in the legal community, and today part of the normal education of a lawyer is devoted to learning something about such theories, normally at a very abstract level. They purport to deal in reality, with the implication that legal science belongs to the world of myth or fiction. They tell us that the real explanation for a particular decision may not be the brooding omnipresence of the law, but politics, or class, or the relentless operation of the principle of economic efficiency, or even the effects of the judge's breakfast upon his temper—the latter being offered as a parody of the views associated with the American writers who thought of themselves as legal realists. In some versions of iconoclasm it is said that decisions just cannot, as a matter of logic, be determined by legal principles, because the principles are inherently indeterminate and inherently contradictory. Weaker versions may claim that although the legal scientist's ideal picture of legal decision is at least possible of attainment in some cases, it breaks down when we come to borderline cases.

In reaction to the modern sceptics R. M. Dworkin has boldly tried to establish a new version of legal science: there really is a uniquely 'correct' answer to all legal problems, though unhappily no way of telling if it has been discovered.[16] It is all rather like the crock of gold at the end of the rainbow. So today, so far as judicial decisions are concerned, there are plenty of competing theories of

---

[14] (1879) See below 158.
[15] See my 'Legal Iconoclasts and Legal Ideals' (1990) 58 *UCINLR* 819.
[16] Various versions of his views are to be found in R. M. Dworkin, *A Matter of Principle* (Cambridge, Mass., 1955), 115, 'Is There Really No Right Answer in Hard Cases?' in *Law's Empire* (London, 1986); and in M. Cohen (ed.), *Ronald Dworkin and Contemporary Jurisprudence* (London, 1984), where he replies to critics.

judicial decision on offer, and you pays your money and you takes your choice. None of this theorizing has, of course, the least effect on the actual practices of courts. Its function is primarily either that of legitimating or that of de-legitimating court decisions. It is conceivable that some such theorizing might, over a long period, alter the conventions of legal argument and justification, or even affect the outcome of cases; in one essay R. M. Dworkin has tried to persuade the English profession to be more like the American.[17] It is also conceivable that iconoclastic theories may, by offering alternative ways of thinking and talking about legal decisions, enhance understanding of them, though I rather doubt this: it surely does not require philosophy to tell us, for example, that if a judge is in a bad temper, or has been offered a bribe, or has a hangover, or dislikes women—this may affect his decisions.

Empiricism and the Study of Cases

One might expect that those who theorize about judicial decisions would seek confirmation, or at least illustration, of their theories in careful empirical studies of cases, which tried to flesh out the idea that decisions might, or might not, be the product of forces other than commitment to some ideal of the rule of law. Some theorists have claimed to do this; thus Dworkin opens one essay by asking 'first . . . a practical question about how judges *do* and should decide hard cases. *Do judges in the United States and Great Britain make political decisions?*'[18] In practice, however, they have shown little dedication to such investigations, and the reality of the matter seems to be that theories of judicial decision are, in general, not empirical in character at all, but philosophical. They deal, that is to say, in a curious sort of therapy, whose function it is to allay intellectual anxieties generated by the language we use to talk about the activities of courts, or to participate in the process of legal argument and justification. Many of these anxieties can be expressed in the form of conundrums. How can courts be said to be bound by earlier decisions if they decide which decisions are binding? How can the theory that courts ought not to make law be reconciled with the admission that cases are a source of law? How can tricky cases be decided under the rule of law if there is no right answer to all legal problems? How can we be sure that the reasons a court gives for its decision are the real reasons, given the fact that a judge may not reveal what his real reasons are, or even, sometimes, be aware of them?

There have been exceptions to the general lack of interest in empirical investigation of cases. The most notable modern example is J. A. G. Griffith's *The Politics of the Judiciary*.[19] In part this is philosophical in character; it attacks the

---

[17] *A Matter of Principle*, ch. 1.   [18] Ibid., 9 (my italics).
[19] It is difficult now to appreciate the hostile reaction in some quarters to this book when it first appeared.

'myth' of judicial neutrality, that is to say a certain conventional way of talking and thinking about the process of judicial decision, and part of the argument consists in an attempt to show, by the analysis of a considerable number of legal decisions, mostly of fairly recent date so that their historical context is part of common knowledge, that judges have given effect to a certain shared vision of the public interest which can sensibly be called a political view. There have been other examples of such work, but they have not been common. One distinguished study of the significance of the notion of the rule of law which is empirically based is the by-product of a piece of history—E. P. Thompson's *Whigs and Hunters: The Origin of the Black Act.*[20]

It is perhaps a matter of preference, but it seems to me to be far more illuminating than the philosophical writings on the subject, which are largely unconnected with reality.

Vulgar Curiosity and its Theoretical Antidote

The starting-point for the study of a number of leading cases which are presented in this book has not been the desire to develop some general philosophical theory of judicial decision, as therapy either for myself or for others. Instead it was initially mere curiosity. I first embarked upon work of this kind through curiosity about *R. v. Dudley and Stephens* (1884),[21] the case in which the sailors killed and ate the ship's boy and were tried and convicted of murder. It was the first law case I ever studied. Who were these men? What on earth were they doing in the South Atlantic in a yacht? Why did it founder? Why did they not keep quiet about the whole affair, given the fact that the principal evidence against them had been consumed? Why just six months' imprisonment? What became of them afterwards? Only, as it seemed to me, by answering these questions could this weird case be understood. A more recent book on wartime detention without trial[22] again started with curiosity about the case of *Liversidge v. Anderson* (1941),[23] curiosity heightened when I discovered that Professors R. F. V. Heuston and De Lloyd Guth had located Robert Liversidge in Vancouver alive, well, and still very understandably cross about his detention. Who was he? Why was he detained? Why were the authorities so keen to withhold information about detainees from the judges? What had they got to hide? And once you begin to investigate such matters new questions emerge—in the case of wartime detention, for example, why did the law officers present one view of the relationship between regulation 18B and the courts in the case of Aubrey Lees in 1940,[24] and an entirely different one in the cases of Robert Liversidge and Ben

---

[20] See Ch. 10.   [21] 14 QBD 273. See my *Cannibalism and the Common Law*.
[22] See my *In the Highest Degree Odious. Detention without Trial in Wartime Britain*.
[23] [1942] AC 284.   [24] [1941] 1 KB 72.

Greene[25] in 1941? And who, for that matter, was Ben Greene, and why was he locked up?

There is indeed something at first very peculiar about the tradition, in legal academia, of suppressing curiosity about cases. Both modern and ancient cases are, at least as a general rule, studied without anyone knowing or indeed caring who the litigants were, why they litigated, what they were trying to achieve, what they did achieve, except in so far as this happens to be public knowledge, as it often will be with very modern cases. Much less is it the general practice to relate cases to their general historical context, which is often quite unknown to those who read older decisions. Was Christopher Hill perhaps correct when he described Chief Justice Coke as a lawyer, but not an intellectual? Is the explanation perhaps architectural: that the law library is not simply the lawyer's laboratory but also his intellectual prison? Or is it perhaps mere inertia, or the cost of rail travel, which explains the fact that the case papers relating to the House of Lords decision in *Duncan* v. *Cammell Laird* (1942),[26] the starting-point for the modern law on Crown privilege (as I write a subject of considerable public interest), have remained unconsulted in the Public Record Office for years.

I prefer an explanation which is theoretical. In the received theory of adjudication, most contextual information about cases is simply irrelevant. As I have said, most lawyers, and indeed most academic lawyers, have little interest in high theory, and function satisfactorily without possessing a very fully worked-out theory of judicial decision. Like bumble bees, they manage to fly in spite of the theoretical difficulties in explaining how they manage to do it. But they do have a theory in the sense of a belief that certain factors, loosely defined by the conventions of legal argument, ought to be irrelevant to the decision of cases. And from this it is a small step to suppose that they are irrelevant to the doctrinal understanding of cases. For lawyers, to quote E. P. Thompson, writing in 1975 of what he calls 'the greatest of all legal fictions', 'the law itself evolves, from case to case, by its own impartial logic, true only to its own integrity, unswayed by expedient considerations'.[27] There is, of course, a sense in which nobody really believes this any more, but it remains the case that much legal behaviour proceeds on the assumption that the law is like that. For example, all legal argument in court makes this assumption.

Law Reports as Sources

Once you begin to ask intelligent questions about cases, questions directed to understanding the case as a historical event, it is fairly obvious that you have to

[25] *Greene* v. *Secretary of State for Home Affairs* [1942] AC 284.

[26] [1942] AC 642. The papers are TS 32/101–117.

[27] E. P. Thompson, *Whigs and Hunters. The Origin of the Black Act* (New York, 1975), 250.

seek for answers in sources other than law reports—if, of course, such sources can be located. For law reports, as sources of information, suffer from two fundamental and inherent defects. One derives from the theory underlying their production, the theory of legal science, which leads to the exclusion, on the ground of its irrelevance, of much information which has explanatory value. Law reports do not, for example, note that the judge was suffering from tooth-ache that day, or had become senile, or whatever. This notion of relevance also leads to the exclusion of material which would locate a case in its contemporary context. Often, of course, such contextual information was available generally at the time, but in the course of the years has come to be forgotten. The context of a case may take various forms—for example, what looks like an isolated piece of litigation may be in reality a mere skirmish in a long-standing feud, or an agreed test case—and in general the more ancient the case the more difficult it will be to discover much about it.

The second basic defect in law reports as historical sources arises from the nature of litigation. Litigation entails a process of fitting—sometimes pushing and shoving—the messy and untidy business of life into artificial legal catego-ries. Even if we leave on one side the fact that litigants normally tell lies, the picture of reality presented in a law report is more or less bound to be to some degree distorted. Indeed the incidents recorded in law reports may never, in any sense, have happened at all. The law report may be simply a forgery, as apparently is the case of the Earl of Huntingdon, reported in the year book for the first year of Henry IV. The report gives an account of the trial of the Earl for treason: in fact he was summarily executed.[28] The case may have been forged to provide a precedent for the possibility of conviction by majority decision. Or the parties may be litigating a fictitious dispute to obtain a judicial ruling on the law, as seems to have happened in *Corbet's Case* in Coke's *Reports*.[29] No doubt the same criticism may be made of many other historical sources; even in private diaries— were they really never intended for publication?—people may censor their thoughts and emotions. But the point is merely that we need, so far as is possible, to try to supplement law reports with other material in the hope that this will at least bring us closer to historical reality, even if we remain a little sceptical of the possibility of ever being sure that we can get the story of a case absolutely right.

So, all in all, it is no more than common sense to appreciate that it is mis-guided, if other relevant materials exist, to rely upon law reports alone to tell us what happened in the case, how the dispute arose, what the persons involved conceived the dispute to be about, how it came to be litigated, how it came to be decided the way it was, much less what the consequences of the decision were to the people involved, or to others indirectly affected by the decision. You

[28] See L. O. Pike, 'The Trial of Peers', 23 *LQR* 442; L. W. Vernon Harcourt, 'The Trial of Peers', 23 *LQR* 43.
[29] (1599) 1 Co. Rep. 83b.

cannot understand litigation simply by reading law reports. So in the studies which follow I have tried to find sources outside the reports which will throw light on the case. The aim is a fuller understanding not simply of the particular decision discussed, but of more general issues about the nature of judicial decision in the common law system, the extent to which the evolution of legal doctrine and its persistence over time require separate explanations, the degree to which decisions can be shown to be politically motivated, or the products of accidental circumstances. I shall, however, try in the main to let these issues emerge from the stories told, and offer no general theories of judicial decision in the course of telling them. Greater understanding of cases does not generate general theories; instead it brings out the complexity of affairs and the extreme difficulty of producing generalizations which have any empirical validity.

Legal Archaeology

My former colleague Professor Peter Fitzpatrick suggested that I should use the expression 'legal archaeology' in the title of this book, aiming boldly to invent, or at least to name, a new category of legal scholarship. Although I have not done so, the suggestion was a tempting one. The analogy between the contextual study of legal cases and archaeology is admittedly by no means perfect. Archaeologists, for example, regularly destroy the evidence upon which their reconstructions of the past are based: legal historians do not. But a reported case does in some ways resemble those traces of past human activity—crop marks, post holes, the footings of walls, pipe stems, pottery shards, kitchen middens, and so forth, from which the archaeologist attempts, by excavation, scientific testing, comparison, and analysis to reconstruct and make sense of the past. Cases need to be treated as what they are, fragments of antiquity, and we need, like archaeologists, gently to free these fragments from the overburden of legal dogmatics, and try, by relating them to other evidence, which has to be sought outside the law library, to make sense of them as events in history and incidents in the evolution of the law.

2

Politics and Law in Elizabethan England
Shelley's Case *(1581)*

The Rule in Shelley's Case

The first case I discuss in this study is *Wolfe* v. *Shelley*.[1] For most people the name Shelley is firmly associated either with the poet, Percy Bysshe Shelley, or with the gothic novelist Mary Shelley, his second wife. But for lawyers the association is with this case, decided in 1581, usually simply called *Shelley's Case*. It gave rise to one of the weirder dogmas of the law of property, the 'rule in *Shelley's Case*'. This concerned the meaning of the word 'heirs' when used in a legal document in which an interest was given to a person, and this was followed by a purported gift of an interest to that same person's 'heirs'. For example, suppose a will gave a life interest in a farm to Peter, and then a 'fee simple'—that is ownership—subject to the life interest, to Peter's 'heirs'. The word 'heirs' were 'words of limitation', that is they delimited what was given to Peter, and not 'words of purchase'—words which gave any interest to Peter's heirs.[2] The ramifications of the rule became immense, but a relatively simple formal statement of it is provided by an early nineteenth-century conveyancer:

The rule is, that when by the same instrument in which a life estate is given, the remainder is limited to the heir or heirs of the body of the tenant for life, whether immediately or subject to other estates, the life estate and remainder shall unite, and the intended tenant for life shall be entitled to an estate in fee simple or fee tail, but so as not to prejudice any intervening interests.[3]

So, in our illustration, Peter obtained the 'fee simple'—that is, became an absolute owner, not a lifetime owner only. In consequence he could do what he liked with the property, contrary to the obvious intention of the testator. And if he died in possession, and made no other provision by will, the property would *descend* to his heir by way of inheritance. The rule was first stated in a report of *Shelley's Case* by Edward Coke, in print in 1600, and earlier in circulation in manuscript.

---

[1] 1 Co. Rep. 88b, 76 ER 199, with record from KB 27/1269 m.58, 1 And. 69, 123 ER 358; Moo. KB 136, 72 ER 490; 3 Dyer 373b, 73 ER 838.
[2] A 'purchaser' in legal jargon was someone to whom an interest was given, not someone who bought an interest.
[3] J. Tyrrell, *Suggestions Sent to the Commissioners Appointed to Inquire into the Laws of Real Property* (London, 1829), 334.

The Shelley Family in West Sussex

Shelley's Case involved a dispute in a prominent Sussex family. One of the curiosities of medieval land law was that women, notwithstanding their generally subservient legal position, could own and inherit landed property, though only if there were no males of equivalent degree. Hence the medieval world produced highly marriageable heiresses.[4] One such was Elizabeth, only daughter of John de Michelgrove, alias Fauconer, who died in 1458. The Michelgrove family was ancient and well endowed long before the fifteenth century; it had been represented at Agincourt. Originally Fauconer (today Falconer),[5] the family took to identifying themselves with their principal manor in West Sussex, Michelgrove, in the parish of Clapham. Shelley also is from a place name, possibly Shelley Park (today Shelley Plain), south of Crawley, not far from Gatwick airport. The Shelleys, too, were well established in the area in the fourteenth century; two had been beheaded in Henry IV's time, a sure sign of importance.

In 1474 Sir John Shelley married Elizabeth de Michelgrove, then 14, uniting two family endowments in West Sussex. Effectively he became Lord of the Manor of Michelgrove: as Blackstone grimly explained: 'By marriage, the husband and wife are one person in law: that is, the very being and legal existence of the woman is suspended during the marriage, or at least is incorporated and consolidated into that of the husband.'[6] Sir John at one time or another owned extensive landholdings around Clapham and further afield, such as the Manor of Applesham, part of Denton, Hoope in Rudgwick, Sullington, and the advowson of Combes and lands there.[7] His magnificent manor house, in Elizabethan times a brick building surrounding a courtyard, with hexagonal towers at each corner, lay near Patching, at the head of a wooded valley beneath the Downs.[8] The landed estate surrounding it occupied most of the parishes of Patching and Clapham, and a considerable portion of Angmering, constituting Angmering Park, today the Angmering Park Estate.

Elizabeth died on 30 July 1513 aged around 53. Her husband survived her unmarried until 3 January 1526.[9] They had at least seven sons and three daughters; others may have died, for in the sixteenth century wealth was no protection against the continuous ravages of death.[10] The first-born son John did

---

[4] See E. Spring, *Law, Land and Family* (London, 1994).
[5] Also de Fauconer and Fawkenor; see SRS XIV 926.   [6] *Commentaries*, i. 430.
[7] SRS XIV (IPM) No. 925 (John Shelley), 926 (Elizabeth Shelley).
[8] D. G. C. Elwes, *A History of the Castles, Mansions and Manors of Western Sussex* (London, 1976), 65 ff.
[9] SRS XIV 925, 926, PROB 11/22.
[10] Heralds' Visitations of Sussex in 1530, 1570, and 1633–4 (various MSS in BL and College of Arms, e.g. Harleian 1484, 1562, CA MS D.13, BL Add. MSS 17065). Pedigrees in *Harleian Society Publications*, liii. J. E. Mousley, *Sussex Country Gentry in the Reign of Elizabeth* (London, 1955), studies 70 families, but not the Warminghurst Shelleys. The pedigree by J. Comber, Comber MSS, West Sussex Record Office (hereafter WSRO) MP 3008 lists William, Richard, Edward, and George,

not survive, and so the name was recycled for the second son. He became a knight of the order of St John, but was killed in battle with the Turks in Rhodes in 1522.[11] The inheritance passed to William, born in 1479 or 1480.[12] In about 1500 he was sent to the Inner Temple to study the law, but not with a view to practise; he was 'put to the Innes of Court to learn to understand his onne evidense'.[13] But William did practise and, encouraged by King Henry VIII, prospered greatly, becoming Recorder of Coventry (1512–15), Autumn Reader elect of his Inn (1517), and Lent Reader (1518). He was made Recorder of London in 1520. He became associated with the Royal Court and, as his son explained:

King Henry the Eight knew my father, whom in his youth he loved very well. And albut in my Lord Cromwell's tyme he passed stormes and with great lose (which after was recompensed liberalie) yet fynale, the King made muche of him agayne.

In 1521 he was placed on the commission for the trial of Edward Stafford for high treason; in the same year he hecame a Serjeant at Law, and five years later a Justice of the Court of Common Pleas. He took part in the trial of the Carthusians, and of John Fisher, Bishop of Rochester, in 1535, and of Queen Anne Boleyn in 1536.[14] In spite of quarrels with Thomas Cromwell, for he disapproved of the reformation, he remained a faithful and favoured servant of the King. In *Dacre's Case*, where the other judges capitulated to Royal pressure, he preserved his integrity by dissenting, and he contrived not to be present for the final decision through being sick. At some point—one source gives 1534, but the work would take many years[15]—he rebuilt the house at Michelgrove on its ancient foundations. He entertained Henry VIII there, and the King particularly praised the quality of the venison which was served to him. I know of no other common law judge of the period who achieved the honour of entertaining his Sovereign.

In about 1502 or 1503, following family practice, William married an heiress, Alice, one of the three daughters of Henry Belknap, and a descendant of Chief Justice Robert of Belknap. He thereby acquired the Manor of Great Knelle, Beckley. On the occasion of this marriage his father settled the Manors of

missing two Johns, and Elizabeth, Jane, and Anne. M. A. Lower, *The Worthies of Sussex: Biographical Sketches of the Most Eminent Natives or Inhabitants of the County . . .* (Lewes, 1865) claims 6 children. J. Dallaway, *A History of the Western Division of the County of Sussex*, ii, Pt. 2, 77, gives 4 sons only.

[11] Married Elinor, daughter of Sir Thomas Lovell of Harling, who bore a son and a daughter who must not have survived into adulthood.

[12] SRS XIV 925. See Dallaway, ii, Pt. 2, 85.

[13] His son Richard to Lord Treasurer Burghley in BL MSS Harley 6993, Art. 14, quoted Dallaway, ii, Pt. 2, 77.

[14] J. H. Baker, *The Reports of Sir John Spelman* (London, 1977), i. 57, 59, 68–71, 229.

[15] T. W. Horsfield, *The History, Antiquities and Topography of the County of Sussex* (Lewes, 1835), ii.

Applesham and Denton, lands known as 'Sakam' (now Sakeham Farm) in Shermanbury, and lands in Combes, on the new branch of the family.[16] The Michelgrove estate, too, was settled on William and Alice in 1511.[17] William also acquired lands in other counties, such as Suffolk and Hertfordshire. His local town house was Kingdom House in Chichester. He died in 1548, and his will, with its extensive bequests to the churches of Clapham and Patching, and to the Cathedral at Chichester, as well as to his retainers, such as his private chaplain, is that of an enormously wealthy individual.[18]

Alice bore William seven sons and seven daughters, all of whom are depicted in his funeral monument in Clapham Church, one, Elizabeth or perhaps Frances, in the habit of a nun. Of these children four sons and four daughters are mentioned in his will.[19] He was succeeded by his eldest son, John, who died on 16 December 1550.[20] John's wife, Mary, daughter of Sir William Fitzwilliam,[21] bore twelve children.[22] Three sons[23] and five daughters[24] appear to have survived him. At the time of John's death, his uncle Edward was at Warminghurst, Richard was in Rudgwick, and parson George Shelley was Rector of Wiston and Parnham, and incumbent of Combes, so the area was well peopled with Shelleys.[25] John was succeeded by another William, 12 when his father died.[26] William took possession of Michelgrove in 1558, and at the time of *Shelley's Case* was the head of the family.[27]

Justice William was only one of the children of Sir John who received great advancement from him. Thomas became lord of the manor of West Mapledurham in Hampshire, which his father had acquired in 1533.[28] Richard, his fourth son, established the Patcham (and Lewes) branch of the family.[29] Richard died in 1552.[30] It was Edward, probably the fifth son,[31] who established the Warminghurst (or Worminghurst) branch, to be involved in *Shelley's Case*.

---

[16] SRS XIV 925.   [17] SRS XIV 926 (10 July 1511).

[18] PROB 11/32 (25 Populwell). On the Subsidy Roll of 38 Henry VIII (E 179/190/268) he is noted as having £400 in lands and goods.

[19] Sons included John, James, Richard, Edward, and Thomas. James became a Knight of Malta, and lived abroad. Richard (died *c*.1589) became Turcopolier of the Order of St John in 1557 and in 1566 Grand Prior; he lived abroad and died in Venice. Edward died in battle with the Scots at Pinkie near Musselburgh in 1547. Horsfield, n. 15 above, i. 376 has John, wrongly, dying before his father. Dallaway, n. 10, ii, Pt. 2, 77, has a pedigree with 4 daughters, Catherine, Elizabeth, Frances, and Margaret. Comber has 3 daughters (Catherine, Margaret, and Elizabeth).

[20] Will PROB 11/34 (12 Bucke).

[21] He owned the manors of Stondon Hall in Essex, Wolston and Marston in Warwick, Exton Bassett and Luces in Wiltshire.

[22] Brass in Clapham Church depicting 4 sons and 8 daughters.

[23] William, John, and Richard. Comber has another son, James.

[24] Bridget, Eleanor, Elizabeth, Mary, and Margaret.

[25] George died in 1557. Brother Thomas and sister Margaret were also alive.

[26] SRS XIV 927.   [27] SRS XIV 929. On 19 Sept. 1559 aged 21 years and 5 days.

[28] VCH Hampshire and Isle of Wight, iii. 88.   [29] WSRO MP 3008.

[30] PROB 11/35 (28 Powell). He appears to have been survived by one son, John, and one daughter. John died in 1587 (will in PROB 11/71 (74 Spencer)).

[31] M. A. Lower, n. 10 above, 128 ff. is confused, also Dallaway, n. 10, at ii, Pt. 2, 77.

The Warminghurst Branch of the Family

The tiny parish of Warminghurst, with its Church of the Holy Sepulchre,[32] once a sanctuary, lies five miles or so north of Michelgrove. Edward became a Master of the Royal Household to Henry VIII, Edward VI, and Queen Mary. There is a brass in the church, but two coats of arms and a depiction of the Trinity have been stolen in modern times. He married Johan, sole daughter and heiress of Poll Iden (i.e. in modern spelling Paul Eden), of Penhurst in Kent.[33] Edward acquired extensive landholdings in Sussex, including Warminghurst Place and Park, some in the surrounding area, at Findon, Angmering, Ashington, Ashurst, Steyning, Sullington, Thakeham, Washington, Wiston, and Wiggenholt. His manors included Cobden, Findon, Muntham, and Sullington, as well as Warminghurst, which he purchased in 1540 for £391 10s., subject to a life interest in favour of Anne Cobham, a widow and presumably a relative; she may have been a daughter of Sir John Shelley.[34]

Warminghurst had been the property of the Abbey of Fécamp, but in 1414, when the alien foundations were seized, it passed to Syon Abbey of the order of St Bridget, founded by Henry V. About 1540, Edward also acquired the manor of Findon from Thomas Cromwell; it, too, had belonged to Syon.[35] Initially his home was Findon Place, near the Church of St John the Baptist there. Anne Cobham apparently then lived at Warminghurst Place, but died by 1547. Edward then moved in.

In 1540 Edward bought part of another manor, Ecclesden, in Patching, which also once belonged to Syon. These directly featured in *Shelley's Case* in 1581, and were called Barhamwyke (a 'reputed' manor) and 'Sir John's lands'. Sir John Shelley presumably held them on lease from the nunnery before the dissolution. The property amounted to some 113 acres, and constituted a farm with a farmhouse, of which no trace survives, so far as I could tell on a brief visit.[36] In modern times these lands appear as Barnstake Copse and Surgeon's Fields; 'surgeon' is a corruption of 'Sir John'. Local tradition has it that they came to be known as Surgeon's Fields when wounded prisoners from the Napoleonic wars were encamped there; present-day France Cottages derive their name from this time.

[32] Fabric from *c.*1220; a church there in 1086. See F. W. Steer, *Guide to the Church of the Holy Sepulchre Warminghurst* (Chichester, 1960).

[33] Brass to 'Pawle Yden, Gentilman & Agnes his Wife' at Penhurst dated 1564: W. D. Belcher, *Kentish Brasses* (London, 1888), i, no. 180.

[34] M. A. Lower, *A Compendious History of Sussex Topographical, Archaeological and Anecdotal*, ii. 228.

[35] Dallaway, n. 10, ii, Pt. 2, 88 has it that Edward acquired Findon in 1528 from Sir John Dudley, and conveyed it back to him in 1531, taking a lease of the manor farm (presumably now Findon Park Farm) for 31 years at £13 6s. 8d. p. a. The reference may be to a different property. The *Letters and Papers of Henry VIII*, vi. 228, refers to Edward paying Cromwell £16 0s. 2d. for the farm of the manor in 1533; see also v, 394. H. R. P. Wyatt, *Fragments of Findon* (Worthing, 1926), has the manor acquired by the Crown in 1515.

[36] I have relied on the Tithe Map of Patching of 1847.

The farm had been granted by Henry VIII to the same Anne Cobham for her life, and then, by way of remainder (to use the technical expression), to Edward Shelley and his wife, and the heirs of their bodies begotten. This entailed the lands. Unless the entail was broken, they would pass after the death of Edward and Johan to the direct descendants of their marriage—to their lineal heirs. The final provision of the letters patent of 1540 was a remainder in fee simple to 'the right heirs of Edward Shelley'. The effect of this was that, if the entail came to an end, as it would do if Edward and Johan had no children or if their lineal descendants died out at some later date, the lineal heir of Edward Shelley would become absolute owner of the property. In the absence of such an heir, his collateral heir, such as a nephew or great nephew, could inherit.

So far as Edward Shelley's other landholdings are concerned, it is reasonably clear that most were also entailed. But the manors of Sullington and Cobden, and three properties in Findon called Palmers Combe,[37] Deanelands,[38] and Pullet's Furze,[39] were not originally entailed.[40] As for those that were, the entail might have been in favour of Edward and Johan jointly, and their descendants— either confined to males, or open to children of either sex—or to Edward alone and his descendants by any marriage. One cannot tell.

Edward and Johan's marriage would have been in about 1515. Johan bore six or seven sons and three daughters. The sons are identified on the funeral brass as 'Ric H T E J R E', presumably Richard, Henry, Thomas, Edward, John, Richard again (perhaps counted twice), and Edward; Richard, not the eldest son, but the fifth, is thus given prominence. The daughters are fully named as Mary, Elizabeth, and Katherine. Only three sons, Henry, Richard, and (possibly) Edward, and two daughters, Mary[41] and Elizabeth,[42] seem to have reached adulthood.

Henry, the eldest son, must have been born about 1517 or so. He certainly married Anne Darknoll (Darkenold etc.),[43] a widow. Her parents were John and Agnes Leades (or Ledes) of Warminghurst.[44] Some pedigrees, including one contemporary one by Lord Burghley, identify his wife as Anne Sackville, daughter of Richard Sackville of a prominent Sussex family.[45] This marriage to a Sackville,

---

[37] On the Findon Tithe Map as Great and Little Palmers Comb, 31 acres south of Findon Place; on the modern OS 1:25000 Sheet 1306 called Church Hill Shaw.

[38] Not located.

[39] Also Pelletes Firs, not located. A William Pellet of Steyning, where there is a property called today 'Shelleys', left money to Warminghurst Church in 1503; see F. W. Steer, n. 32 above. Presumably the name derived from this family.

[40] See C 2/Eliz/S7/53.

[41] Pedigrees by Berry and Comber have her marrying a John Wintershall.

[42] Berry (following BL Harleian MS 1562) and Comber have her marrying John Apsley of Pulborough (died 1594) and the latter as her having 5 sons and 2 daughters.

[43] Also Darknold and other spellings.   [44] C 2/Eliz/S7/53.

[45] SP 12/185 No. 46, *Harleian Society Publications*, liii. 36, has both Henry senior and his son marrying Anne, and another Henry is confused with Henry junior. W. Berry, *County Genealogies, Pedigrees of the County of Sussex* (London, 1830), follows this. Comber has Anne as the daughter of Richard Sackville of Chipstead in Surrey, and as subsequently marrying Thomas Matson. J. B. Burke, *A Genealogical and Heraldic History of the Peerage and Baronetage etc.* (London, 1861),

if not an error, must relate to an earlier childless marriage ending in Anne's death; if so Anne Darknoll would be his second wife. Anne produced a granddaughter to Edward, Mary. She was alive, but still an infant, in 1554.

Richard, the second surviving son, was born in about 1536. He was probably the fifth-born son. He did not marry in his father's lifetime, and was 18 when his father died in 1554.[46] Edward, an elder brother to Richard, and probably the third son, had married, but apparently died childless some time before 1554.[47]

The Sickness visits Warminghurst

No doubt, had fortune smiled on the family of Edward and Johan, there would have been other children and grandchildren. But in 1554 illness—we cannot tell what form it took—struck the Shelleys of Warminghurst. The first to die was Johan, on 5 February. Then Henry, who was heir apparent to his father in regard to both entailed and non-entailed lands, died at some time during the summer.[48] In late September, the patriarch Edward began to sicken; we can tell this because the legal transactions associated with his fear of impending death date from 25 September. The future of the Warminghurst branch of the family had become uncertain. Mary, the granddaughter, was the heir presumptive to lands not entailed, and to entailed lands where the entail was not limited to males; these included the farm of Barhamwyke. But Mary was an infant, and even if she survived to marry she would not, of course, in the conceptions of the time, perpetuate the Shelley family of Warminghurst. As an heiress she would marry, and the lands would pass into the control of her husband.

Richard was next in line, and would bear the Shelley name, but he was unmarried. As for Edward's two daughters, Mary and Elizabeth, neither is mentioned in any of the documents connected with the family dispute. They were no doubt already married into other families: Mary may not have been alive.

The position was by no means desperate; there was, in Richard, a male Shelley to perpetuate the family, and a glimmer of hope. For at his death Henry had left his wife, Anne, pregnant. She might, with good fortune, produce a boy who would survive into adulthood.

960 and later editions, in its pedigree of Shelley of Castle Goring adds that Richard Sackville was great uncle of Thomas Sackville of Knole, first Baron Buckhurst (1568), later first Earl of Dorset. It also wrongly has Edward Shelley succeeded by his eldest son, Henry. R. B. Manning in 6 *JRH* 267 has Henry Shelley Jr. marrying a daughter of Thomas Walsingham (citing SP Dom. Eliz. CLXXXV no. 46) and then Anne Sackville, daughter of Richard Sackville of Chipstead, citing the Comber Pedigree. In fact, his second wife was Barbara Cromer, daughter of Sir William Cromer.

[46] Co. Rep. 101a.

[47] Comber has Edward junior as dying young before 1565; he certainly died before 1554. Harley 1562 (*Harleian Society Publication*, liii. 36) has an Edward Shelley, presumably the same, married to one Mary.

[48] No surviving will or administration.

The Deathbed Plans of the Patriarch Edward Shelley

The family dispute which generated *Shelley's Case* also provoked other litigation: cross-petitions in Chancery, cross-complaints in the Star Chamber, and
criminal proceedings at the Assizes. A considerable but incomplete body of
material survives. But it is not easy, from the stories set out in the pleadings of
Shelley's Case,[49] from the allegations made in the Chancery suit, *Richard Shelley*
v. *Henry Shelley*,[50] and from the incomplete Star Chamber papers in *Henry Shelley*
v. *Richard Shelley and others*[51] and *Richard Shelley and Nicholas Wolfe* v. *Henry
Shelley and others*,[52] to reconstruct precisely what was done about the Shelley
estates in the dying days of the patriarch Edward. Then, as now, there were two
sides to any account of a family dispute. I shall do my best.

We must distinguish Edward's freely owned land from his entailed lands. So
far as the former are concerned, at some earlier point, probably before the
marriage of his elder son Henry to Anne Darknoll, Edward Shelley made a will.
In it he left this freely owned property—the manors of Sullington and Cobden,
and the lands called Palmers Combe, Deanelandes, and Pullet's Furze—to three
trustees. One, John Carell, was an Inner Temple lawyer of considerable prominence, in 1555 considered by the Privy Council as a possible Chief Justice.
The Carells adhered to the old religion, and became a noted Sussex recusant
family; consequently, under Elizabeth I they fell out of favour.[53] The other
trustees were Edward Darknoll, presumably Anne's father-in-law, and John
Apsley, a yeoman of Slynford. John lived at Thakeham Place, about half a mile
west of Warminghurst Place.[54] The trust was to last 'until the next heir male of
Edward Shelley shall be twenty four'. The property was then to go to that heir
and the heirs male of his body begotten, thus granting an entail in tail male,
heritable only by male lineal descendants.

Subsequently, in the negotiations over the marriage of Henry to Anne Darknoll,
perhaps sometime around 1550–2, Edward covenanted to grant at least some of
these lands to Henry and Anne in tail male special—that is, with inheritance
limited to male descendants of their marriage only. The documents suggest that
at some point he did so, possibly retaining a life interest in his own favour:

---

[49] 1 Co. Rep. 88b, 76 ER 199 (taken from KB 27/1269 m.58).

[50] C 2/Eliz/S7/53, petition of Richard Shelley of 11 June 1580 put in by his counsel, Edward
Fenner, and answer of Henry Shelley put in by Edward Coke.

[51] STAC 5/S34/27 and STAC 5/S61/6.

[52] STAC 5/S24/29, STAC 5/68/8, STAC 5/S77/21, STAC 5/S32/28.

[53] Mousley, n. 10 above; the family's secret Priest House is in West Grinstead. John died 1567,
will PCC 34 Stonarde. See my article 'Keilwey's Reports, Temp. Henry VII and Henry VIII', 73
LQR 89 at 98–100. Spellings of the name of course differ. See *Acts of the Privy Council* (hereafter
APC), v. 138.

[54] Now the site of Thakeham Place Farm. Dallaway, n. 10, ii, Pt. 2, 243, has a pedigree. John died
on 14 May 1587 and is buried at St Mary's Church, Thakeham. The church contains a monument
to John. See G. M. Powell, *Guide to St Mary's Church Thakeham* (Brighton).

he must have retained control over the property or some considerable part of it, but the precise nature of the transaction is obscure.

Later, and this must have been in September or early October 1554, as death was coming on, and after his son Henry had died, Edward Shelley executed, and on 6 October published, a fourteen-page declaration of his intent—in effect a new will—to his three trustees. This does not survive. In it he revoked his earlier will, and said that the trustees were to hold the properties themselves for a term of twenty-four years, and then hold them for the heir male and his heirs male of his recently deceased son Henry. Now in October 1554 no such heir male apparent existed, but Henry's widow was pregnant, and the child might turn out to be a boy.

The other lands were entailed. Edward Shelley could break the entail, and secure a free power to dispose of the lands as he wished, only by taking appropriate action in his lifetime: you could not break an entail by your will. Late in September Edward must have decided to break the entail—the principal lands involved were the manors of Warminghurst and Findon and the farm at Barhamwyke, which was at this time let on a long lease to one Richard Belchamber. In order to break the entail, the law required Edward, through his lawyers, to go through a bizarre rigmarole known as 'suffering a common recovery'. I have elsewhere described this process, and will not repeat the description here. Briefly what had to happen was this. Edward Shelley had to initiate a charade in the Court of Common Pleas, in which one or more trusted persons sued him, alleging an entirely fictitious title to the entailed property.[55] With his acquiescence the claimants 'recovered' the lands from him with an absolute title (technically for an estate in fee simple). So the entail was broken. Legal arrangements were made, at the same time, to transfer the property from the successful claimants, in accordance with Edward's wishes, to whomsoever was intended to benefit. To achieve this result the recovery was expressed to be 'to the use of' the people who were really to obtain interests in the property. The effect of the Statute of Uses of 1536 was that the legal title passed automatically to them by a sort of legal magic the very second that the judgment in the recovery was executed. The recovery was 'executed' by the delivery of possession to the recoverors.[56] The fictitious legal suit involved elaborate formalities, extensive paperwork, and handsome legal fees, but did not require a personal appearance by Edward Shelley in the Court of Common Pleas in London.

The recoverors in this instance were Richard Cowper and William Martin. Richard was a barrister and appears as a beneficiary in William Shelley's will. From the Star Chamber documents we can tell that William Martin was wholly illiterate and could only make his mark; he would be some sort of personal servant.

There was, however, a complication which was very worrying to the dying

---

[55] My *A History of the Land Law*, 129–137.   [56] Ibid., ch. 7.

Edward: you could only suffer a recovery during the law terms, and the next law term did not begin until 9 October. Hence it was essential for Edward to survive until that date if the entail was to be broken; you cannot litigate once you are dead. Furthermore, in order to be effective the suit in the Court of Common Pleas had to be followed by the execution of the Court's judgment, with the local sheriff ritually delivering possession (technically 'seisin') of the property to Cowper and Martin. Until this was done the procedure was incomplete and ineffective. There was bound to be some considerable delay between judgment in London and execution in Sussex, given the distance and the state of Tudor roads.

The writ initiating the suit was issued on 20 September, and *Cowper and Martin* v. *Shelley and Siliborn* was to take place on 9 October, the very first day of the term. Henry Siliborn was a defendant because the charade involved recording an unenforceable judgment against the court crier of the Court of Common Pleas, who must at the time have rejoiced in this odd name. Edward's lawyers prepared a document, an indenture, signed and sealed on 25 September, but not delivered so as to become effective until 6 October. This set out what was to become of the lands once the entail was broken.

The indenture distinguished two segments of the lands. So far as the manor (but not the park) of Findon was concerned, the lands were to be entailed back to Edward Shelley in tail male. He might, after all, recover. The effect of this was to cut Mary out from any chance of inheriting; the heir presumptive was now Richard, but he would be displaced if Anne's baby turned out to be a boy. This was followed by complicated fail-safe provisions.[57]

So far as the other entailed lands were concerned—these included Warminghurst, the park of Findon, and the farm of Barhamwyke—the arrangement made to cope with the possibility that Edward might survive was different. The indenture provided that they were to go to Edward Shelley for life, and on his death to the three trustees for a term of twenty-four years, and then 'to the only use, profit and behoof of the heirs male of the body of Edward Shelley lawfully begotten, and of the heirs male of the body of the heirs male lawfully begotten'. The effect of this was to give the possession of the land, once Edward died, to the trustees. But the gift to the heirs male operated as an immediate gift of the freehold to the heir male (technically a vested remainder) on the death of Edward, though the right to take possession was postponed for twenty-four years.

---

[57] In case Edward Shelley's male line died out there followed an entail in favour of the heirs male of the body of Edward's father, Sir John Shelley. In 1554 the heir apparent entitled under this provision was William Shelley of Michelgrove, who was a minor, aged 14; he was the grandson of Sir John and Elizabeth. Finally, in case Sir John's male line became extinct, there was a gift to 'the right heirs' of Edward Shelley; this would include females and collaterals, and gave an absolute title in fee simple. In 1554 the 'right heir' or heir general presumptive of Edward Shelley was Mary, not Richard. In the common law system children stand in the shoes of their parents for inheritance purposes: Mary's father, Henry, had had a better claim than Richard, since he was the eldest son; Mary takes over this priority and so trumps Richard.

As we shall see, the meaning and effect of this provision was the central question at issue in *Shelley's Case*. This again was followed by fail-safe provisions.[58]

Quite why the manor of Findon was entailed on Edward Shelley, and these other lands granted to him for life only, is not explained. Had Edward Shelley survived his illness, the effect, if the provisions had been literally interpreted, would have been to enable him to continue to enjoy the possession of all the lands during his lifetime, and to give him a free power of disposition over the manor of Findon, but not over his other lands.[59] It may also seem curious that the trust for twenty-four years, which provided for the care of the property for rather longer than the minority of Anne's baby, if it turned out to be a boy, was not imposed on the manor of Findon too. The explanation must be that the manor of Findon was held 'in chief' of the Crown as immediate feudal lord. Consequently, if an infant heir succeeded, both the land and the heir would be in the guardianship of the Crown, in wardship as it was called. The Crown was entitled to manage the land during the minority.

If these transactions accurately carried out Edward Shelley's intentions, there is no doubt as to their purpose. The dying patriarch was pinning his hopes on Anne's baby, his unborn grandchild, turning out to be a boy. He wanted to make sure that if this happened his estates would pass down to that male grandchild, as representing the senior male line, rather than to Richard, his living son. The reply to the Chancery petition puts it that he was 'desirous that his name and family should continue'. A purist in the custom of primogeniture would prefer the senior male line. The trust for twenty-four years makes good sense if this is the plan, but no sense if the baby turned out to be a girl, and the lands passed to Richard, who was already 18; for him a trust of six years would have done the same job. But the reply to the Chancery petition tells us that the trustees knew that in this eventuality they were trusted to let Richard take over the lands, presumably when he reached the age of 24. The reply further argues that if Edward's primary intention had been to pass the lands to Richard, he would surely, with the assistance of counsel, have used 'a more certain form of words'. He could indeed have expressly entailed the lands in favour of Richard by name, for example. The fact that he did not do this seems to make his intention to prefer the baby, if it turned out to be male, perfectly clear.

Richard Shelley's Story of his Father's Plans

But there is another story—Richard's story—as to what went on at Warminghurst in the dying days of Edward Shelley.[60] As illness came upon him, Edward

---

[58] A gift 'for lack of such issue' in similar terms to the heirs male of Sir John Shelley, and finally a gift to the rights heirs of Edward Shelley for ever.

[59] Once the rule in *Shelley's Case* was invented, the position would have been different.

[60] Deduced from interrogatories, in particular those to be administered to William Martin, STAC 5/S68/8, and from the Chancery Petition C 2/Eliz/S7/53. Quotations have the spelling modernized.

Shelley had firmly decided 'to bestow the manor of Warminghurst and all other his lands and inheritance upon his son Richard Shelley'. He therefore set out to the house of John Carell in Warnham,[61] eleven miles north of Warminghurst, 'to request his advice and counsel thereto'. The conference was also attended by a Mr Apsley of Pulborough, probably Michael Apsley, brother to the trustee John Apsley, and Edward's son-in-law; he had married Edward's daughter Elizabeth.[62] William Martin, the servant, was also there. Carell and Apsley persuaded the failing Edward, against his better judgement, to prefer the issue of his eldest son, Henry, so long as a male child was born to Anne, to his younger son, Richard. Carell argued that by the law of nature 'when the cock was gone the hen should keep the chicken'; presumably this was a proverb current at this time. Indeed Carell held his view so strongly that he said he would not be of counsel to Edward unless his advice was followed.

The outcome of this conference and Carell's bullying was the lost fourteen-page declaration of intent, and revocation of the earlier will. But afterwards Edward 'lamented . . . that he should be constrained to pass that which he had gotten with the travail of all his life to such as he knew not at the pleasure of others from those that he knew and well liked'. On his return to Warminghurst, Edward changed his mind; Carell was summoned to Warminghurst Place, and a secret conference took place between Edward and his lawyer, with everyone else excluded from the bedchamber. After this conference Edward 'openly said that no bird of his daughter-in-law should ever sit in his seat'. This remark is quoted in a number of the surviving documents. He also spoke 'many loving natural and fatherly words' of Richard, who was, no doubt to his subsequent regret, for some reason absent from the deathbed at Warminghurst. What his father said showed 'that he had reposed his singular and especial hope in him that he protested that he would pass his lands to him if he mayeth live thereto', this being a reference to the need for him to survive until the first day of the law term. Mistress Agnes Leades was present, lobbying for her daughter and grand-children, but Edward ordered her 'not to be suffered to trouble him'. On 6 October, Sir John Gyfford, John Apsley of Thakeham, and his brother Michael Apsley, late servant to the Duke of Somerset, were summoned to witness the delivery of the legal documents, needed to make them effective. After this Edward protested that this would be 'the last of all his worldly causes'. He then dramatically pulled off his signet ring, and gave it to Edward Darknoll to give to his son Richard. Nothing could make his wishes clearer.

Soon after, local rumour, put about by his daughter-in-law and her friends, had it that he had indeed died before the critical day, 9 October, but that he had 'suborned his servants and friends to make show of his life after his departure until the day were passed'. So friends came to check that he really was still

---

[61] Described as of Thakeham in the pleadings in *Wolfe* v. *Shelley*, but his home was Warnham Place, now Warnhamplace Farm; see *VCH Sussex*, vi, Pt. 2, 203 ff.

[62] *c.*1533—30 Apr. 1593 (Comber). Will is PCC 4 Dixy.

alive, as he apparently was, though it is not clear when precisely these outsiders last saw him alive. It is said that capacious deep freeze cabinets are maintained in the better organized homes of the wealthy to guard against similar problems of survival today. The new documents were sent off to London the same day, 6 October; it was vital that they arrive by 9 October.

If Richard's story is accepted, it is again quite clear what Edward's wishes were: to favour him, the son his father knew and loved. In the Chancery proceeding there is a hint from Richard's side that certain documents which would have furthered his case were subsequently suppressed. Be that as it may, the provisions in those that reached London were those of the indenture of 25 September, as described in the pleadings in *Wolfe* v. *Shelley*: I have already set them out. Whatever his suspicions, Richard was unable to lay his hands on any other relevant documents.

Whichever story is accepted, it is clear that the dying Edward had cut things rather fine, for between the hours of five and six in the morning of the very first day of the law term he died. Or so it was said. One cannot but wonder whether Edward really died the night before, or even earlier. The proceedings in London, where his death would not be known, went ahead. Edward was in due course buried at Warminghurst. And on 19 October the Sheriff of Sussex, Sir Thomas Saunders, delivered seisin of the lands involved to the recoverors, Richard Cowper and William Martin. But Edward Shelley's premature death inevitably cast a doubt over the legal validity of what had been done.

The Birth of Henry Shelley Junior

On 4 December Anne was delivered of a healthy baby boy, who was named Henry, after his father. Baby Henry, as everyone would know, and as the inquisition *post mortem* formally recorded,[63] was the heir to his grandfather, Edward. A posthumous child was able to inherit, and to displace the claims of individuals who would otherwise have inherited. So, in contemporary understanding, baby Henry displaced any claims his sister Mary or his uncle Richard might have had. Henry's moral claim would seem even stronger if his father had intended him to succeed.

But, if Richard's story was true, the position became somewhat ambivalent, since his father's desire that he should succeed would then give him a moral claim. This would be strengthened if there had been some sort of incompetent or even dishonest failure on the part of the lawyers to implement the dying patriarch's wishes. When Edward gave his instructions, there was only one person who could be called his 'heir male'—Richard. Consequently, if the effect of the transactions was a gift of the lands to Richard, the only heir male in

---

[63] SRS, xxxiii. 59.

existence when Edward died, then Richard had the better claim. It was surely Richard who commissioned the funeral brass in Warminghurst Church and, as we have seen, it was he who was given prominence on it. Through the brass founder he was asserting his claim, and if you visit the church today you can see him doing just that.

For the time being peace reigned, and baby Henry was in no position to assert any claim. He became one of the Queen's wards, and passed into the control of Edward Lewknor, who had purchased the wardship.[64] The Lewknors owned the manor of Hamsey in Sussex, just north of Lewes, and Edward's father, who must have approved the Protestant reformation, had died in the Tower in 1556, having been in rebellion against Queen Mary.[65] Henry survived the perils of Tudor childhood; indeed he was to live to the age of 68 or 69, eventually dying in 1623.[66] Edward Lewknor would have controlled his marriage, and select his first wife, who was Friswide or Frideswide, the fourth daughter of Sir Thomas Walsingham.[67] Sir Thomas came from a Kentish family based on Chislehurst: he was a Justice of the Peace and Sheriff of Kent in 1563. He was related to Sir Francis Walsingham, Principal Secretary of State to Elizabeth I, who ran the Elizabethan secret service.[68] So Henry became linked to a family which strongly supported the Queen, and the reformed religion, in which he must have been reared. Henry came of age in 1575. On 12 May 1576 he was licensed to enter the Manor of Findon.[69]

So far as the other lands not in Crown wardship are concerned, the three trustees took possession of them. John Carell died in 1567, and since he made his will in March of 1565 he probably began to fail in that year; at some uncertain point, Edward Darknoll also died, leaving John Apsley as the sole trustee.[70] Richard would attain his majority in 1557 or 1558, and become 24 in 1560 or 1561. He moved into Warminghurst Place in about 1565, with, he claimed, the consent of the trustees.[71] This could be evidence that it really had been his father's wish to favour him, for the trustees would surely know.

---

[64] CPR (Phillip and Mary), vi (1555). For the system see J. Hurstfield, *The Queen's Wards. Wardship and Marriage under Elizabeth I* (London, 1973), and H. E. Bell, *An Introduction to the History and Records of the Court of Wards and Liveries* (Cambridge, 1953). On the Lewknor family in Sussex see Mousley, n. 10 above, 575 ff.

[65] *VCH Sussex*, vii. 83 ff., CSP Dom. Mary, 81 (1556); the manor was granted back to the family by Elizabeth, CSP Dom Eliz., vi, 31 Mar. 1573.

[66] 19th-century extracts from the lost parish register of Warminghurst show him buried there on 9 Dec. 1623 (WSRO MF 483); IPM, 15 Jan. 1625 (SRS XIV No. 931); will proved Chichester, Storrington Deanery 13 (WSRO MF 819).

[67] WSRO MP 1308.

[68] See CAR Kent *passim* for him as a Justice and the *DNB* article on Sir Edmund Walsingham; also E. A. Webb, G. W. Miller, and J. Beckwith, *The History of Chislehurst, Its Church, Manors and Parish* (London, 1899).

[69] CPR Eliz. I 1575–8, 1115, at 150. See also CPR Eliz. I, ii, 1560–63, 117, 11 Feb. 1561.

[70] See C 2/ELIZ/S7/53.

[71] STAC 5/S24/29, S61/6. His son John was baptized there on 22 Dec. 1567 (WSRO MF 483). CPR Eliz. ix, 1580–2, no. 752 of 1 Dec. 1580 describes him as of Warminghurst.

Henry Claims the Shelley Lands

Until June 1580, when Richard began a Chancery suit against him, Henry seems to have been untroubled in his possession of Findon and the other lands which had been in ward. Henry does not seem actually to have lived at Findon Place— in early 1579 he is described as being of Henfield, a village some twelve miles or so east of Warminghurst, and about the same distance from Findon.[72] Henry, however, took legal advice, and was told that Richard was entitled to inherit none of his father's lands. So, in 1578, when the term of twenty-four years ended, Henry set about asserting his claim, and soon the dispute with his uncle erupted into open violence.

Henry's first move was an approach to the Privy Council, which at once took his side, without any sort of hearing. In October the Council wrote to Richard, instructing him to deliver possession of the manor of Warminghurst and other lands to his nephew Henry, or appear on 28 October.[73] Richard did not appear, and on 26 October the Council wrote to the Lord Keeper for advice on some way of helping Henry against Richard, who was 'going about to defraud him of certain lands in Sussex'.[74] In 1578, presumably in consequence of this advice, Henry brought a Chancery suit, and obtained an injunction against Richard, probably relating only to the farm of Barhamwyke: no documents survive. In October 1578, as soon as the earlier lease to Richard Belchamber ended, this property had been leased by Richard to Nicholas Wolfe of Ashington, who appears to have been a friend of his.[75] On 14 August there was some sort of conference between Henry and Richard, at which, according to Richard, Henry undertook not to pursue his claim forcibly. But he went back on this, and on 6 November arrived at the farmhouse with his sword drawn, accompanied by a number of armed supporters. They included Richard Agates of Henfield, 'a lewd and ill-disposed person and an ancient enemy unto the said Nicholas Wolfe' who was also suspected of the brutal killing of one of Wolfe's cattle. Wolfe was not at home, which was as well since it was said that 'if he were he shulde be cutt in pieces and hanged up'. After threats had been delivered through a window, Wolfe's servants decided that discretion was the better part of valour and let Henry in. A special session of the Justices of the Peace was soon after held at Arundel, with learned counsel appearing, and the Justices apparently found that there had indeed been a riot and forcible entry. But they decided against action because of the legal doubt surrounding the title. So Henry remained thereafter in possession of Barhamwyke.

Henry next turned his attention to recovering Warminghurst. Early on 28 September 1579 he entered the park with an armed and mounted band of ten

[72] STAC 5/S61/6.   [73] APC, 1577–8, 345 (14 Oct. 1878).
[74] APC 356 (26 Oct. 1578).   [75] Answer of Henry Shelley, 8 Feb. 1579, STAC 5/S77/21.

supporters.[76] They began to drive out sixty cattle belonging to Nicholas Wolfe, which were grazing there. Henry's story was that he was merely exercising his legal right to distrain the cattle which were consuming *his* grass—in legal jargon impounding them as a distress *damage feasant*. Richard, more plausibly, thought this was simply an attempt to take violent possession. Richard assembled his supporters, who included Nicholas Wolfe, the owner of the cattle, and Edward Shelley. Edward would be his son. For Richard had by now married Katherine Devenish, the daughter of Thomas Devenish of Kelinglye in Sussex, and they had three children, Edward, Elizabeth, and Mary.[77] George Apsley, presumably a relative of the trustee, and Richard Hudson, who was a servant of another Richard Shelley, the son of John Shelley of Patcham, were present. There was some violence, though it does not seem, by the standards of the time, to have been very serious, and the constable was summoned to restore the peace.

The outcome of this fracas was that in late 1579 both Henry and Richard complained to the Star Chamber, and Henry and his companions were indicted for trespass and riotous assembly before the Justices of Assize at East Grinstead on 7 March 1580; the Grand Jury found a true bill for riot, but expressed their uncertainty as to the title, and the case appears never to have proceeded to a verdict. There must have been a similar incident at Sullington. In June 1580 Richard petitioned the Court of Chancery, claiming that Henry had wrongly entered into the manors of Findon and Sullington as well as Barhamwyke, and was wrongly withholding a will and other evidences from him. He wanted an order against both Henry and John Apsley, the remaining trustee, which suggests that Apsley was now on Henry's side. None of these proceedings appears ever to have been brought to a conclusion. It is impossible to be certain, since the court records are incomplete, and the Privy Council records from June 1582 to February 1585–6 are missing too. However, in Hilary Term 1579 Richard and his lessee, Nicholas Wolfe, initiated the common law action of trespass for damages, *Wolfe* v. *Shelley*. Of all the litigation, this suit alone was eventually brought to a conclusion in the summer of 1581, and immortalized as *Shelley's Case*.[78]

But before we consider it there is a preliminary puzzle—what was this violent dispute really all about?

---

[76] CAR Sussex no. 77, 150, East Grinstead Assizes before Southcote and Gawdy JJ, 7 Mar. 1580, ASS 35/22/8. See also no. 696 where another Shelley, John of Patcham, was involved in a similar escapade in Danny Park, owned by Gregory Lord Dacre.

[77] SP 12/185 no. 46 (1585), Berry, n. 45 above, 66. Comber is similar, also The Visitation of Sussex (1530 and 1633–4) in BL MS Harleian 1562. A list of recusants of 1582 lists at Warminghurst Richard, Edward, Elizabeth, and Mary Shelley. See CRS, liii. 5. Berry notes an Edward Shelley, only son and heir of Richard Shelley of All Canning, near Devizes in Wiltshire, Richard being the second son of Edward of Warminghurst. Comber follows this, but probably refers to a different person, unless our man held lands there. There was, however, connection between All Cannings and the Shelley family (see *VCH Wiltshire*, x. 26 for a reversionary lease of land there to Edward Shelley).

[78] Debated in Easter Term, 23 Eliz. (1581), and decided Trinity Term, 23 Eliz. (1581). The Privy Council order arising from the decision is 4 July 1581.

The Rift in the Shelley Family

At one level, no doubt, Richard and Henry disagreed over the intentions of the dying patriarch, Edward, and had conflicting understandings of legal and moral rights to inherit the family lands. There was some independent support for Richard's claims, for example, from Richard Martin, Edward's servant, and from the trustees, particularly John Apsley, though perhaps he changed sides. Letting Henry have Findon and Sullington, and Richard have Warminghurst and Barhamwyke, may have been a compromise which Henry was not prepared to accept. Personal animosity also played a part. There is an indication in one of the interrogatories of the depth of feeling involved; one question to be put to a number of witnesses on behalf of Richard was whether they had not heard Henry say 'that he hathe hated loathed abhored and detested his uncle Richard Shelley'.[79] But this hatred could well be the consequence rather than the cause of the litigation.

It seems likely that the intensity of the dispute, and its outcome, has a deeper explanation in religious conflict, which at this period could create terrible divisions within families, the more so because the line between religious dissent and treason was at this time very uncertain. The dispute erupted just at a time when the harassment of Catholic recusants in Sussex, and indeed elsewhere, was being intensified. The first proceedings against a number of prominent recusants date from 1581.[80] There is clear evidence of a religious rift in the Shelley family.

The senior branch, the Shelleys of Michelgrove, adhered faithfully to the old religion. William, the grandson of Justice Shelley, who succeeded in 1550, came of age in about 1558.[81] He was before the Privy Council on account of religion in August 1580, and between 18 March and 6 July 1581 he was a prisoner in the Fleet. He was released on bail, and tried for recusancy at Newgate on 9 April 1582.[82] Michelgrove long continued to be notorious with the Council as a haven for priests.[83] The Shelleys of Mapledurham were also recusants: Thomas Shelley, the brother of Edward Shelley of Warminghurst, became a fugitive, and died abroad in 1577, and his son Henry was in the White Lion prison in 1581, and died in prison in 1585.[84] Richard Shelley himself appears in a number of records as a recusant.[85] In 1577 he was so listed for the Privy Council by the Bishop of

---

[79] STAC 5/S24/29.

[80] CAR Sussex 936 and 925. There was one indictment for recusancy in 1571, no. 354.

[81] SRS 929.

[82] APC 1580, 11 and 13 Aug., 26 June 1581. See also CAR Sussex 936, 940, 975, 980.

[83] See JRH 16 at 192, CSP For. 1582 75, CSP Dom. 1591–4, 176 (1592).

[84] W. R. Trimble, *The Catholic Laity in Elizabethan England 1558–1603* (Cambridge, Mass., 1964), 87 and 112, citing SP 12/118/6, APC XIII 129, *VCH Hampshire and Isle of Wight*, iii. 88 ff. The Catholic Henry Shelley, son of Thomas, must be distinguished from Henry of Warminghurst. Thus, CRS lxxi (1986) at 152 is confused, thinking that a Henry Shelley, who was in prison in 1580 and later, was the son of Richard of Warminghurst; he had no such son.

[85] See SAC 3 90n. (1876, where he is described as late of Warminghurst), SAC 12 202 (1584). In the Burghley pedigree of 1576 he is described as a recusant: SP 12/185, No. 42.

Chichester.[86] He was summoned before the Privy Council in 1580 on this account and committed to prison for his 'obstinacie in popery'; this was during the litigation over the family lands.[87] Edward, Elizabeth, and Mary Shelley of Warminghurst, his children, but not his wife Katherine, who may by then have died, were also listed as recusants in 1582.[88] Nicholas Wolfe of Ashington and his wife, Mary, were also recusants.[89]

Not all the Shelleys remained loyal to the old faith. Richard Shelley of Patcham and Lewes, one of the Sussex Justices of the Peace in 1575–94,[90] enthusiastically enforced the laws against recusancy,[91] often in company with the wealthy *parvenu,* Justice of the Peace, and Sheriff, Thomas Bishop. In 1583 he was engaged in investigations at Warminghurst into allegations of recusancy, dangerous words against the Queen, and possession of seditious books, by Nicholas and Mary Wolfe. This incident, which rumbled on until 1584, reflected another family division, for the charges were brought by Edward Wolfe, and the books had been handed to Mary by John Hudson, recently deceased, servant to Richard Shelley of Patcham, and presumably an *agent provocateur.*[92] Nowhere is Henry described as a recusant. He would surely, as we have seen, have been brought up by Edward Lewknor in the reformed religion. The fact that he later became a Justice is conclusive that he was Protestant; Catholics were excluded from the commission after 1575.[93] In one of the documents connected with the Star Chamber proceedings it is suggested that Thomas Bishop JP, the scourge of Sussex recusants, had taken the side of Henry.[94]

The religious background surely explains the official support of Henry in his efforts to recover the Shelley lands from his papist uncle, a member of a faction which was dangerous to the Queen. When, in 1585, after William of Michelgrove had, as we shall see, been detected in treason, Lord Burghley compiled his pedigree of the dangerous Shelley family, he noted on it that Henry had recovered Warminghurst, and that Richard was a recusant, and he crossed out 'of

[86] See SP 12/117/5.
[87] APC 1580, 158, 11 Aug. and 13 Aug. See also CSP For. 1583–4, 652 (1583) noting the arrest of Mr Shelley, a rich gentleman of Sussex. Also BL MS Harleian, 360, fo. 1.
[88] CRS, liii. 5, based on Cecil Papers 238/1.
[89] CAR Sussex 1223, 1341, 1483, 1523, and elsewhere; SP 12/184/45 (Nov. 1585) Also John Shelley, his wife Anne, and John and Anne Leades. See SP 12/183/38 (Oct. 1585), SP 12/184/45 (Nov. 1585). See also BL Harleian MS 7042 211b, and Harleian MS 703 fo. 67, where John Leades and Nicholas Wolfe are included with William Shelley, Richard Shelley, Edward Shelley, and John Shelley of Clapham in a list of recusants to be disarmed. See also CRS lxxi (1986), 194.
[90] See CAR Sussex generally; Mousley, n. 10 above, 724. Richard was one of the 12 children of John Shelley (died 1587, will PCC 74 Spencer) and Ann; he died in Oct. 1594. His father was apparently a recusant.
[91] CAR Sussex *passim.* See also APC 1580 where he was involved in proceedings against William Shelley, John and Edward Gage, and Richard Shelley, and APC 1592 329.
[92] SP 12/163/86, 164/10, 177/17. On Bishop, owner of a magnificent house at Parnham, see Mousley, n. 10 above, at 84.
[93] See e.g. CAR Sussex 1453 where he is acting with Thomas Bishop. For exclusion see Trimble, n. 84 above, 71.
[94] STAC 5/S77/21.

Worminghurst' under Richard's name.[95] The dispute was thus not of merely local significance. To the authorities the issue in the case was one of state, not of property law.

The Case of Wolfe v. Shelley

The common law case of *Wolfe* v. *Shelley* has all the appearance of a contrived test case, designed to settle the whole dispute. It was based upon Henry's violent entry into the farm of Barhamwyke in 1578; Nicholas Wolfe sued as lessee of Richard Shelley, and his title depended upon the validity of Richard's title. For the purposes of the action the incident was dated 7 November, and the forcible nature of the entry was concealed, for it would have complicated the proceedings: a claim forcibly pursued could be lost for that reason. The jury formally found a special verdict—that is, they did not find the defendant guilty or not guilty of the trespass, but made an elaborate finding of the facts, leaving the decision to the judges. The special verdict would have been settled by counsel as an agreed statement of facts.

In the case, the dispute between uncle and nephew over the dying intentions of Edward Shelley, a quarter of a century earlier, was necessarily distorted by the lawyers, principally Edward Coke for Henry, and Edward Fenner, a Sussex man, for Richard. They could make no use of stories about skulduggery over suppressed documents, or remarks attributed to the old man on his deathbed. Edward's intentions were, in the theory of the law, to control the case if they lawfully could, but they had to be divined from the formal documents—in particular the indenture of 25 September 1554 and the common recovery in the Court of Common Pleas. Whether because documents were not available, or because it was agreed between the lawyers that they were ineffective, nothing was made of Edward's earlier will, of the covenant in favour of Henry and Anne on account of their marriage, of the conveyance in their favour, or of the fourteen-page declaration of intent. These played no part in *Wolfe* v. *Shelley*. So the dispute, though in reality moral and religious in nature, and related to conflicting stories of the last days of Edward Shelley of Warminghurst, became transmuted into a disagreement as to the technically correct interpretation of some legal documents.

Henry seemed to have a good case. He was certainly both the heir general and the heir in tail to Edward Shelley. It followed that, if the deathbed dispositions of Edward Shelley were not effective, Henry was entitled to all the lands by way of inheritance. If, however, the dying transactions were valid, then Barhamwyke, after the twenty-four-year term, had been given 'to the only use, profit and behoof of the heirs male of the body of Edward Shelley lawfully begotten, and of the heirs male of the body of the heirs male lawfully begotten'. Since Henry

[95] SP 12/185 no. 46.

was the 'heir male of the body of Edward Shelley lawfully begotten', surely he should take the lands. The fact that, for a couple of months after Edward's death, Richard appeared to be the heir male was neither here nor there, since a post-humous child could trump the claims of such a person. Such was the case for Henry.

But Richard's case was both ingenious and plausible. It was that, although he was claiming as heir male of Edward Shelley, he was not claiming the lands as an *inheritance* from his ancestor Edward at all. He claimed the lands because Edward gave them to him, identifying him by the description 'heir male of the body of Edward Shelley lawfully begotten'. He was not claiming the lands 'by descent' but 'by purchase', a 'purchaser' bearing the technical meaning of some-one who acquired lands by grant or gift. As it was put in a document connected with the Star Chamber proceedings, Richard claimed 'as purchaser by the name of heir male'.[96] If the matter was looked at in this way, then the critical moment was when the dying Edward's gift took effect—either on 9 October, the day the common recovery was suffered, or perhaps ten days later, when the sheriff de-livered seisin to the recoverors. At either moment the only person who fitted the description 'heir male of Edward Shelley' was Richard, for Henry had not yet been born. And once you acquired property as a grantee—'by purchase'—there was no question of your being retrospectively deprived of your property, as you could be if you took by descent.[97] There was no doubt that a person could take lands 'by purchase' by the name of heir, and at a common-sense level the 'heir male' who was, according to the indenture, to take the property, subject to the twenty-four year trust, had been *given* it, and should not therefore be regarded as *inheriting* it.

Yet in reply it could plausibly be argued that, if the indenture and the recovery really carried out the intentions of the dying Edward, it did look pretty obvious that Edward's primary plan was to pass the property to Anne's baby if it turned out to be a boy, rather than to Richard. Otherwise the twenty-four-year trust made no sense. And the court had before it no other evidence of those intentions except these legal documents. The fact, if it was a fact, that the old man had said that no bird of his daughter-in-law would ever sit in his seat, if he had indeed said it, was neither here nor there.

Wolfe v. *Shelley* was elaborately argued for three days before the Justices of the Court of Queen's Bench; three serjeants, Anderson, Gawdy, and Fenner, appeared for the plaintiff, Nicholas Wolfe—that is, for Richard's side—and

[96] STAC 5/S61/6.

[97] R. Brooke, *La Graunde Abridgement* (London, 1576), Discent 58, has this extreme example: 'See in the first book of *Doctor and Student* that where there is a father and son, and the son purchases lands and dies without issue, the uncle enters, and two years later the father has another son by the same woman as was mother to the first son, this younger son may enter and oust the uncle. As when a man dies seised having issue a daughter, and the daughter enters, and then a son is born, he will oust the daughter, and this in descents, the contrary in remainders, purchases, and such like.'

Solicitor-General Popham, with Cowper and Coke, for the defendant, Henry Shelley. Then, so Coke tells us:

the Queen hearing of it (for such was the rareness and difficulty of the case, being of importance, that it was generally known) of her gracious disposition, to prevent long, tedious and chargeable suits between parties so near in blood, which would be the ruin of both, being gentlemen of a good and ancient family . . .

directed Sir Thomas Bromley, the Lord Chancellor, to summon all the judges to confer upon the case 'to give their resolutions and judgements thereof'. Coke must, of course, have known all about the background to the case and the political reason for the interest of the Queen and her Privy Council; his account of the Queen's intervention had to be diplomatically phrased. His report of the case was first published in manuscript in 1582, and dedicated to Lord Buckhurst; perhaps he was trying to curry favour by rationalizing a somewhat puzzling legal decision, as well as drawing attention to his success in the case. Lord Buckurst, formerly Thomas Sackville, was a Privy Councillor and Lord-Lieutenant of Sussex; as we have seen he may have been related somewhat distantly by marriage to Henry Shelley senior. He would certainly have been interested in the case and know all about the background to it.[98]

The judges convened at York House, where the case was again argued by Fenner and Coke, and Lord Chancellor Bromley, who had no real business to be there at all, gave his opinion in favour of Henry Shelley. But the judges remained undecided, and argued the case again amongst themselves at their lodgings in Serjeants Inn. They then postponed a decision until the following Trinity Term. It seems likely that the real reason for the intervention of the Queen and her Chancellor was to bring pressure to bear in favour of Henry Shelley. In Trinity Term most of the judges came out in favour of Henry.

It is not, however, possible to say with complete certainty what the legal justification for the decision actually was. At this period the judges normally argued a case amongst themselves publicly: today they argue privately. They did not necessarily make public the reasons for their eventual decision: today, of course, they do. Sometimes at this period counsel would ask for an explanation, and be provided with a brief one, as when Edmund Plowden in *Sharington* v. *Strotton* (1565) asked Chief Justice Catlyn, 'May it please you, my lord, for the sake of our learning, to show us the reasons of your judgement?' and the Chief Justice obliged.[99] According to the reports of the case by Coke and by Moore, chief Justice Wray did, in this instance, provide a short explanation.[100] If we accept their reports, the judges upheld the transaction carried out on behalf of the dying

---

[98] See J. H. Baker, 'Coke's Notebooks and the Sources of His Reports' [1972A] *CLJ* 59 at 71; on Buckhurst, see above, n. 45.

[99] Plowden 298. J. H. Baker and S. F. C. Milsom, *Sources of English Legal History. Private Law to 1750* (London, 1986), at 492.

[100] 1 Co. Rep. 106a, 76 ER 238; Moo. KB 140, 72 ER 492.

Edward as valid even though the recovery was suffered on the very day he died, and the judgment not executed until after his death, on 19 October.[101] But they ruled that the recovery did not take effect until the seisin was delivered by the sheriff. At that moment, under the Statute of Uses, the three trustees acquired their twenty-four-year leasehold interest, and Richard, who was then the only heir male in existence, acquired the entailed interest. But they also agreed, unanimously according to Moore, but with one dissent according to Coke,[102] that Richard should not be treated as taking the entailed interest in the land as a purchaser; he was 'in, in course and nature of a descent'. This was the critical ruling in the case, and the reports of the case by Coke, Moore, and Dyer agree on this. In consequence, Richard lost his rights the moment his nephew Henry was born. Edmund Anderson's report also treats the contention that Richard took his interest by purchase as *le grand point*. He says the judges ruled that Henry should have the lands, but adds 'mes le reason ne fuit publish per le Court'. What I take this to mean is that the judges ruled that Richard took by descent, which agrees with the other reports, but that Chief Justice Wray in his brief explanation did not say why. Francis Moore's report agrees. Anderson adds: 'Note the Attorney Master Coke has now made a report in print of this case with the arguments and agreements of the Chancellor and other judges but nothing of what was said in the Court is shown there.' So Coke's account of what Chief Justice Wray said on this central point was embellished.[103] Coke gave four separate reasons for the holding that Richard took by descent, the fourth of which was 'because the uncle [i.e. Richard] claimed the use by force of the recovery, and of the indentures by words of limitation, and not of purchase'. This became 'the rule in *Shelley's Case*', and Coke's report therefore assumed that the Court must have accepted his own argument. It was that there was a rule that:

when an estate is made to a man [i.e. the life estate to Edward], and after in the same deed, (to limit the quality of the estate) a further limitation is made to his heirs, or to the heirs of his body; in all these cases his heirs, or his heirs of his body, shall never take as purchasers, but in this case these words 'heirs male of the body of Edward Shelley', were words of limitation.

By 'limitation' is meant that the words delimit or define the nature of the interest given to Edward, in effect giving him an entail rather than a life estate, which would pass down to whoever turned out to be his heir male, here Richard until the baby Henry was born, and then to him. Of course, because the judgment in

---

[101] According to Moore, Meade J dissented in thinking that the recovery could not be executed after his death against the tenant in tail; Coke indicates that more than one dissented on this point, and the report by Dyer indicates dissent by Dyer and Periam.

[102] An unidentified Justice of the Common Pleas. Both William Periam and Thomas Meade were Common Pleas judges.

[103] 1 Co. Rep. 106b, 79 ER 239.

the common recovery was not actually executed in Edward's lifetime, Edward never did take any interest under it, but, had he not died on 9 October but lived until 19 October, he could have, and the other reasons for the judgment given in Coke's report are all directed to the contention that the outcome of the case ought not to be affected by the fact that Edward happened to die before any steps could practically be taken to execute the judgment. The proceedings should all, as it were, relate back to the day on which Edward was still alive, and the judgment given, and the law ignored parts of a day.

Whether all the judges, or some of them, actually did accept Coke's argument must remain uncertain. Chief Justice Dyer, who took part in the case, kept his own private notes, and these contain what was at least his reason for favouring Henry, and this differs from Coke's rationale. His account reads:

the son, s. [scilicet] the posthumous, shall have the land, as the nearest and eldest heir male: and that seems also to have been the intent and will of the creator of this special tail. And the uncle cannot have it as purchaser, because he is not heir of the body of his father, for the daughter of the eldest son [i.e. Mary] is heir general, therefore he is not heir male of the body of his father to purchase unless he was as well heir as male, which he is not; but he took the limitation of the said entail by descent until the son was born.

The pseudo-logical argument in this admittedly obscure passage is that to take 'by purchase' Richard must be *both* the heir, meaning the heir general of Edward, *and* male; he was male all right, but Mary was the heir general. If you tell someone to give milk to the black cat, the pussy to be benefited must be both black, and a cat. So, Dyer's theory goes, if Richard did not take by purchase, he must have taken by descent, and one who took by descent could lose out to a posthumous child. For Dyer's theory there was some barely intelligible authority.[104] Perhaps other judges had other technical justifications for holding that Richard had taken by descent and not by purchase; at the end of the day we really cannot tell whether the rule in *Shelley's Case* was applied in *Shelley's Case* or not.

We can be quite sure that the judges would all be perfectly well aware of the politics of the dispute, and of the wishes of the Queen and her Privy Council; it is perfectly possible that the decision was politically motivated, but here again there is just no clear evidence one way or the other.

So *Shelley's Case* classically illustrates a methodological problem commonly ignored—in the nature of things theoretical explanations of judicial decisions rest upon extremely fragile foundations.

[104] Brooke, n. 97 above, Done 61 (1546) (a case otherwise not reported), *Taile et Dones in Taile* 3 referring to YB 9 Hen. VI, Trin. fo. 23, pl. 19 at fo. 24 *per* Elderkar: he argued that if land was given to the right heirs female of B after a life interest to A, and B is dead, leaving a son and daughter, the daughter would not take the land since she was not the heir of B. No reason is given, and in the case in 1546 the doctrine is repeated by Hare, an ancient apprentice and Master of the Rolls.

The Later Fortunes of the Shelleys

Henry Shelley, having won his action, was only entitled to damages. But on 4 July 1581 the Privy Council wrote to the Sheriff and Justices of the Peace in Sussex, ordering them to put him in possession of Barhamwyke.[105] Sometime before 1585 he acquired Warminghurst and the remaining Shelley lands.[106] Between September 1582 and 1604 six sons and four daughters of his were baptized in the Church of the Holy Sepulchre there, his second son, rather oddly, being named Richard.[107] His first wife died leaving no issue, and all his children, twelve in all, were born to his second wife, Barbara, daughter of Sir William Cromer. She died in 1612.[108] Henry died in 1623, apparently at Sullington Place, but was buried at Warminghurst. By then he had sold Findon and appears to have been seriously in debt through some unhappy speculative venture in Scotland.[109] In 1637 the family lost its connection with Warminghurst. Warminghurst Place, after 1676, became for a while the home of no less important a person than the Quaker, William Penn, who drafted the first constitution of Pennsylvania there.[110]

As for Richard Shelley, the loss of the action began a progressive decline in his fortunes.[111] He was already in trouble with the Privy Council over religion, and in 1581 a special search was made in Warminghurst for his children Edward, Elizabeth, and Mary, who at first could not be found.[112] Shortly after he lost the action he became a prisoner in the Marshalsea.[113] He was still there in 1582.[114] A report on Sussex in 1583 says of the 'gentlemen' there: 'most of the greatest revenue ill affected, as Gages, Carrels, Shellyes etc.'.[115] His son, Edward, was sent to the Clink prison on 5 July 1581, and was still there a year later.[116] The worst suspicions of the Shelleys were confirmed when William Shelley of Michelgrove, already, as we have seen, in trouble as a recusant, became involved, with the Earl of Northumberland, in the Throckmorton plot to establish Mary Queen of Scots as Queen. One plan involved an armed landing in Sussex.[117] On

---

[105] APC 1581–2, 117.   [106] SP 12/185, no. 46 (Burghley Pedigree).
[107] WSRO MF 483.   [108] Comber pedigree; that by Berry has 11.
[109] Will dated 20 Jan. 1623, Chichester Storrington Deanery WSRO MF 819; IPM PRO C 142/438, SRS, iv. 931.
[110] *VCH Sussex*, vi, Pt. 2, 49 ff. Penn sold the property in 1702.
[111] See B. Manning, 'Richard Shelley of Warminghurst and the English Catholic Petition of Toleration of 1585', 6 *JRH* 265. This article seems to me to sometimes go a little beyond the evidence.
[112] DRO (Chichester) Ep.1/37/1, no. 2 and no. 9, quoted by Manning, n. 111 above. The first document includes a valuation of property, and it is noted that Richard's lands are the subject of a legal dispute.
[113] St G. K. Hyland, *A Century of Persecution Under Tudor and Stuart Sovereigns from Contemporary Records* (London, 1920), list of 27 July 1581 from Loseley MSS, 319.
[114] CRS, xxi (1919) 71; CSP Dom. Eliz. 1581–90, 68 CLV no. 27.   [115] SP 12/165 no. 22.
[116] Hyland n. 113 above, 319, 391 (citing Loseley MSS, xii, no. 53).
[117] Mousley, n. 10 above, at 257 ff. gives a full account. There are further details in SP Eliz. For., iv, 613. See also Conyers Read, *Mr Secretary Walsingham and the Policy of Queen Elizabeth*

15 December 1583 William was indicted for treasonable plotting with Charles Paget, whom he met in Patching Copse on 16 September 1583; it was said that he

had a secret conversation with Paget how and in what manner and where the kingdom might be invaded by the Queen's enemies, and by what means Mary late Queen of the Scots could be delivered, and how the pure religion established in the country could be changed.[118]

In 1584 he was ordered to be racked to secure further information, and he was again examined in 1585.[119] He confessed and implicated the Earl, who committed suicide on 21 June 1585. An indictment was found against him at East Grinstead Assizes on 5 February 1586, and a special commission appointed to try him in London.[120] On 12 February 1586 he 'humbled himself very lowly and dutifully to the Commissioners' in Westminster Hall and admitted his guilt, whilst blaming the Duke, gloomily remarking that 'these actions I have entered into I fear me will be the undoing of me and my house'. Chief Justice Anderson, who as a serjeant had represented Richard's side in *Shelley's Case*, formally sentenced him to the appalling death reserved for traitors at Tyburn. The Michelgrove estates were confiscated; there is an inventory of the house made in 1585 by the Sheriff of Sussex.[121] John Shelley, William's recusant brother, appears to have continued to live in the semi-derelict mansion. The Michelgrove estates were leased back to John[122] and Henry Shelley, the winner in *Shelley's Case*; John had conformed in the 1590s.[123] They were not to be fully restored to the family until 1604, when William's nephew John took over.[124]

However, William was not executed, but held in prison to await the Queen's pleasure. In November 1586 she formally respited his execution; he became a hostage to control the Shelley family.[125] His wife, Jane, reduced to pawning her belongings, spoke in 1592 of him to one Alice Haydon; she 'wished he might dye in his bedd' but feared he might soon be 'drawn on a hurdle'. She added that 'she was undone by him'. In desperation she visited John Fletcher, a Fellow of Gonville and Caius College in Cambridge, for astrological advice as to whether

(Oxford, 1925), ii. 388, 'A True & Summarie Reporte of the Declaration of some part of the Earle of Northumberland's Treasons' reprinted A. F. Kinney, *Elizabethan Backgrounds* (Hampden, Conn., 1975), 168.

[118] KB 8/47 *Baga de Secretis*. BL Landsdowne MS 45 fos. 164–75 (an incomplete account of the trial).

[119] CSP Dom. 1581–90, 159. See also 13, 64, 68, 86, 136, SP 12/178 no. 74 (27 May 1585).

[120] SP 12/178, no. 174 (27 May 1585) has him with the Earl of Northumberland in the Tower.

[121] 'An Inventory of the Goods and Chattels of William Shelley of Michelgrove, 1585', published by H. Michell Whitley, SAC LV 284.

[122] William's brother, who died in 1592. He and his wife, Elizabeth, were recusants too. See CAR Sussex 1223 (1587) and 1341 (1586); Trimble, n. 84 above, citing SP 12/189/54, 200/61.

[123] Trimble, n. 84, above, 163–4.   [124] Born c.1586. He became a baronet in 1611.

[125] SP 12/195/31 and 32. 189/54 list him with another Catholic, John Bamford, in the Tower of London.

things might yet look up (as no doubt by the death of the Queen); she also wanted to recover some property. He fed her gooseberries from the College gardens, but had little else to offer once he discovered she was wife to William, now in the Gatehouse Prison 'and a dead man in law', and not a marriageable widow. She ended up in trouble with the Council over this visit, being for a while imprisoned.[126] William died in prison in 1597.

Richard, too, was still in the Marshalsea Prison in November 1583;[127] he would come under suspicion of treason. But in early 1584 he seems to have been released, and in August 1584 he is noted as being at the house of his father-in-law, Mr Devenish, in Chichester. In February 1585 he is listed with Edward and William Shelley as a Sussex recusant.[128] In March 1585 he was in trouble again for presenting a petition for toleration to the Queen in person.[129] He was asked whether he would subscribe to the sentence: 'Whosoever being a born subject of this realm doth allow the Pope has any authority to deprive the Queen Elizabeth of her estate and crown is a traitor.' He declined: 'He saith that it is very hard for him to decide what authority the Pope has and therefore can answer no further.' He was in the Marshalsea Prison again on 15 March; also in prison was his friend Nicholas Wolfe, who was suspected of 'designs against Her Majesty'.[130] He was still there in October.[131] One form of persecution of recusants was to subject them to special taxes, and in November 1585 Thomas Bishop reported that Richard had not paid: 'I fynde him to be of very meane ability and not able to contribute anythynge'.[132] Wolfe, also of mean ability, had paid in part. In a list dated May 1586 Richard is recorded as 'mort'.[133] His name and Nicholas Wolfe's are missing from a comprehensive list of religious prisoners of November 1586.[134] He had died in prison. One undated list describes him as recently dead in the Marshalsea.[135] A printed version of the petition he presented to the Queen, dating from 1621, also claims that he died in the Marshalsea.[136] His name as being 'of Warrenhurst' does appear in a 1592 list of recusants to be disarmed,[137]

---

[126] SP 12/244, no. 42, CSP Dom. 1591–4, at 470–2. See also SP 12/148/39, cited Trimble, n. 84 above, 105, where Jane petitions for the return of some property.

[127] SP 12/163, no. 43.   [128] BL Harleian MS 703, fos. 19 and 21.

[129] CRS xxi, 71; *Recusants in the Exchequer Pipe Rolls* by Dom. H. Bowler, edited T. J. McCann, CRS lxxi (1986), nos. 3 and 4. Examined 12 Mar. 1585, SP 12/177/17. Lord Vaux, Sir John Arundell, Sir Thomas Tresham, and Sir William Catesby were also involved. His examination on 9 Apr. 1585 is also described in BL Landowne MS 45 fos. 176–9. Text of petition in BM Add. MSS 39 and 28–38. See also R. Challoner, *Memoirs of Missionary Priests* (ed. J. H. Pollen, London, 1924), 107.

[130] SP 12/164/10 (Dec. 1583), 180/64, 183/38.   [131] SP 12/183, CSP Dom. 1581–90, 276.

[132] SP 12/184/45.

[133] SP 12/189/54, list compiled by Thomas Bishop, Richard Shelley of Patcham and others.

[134] SP 12/195, no. 34. See also SP 12/180, no. 64.

[135] Loseley MS, v, no. 28, printed Hyland, n. 113 above, 402; list was by Sir William More, undated, but must be 1586.

[136] Quoted by Manning, n. 111 above, at 265; it says that Master Shelley 'was by Sir Francis Walsingham then chiefe Secretarie, committed close prisoner to the Marshallsey where he died'. I have not seen a copy of this pamphlet.

[137] HMC Salisbury, iv. 263, BL Harleian MSS 703, fo. 67.

together with Edward Shelley, gentleman, William Shelley, esquire,[138] and John Shelley of Clapham.[139] But this is obviously simply a copy of an out-of-date list. A Richard Shelley features as a recusant suspect in Sussex records in 1595[140] But this was a son of Henry Shelley. He died on 15 December 1623, leaving a widow Joan, daughter of Henry Darknoll, who settled lands forming part of the manor of Sullington on them.[141]

As for our Richard's son, Edward, an Edward Shelley, gentleman, of the Sussex family of Shelleys, who may be the same person, was executed at Tyburn on 30 August 1588 for harbouring a seminary priest. The priest, William Deane, was also executed, but at Mile End.[142] There are other references to an Edward as a recusant and prisoner, and although the identification is uncertain it is quite likely that the martyr Edward Shelley was indeed Richard's son.[143] Richard's family thereafter fades from the records.

The Rule in Shelley's Case

One of the basic characteristics of the common law system is that in general it does not consist of rules, in the sense of propositions of law whose text is canonical. But to this there are notable exceptions. Edward Coke was himself somewhat given to this practice; for example, he formulated a notable rule encapsulating the doctrine of consideration in contract law.[144] Through his report, *Shelley's Case* came to stand for 'the rule in *Shelley's Case*'. Coke cited very little authority for his 'rule',[145] and it cannot be found earlier. But with publication in print in 1600 it became part of the received legal culture. I have discussed elsewhere the medieval background to related doctrines, which then served two quite different functions—the prevention of the evasion of feudal obligations which arose when land was inherited, and the validation of transactions

---

[138] The only known William was the traitor, still in prison.

[139] This would be the brother of William, the traitor; he died on 27 Aug. 1592, and his son became the first baronet.

[140] BL MS Harleian 703, fo. 67, CAR Sussex 1550.

[141] C 142/417 (IPM), giving his heir as John. See Dallaway, n. 10 above, ii, Pt. 1, 38.

[142] 19 JRH 218, 229; see R. Challoner, n. 130 above, 134; CRS v (1908) at 290 (MS cat. of martyrs probably by Father John Gerard), R. Challoner (ed. J. H. Pollen, *Memoirs of Missionary Priests*, 134 and 141. In BL MS Harleian 7042, fo. 209b, describes him as *nuper de London generosus*; CAR Surrey, No. 1333 and 1422 mentions proceedings against recusants Richard Shelley, esquire, and Edward Shelley, gentleman, of Southwark (where the Clink prison was), at Croydon Assizes in 1582 and 1583. Probably this would be our Richard and his son.

[143] Hyland, n. 113 above, 381, 391, 402, 404, prints documents from the Loseley MSS showing one Edward Shelley a prisoner in the Clink and later the Counter sometime after 1584. The documents also refer to one Henry Shelley as a recusant who died in prison about this time. See n. 84 above. I have not examined the original MSS.

[144] See *Stone* v. *Wythipol* (1588), discussed in my *A History of the Common Law of Contract*, 487.

[145] 40 *Lib. Ass.*, pl. 19, T. Littleton, *Tenures* (London, 1481 and numerous later editions); *Brett* v. *Rigden* (1565) 1 Plowden 340, 75 ER 516; *Nichols* v. *Nichols* (1574) 2 Plowden 477, 55 ER 717.

which would otherwise have foundered because of the law's refusal to allow contingent gifts to be valid. I there suggested that the revival of this old doctrine in *Shelley's Case* might have been in part explained by a judicial desire to favour freedom of alienation, and by a Royal desire to prevent the evasion of feudal obligations.[146] So far as the case itself is concerned I now incline to think both explanations to be wrong; though we cannot be sure, the judicial interest was perhaps in upholding the intention of the patriarch, and perhaps pleasing and protecting the Queen, and the Royal interest was in favouring the politically correct branch of the Shelley family against a dangerous papist. But these explanations are inherently speculative.

Soon the rule in *Shelley's Case* took on a life of its own, and an enormous body of arid doctrine accumulated around it. It was even put into verse:

> *Shelley.* When ancestors a freehold take.
> The words 'the heirs' a limitation make.[147]

It became a rigid rule of law for the interpretation of documents to be applied, however silly the result. Normally in legal thought we allow the supposed purpose of the law to influence, within limits, the application of the law. The subsequent history of the rule in *Shelley's Case* is an example not so much of the divorce between rule and purpose, but of the survival of a rule which was no longer supposed to have any purpose at all. In so far as it favoured freedom of alienation it was superseded in the late seventeenth century; in so far as it protected feudal obligations it became redundant when they were finally abolished in 1660. From about the 1680s the rule ceased to perform any useful function at all. Competent lawyers could always, by appropriate draftsmanship, avoid its application; where it did apply, this tended to be an accident.

In the eighteenth century the great Chief Justice Lord Mansfield attempted, in the fictitious case of *Perrin* v. *Blake* (1770–2),[148] to treat it as a rule of construction only, which could give way to other evidence of the settlor's intent. This provoked a major legal dispute, and induced Charles Fearne to write an excruciating book, *An Essay on the Learning of Contingent Remainders* (1772). Some thought, as Fearne did, that Mansfield was playing fast and loose with the law—fidelity to silly though well-established rules really separates those who respect the rule of law from those who do not. Fearne, who became the high priest of the rule, was somewhat dismissive of those who wondered what its point had ever been; he confined his attention to:

---

[146] *A History of the Land Law* (Oxford, 1986), 99–100.
[147] Anon. (probably J. Worrall), *The Reports of Sir Edward Coke, knt., in Verse etc.* (London, 1742).
[148] 4 Burr. 2579, 96 ER 355; 1 Blackst. 672, 96 ER 392; the case arose out of a dispute before the Privy Council over an estate in Jamaica, and this could not go to Mansfield's court. Hence the legal issue was raised there by litigating a fictitious case. The decision of Mansfield's Court of King's Bench (Yates J dissenting) was reversed in the Exchequer Chamber; an appeal to the House of Lords was compromised: see J. Oldham, *The Mansfield Manuscripts and the Growth of English Law in the Eighteenth Century* (London, 1992), 1353–5.

the present extent and prevalence of that rule; abstracted from the remote *origin* of the rule itself, at a period and on principles, now problematical: WHAT THEY WERE, may be left to the investigation of erudite curiosity, or the representations of prolific ingenuity.[149]

In the early nineteenth century the heretical idea came to be expressed to the Real Property Commissioners that nothing whatever would be lost if the rule, which 'has produced more elaborate discussion and greater differences of opinion than any other principle of law' might in fact be abolished without anyone being the loser.[150] Even earlier than this, in 1821, Connecticut abolished it. But in its country of origin it survived until 1 January 1926. Yet when I studied property law in Oxford in 1952 we still had to know what it was, since otherwise, it was argued with perverse but yet compelling logic, we could not understand what precisely had been abolished. And the rule could and indeed still can apply to legal instruments executed before 1 January 1926.

Elsewhere in the common law world the rule in *Shelley's Case* still enjoys a curious twilight existence. In legal education it flourishes in the American law schools; its archaic nature and sheer incomprehensibility positively attracts some students of property law, who are fascinated by the absurd, whilst utterly repelling others. Those who teach property law can always establish their dominance by teaching the rule, since a high proportion of their class can be relied upon to misunderstand it, and their confusion can always be enhanced by teaching the doctrine of worthier title, another Gothic relic, at the same time. Outside the classroom its status resembles that of the Big Foot, the Yeti, or the Tasmanian Tiger; sightings are still possible. Many juridictions have abolished it by statute: Michigan, for example, in 1838, Texas in 1964, though not retrospectively, so that from time to time it continues to frustrate the intentions of testators. Although American courts cheerfully invent new constitutional and common law doctrines, and abrogate old ones, as the whim takes them, they shrink with a sort of superstitious awe from disrespectful treatment of the sacred rule in *Shelley's Case*. A computer search of American cases produced eighty-one cases since 1970 in which the rule is mentioned or applied. It certainly survives in some jurisdictions, Arkansas, for example, whilst it is certainly extinct in others. Nobody quite knows which all these jurisdictions are. In such places as Tristan da Cunha, Pitcairn Island, or the Gambia, which have to some degree enjoyed the reception of the common law, it is wholly obscure whether it ever did exist, and nobody there very much cares.

The Ghosts of West Sussex

West Sussex has, of course, changed greatly since Elizabethan times, and only the bones of the Shelleys remain at Clapham, Patching, Findon, or Warminghurst.

---

[149] Fearne 290.

[150] See J. Tyrrell, *Suggestions Sent to the Commissioners Appointed to Inquire into the Laws of Real Property* (London, 1829), 334.

But a visit can still be worthwhile, especially to those who claim psychic powers, and can be enlivened by stopping, *en route*, at the Shelley Arms in Nutley or Horsham, or one of the other houses which bear the name or display the canting device of the family, sable, a fess engrailed between three whelk shells or, or their crest, a griffon's head, erased, argent, beaked, and ducally gorged, or.[151] Many of the places I have mentioned can still be easily identified—Barhamwyke and Sir John's Fields in Patching, now Barnstake Copse and Surgeons Fields (today wooded), close to Patching Copse where William Shelley plotted treason and brought his house and his wife, Jane, to ruin. To the south, Ecclesden Common and Farm preserve the name of the manor of which they formed part. The church at nearby Clapham, which, like many Sussex churches in this area, stands a little way apart from the present-day village, rests on the mortal remains of generations of Fauconers and Shelleys; their memorials are all around you. If you visit it you must lift the carpet in front of the altar to see the magnificent memorial brass of John in his armour, and the heiress Elizabeth, whose union established the family at Michelgrove;[152] it was saved from the iconoclasts by being buried for some years. Elizabeth wears a robe with the arms of the Shelleys on the dexter side, and the falcons of the Fauconers on the sinister, quarterly or and azure, a falcon rising, argent. To the left of the chancel is Justice Shelley in his coif and judicial robes, kneeling with his wife, Alice, the Belknap heiress, and their many children. A short walk up the valley above Patching brings you to the site of Michelgrove House. The descendants of the fallow deer whose venison so pleased King Henry VIII are still there in the woods, though you will be fortunate if you see more than their slots, but the great house is no more. In the late eighteenth century it was extended and modernized by Sir John Shelley— a claim it was demolished and moved to a position higher up the valley is plainly incorrect[153]—but in 1800 the family sold to Richard Walker of Liverpool, whose son 'became interested in the running of coaches between London and Worthing, and elsewhere. This contributed to his insolvency'.[154] Before this he engaged Humphrey Repton, the landscape gardener, to improve the place, but his proposals were never executed. He was intrigued by the architecture, and recorded what was then supposed to be the origin of the house, which he much admired: 'The house is said to have been built by a knight of Malta,[155] in the reign of Henry VIII, in imitation of a Morisco palace which he had seen in Spain; if this be true it accounts for the singular style of architecture.'[156]

---

[151] There is a Shelley Hotel in Worthing, another in Lewes, and a Shelley House Antiques in Arundel.

[152] H. R. Moss, *The Monumental Effigies of Sussex* (Hove, 1933).

[153] Derived from D. G. C. Elwes, *A History of the Castles, Mansions and Manors of Western Sussex* (London, 1876), 65 ff. Inspection of pictures dating from 1782 (by Lambert) and of 1827 by Hewetson, No. 54 in R. Ackerman's *Repository of Arts, Literature, Commerce, Manufactures, Fashions and Politics* (London, 1809–28) clearly shows alterations, not complete rebuilding.

[154] Caption to the print in Ackerman; n. 153 above.   [155] See above, n. 19.

[156] H. Repton, *The Landscape Gardening and the Landscape Architecture of the late Humphrey Repton Esq.* (London, 1840), 273–5. This has Repton's drawings of the house.

Michelgrove was sold in 1828 or so to Bernard Edward, Duke of Norfolk, who for some reason hated the Shelley family:

> That nobleman, to the grief of the district, pulled down the time honoured mansion of Michelgrove, which had been built on the ancient foundations by Judge Shelley, and honoured by the presence of royalty in the person of King Henry VIII . . . *Sic transit* etc.[157]

In Findon the manor of Muntham, once emparked, lost its manor house in 1953, and unromantically became the site of the Worthing Municipal Crematorium; the farmhouse remains. Of the other mansions, Findon Place still exists. The present house possesses thirteenth-century cellars, but is principally from 1740–60. A Tudor chimney, built when the property was owned by Richard Rich and Thomas Cromwell, survives.[158] In Sullington, the manor of Cobden is recalled in the buildings of Cobden Farm, and the manor house, where Henry Shelley died, survives as Sullington Manor Farm, partly medieval, next to the Church of St Mary, which contains an effigy of the crusader, de Covert, who died at the siege of Acre with Ranulf de Glanvil of legal fame.

You approach Warminghurst, where there is no village, up the shaded Park Lane, and the park, whose ancient medieval boundaries are easy enough to locate, lies to the west, overlooked from the vacant site of Warminghurst Place. The latest mansion to stand on the site was not Tudor; it was built by James Butler in the eighteenth century.[159] This mansion, too, was destroyed by the same Duke of Norfolk in his vendetta against the Shelleys; he acquired the property in 1805 and had even grubbed up a Spanish chestnut tree which, being around 270 years old, had been planted about the time the Shelleys first came to Warminghurst.[160] Within the deserted Church of the Holy Sepulchre you will see the Shelley memorial, and you may, if you are devout, obey the injunction:

> of your charite pray for the soules of Edward Shelley Esquyer sumtyme one of the fowre masters of the Howsehold withe the most victorius Princes Kyng Henry the viiith. and Kyng Edward the vith. and oure sou'ayn Lady Quene Marye, and Johan his wiffe daughte and heyre of Poll Iden of Kent . . .

and even ask for a sign of what Edward's intentions really were as he lay dying across the lane in Warminghurst Place 400 years and more ago. And in addition to this monument Edward and Johan have their memorials both in the rule in *Shelley's Case*, and in their direct descendant, the poet. And when you have

---

[157] M. A. Lower, n. 34 above, i. 65 ff. Present-day Myrtlegrove Farm to the east was originally called Michelgrove Farm; I do not know why or when its name changed.

[158] I am indebted to a MS account of the house by the daughter of Dr R. K. Middlemass of Sussex University, who owned Findon Place 1965–72. The house was offered for sale in *Country Life* (10 Feb. 1994, with photograph).

[159] A 1707 map of Warminghurst by Francis Hill (BL Add. MSS 37420) has a depiction of the Tudor House.

[160] T. W. Horsfield, n. 15 above, i, 239; E. Cartwright, *The Parochial Topography of the Rape of Bramber in the Western Division of Sussex* (London, 1830), ii, Pt. 2, 256.

concluded your visit to the church you should sit for a while very quietly in the hollow way of Park Lane, for if you are there at the right time of the day and year you will hear the turtle doves calling gently in the trees above—could it be that they are telling you something about words of limitation, and not of purchase?

3

The Timeless Principles of the Common Law: Keeble v. Hickeringill *(1707)*

Ducks and the Common Law

The contribution of ducks to the common law system has been limited, but significant; they have concentrated the minds of lawyers upon fundamental issues of timeless principle. Nobody who has ever read the case is likely to forget the decision in *Regina* v. *Brown* (1888),[1] in which the Court of Crown Cases Reserved was initially somewhat puzzled by the earlier unreported decision in *Regina* v. *Dodd* (1877). In this, it was thought, the judges had reorganized the natural world into a new scheme of categories, and ruled that a duck was not an animal. *Brown's Case*, arising as it did in Essex, involved a tale for which the world was not yet prepared, though it did provoke from Lord Chief Justice Coleridge an expression of sympathy for 'the poor birds' concerned, coupled with a decision that they were indeed animals. But the most notable legal achievement of the *anatinae* must surely be the decision of the Court of Queen's Bench in the case of *Keeble* v. *Hickeringill*, judgment being given on 20 December 1707 in Michaelmas Term of the sixth year of Queen Anne.[2]

It involved an action for damages for frightening ducks, then, as now, timorous creatures. Although the case is still an authority of some importance in English law, its true home is now the United States, where it features very prominently in the teaching of both the law of property and the law of torts through the case method of instruction, which, for those who have not suffered under it, can be studied in the privacy of one's own home by renting the film *Paper Chase*. But few indeed of the hundreds of law professors who have made use of the case in legal instruction can have possessed any clear idea of what the case was actually about. For the ducks involved in the case were frightened away from a duck decoy, and today, especially in the United States where they are both made, collected, and indeed used on a large scale, a duck decoy means

---

[1] CCC XVI 715.

[2] The parties appears as Keable, Keeble, and Keble, and as Hickeringall, Hickringill, Hickeringill, Hickeringell, and Hickeringal; the *DNB* has Hickeringill or Hickorn-Gill. For reports see Holt KB 14, 17, 19, 90 ER 906 (Case 16), 907 (Case 17), 908 (Case 18), 11 Mod. 74, 130, 88 ER 898, 945, 3 Salk. 9, 91 ER 659, note to *Carrington* v. *Taylor* (1809) 11 East 574, 103 ER 1127, W Kel. 273, 25 ER 610; Buller, *Nisi Prius* 79. The pleadings are in PRO KB 122/13 at m. 346 (Trinity 3 Anne, 1704). There is a report in Harvard Law School MSS 1109. 1 at 23–5 which wrongly says there was a special verdict found. I am indebted to Prof. Charles Donahue for a copy.

a model duck, which may be floated on a pond, or set down upon the ground, to lure other members of this sociable race to their doom. This, however, was not the sort of duck decoy involved in *Keeble* v. *Hickeringill*. It was a much more elaborate device, of which one of the barristers engaged in the case, Montague, remarked enigmatically: 'decoys are not of any long standing, but against the laws of the land, to allure fowl and take them there in large quantities'.[3] To make sense of this statement, and to understand the significance of the litigation, requires a short incursion into the history of duck decoys.

Ducking and Other Systems for the Capture of Ducks

The principal English historian of the duck decoy was a baronet, Sir Ralph William Frankland Payne-Gallwey,[4] described by himself in *Who's Who* as a 'well known, experienced and enthusiastic wild fowler'. In 1886 he published a sumptuous volume entitled *The Book of Duck Decoys. Their Construction, Management and History*; characteristically this work appeared as the duck decoy was everywhere in fatal decline. Sir Ralph, like many of the landed gentry of his time, had absolutely nothing to do. So, apart from short service as a Lieutenant in the Rifle Brigade, he devoted his life to cricket, golf, fishing, and shooting wild birds, and to writing books. Although of catholic interests, including the cross-bow[5] and projectile weapons of the ancient world[6] in his repertoire, his books chiefly belong to the enormous and largely forgotten literature of field sports. They were, in Britain, the preserve of the upper classes, who regularly engaged in grotesque orgies of slaughter. The principal victim was the pheasant, but little that moved was safe, and rare creatures were shot to simplify identification. Perhaps his most successful publication was his three volumes of *Letters to Young Shooters*;[7] the most intellectual was surely *High Pheasants in Theory and Practice*, published in 1913.[8] High pheasants certainly did present a problem, and one that provoked one of the few jokes, if indeed it was a joke, attributed to the aristocratic Lord Halifax, 'the Holy Fox', Britain's Foreign Secretary from 1938 to 1940. When asked whether the interminable late-night

---

[3] Holt KB 17, 90 ER 908. Cf. Powell J in W Kel. 275, 25 ER 611: 'He thought Decoy Ponds were new Things'.

[4] 19 Aug. 1848–24 Nov. 1916.

[5] *Crossbows, Medieval and Modern, Military and Sporting . . . with a Treatise on the Balista and Catapult of the Ancients* (London 1903).

[6] *A Summary of the History, Construction and Effects of the Projectile Throwing Engines of the Ancients with a Treatise etc.* (London, 1907).

[7] (1890–4).

[8] His other books were *The Fowler in Ireland* (1882), *The Mystery of Maria Stella, Lady Newborough* (1907), *The History of the George worn on the Scaffold by Charles I* (1908), *The Pedigree of Frankland of Thirkelby* (1910), and *The War: A Criticism* (1915), a plea for conscription; his son was killed at the very beginning of the war. He also wrote a joint work on shooting with Lord Walsingham.

meetings at the time of Munich were not wearing him out he replied, 'Not exactly. But it spoils one's eyes for the high birds'.[9] Sir Ralph was not averse to killing a wide variety of wild creatures, but his chief enthusiasm was for the destruction of ducks, for whom he had a deep if somewhat curious affection. At his country seat, Thirkelby Park in Yorkshire, he constructed his own duck decoy, and although I have not visited the site this can still be located in Pond Wood from the current map of the area.[10] For duck decoys were substantial constructions, which leave traces on the landscape, both physical traces, and place names, long after they have fallen into disuse.

In the past there were in Northern Europe enormous stocks of wild ducks, an important source of food. Wild ducks, *canards sauvages*, are highly edible, and my *Nouveau Larousse gastronomique* describes the flesh of the commonest duck, the mallard, known in France as simply *un sauvage*, as 'exquisitely flavoured'. So significant was the wild duck as food that the canonists classified the pintail, the teal, and the garganey as not meat at all, and therefore suitable fare for Lent. But ducks are shy and elusive; in consequence they are hard to capture in large numbers as a commercial operation. They may, of course, be shot, but there are no free ducks, and a solitary bird, or even a small number of propinquous ducks, if dispatched by fowling piece, are likely to die in debt, unless of course killed in sport, when the sinful pleasure derived from the pursuit of the creatures is entered into the equation.

In medieval Britain a technique was, however, developed which enabled ducks to be captured in very considerable numbers. It could only, however, be used in areas of wetland. It depended upon the fact that during the summer months young ducks were still unable to fly, and their parents, during the moult, were also more or less flightless. As Sir Ralph explains:

The ducks were beaten out of the reeds and marsh into the water, and then the young birds, being unable to fly at all, and the old ones but little, owing to their 'moulting' condition, were all easily edged to their capture by a compact line of men and boats, just as a net surrounds a shoal of fish.[11]

By this technique, which was known as 'ducking', thousands of ducks could be captured in a single drive.[12]

But the practice had three disadvantages. One was that it required many people; it was a communal activity, involving a 'Company of Duckers', and someone to act as accountant for the division of the spoils. The second was that

---

[9] P. Johnson, *The Oxford Book of British Political Anecdotes* (Oxford, 1989) 213.

[10] Sheet 100; map reference 472792. There is a description in J. Whitaker, *British Duck Decoys of To-day* (London, 1918), 91. It had 3 pipes and the pool covered an acre; in 1918 it was catching about 50 ducks a year.

[11] Payne-Gallwey, *The Book of Duck Decoys etc.* (hereafter referred to simply as 'Payne-Gallwey'), 5.

[12] T. Southwell, 'Wild-Fowl Driving in the Sixteenth Century' *Transactions of the Norwich and Norfolk Naturalists Society*, vii (1899–1904), 90.

such drives caused extensive disturbance and could not be repeated in the same area. The third was that they were extremely destructive of stocks, involving the killing of many immature birds, being carried out when 'the seid olde fowle be mowted and not replenysshed with feathers to flye, nor the yonge fowle fully feathered perfyctly to flye . . . in such wyse that the brode of wylde-foulle is almost thereby wasted and consumed'. Consequently it was made illegal by an Act of Parliament of 1534, from which this is a quotation. The Act forbad the taking of duck eggs between 1 March and 30 June, and the netting of ducks between 31 May and 31 August, when such drives took place.[13] This Act was, however, repealed in response to pressure from the Fenland commoners in 1550,[14] and was in any event hard to enforce in the remote areas where the practice went on. The driving of ducks continued into the seventeenth and early eighteenth centuries; at the ducking on Deeping Fen in Lincolnshire in June of 1728, 13,032 ducks were captured in three days.[15] It passed out of use as individual private landholding of drained wetlands supplanted their use as commons, and it became illegal again in 1603 under temporary legislation which was probably impossible to enforce.[16] In 1710 a close season between 1 July and 1 September was introduced,[17] and this was amended to one beginning on 1 June in 1737.[18] Eventually, in 1831, earlier laws were repealed and conservation left to the initiative of private landowners, and this remained the state of affairs until modern times. By now ducking was long dead.[19] Counsel's statement in *Keeble* v. *Hickeringill* that decoys were illegal is a confused reference to the legislation passed to control ducking.

There were a variety of other techniques employed to net, trap, or snare ducks individually or in small numbers, and many of these are described and illustrated in a seventeenth-century work, *The Ornithology of Francis Willughby*, which incorporated *An Epitome of the Art of Fowling* (1678).[20] They could be shot relatively inexpensively by the skilful with a bow and arrows. Shooting ducks with hand-held fowling pieces was practised primarily for sport. For commercial exploitation there was evolved, probably in the eighteenth century, the punt gun. This was a miniature cannon, discharging up to a pound or more of lead shot; the gun, which might weigh as much as 150 pounds, was normally built into a shallow boat or punt which could be paddled or poled within range of an unsuspecting flock of ducks or gaggle of geese. With good fortune a considerable number of birds could be killed or maimed by a single shot, and then collected by the gunner and his water dog.[21] The late Sir Peter Scott, eventually the principal conservationist of wild fowl in Britain, was in his youth a punt gunner, and

---

[13] 25 Henry VIII c.11.   [14] 3 & 4 Edw. VI c.7.   [15] Southwell n. 12 above, 91.
[16] 1 Jac. I c.27, s. 2, on which see below at 68.   [17] 9 Anne c.25, s. 4.
[18] 10 Geo. II c.32.   [19] 1 & 2 Will. IV c.32.
[20] The epitome was by one John Ray. See also R. Blome, *The Gentleman's Recreation* (London, 1686), Pt. II.
[21] See J. Wentworth-Day, *A History of the Fens* (London, 1954), chs. 12 and 13; *Coastal Adventure* (London, 1949).

describes the practice in his autobiography, *The Eye of the Wind*, as does J. Wentworth-Day. The most bloodthirsty and extensive account of punt gunning I know is, however, by a Lincoln's Inn barrister, H. C. Folkard, who came from Mistley in Essex. He wrote a legal treatise on libel and slander, and *A Guide to the Law of Loans and Pledges*, not, I suspect, a gripping work; he became more generally known for his *The Sailing Boat*. His most ferocious work was *The Wildfowler. A Treatise on Fowling, Ancient and Modern. Descriptive Also of Decoys and Flight Ponds*;[22] the literature of field sports in the nineteenth century was at times quite remarkably sadistic. He thus describes the critical moment:

On pulling the fatal trigger a cloud of smoke rises before the shooter, through which he dimly sees hundreds of ducks flying off in line . . . on the smoke clearing he beholds, as it were, a pathway of dead and dying ducks . . . the imaginary pathway soon becomes a broken and scattered extent of dead, dying, and disabled victims.[23]

Hence a chapter of his book is devoted to what he calls, with a certain lack of charm, 'The Cripple Chase'. He explains that where a gun is mounted on a yacht, a practice he describes, 'the cripple chase offers fine fun for young sailors and cabin boys'. As many as a hundred ducks could be brought down by one shot. Punt gunning was widely practised, sometimes by fleets of gunners, who co-ordinated their assaults on the unfortunate ducks. The commercial use of punt guns continued into quite modern times, even as late as the 1950s, and punt gunning also flourished as a slightly eccentric form of upper-class sport. It had the disadvantage that, once the gun was fired, all other birds in the area were put to flight, so that a considerable period had to elapse between shots. It could also be hazardous to the gunner, who might drown or be injured by a burst gun.

The Introduction of the Duck Decoy

In the sixteenth century the Dutch developed an entirely new technique for capturing wild ducks on a commercial scale, known as an *eendenkooi*, which means duck cage. There were two such *eendenkooien* on Texel as early as 1561, and in all something like 120 were constructed in Holland.[24] In the late sixteenth or early seventeenth century they were introduced into Britain.[25] The English term

---

[22] See in particular chs. 21 ff.   [23] At 140.

[24] On the Dutch history see G. D. van der Heide and T. Lebret, *Achter de Schermen* (*Behind the Screens*) (Kinheim-Uitgeverij–Heiloo, 1944) and Sietmu Dykhinen, *Endenkooien* (Terra, Lutfen, 1980). Gerard Mast, secretary to the decoymen's association of Friesland/Groningen in 'Endenkooien op de waddeneilanden' ('Duck Decoys of the West Frisian Islands'), *Waddenbulletin* 1992. I am indebted to Dr R. F. van der Sluis and Gerard Mast for information.

[25] Wentworth-Day, *A History of the Fens*, n. 21 above, ch. 10. Earlier accounts include F. Willughby, *The Ornithology of Francis Willughby of Middleton in the County of Warwick Esquire* (London, 1678), which includes a primitive plan; R. Blome, n. 20 above, who in ch. 6 at 128 gives a very brief account; W. Stukeley, *Itinerarium Curiosum or an Account of the Antiquitys* (London, 1724), which includes a plan, R. Bradley, *A General Treatise of Husbandry and Gardening* (London, 1726), *The*

for them was originally 'coy', or 'koye', taken from the Dutch, but they came to be called 'decoys'; the 'de' may come from Dutch *eendenkooi*, from *de kooi* or from 'duck coy'.[26] Whatever the origin of the term, a coy was not a model duck designed to entice other ducks, but an elaborate duck trap. Sir Henry Spelman (1564?–1641), as quoted by Payne-Gallwey, wrote: 'Sir W. Wodehouse (who lived in the reign of James I, 1603–25) made among us the first device for catching DUCKS, known by the foreign name of a *koye*.'[27] Sir William, whom Spelman describes as a reviver of James I by his jests, was the son and heir of Sir Henry Wodehouse, who had 'greatly wasted his estates'. He, too, was cheered up by his jocular son. Sir Henry died in 1638.[28] Sir William succeeded his father in 1624, but when he introduced the decoy into Norfolk is uncertain, though probably it was after 1624.[29] Decoys were not his only link with Holland; his eldest son, Thomas, was reputed to have committed incest with his sister, Elizabeth, there. The resulting child, discretely called Elizabeth Smith, was provided for in her father's will. The decoy was at Waxham in Norfolk, earlier called Waxstonsham, where the family had been settled since Tudor times. The site can still be identified.[30] The other pioneer enthusiast for decoys about whom something is known was Sir William Brereton (1604–61), who became a Parliamentary General during the civil war. His *Travels in Holland The United Provinces England Scotland and Ireland*, eventually published in 1844, but describing travels in 1634 and 1635, contain many references to 'coys' both in Holland and England.[31] Those mentioned in England were one between Newcastle and Morpeth on Point Island, owned by Mark Arington,[32] one built by a Mr Swan somewhere

---

Universal Magazine of Knowledge and Pleasure (April 1752), O. Goldsmith, *A History of the Earth and Animated Nature* (Edinburgh, 1840), ii, 235–6; T. Bewick, *A History of British Birds* (London, 1797 and 1804); T. Pennant, *British Zoology* (London, 1812), ii, 259–63; R. Lubbock, *Fauna of Norfolk* (London, 1879), 134 ff., all cited by Payne-Gallwey, 8. He reproduces the earliest picture of one, dating from 1665, at 9; the source is J. Ogilby, *The Fables of Aesop paraphras'd in verse* (London, 1665), at 200; the picture illustrates the fable of the Husbandman and the Stork. T. Southwell, 'Norfolk Decoys', *Transactions of the Norwich and Norfolk Naturalists Society*, ii (1874–9), 538, contains much information. Decoys were also constructed in France, Belgium, and Denmark.

[26] The *SOED* (2nd ed.) points out the earlier recorded use of decoy to mean a swindler.

[27] Payne-Gallwey, 2. Spelman actually wrote in his *Icenia sive Norfolciae Descriptio Topographia*: *Hic Gulielmus Woodhouse Eques, Jacobo Regi nuper in facetiis, & Familiae corruentis Suscitator, primum apud nos instituit Discipulum Anatorium, peregrine nomine a Koye, ie. Cors seu Cavea nuncupatum.* See *The English Works of Sir Henry Spelman* (London, 1723), ii. 153.

[28] W. Rye, *Norfolk Families* (Norwich, 1913), 1026–9. For Sir Henry's will see PROB 11/145 (PCC Clarke 15); for Sir William's PROB 11/181 (PCC Harvey 175).

[29] John Speed (c.1552–1629) used a description of Norfolk by Spelman in his *The Theatre of the Empire of Great Britaine* (London), of which the British Library has an edition of 1611 (shelfmark G.7884), at Book I, 35. However this does not include any mention of decoys.

[30] OS map reference 436255, where the early nineteenth-century OS map (Sheet 38) marks Decoy Covert. The site is south of Waxham at the end of a small dyke which feeds into New Cut, approximately 400 yards from Waxham Bridge Farm.

[31] Edited E. Hawkins for the Chetham Society. See 17, 22–3, 37, 43–4, 89–90, 153, 171. Evelyn notes decoys in Holland near Dort 'where they catch innumerable quantities of Fowle' in 1641; see *The Diary of John Evelyn* (ed. E. S. de Beer), ii. 59.

[32] Not listed by Payne-Gallwey; possibly the reference is to the Pont River. I have not identified the site.

near Newcastle, one called Orion's Coy, half a mile from Rodney-Stoke in Somerset,[33] and his own coy, run by a coy man called John, who was probably Dutch, situated in Cheshire near Dodleston; Decoy Farm today marks the site.[34] It was a *koye* which was involved in *Keeble* v. *Hickeringill*. Four apparently remain in working condition,[35] used to capture birds for ringing.[36] A number still operate in Holland.

The basis of a decoy is a pool, which could be of considerable size; that of the Borough Fen decoy covers two and a half acres. Fritton Lake in Suffolk, which at one time had twenty-one pipes, is a lake three miles long. Pools of around two acres were most effective; a decoy man named Old George Skelton (*c.*1760–1840), whose family was celebrated for their expertise, and who designed many decoys, popularized small pools.[37] Radiating from the pool were a number of channels; there might be as many as eight of these, though more commonly there would be three or four. These would be around twenty feet across where they joined the pool, tapering to a mere two feet or less. They were up to around 400 feet long, and were curved, so that from the pool it was impossible to see down them for more than about half their length. They were roofed with netting, supported by hoops, and were called pipes. At the junction with the pool the pipe might be fifteen or twenty feet high, but at the end of the pipe the diameter would be around two feet. Arrangements had to be made to supply the pool with water, and to direct a current down a selected pipe towards the pool; decoys were therefore built near a natural stream, and an elaborate system of supply channels had to be constructed to operate the larger ones. To prevent disturbance a decoy needed to be surrounded with a considerable area of woodland.

Isolation was critical to success. Willughby, one of the earliest writers to give an account of decoys, in 1678, explains: 'A place is to be chosen for the purpose remote from Common High-ways and all noise of people.'[38] Ducks have an acute sense of smell, and decoy men concealed their own scent with burning peat. There were concealed paths which enabled the decoy man to move about without disturbing the ducks on the pool. So duck decoys were considerable capital works. The Borough Fen decoy covers seventeen and a half acres.

The method of working a decoy was ingenious. The pool, and such ducks, whether wild or tame, which happened to be on it, attracted others; decoys

[33] Listed by Payne-Gallwey as Stoke Decoy. On current OS map Sheet 182 there is Decoy Pool Farm near the site at 455505; on the early OS map (Sheet 76) the decoy itself is marked and another decoy 21/2 miles NE at 431526 on Sheet 182.

[34] Sheet 117 at 381629. On the old OS map, (Sheet 25) the farm is called Lache Farm. This was a 5-pipe decoy. The site is discussed in T. A. Coward and C. Oldham, *Birds of Cheshire* (Manchester, 1900), 162. The authors refer to a pool behind the farm and some curious depressions radiating from it, but unconvincingly argue against this as the site.

[35] See below 56.

[36] I am indebted to Mr Richard Chappell, decoy man at Slimbridge, for information.

[37] Lubbock, n. 25 above, 138; Southwell, 'Norfolk Decoys', *passim.* Payne-Gallwey gives a picture of his son, Young George.

[38] F. Willughby, n. 25 above.

worked best if there were not many other pools in the area. The task of the decoy man was to persuade some of the ducks which had settled to swim into a pipe, whilst not disturbing those remaining on the pool. Since ducks like to swim into the wind, the pipe selected itself; they also like to swim against the current, and this too could be arranged. The ducks could be lured into a pipe by the use of tame trained ducks, or by feeding the pipe with corn. In early accounts of decoys the use of tame ducks seems to have been the norm, and Daniel Defoe in his *A Tour Through the Whole Island of Great Britain* gives an entertaining account of the use of these 'traytors that drew the poor ducks into this snare'.[39] Tame ducks were indeed used by Samuel Keeble, the decoy man in our case.

Dogging with Coy-Dogs

Although tame ducks were always used to attract ducks to the central pool, the preferred method of attracting them into the pipe was by 'dogging'. An elaborate arrangement of screens was built alongside each pipe, which enabled the decoy man, without being seen or smelt, to control a dog, know as a 'coy-dog' or 'piper'.[40] The dog contrived to appear and disappear, jumping over some low screens in a puzzling manner which excited the curiosity of the ducks. The piper began its antics by leaping over a screen called the 'yackoop', this and some other terms being of Dutch origin.[41] The dog was trained to retreat further and further up the pipe, always under the silent control of the decoy man. The curious ducks followed.

Decoy men were notoriously secretive:

The Decoymen kept their secrets well, and were indeed forced to do so in their own interests, for it stood to reason they knew that the greater the number of Decoys in use the less would be each owner's proportionate share of birds . . . was he not fearful of some covetous neighbour setting up a Decoy for himself hard by, and so robbing him perchance of half his profits?[42]

Dogging was something of a trade secret; the Revd R. Lubbock, writing in the early nineteenth century, said:

it is not always an easy task to obtain admission to a decoy when in the hands of an illiterate man, it is almost unapproachable by anyone: *Procul o Procul este profani*[43] is the cry, for they hide their manœuvres against the wildfowl in as much mystery as the Rosycrucians throw around their search for the philosopher's stone.[44]

---

[39] Edn. of 1974, ii. 97–100.   [40] Brereton uses the former term; see 23.

[41] Perhaps formed from Dutch *jacht* and English coop, meaning a basket work screen for hunting the ducks.

[42] Payne-Gallwey 1.

[43] 'Keep away, keep away, you uninitiated ones!' This was the cry of the Sybil in the *Aeneid*, Book VI.

[44] N. 25 above, at 134.

He nevertheless managed to inspect the workings of Ranworth Decoy in Norfolk. Some early writers, such as Defoe and Sir Henry Spelman, the earliest English writer on the subject, wrongly suggest that dogs were used merely to frighten the ducks up the pipe:

Then, when a cunning dog, trained for this purpose, appears cautiously at the farther edge of the wide end of the pond, the wildfowl move off toward the narrow end, and when the dog presses them in that direction, but from a distance, and sometimes gets into the water and sometimes secretly gets out again, they strive to reach only the same narrow end. The dog now openly jumps about, and on seeing this the decoy ducks settle, while the new arrivals take to their wings and crash into the fowler's nets.[45]

Willughby, the earliest to give a full account, gives an entertaining but slightly fanciful account of the work of the dog:

The Whelp in compassing the hedges ought always to keep his tail directed towards the Pool, his Head toward the Pipe, and so he terrifies the Birds before him, and drives them forward; Those behind him he allures and tolls forward they following him to gaze at him as a new and strange thing.

Views as to the best type of dog varied, though dogs which resembled foxes were usually preferred; Lubbock thought a red or brown dog was best.[46] Brereton, who took a special pride in his own dogs, wrote: 'Coy-dogs best that are either white or red, and the more hairy the better.'[47] Sir Ralph Payne-Gallwey, in a spirit of experiment, tried the use of a cat, a ferret, a rabbit, and even on one occasion a monkey, but found these creatures too difficult to control.

Whether by dogging or feeding, or some combination, a number of ducks, if all went well, would enter the pipe, and swim up it until they could no longer be seen by their friends back on the pool. The decoy man, who had until this moment remained out of sight behind the screens, now appeared behind the ducks, whilst remaining concealed from the pool. Willughby explains: 'The whole art consists in this, that the Birds within the Pipes may see the Fowler, those in the Pool not seeing him.'[48] The natural reaction of most frightened ducks—though not diving ducks such as pochards—was to take off into the wind; flying up the ever narrowing pipe they were trapped at its end, and could be removed alive and undamaged. They could then be immobilized by having their wings interlocked and their feet tied, and thus taken considerable distances to market or, of course, killed. Seventeenth-century ducks did not, I fear, have rights. The whole process could then be begun again, so that the decoy was in continuous operation; uncaptured ducks served to attract others to the pool.

Duck decoys employing pipes of the type I have described must be distinguished from more or less elaborate duck cages built on the edge of pools, into

---

[45] *The English Works of Spelman* (London, 1727), Posthumous Works, 153. Cf. T. H. Allen, *The History of the County of Lincoln from the Earliest Period to the Present Time* (London, 1834), i, 60.
[46] N. 25 above, 142.   [47] Brereton, n. 40 above, 23.   [48] N. 25 above, 373.

which ducks were attracted by feeding or the use of tame ducks, and imprisoned by closing the entrance. Many pools in the past had such traps, and some remained in use in modern times, but their ability to catch ducks commercially in large numbers was very much less than that of decoys.[49] They principally existed to supply ducks for the owner's table. Descriptions of decoys in operation in 1918 by Whitaker also indicate that some decoys were operated without the use of a dog, the ducks being induced to pipe simply by feeding, or by the use of tame ducks.[50]

So long as considerable stocks of wild ducks existed, the duck decoy was an efficient mechanism for their commercial exploitation. Decoys could also be built and used by rich landowners simply to provide for their own needs. Charles II, for example, had one built in St James Park in central London. It was constructed by a Dutchman, Sydrach Hilacus. The decoy man was called Storey, and his name is preserved in the place-name Storey's Gate.[51] The craft of decoy man, now all but extinct, was commonly passed down from father to son, and preserved, so far as possible, as a mystery. The Borough Fen decoy, for example, was operated by the Williams family from around 1670 until 1958; the Skeltons operated numerous decoys in the eighteenth and nineteenth centuries.[52] The larger commercial decoys seem to have been usually held on lease from the landowner by the decoy man, and although considerable initial outlay was required a decoy could thereafter be worked by a single individual. The winter was the period when large numbers of ducks migrated to Britain, and in the summer months the decoy man could devote his time to maintenance and repair.

The Rise and Decline of the Duck Decoy

According to W. Page and J. H. Round, writing in 1907, about 192 decoys were constructed in England, nineteen in Ireland, and a few in Wales; they nearly all date from the seventeenth or eighteenth centuries.[53] To day the location of many can be discovered from place-names, or from the remains of the pool. The current *Ordnance Survey Gazetteer of Great Britain*, which lists all names on the 1:50,000 maps, has fifty 'decoy' names, such as Decoy Farm, The Decoy, and so forth; there are also numerous 'pond' names, some connected with decoys, Coy's Bridge in Lincolnshire and Coy's Grove in Suffolk. There is an

---

[49] Payne-Gallwey describes them; see 3 and 71–2. Whitaker notes examples, as at Groby Park in Leicestershire.

[50] e.g. Abbotsbury in Dorset.

[51] Evelyn records this in his memoirs on 29 Mar. 1665; see iii, 398; H. B. Wheatley (ed.), *The Diary of John Evelyn* (1906); J. Wentworth-Day, *History of the Fens* 117. Evelyn also mentions decoys at Pyrford (see *VCH Surrey*, iii, 431) and elsewhere (see vol. iv, 114, 118, 255).

[52] T. Cook and R. E. M. Pilcher, *The History of the Borough Fen Decoy* (Ely, 1982), chs. 2 and 7. On the Skeltons see Payne-Gallwey, *passim*, and Southwell, 'Norfolk Decoys', 542.

[53] *VCH Essex*, ii, 588–9. Payne-Gallwey at 59 lists 186 in England and 22 in Ireland.

example in the Shelley country, just to the east of Angmering, identified on the map as Decoy Pond, in Decoy Wood.[54] Many more can be located on old maps. Most decoys were close to the east coast, in Lincolnshire, Norfolk, Suffolk, and Essex. Ideally they were situated near mudflats. Payne-Gallwey lists twenty-nine decoys in Essex, where the dispute litigated in *Keeble* v. *Hickeringill* arose.

They could be extremely profitable. Thus the Revd W. B. Daniels in his *Rural Sports* (1802) records that 'the number of *wild fowl* taken in *decoys* is amazing; these birds have of late years been all contracted for by the London Salesmen and Poulterers, at so much per dozen, formerly *eighteen shillings*, now from about a *guinea* to *four and twenty shillings*'. He recorded that in 1795 the Tillingham decoy on the Essex coast—known as the Marsh House decoy and still in existence in a decayed state—made a clear profit of £800.[55] In 1799 another Essex decoy caught 10,000 birds. It was then owned by the Revd Sir Henry Bate Dudley, 'the Fighting Parson', a noted duellist, sportsman, journalist, and 'man of pleasure'.[56] This was the Glebeland Decoy, situated in the same area about a mile to the north, near Bradwell on Sea.[57] The numbers caught would indeed have been considerably larger, since for accounting purposes mallards (often simply called ducks) counted as one, but smaller ducks, such as widgeon or teal, as a half only.[58] Wentworth-Day gives detailed figures for the Ashby Decoy in Lincolnshire between 1833 and 1868; in three years, over 6,000 birds were captured.[59] Whitaker states that in 1714 the Steeple Decoy in Essex took 7,364 birds; the costs of construction in 1713 was £176 11 *s.* 4 *d.*, and the first year's catch sold for £150.[60] He also says that Great Oakley in the same county took 12,000, and that Ashby in North Lincolnshire once took 2,300 ducks in a single month.[61] But the stocks of duck were over-exploited, and many areas of wet land drained and brought into cultivation.[62] The decline was very rapid. Thus the Glebeland decoy was abandoned in 1822, though the problem there may have been the existence of two other decoys within the same coastal area, and the location of houses rather too close to the decoy.[63] The greatest of the decoy men,

[54] Listed by Payne-Gallwey at 59 as one of 7 in the County, and no longer in use.

[55] Listed by Payne-Gallwey as still in use. On the current 1:50000 OS map (Sheet 168) marked at 020042, about half a mile from the sea coast and the extensive Dengie Flat.

[56] See *DNB* entry and Wentworth-Day, *Coastal Adventures*, n. 21 above, 73. He edited the *Morning Post* and later the *Morning Herald*, and was at one time Vicar of Bradwell.

[57] A third decoy, Grange Decoy, was located 11/2 miles to the south of Marsh House Decoy. All three decoys are shown on the 1952 OS map of the area (Sheet 162) at 019056 (Glebeland, to the west of Glebe Farm), 019042 (Marsh House), and 020019 (Grange). In the current map (Sheet 168) only Marsh House Decoy remains.

[58] W. B. Daniel, *Rural Sports* (London, 1802), ii. 469, 471; Payne-Gallwey, 78.

[59] *History of the Fens*, n. 21 above, 129.

[60] Enlarging it in 1721 cost £130 3*s.* 0*d.* See Wentworth-Day, *Coastal Adventure*, n. 21 above, 89–90.

[61] Ibid. 105.

[62] See T. H. Allen, n. 45 above, i. 60: J. Wentworth-Day, *History of the Fens*, n. 21 above, ch. 10 and *passim*.

[63] Payne-Gallwey, 78.

the diminutive George Skelton, succumbed to cold and drink in February 1857, expiring in a four-poster bed in the decoy house of the Dersingham decoy, appropriately surrounded with curtains formed by strings of dead ducks.[64] By the 1880s twenty-six of the Essex decoys were out of use, and only three were still operating. In England and Wales only forty or so of the 200 or more which had been built were still in use when Payne-Gallwey published his book.[65] By 1918 the number had dropped to twenty-eight,[66] and by 1936 to only five; this was about the number still operating in 1954. Those commercially operating were Marsh House in Essex, Orwell Park and Fritton Lake in Suffolk, Borough Fen in Lincolnshire—already partly in use for bird ringing—and possibly Wretham in Norfolk. Orielton in Wales was in use for bird ringing (there is now a Field Studies Centre there), and Berkeley Old Decoy was in the course of being brought back into use for this purpose.[67] Eventually the few remaining decoys were either abandoned, or taken over entirely by conservationists. The Wildfowl Trust acquired Berkeley Old Decoy at Slimbridge in 1947, and the Nacton decoy in Suffolk, which had long remained profitable, in 1968. Borough Fen Decoy was acquired in 1951, and from 1954 used exclusively for ringing birds. The only other decoy still in working condition in Britain, so far as I am aware, is Boarstall Decoy near Brill in Buckinghamshire, which is owned by the National Trust; it dates from the eighteenth century, and is located in thirteen acres of woodland. The Protection of Birds Act of 1954 made the future use of decoys for capturing ducks except for ringing or scientific purposes illegal, though decoys in use immediately before 1954 were exempted, as they still are.[68]

Problems of Competition

As the number of decoys increased, problems over competition between them were bound to arise, particularly because suitable locations were fairly limited. The decoys—for there were three of them—involved directly or indirectly in *Keeble* v. *Hickeringill* have long since ceased to operate; none was in use when Payne-Gallwey published his book in 1886, though he states that one, the first which I describe, had operated in living memory. It was the decoy directly involved in the case, operated by the plaintiff, Samuel Keeble. It was called the Jacques Hall New Decoy, and was in the parish of Wix in Essex, about a mile south of the estuary of the River Stour.[69] It lay approximately 300 yards to the

---

[64] The story was told to Thomas Southwell by a gentleman who visited the dying decoyman. See T. Southwell, 'Norfolk Decoys' in *Trns. of the Norwich and Norfolk Naturalists Society* (1874–9), ii. 543.

[65] Payne-Gallwey, 76. The Essex decoys in use in 1886 were Marsh House, Grange, and Old Hall.

[66] J. Whitaker, n. 10 above, preface.

[67] Wentworth-Day, *History of the Fens*, n. 21 above, 16.

[68] The Protection of Birds Act has now been overtaken by the Wildlife and Countryside Act 1981.

[69] See Chapman and André's map of Essex of 1777 and the OS map (1805).

east of the present-day Bluehouse Farm; nobody would site a decoy so close to habitation, and this farm, which does not appear on the map of 1777, was either built after the decoy had ceased to operate, or perhaps its construction caused the decoy to be abandoned. Minott's meadow, mentioned with Minott's Hill in the pleadings and in reports of the case as the site of the decoy, is shown as woodland or scrubland on the tithe map of Wix of 1837.[70] We may guess that a piece of what had been swampy meadow land was used as the site of the decoy. This map does not show the pool or pipes, which had presumably been obliterated by 1837.[71] The approximate position can be identified on the ground today. It lay across a small stream 800 yards north east of an imposing house, externally eighteenth century in appearance, but with an earlier seventeenth-century interior. The house was then and still is called Pond Hall. It was the home of the defendant in the case of *Keeble* v. *Hickeringill*.

Considerably further away, about 2,000 yards from Pond Hall, a little to the east of north, is Jacques Hall, from which the decoy had its name, close to the River Stour, where there is a Jacques Bay. The name is sixteenth century. The present house, built on an older site, and incorporating medieval fragments, dates from 1834, and earlier maps show a house there, though I have been unable to discover much of its history. In the very early eighteenth century, Jacques Hall was owned by the Earls of Oxford until the partitioning of the De Vere estates after the death of the last Earl in 1703.[72] Jacques Hall is currently the home of a therapeutic community for disturbed teenagers. About 1,100 yards to the east of Jacques Hall, and 2,700 yards north east of Pond Hall, is the site of a second decoy, Jacques Hall Old Decoy, only very indirectly connected with the litigation. Payne-Gallwey notes that in 1886 'the pond is quite filled up and its enclosure alone remains'. On the Bradfield tithe map of 1837 two field names, Decoy and Decoy Pond Pightle, relate to it, and the site, which can readily be identified, is now a swampy and overgrown area with a small stream running through it, to the west of Wheatsheaf Lane, and close to the railway line. This decoy is not shown on the map of 1777, and we may guess that it had by then been long abandoned. As we shall see, it had probably been superseded by the time of the litigation.

The third duck decoy indirectly involved in the case was owned by Hickeringill, and was known as Pond Hall Decoy. It lay on a small stream almost due north

[70] The tithe apportionment was confirmed in 1843; the reference to the copy is the ERO Acc. C231. There was also a field called Little Minott's.

[71] Re-issues of the OS map continued to show the decoy, relying upon the original survey.

[72] The Hall is on the site of a hamlet also called Bradfield Manestune, Monaston, Mountherd, or Manston. Before the dissolution there was a nunnery there, a daughter house to the Abbey of Wix, with a chapel dedicated to Our Lady in the Oats. Sir Henry Rainsford of Bradfield acquired the property at the dissolution and gave it to his son Jakys (brass in Bradfield Church). See T. Wright, *History and Topography of the County of Essex Comprising its Ancient and Modern History* (London, 1831 and 1835), ii. 783; P. Morant, *History and Antiquities of the County of Essex* (London, 1768), i. 465. After being considered as the site of a zoo, Jacques Hall was sold in 1963 to the Spastics Society, which was unable to find sufficient funds to retain the property.

of the Hall. The name of the Hall must be associated with the existence of the decoy, and conceivably Hall and pond were built about the same time, when duck decoys were something of a novelty in England. According to Payne-Gallwey[73] the remains of Pond Hall Decoy were half a mile to the east of Jacques Hall Decoy, and half a mile to the south of the village of Bradfield. 'East' here is an obvious slip for 'west'; in fact the decoy was on a small stream which runs to the west of Pond Hall, and which joins the stream used for the Jacques Hall New Decoy further to the north.[74] The decoy would be in or close to what is still called Pond Hall Wood. The Wix tithe map of 1843 has a Decoy Field adjacent to this wood. Pond Hall Decoy does not appear on the map of 1777, and must by then have been long abandoned. If any reader visits the site, it is important not to confuse the long-abandoned decoy with a duck pond which is close to the Hall. It was much closer to Jacques Hall New Decoy than Payne-Gallwey supposed—approximately 350 yards to its west. As these things go, this is very unusual; duck decoys were normally well dispersed. It is apparent from one of the reports of *Keeble* v. *Hickeringill* that the quarrel which provoked the litigation involved two decoy ponds, and that the plaintiff's was 'pretty near' that of the defendant.[75] The reference is to Jacques Hall New Decoy and Pond Hall Decoy.

Once, however, it becomes clear that there were really three decoy ponds involved in the story, and their approximate location is established, it becomes reasonably clear why the dispute arose. The original Jacques Hall Old Decoy was situated a long way from the Pond Hall Decoy, and consequently was not thought to be in direct competition with it. Perhaps because it had been built close to a highway, or perhaps because it was rather too near the Stour estuary, and subject therefore to disturbance from punt gunning, it did not prove to be successful. So a decision was taken to construct a new decoy well inland in Minott's Meadow. Apart from the fact that it lay on a small stream, we cannot tell quite why this site was selected, except that it would be fairly secluded. But it is easy to see why its selection would irritate the owner of Pond Hall Decoy, for it was provocatively close to his decoy, and thus in direct competition with it.

Messrs Keeble and Hickeringill

As for the individuals involved in the case, a little is discoverable about Samuel Keeble, the plaintiff. He was a yeoman of Bradfield, and his will, dated 3 January 1719 and proved in May 1720, shows him as a married man—his wife's

[73] Payne-Gallwey, 92.

[74] Payne-Gallwey's location, probably based on the OS map of 1805, which is unclear, is on elevated sloping land, and is quite impossible.

[75] Holt 14, 90 ER 906.

name was Bridget—who owned three freehold properties in Bradfield and some copyhold property held of the Lord of the Manor there, and who also held two fields on lease from one Richard Rigby.[76] It contains no explicit reference to the decoy, which he may have operated as a tenant. However, his will records that his copyhold property had been purchased from William Peck, and Peck had been entitled to a share of the De Vere lands (which included Jacques Hall) when they were partitioned, and it may well be that the decoy was on these lands.[77]

Considerably more is known about the defendant, the Revd Edmund Hickeringill, who is described by two sober scholars in the Victoria County History as 'a half crazy minister and controversial pamphleteer'[78] and in the *Dictionary of National Biography* as 'the half-crazy rector of All Saints, Colchester'.[79]

Edmund Hickeringill (1631–1708) had begun his religious life as a Baptist, but after being excommunicated he became a Quaker and then, later in the same year, a Deist; this was all in the heady days of the Commonwealth, towards the end of which he embarked upon a military career. In the course of this he spent some time in Jamaica, about which he wrote a successful book, extolling its 'suitableness to English complexions'.[80] Curiously and perhaps significantly this book contains the earliest use of the verb 'decoy', though differently spelled: 'to allure and Duckoy the unwary world'.[81] After the Restoration he was unwisely ordained in the Church of England by the then Bishop of Lincoln, to the eternal regret of Bishop Henry Compton of London. He contrived to obtain preferment in Essex. He became for a short time Vicar of St Peter's, Colchester, in 1662, and soon after Rector of All Saints, Colchester, where he continued from 1662 until his death at the age of 78 on 30 November 1708: there is a monument to him there. He was also Vicar of Boxted in 1662–4 and Vicar of Fingrinhoe in 1692–1703. He owned land in Wix, where he was Lord of the Manor, and lived in Pond Hall. The family continued to live there throughout the eighteenth century, and his son Thomas assumed a coat of arms—three horses, appropriately rampant—to which he was not entitled, which may still be seen there.[82]

Edmund was opinionated and litigious, and fell to quarrelling with his bishop,

[76] ERO D/ABR 18/37. ERO D/DFI E3, a 1704 survey of the estates of the co-heirs of Viscount Bayning, has a John Keeble occupying Creek's Tenement in Bradfield, and Mr Hickringale as tenant of the Parsonage Land.

[77] I am indebted to P. R. J. Coverley of the Essex County Record Office for this information. The partition was confirmed by Act of Parliament in 1710.

[78] *VCH Essex*, ii. 72.

[79] In the articles on Hickeringill and on Henry Compton, Bishop of Oxford and later of London.

[80] *Jamaica Viewed: with all the Ports, Harbours, and their several soundings, Towns etc.* (London, 1661).

[81] Quoted *SOED* (2nd ed.) from the Preface.

[82] Edmund's wife died on 6 Apr. 1708; he left 2 sons and 4 daughters. See P. Morant, *The History and Antiquities of the . . . Town and Borough of Colchester in the County of Essex* (1748), App. to Book III, 51. The last member of the family there died on 21 Aug. 1799; there are memorials in Wix Church. The Bradfield Historical Society possess material, which I was kindly allowed to see. I am grateful to Mr Nigel Klammer.

Henry Compton, who he thought was soft on nonconformity; in a celebrated sermon in London in May of 1680 he invoked the curse of Meroz against him.[83] In March 1680, after attempts by the Court of King's Bench to control him, he was tried at Chelmsford Assizes for barratry, the common law crime of habitually stirring up suits and quarrels. He represented himself, and was acquitted.[84] As he put it in a later pamphlet: 'How has this Defendant been pestered within Twelve Months? Four and twenty great Heads of Barretry preferred against him in the Crown Office, about fifty witnesses subpoena'd to prove this, yet, scarce ten of them sworn.'[85] Bishop Compton proceeded against him for *scandalum magnatum* at the Colchester Assizes on 8 March 1681 before Chief Justice Pemberton, and obtained an award of the huge sum of £2,000, which the Bishop proposed to contribute towards the building of St Paul's. He said that the Bishop 'is a bold daring impudent man, for sending some Heads in Divinity to all his Clergy in these parts, which are contrary to law . . . His Lordship is very ignorant . . . I can prove his Lordship to be concerned in the Damnable Plot late discovered'. The damages were remitted in 1684 on his public confession of his offence before the Court of Arches.[86] In his pamphlet account of the trial he included poems on:

> Those fatal Rocks (in sea) that stand,
> Near th'Isle of Silly, nigh the Land,
> (By Marriners so shunned and blam'd),
> *The Bishop and his Clerks* are named.

In June 1681 he was proceeded against in the Court of Arches for celebrating clandestine marriages, and irritated the Court by keeping his hat on, and by telling it: 'Toads had poison in them, but had an antidote also; that vipers had poison in them, but the flesh was an extraordinary medecine . . . that even the vilest and worst of God's creatures had something of good in it, saving, that Court.' He was then taken before the King's Bench by writ of *supplicavit*, and bound over in the sum of £200 to be of good behaviour. He was involved in a variety of other legal proceedings. Thus he was fined £400 in 1696 for illegally altering the Parochial Rate Book, and in 1705 the Bishop cited him before the

---

[83] *Curse ye Meroz or the Fatal Doom. In a Sermon Preached . . . before the Lord Mayor etc.* (London, 1680). There was a related pamphlet literature. The reference is to the *Book of Judges*, v. 23.

[84] *The Late Famous Tryal of Mr Hickeringill . . . Author of The Naked Truth* (London, 1681). The offence was abolished by the Criminal Law Act 1967. The last indictment for this offence was of Fred Bellgrove, 'compensation agent' (i.e. ambulance chaser) in July 1889 at Guildford Assizes; he was convicted of conspiracy to defraud in connection with a fraudulent damages claim against the London and South Western Railway, which was behind the prosecution. The charge does not appear to have been pursued. See *The Times*, 8 July 1889, 11.

[85] *Scandalum Magnatum: or, the Great Trial at Chelmnsford Assizes etc.* (London, 1682).

[86] See anonymous article in *DNB*. See also *News from Doctors Commons: or, a true account of Mr Hicheringill's appearance there, June 8 1681 Upon a Citation for Marrying People without Bannes of License* (London, 1681). There is a pamphlet account of his confession in 1684.

Court of Arches for a pamphlet, *The Vileness of the Earth.*[87] He published many pamphlets, and his last work seems to have been *A Burlesque Poem in Praise of Ignorance. The Greatest Part Thereof Composed Eight and Fifty Years Ago*, which appeared in the year of his death (1708). It was critical of lawyers:

> Then give the Lawyers Writs of Ease,
> Let the Breath-selling Trade surcease.

The style of his writings is perhaps well caught by this verse of his jocular poem on self-important Bishops:

> Or wasn't Tom Beckett in a huff,
> With his most right and lawful King,
> From whose posteriors came a puff,
> That him upon his knees did bring.[88]

Bishop Compton, it is said, had some laudatory remarks on his funeral monument chiselled off.[89]

Given his character, it is not perhaps surprising that Edmund, confronted with the construction of the Jacques Hall New Decoy so close to his own decoy, retaliated by taking direct action. And, given the identity of the parties to the litigation, it involved overtones of the class war—Hickeringill was very much a gentleman, and Keeble a mere yeoman. It is possible, too, that the function of their two decoys differed; Keeble's was certainly a commercial enterprise, and Hickeringill's may have merely provided ducks for his own table.

Self-Help and the Pursuit of the Wild Duck

The particular incidents which gave rise to the litigation occurred on 8, 10, 11, and 12 November, in 1703. It was alleged by Samuel Keeble that he was possessed of land called Minott's Meadow, and in it of a decoy pond, and that Hickeringill, intending to harm the plaintiff, to frighten away the wildfowl which resorted to the decoy, and to deprive him of his profit, went to the head of the pond and fired off six guns, which frightened off the ducks, including some decoy ducks, and behaved in the same way on two subsequent occasions; there was no allegation that Hickeringill actually entered the plaintiff's property. The Essex Quarter Sessions Records make it clear that this was only one skirmish in a protracted war. On 15 September 1704 Samuel Keeble was bound to appear at the next sessions 'to shew a bill of indictment against John Osborn and Robert Pammont for breaking his hedges and entering into his closes and grounds to

---

[87] See *VCH Essex*, ii. 72, and *DNB*. See also *R.* v. *Hickeringill* (1706) 11 Mod. 113, 88 ER 934, where an indictment for altering a Land Tax Assessment was quashed.

[88] N. 85 above, 83.

[89] Morant, n. 82 above—'The fulsome and false stuff . . . hath been chiseld out, by order of Compton, it is said'.

scare away the wild fowle out of his decoy pond there and thereupon to give such evidence as he knows concerning the same'. On the same day John Osborn, Robert Pammont, and Thomas Hickeringill were bound in the sum of £40 to appear to answer the charges, and to be of good behaviour in the meanwhile. Apparently they did not behave themselves, and the bonds were forfeited; this in effect imposed a heavy penalty, and no indictment was preferred.[90] The Thomas Hickeringill involved was Edmund's son. The records of the King's Bench for Michaelmas Term 1704 also contain indictments against William Copsey, Robert Pammont, John Osborn, and Mary and Francesca Hickeringill for forcible entry onto the site of the decoy in December 1703 and 1704.[91] In 1705 there was further trouble, and Samuel Keeble, together with Robert Kerrington, yeoman, and William Mason, a glazier, were bound over to keep the peace towards Robert Pammont of Wix.[92] It is notable that Edward Hickeringill himself seems to have prudently avoided any actual entry upon the property, leaving others to undertake his dirty work for him.

Aggressive activity between rival decoy men was apparently not unusual. Thus the Revd W. B. Daniel in his *Rural Sports* (1802) records:

The tricks which the *decoy-men* employ to destroy the haunt of the birds in each other's ponds are various, and as well calculated to produce the mischievous effects they intend, as can well be devised; such as putting a slightly wounded bird or two in the pond, not a bird will *pipe* until the *stricken Deer* is removed; and the natural shyness of the bird is so awakened by the pain of his wounds, that it is sometimes the labour of two or three days to secure him and restore tranquillity. A second manœuvre is, thrusting a feather into the nostril of a wild fowl, and launching it into the decoy: here again not a fowl can be caught until the deformed stranger is got rid of. A third, and perhaps the most decisive, is starting *train oil* into the brook or rill which supplies the pond at some distance from it; some portion of this will be carried by the current into the decoy, and in an instant the fowl, however numerous, quit, and will not resume their haunt until every taint is removed.[93]

As we shall see, another form of chemical warfare was used in later dispute. But we may assume that none of these competitive mechanisms was employed in our case, or they would surely have been mentioned in the pleadings.

The Case of Keeble v. Hickeringill

Samuel Keeble's civil action, which was for damages, was tried before a jury at *nisi prius* at the Essex Autumn Assizes on 30 October 1704 at Chelmsford.[94]

---

[90] There were 2 bonds, with Hickeringill bound in total in the sum of £80.

[91] KB 11/20 (Box containing Part II); references in IND 1/6657.

[92] ERO, Calendar of County Records. Sessions Roll 521, Michaelmas 1704, Nos. 27, 28, and 31; and Roll 526, Epiphany 1705/6, No. 29.

[93] W. B. Daniel, *Rural Sports* (2 vols., London, 1802), ii. 471.

[94] ASSI 34/3. An action against Hickeringill by one Warner was listed, but apparently not proceeded with.

The defendant pleaded the general issue 'not guilty'. The jury found for the plaintiff Keeble, and awarded £50 in damages. The next step was for the plaintiff's counsel—he was represented by Serjeant Brodrick and Robert Raymond—to ask the Court, sitting in Westminster Hall in London, to enter judgment in his favour, and this gave an opportunity for the defendant's lawyers, Serjeant Sir John Darnall and Sir James Montague, to make a motion in arrest of judgment, raising legal objections to the verdict, based upon what was formally included in the record of the Court. The case was regarded as 'a new case'; one report notes that 'Gold remembered such a case in Somersetshire, but it was never debated'. Consequently the case was argued on a number of occasions.[95]

In the course of these arguments a number of uninteresting technical points were raised, but the basic reason for long debate was the novelty of duck decoys: the law relating to them and their interrelations was not yet settled. New technology had to be fitted into old law. But there were two specific reasons why Samuel Keeble's action was tricky and interesting. One was that Edmund Hickeringill had fired the guns on his own land. An attempt was made to argue that the jury must have found that a trespass occurred, which would have disposed of the case, but the judges rejected this suggestion. In the pleadings he is said to have come to the Pond Head, and it could be that some part of the artificial pool, when full, actually extended into Hickeringill's own property. In the absence of any trespass surely a landowner was perfectly entitled to shoot guns off on his own land. The other was that if Keeble were to be given damages, this must surely be because of an interference with his rights as a landowner. But the ducks were not his ducks until he caught them, and he surely had no right that the ducks should come to his pond. So how could it be said that any right of his had been violated?

Lurking behind the arguments presented in the case, both by counsel and by the judges, was the perception that what the case was really about was the idea that competitive economic activity was to be encouraged, even if it caused loss to other people. As Chief Justice Holt put it: 'and tho' decoys spoil gentlemen's game, yet they are not unlawful, for they bring money into the country.'[96] But it was not entirely clear where this led, for if the decoy man could harm Hickeringill by luring the ducks onto his pond, might not Hickeringill retaliate? As Holt pointed out during the argument, 'if the ducks fly out of the plaintiff's ground into the defendants, then the defendant may shoot them'. The implication was that all that was involved was legitimate competitive activity by Edmund Hickeringill.

[95] The case appears on the record from Hilary 3 Anne to Michaelmas 6 Anne. It was argued in Easter Term 5 Anne (1705), and adjourned (see Holt KB 15, 90 ER 906). It was reargued in Hilary 5 Anne (1706). See Holt KB 17, 90 ER 907. Holt's MS reports (cited 103 ER 1126–7) dates the case Trinity 5 Anne (1705), perhaps another argument. It was determined on 20 Dec., Michaelmas 6 Anne (1707).

[96] Holt KB at 18, 90 ER 908.

Eventually the judges, after publicly arguing the case, ruled in favour of Samuel Keeble; apparently they were unanimous. Chief Justice Holt 'delivered the judgement of the Court'.[97] Whereas at the time of *Shelley's Case* there was no settled practice of revealing the reason for a decision, the *ratio decidendi*, by the early eighteenth century it was normal to do so. But no official explanation of the decision was placed on the record. We have four different unofficial texts of what was said.[98] In addition a notebook, which belonged to Holt himself, contained a text of what may originally have been his own argument. He seems to have used it as the justification for the eventual judgment of the Court.[99] Holt thought that the case should be decided in accordance with reason and principle, and claimed that although the case 'seems to be new in its instance . . . it is not new in the reason or principle of it'.[100] Unhappily, given the state of the texts, it has never been absolutely clear what principle the Court did apply.

Holt, and presumably his colleagues, thought that it was important that operating the decoy pond was Samuel Keeble's trade or profession, and one that was profitable to him. The importance of this was that it gave him standing to sue even though there had been no entry on his property, and even though the ducks which were frightened away were not his ducks. It is possible that the emphasis on the commercial character of the decoy was intended to differentiate the case from one in which a mere sporting interest was involved; there was an old dogma in the common law that it took no account of things of mere pleasure or delight. It also served to categorize the nature of the action as being an action 'in the nature of disturbing him from exercising trade'.[101] In the report in Kelyng Holt says, 'the Plaintiff does not bring his Action for the Property he has in the Wild Fowl (for he had no Property) but for frightning and hindring great Numbers from coming to his Decoy Pond'. In another sense, however, Holt does call the action one for interference with Keeble's 'property',[102] which in this sense means his right, like that of everyone else, to exercise his trade and occupation. He then explains that it would have been perfectly lawful for Hickeringill to compete with Keeble 'as if Mr Hickeringill had set up another decoy on his own ground near the plaintiff, and that had spoilt the custom of the plaintiff'.[103] Either might lawfully 'seduce' or 'allure' the ducks. But what was not lawful was Hickeringill's behaviour, and what remains somewhat obscure is what it was about that behaviour which made it unlawful. The plaintiff had alleged that Hickeringill had intended to damage the plaintiff, and to frighten and drive away

[97] 11 Mod. 130, 88 ER 945.
[98] Holt KB 19, 90 ER 908; 3 Salk. 10, 91 ER 659; 11 Mod. 131, 88 ER 945; W. Kel. 273, 25 ER 610.
[99] 11 East 575, 103 ER 1128.
[100] 11 East 575. Similar language is used in the report in Salkeld.
[101] From the report in Salkeld.
[102] See the report in East. Holt is contrasting interference with a privilege with interference with property.
[103] Report in East.

the ducks, and to deprive the plaintiff of his profit—*machinans et malitiose intendens . . . in vivario suo predicto damnificare.* Two reports indicate that it was because Hickeringill's conduct was 'malicious' that it was unlawful.[104] One adds to this a clearer explanation of what was meant by malicious—'this is a malicious Act purely to do the Plaintiff a Mischief without any Motive of Profit or Pleasure to himself'.[105] And one text suggests that what was critical was that Hickeringill frightened the ducks,[106] presumably in contrast to merely seducing them. The same sort of distinction is critical to courtship.

Clearly the precise line between lawful competition and unlawful interference is not an easy one to draw. Holt's own record of his argument concludes with a statement of what we now call the policy underlying the decision. It makes play with the fact that decoys were not all that new; they had been in use for some time:

And when we know that of long time in the kingdom these artificial contrivances of decoy ponds and decoy ducks have been used for the enticing into these ponds wildfowl, in order to be taken for the profit of the owner of the pond, who is at the expense of servants, engines and other management, whereby the markets of the nation may be furnished, there is great reason to give encouragement thereunto; that the people who are so instrumental by their skill and industry so as to furnish the markets should reap the benefit and have their action.

This passage suggests another rationale—Hickeringill was not so much *competing* with Keeble as *preventing* him from exercising his trade, and there are other hints of this idea.

Other Litigation over Duck Decoys

Keeble v. *Hickeringill* was not the first case about interference with a duck decoy. In the course of argument 'Gold remembered such a case in Somersetshire, but it was never debated'.[107] Payne-Gallwey records the existence of twelve decoys in that county, of which Sharpham Park, Shapwick, and the triple decoy of King's Sedgemoor were still operating in his time.[108] He also gives an account, derived from a note in a pedigree at Aston Hall, of an earlier Chancery suit over a decoy belonging to the Hall, which is two miles south-east of Oswestry in Shropshire. It was constructed by Thomas Lloyd of Aston Hall, who died in 1692.[109] The decoy gave its name to the existing Decoy Farm, a mile and a half away to the north-east of the Hall; it was a little to the north-west of the farm, and the first OS map, based on surveys carried out between 1817 and 1830 has

---

[104] Salkeld and East; the latter adds that either a violent or a malicious act was actionable.
[105] W. Kelyng.   [106] Holt KB.   [107] Holt KB 16, 90 ER 907.
[108] Payne-Gallwey, 59.
[109] *Ibid.* 150–1. The Shropshire Record Office has the Aston papers, but not this pedigree.

a Decoy Coppice which had concealed it.[110] Lloyd, it is said, successfully sued one Mytton of Halston Hall, which is two miles away to the north-north-west, for building a forge 'close by on the opposite side of the River Perry for the purpose of disturbing the ducks for shooting at them'.[111] The Mytton concerned, Richard,[112] was the ancestor of Jack Mytton, an outrageous figure in the late eighteenth-century sporting world, and the subject of an entertaining life by 'Nimrod' (Charles Apperley). He ruined his family by his extravagance, eventually retreating to Calais to escape his creditors. He owned a famous racehorse, Euphrates, and named two of his children after it; his eccentricities included riding a bear into a drawing room when fully attired in hunting pink.[113] A considerable slaughterer of ducks himself, he was noted for sometimes pursuing them in the winter whilst completely naked.

I have attempted without success to locate records relating to this suit. There are records of two other seventeenth-century Chancery suits involving a long-running feud between the Mytton and Lloyd families. One was in 1649, involving amongst others Thomas Mytton[114] and Andrew Lloyd; the dispute arose over extensive enclosures in a large area of waste common lands known as Babbyes Wood,[115] today giving its name to the village of Babbinswood, in which the complainants asserted rights of common.[116] The second, in 1669, involved Thomas Lloyd, with his wife Sarah, embattled with Richard Mytton and others, and again arose out of the same quarrel.[117]

The litigation over the duck decoy may well have been an incident in this feud. A document in the Aston Papers dating from 17 January 1742 rehearses an agreement of 11 October 1678 which was intended to settle a quarrel over interference with the decoy, which had apparently led to common law litigation. An action of trespass on the case had been successfully brought by the guardians of Richard Mytton against Thomas Lloyd to try the title to an area of waste ground known as Kinshall Moor, parts of which had been enclosed, close to where the decoy was situated; the process of enclosing common lands in this area provoked persistent quarrels and litigation.[118] The agreement had not been

---

[110] Sheet 32. The Whittington Tithe Apportionment of 1842 (SRO 3375/10, 102,109) has numerous 'decoy' field names which can be identified on the maps, and Decoy Farm and Decoy Crossing Cottage survive today. The site of the decoy was at 353295 on the present-day OS 1:25000 map sheet number 847; its circular enclosure survives.

[111] The existence of the forge is confirmed by SHRO 2313/109, 28 May 1685.

[112] The Richard Mytton concerned succeeded his father (also Richard) in 1669 and died in 1718. He was still a minor in 1678, and would have been born in about 1658.

[113] Nimrod (Pseud. for Charles James Apperley), *Memoirs of the Life of the late John Mytton Esq. of Halston, Shropshire* (London, 1835).

[114] Died 1656.

[115] Various other spellings. On the old OS map (Sheet 32) Babies Wood appears twice, once relating to a copse at 331290, and once relating to a building at 337301 (references for the modern grid system; see OS map (Sheet 126)).

[116] C 2/CHAS I/M24/10.   [117] C 2/CHAS I/L66/159.

[118] SHRO 2171/92. The agreement involved Roger Kynaston of Hordley Esq. and his son, Edward; Thomas Lloyd of Aston Esq.; Rebecca Mytton, widow of Richard Mytton (who died 1659); and her son Richard Mytton (died 1718).

fully carried out sixty years later, and it was now agreed that Thomas Lloyd would give up his claim to four pieces of enclosed land, and in return John Mytton agreed to lease two acres of land adjacent to the decoy on which there was a small house to Lloyd for 999 years, and demolish and remove a small house on this land 'for prevention an Interruption or Molestation of the aforesaid decoy by the occupier of the aforesaid little house'. There may well also have been a Chancery suit arising out of the same quarrel at some point in the late seventeenth or early eighteenth centuries.

Keeble v. *Hickeringill* was apparently applied in one or two cases on the Norfolk circuit, according to Le Blanc J in *Carrington* v. *Taylor* in 1809. This is the only later reported case.[119] The decoy involved was the Old Moze Hall Decoy, in the parish of Beaumont-cum-Moze, near Walton on the Naze.[120] In the report this is mislocated near the Blackwater River, but was some considerable distance away. The nearby tidal inlet is Hamford Water, and the decoy was near its north-west extremity, at the head of Oakley Creek. It is shown on the earliest OS map three-quarters of a mile north-east of the Hall, and a pond still exists there.[121] On this occasion the dispute was between a decoy man and a professional punt gunner who was shooting in a boat on Oakley Creek; his operations inevitably interfered with the decoy.

Payne-Gallwey records some information which suggests that the story behind the case may have been somewhat similar to that underlying *Keeble* v. *Hickeringill*. This derives from the recollections of a Mr Smith, whose father had been the decoy man fifty years earlier at the Great Oakley Hall Decoy, 300 yards away:[122]

the two Decoymen were sworn and jealous enemies, and the one at Old Mose Hall, to annoy the other, used to buy all the asafoetida he could afford, and building it into a lump on the top of a bonfire when the wind was dead on to the rival Decoy, he used to set fire to it . . . 'The stink was awful, and neither man nor duck could stand it and had to leave the position in the hands of the enemy. No that vile stuff stunk out the whole place, and finally killed my father of grief and destroyed the fine Decoy.'[123]

The Old Moze Hall Decoy was last operated in 1841, and the Great Oakley Hall Decoy ceased to operate about the same date.[124]

[119] Reported at trial before Chief Baron MacDonald on 27 July 1809 in 2 Camp. 258, 170 ER 1148, and before the King's Bench in London on 10 Nov. in 11 East 571, 103 ER 1126.

[120] Payne-Gallwey notes the case at 17, and has information about the decoys involved at 88–91.

[121] Sheet 64. On the current maps the reference is 212265.

[122] OS map at 209270 as a 6-pipe decoy under the name Old Decoy; the site today has two large artificial ponds on it.

[123] Payne-Gallwey is quoting from a letter from an acquaintance of his, Colonel Heathcote, who in turn is quoting Mr Smith, who worked at the decoy as a boy under his father.

[124] The 1841 Census (HO 107/338) for Beaumont cum Moze has Pond Farm occupied by Joseph Serrel, and Decoy, occupied by Mark Pawtrey, an agricultural labourer. Pond Farm still exists and is a long way to the west, and cannot have been connected with the Old Moze Hall Decoy; Decoy must have been a cottage, of which no trace remains. For Great Oakley it records Decoy, comprising four cottages occupied by labourers and their families. These are marked on the early OS map, but no trace remains. No decoy man is recorded.

It was this disagreeable decoy man who may well have been the plaintiff in
Carrington v. *Taylor*. It is possible that Taylor was involved in the dispute
between the two decoys, and was not simply out innocently punt gunning. The
fact, as recorded, that he fired on two occasions tends to confirm this, as a
second shot in the same area could have no legitimate explanation. There is
some other evidence as to the background to the dispute.[125] In about 1800 the
owners and operators of decoys in the Blackwater River area formed themselves
into a prosecution society to protect their rights against those who disturbed
decoys. One William Lawrence, a solicitor of Malden, acted for this society, and
a notice dated 11 September 1800 was published in the papers, addressed to
'gunners and puntmen', announcing the purpose of 'prosecuting such persons as
shall hereafter by fowling, or by any other manner, disturb the wild Fowl in or
near such Decoys, or hinder or prevent their resort thereto'. Five guineas reward,
a considerable sum, was offered for information leading to conviction. The
statement in East's report, presumably picked up from something said in court,
that the decoy in *Carrington* v. *Taylor* was near the Blackwater, could derive
from the fact that this Blackwater River association was involved in the litigation. The gunners and puntmen reacted to the threat by taking the opinion of
learned counsel on two questions:

FIRST. Will an action of Trespass lie against the Gunners and Puntmen for killing and
taking wild Fowl in the River in the Winter Season, or for shooting the wild Fowl,
when on the wing, whilst they are in their boats upon the River?

Counsel's opinion was that no such action would lie, because the birds were
'*ferae naturae*, and not the distinct property of anyone'. The second question
was whether, if an action did lie, it would be maintenance, that is unlawful
meddling in other people's quarrels, for the association, as opposed to the aggrieved individual, to sue; his opinion was that it would indeed be maintenance.
The idea that the shooting of wildfowl was itself a criminal offence, even outside the moulting season, appears to have been based upon a statute of James
I,[126] which if taken literally did appear to make decoys illegal by criminalizing
the taking of ducks 'with any manner of nets, snares, engines or instruments
whatsoever'. But the opinion was that this Act was a limited one and it had
expired. The only relevant legislation still in force only protected wild fowl in
the moulting season, from 1 June to 1 October.[127] It is quite possible that
Carrington v. *Taylor* was in the nature of a test case arising out of competition
between the gunners and the decoy men.

At the trial of the action it appeared that Taylor, who was a professional
gunner, fired his gun when about 400 yards from the decoy, and again when
closer. There was no direct evidence that he had aimed at birds already in the

---

[125] Daniels, n. 93 above, 482.
[126] 1 Jac. I c.27, s. 2, renewed by 3 Car. I c.4 and 16 Car. I c.4.
[127] 9 Anne c.25 and 10 Geo. II c.32.

decoy, or that 'he had fired his piece with the malicious intent of frightening them away'. His lawyer, Garrow, argued that he was just as entitled to shoot the ducks as the plaintiff was to catch them in the decoy. The ducks were 'of common right'—we would say they belonged to nobody, and anyone was entitled to take them. The judge introduced a new way of looking at the rights of the parties. This decoy, he said, was an ancient decoy. Consequently it was protected against interference, just as were ancient lights. This doctrine was rationalized by a fiction:

From long uninterrupted enjoyment, a grant must be presumed from the owners of the surrounding lands, for which an adequate consideration may be supposed to have been originally given; and an ancient decoy will be protected by the law, as well as ancient lights.

Consequently, 'it is privileged in law; and whatever seriously disturbs it is actionable'. The reasoning seems a little odd since the defendant was not on adjacent land, but on a creek in the sea, though it is just conceivable that the explanation was that Taylor was indeed a landowner, perhaps associated with the rival decoy.[128] The judge did think there was evidence of malice: 'If the plaintiff has been injured and aggrieved by what the defendant has done, the law infers that the defendant maliciously intended to injure and aggrieve him.' The jury gave a verdict for the plaintiff with forty shillings damages; we can only speculate why. With local knowledge they may of course have thought that a deliberate attempt to interfere with the decoy was involved. When the case came before the full court in London, it refused to interfere, treating the matter as essentially a jury question. The theory of ancient decoys was repeated by the lawyer H. C. Folkard in his book on wildfowling, who said that it was therefore unlawful to shoot near one.[129] But no later court was given a chance to rule on the matter, for no later dispute over duck decoys ever seems to have been litigated. That competition over wildfowling continued to be troublesome is, however, illustrated by the criminal case of *R. v. Ward* (1872).[130] A punt gunner of Aldeburgh, Samuel Ward, coxswain of the lifeboat there, shot at another at a range of twenty-five yards on a clear moonlit night in a creek on the River Alde. The victim was William Chatten, a Trinity House pilot, and something of a friend of his. There then took place one of those conversations which only exist in reports of legal proceedings: 'I at once said "Who is that?". The prisoner replied "It's me". I said "And a pretty mess you have made of it; you have shot my eye out".' Samuel towed William's punt in, remarking comfortingly: 'You are not dead yet. You are moving about.' He had himself been shot earlier in

---

[128] He had a licence from the Admiralty, apparently then required for the use of an armed vessel at sea.

[129] *The Wildfowler. A Treatise on Fowling, Ancient and Modern. Descriptive also of Decoys and Flight Ponds* (4th ed., London, 1897), 78.

[130] 12 CCC 123, CCCR, tried Suffolk Assizes, Bury St Edmunds, 1 Aug. 1871: *Bury and Norwich Post Supplement*, 8 Aug. 1871.

mistake for a duck. William was indeed blinded in one eye and his arm was badly injured. The jury decided it was no accident; Samuel was intending to frighten his friend away from what he conceived to be his ducks. He was convicted of unlawful wounding and sent to prison for twelve months at hard labour.

From Ducks to Rooks, and thence to Grouse and Foxes

Not many years later, however, in 1824, a new twist was introduced in a case involving rooks. My *Nouveau Larousse gastronomique* gives a recipe for *Pâté de corbeau* taken from A. Suzanne, *La Cuisine et la pâtisserie anglaise* and adopts an encouraging tone: 'Rook pie, in spite of what the sceptics and the incredulous may think, is a dish which is not to be despised, if properly prepared.' No doubt it was because of his liking for this dish that the plaintiff in *Hannam* v. *Mockett* (1824),[131] who had a rookery on his land, was enraged when the defendant succeeded, by firing guns on adjacent property, in driving the rooks away entirely; he put a figure of 1,000 on those that left, and another 1,000 on those that 'were then about to resort to and settle in the said rookery', and which were frightened from coming. In the pleadings the plaintiff alleged that in addition to the profit and advantage he obtained from killing the rooks he derived aesthetic pleasure from simply having them about. The attitude of the defendant, whose conduct was alleged to have been maliciously directed towards injuring the plaintiff, was equally understandable; one man's rook pie is another's laundry bill. A large rookery next door can cause considerable nuisance from the plentiful droppings of the birds, as well as from cawing. At the trial the plaintiff won a verdict and damages of £10.

After argument on a motion in arrest of judgment Bayley J delivered the opinion of the Court of King's Bench, which took an unfavourable view of rooks. He ruled that the plaintiff had no cause of action. To succeed the plaintiff must show that a right of his had been infringed, and since he did not own the rooks:

the question then is, whether there is any injury to any property the plaintiff had a special right to acquire. A man in trade has a right in his fair chances of profit, and he gives up time and capital to obtain it. It is for the good of the public that he should. But has it ever been held that a man has a right in the chance of obtaining animals *ferae naturae*, where he is at no expense in enticing them to his premises, and where it may be at least questionable whether they will be of any service to him, and whether indeed they will not be a nuisance to the neighbourhood? . . . Allow the right to these birds, and how can it be denied to all others?

He was dismissive of the culinary merits of rooks, and argued that whereas some birds—amongst others he instanced swans, ducks, bustards (by this time extinct

[131] 2 B & C 934, 107 ER 629; 4 D & R 518, 2 LJKB 183.

in Britain), and herons—had been well regarded by the law, and entitled to protection, rooks had long been viewed with nothing but unrelenting hostility, ever since the statute of Henry VIII—'An Act to destroy Choughs, Crows and Rooks'.[132] So the situation differed from *Keeble* v. *Hickeringill*; no mention was made of *Carrington* v. *Taylor*. Those who seek a deep explanation for judicial attitudes may note that rook pie is predominantly a northern dish, whilst Bayley J was a southerner, born in Huntingdonshire, where the consumption of rook pie would be regarded as eccentric.

Two later cases moved the discussion on to grouse and silver foxes. *Ibbotson* v. *Peat* (1865)[133] involved a rural battle over the Duke of Rutland's grouse moor. The Duke, Charles Manners,[134] Master of the Belvoir Hunt and a member of the Jockey Club by acclamation, had spent considerable sums of money in the preservation of grouse, and the plaintiff, who farmed adjacent lands, enticed them by placing food out so as to shoot them himself. His Grace decided to retaliate and, on his instructions, his gamekeeper 'fired, exploded and projected, certain offensive, injurious, noxious, terrifying and dangerous rockets, fireworks, missiles, projectiles and combustibles . . .' to drive the grouse off farmer Ibbetson's lands and prevent him from shooting them. He achieved this object, but also caused distress and injury to the plaintiff's farm stock. The Duke's lawyers did not dispute the facts, but pleaded that what had been done had been no more than was necessary 'to prevent the plaintiff from shooting and killing the said grouse so lured and enticed'. It is hardly surprising that the judges were not impressed by this defence. Pollock CB seems to have thought that two wrongs do not make a right; Martin B thought the case was precisely covered by *Carrington* v. *Taylor*; and Bramwell B, whilst reserving his opinion on 'the propriety of such conduct between gentlemen and neighbours', thought that a landowner was perfectly entitled to entice game away from adjoining land: 'where a person's game is attracted from his land, he ought to offer it stronger inducements to return to it.' *Keeble* v. *Hickeringill* was of course mentioned in argument, and it was suggested that there was an important distinction to be made: 'There is nothing unlawful in enticing game by putting down corn; but it is unlawful to frighten them away by firing combustibles.' Silver foxes come into the story in *Hollywood Silver Fox Farm Ltd.* v. *Emmett*; the facts could only have arisen in the 1930s.[135] A Captain Chandler, one of the many veterans of the first war who attempted to respond to the depression by entrepreneurial activities, had purchased Hollywood Cottage at Kingsdown in Kent, where he and his wife set up a silver-fox farm with thirteen vixens and twelve dog foxes. His neighbour, Emmett, was attempting to develop a residential building estate next door. He thought Captain Chandler's notice board 'Hollywood Silver Fox Farm' would reduce the value of his building plots. But Captain Chandler saw no

[132] 24 Hen. VIII c.10.
[133] 1 May 1865. 3 H & C 644, 159 ER 684, 34 LJ Ex. 118, 11 Jur. (NS) 394.
[134] 1815–88.   [135] [1936] 2 KB 468, 19–20 Mar., 8 Apr. 1936.

reason why he should take it down. So Mr Emmett, who seems to have known a thing or two about silver foxes, announced his intention of firing guns loaded with black powder as near as he could to the breeding pens during the breeding season. 'And I guarantee', he added grimly, 'you will not raise a single cub.' He was as good as his word, his young son being charged with the task of doing the horrid deed. A story was told that the shooting was an attempt to reduce the local rabbit population, but nobody believed that.

Silver foxes are temperamental creatures; loud noises put them off mating, induce miscarriages, and even induce cannibalism. Few cubs were born, some vixens gave up sex entirely, and one ate her four cubs.

So Captain Chandler sued, and the judge, Macnaghten, held in his favour, awarding damages and an injunction restraining shooting in the breeding season. His opinion opens by saying that the action 'raises once again the question, which was debated in the case of *Allen* v. *Flood*,[136] whether the decision in the famous duck decoy case, *Keeble* v. *Hickeringill*, was well founded'. He thought it was.

The Relevance of Malice in the Law of Torts

'The question' is a reference to a controversy which had much intrigued legal thinkers in both England and the United States in the late nineteenth century: was there a general timeless principle of the common law whereby actions which were lawful if done with a good or acceptable motive became unlawful if malicious, performed with the sole intention of causing harm? And in any event what motives were acceptable, and what exactly was a malicious motive? O. W. Holmes, in his *The Common Law* (1881), touched on the question, pointing out that 'the law does not even seek to indemnify a man from all harms . . . There are certain things which the law allows a man to do, notwithstanding the fact that he foresees that harm to another will follow from them.' He went on to give a number of examples:

He may establish himself in business where he foresees that the effect of competition will be to diminish the custom of another shopkeeper, perhaps to ruin him. He may erect a building which cuts off from a beautiful prospect, or he may drain subterranean waters and thereby drain another's well; and many other cases might be put.[137]

In *Leon Rideout* v. *David Knox and Another* (1889)[138] Holmes delivered an opinion in which he said at common law 'that to a large extent the power to use one's property malevolently, in any way which would be lawful for other ends, is an incident of property which cannot be taken away even by legislation'. But he and the court nevertheless upheld the constitutionality of a statute against

---

[136] [1898] AC 1.   [137] O. W. Holmes, *The Common Law* (Boston, Mass., 1881), 144.
[138] 148 Mass. 368.

spite fences, viewing the restraint imposed, which only applied to fences over six feet in height, as an insignificant interference with property rights. The legislation only applied, in his view, if malevolence—the pleasure gained from doing harm—was the predominant motive, rather than some legitimate gain, and in the case this seems not to have been the situation, since the fence was used to trail vines. Holmes returned to the topic in his article 'Privilege, Malice and Intent' in 1894,[139] and toyed with the idea that 'there is no general policy in favour of allowing a man to do harm to his neighbour for the sole pleasure of doing harm'. But he conceded it was difficult to imagine such a case, unless *Keeble* v. *Hickeringill* and *Tarleton* v. *M'Gawley* (1793)[140] were examples. The latter case involved a vessel engaged in trading off the Cameroons in West Africa, including slave trading; the defendants fired a cannon at an African trading canoe, killing one of its occupants, with the intention of deterring trade with the vessel, and this was held to be actionable. The defendant did have an economic motive; he was owed money by the Africans and wished to bring pressure on them to pay him. So this was not really a case of *disinterested* malevolence.

The best-known English leading case on this issue is *Mayor of Bradford* v. *Pickles*, decided by the House of Lords the year after Holmes wrote his article.[141] The Bradford Corporation had, in 1854, taken over the waterworks supplying the city from the earlier private utility company. The supply came from the Many Wells Springs on the west of the valley of the Hewenden Beck, the site of the springs being owned by the corporation. The water was collected in the Hewenden Reservoir. Edward Pickles owned land near these springs, and had at one time worked a stone quarry there. Ostensibly to drain the water from his supply of stone, he sank a shaft near the springs, and in 1892 he began to construct a tunnel on his land over 500 yards long which would, if completed, have drained the percolating water from the source of the springs and returned

---

[139] O. W. Holmes, *Collected Legal Papers* (New York, 1920), 117, originally published (1894) viii *HLR* 1. Holmes may have been further encouraged to do so by the cases on the subject collected by J. B. Ames in *A Selection of Cases on the Law of Torts* (Cambridge, Mass., 1893), i, to which Holmes refers. Cases such as *Keeble* v. *Hickeringill* are grouped with *Garret* v. *Taylor* (1620) Cro. Jac. 567; *Ibbotson* v. *Peat* (1865) 3 H. and C. 644; *Tarleton* v. *M'Gawley* (1804) Peake 270, 170 ER 153; *Anon* (1410) 11 Hen. IV f. 47 pl. 21; *The Mogul Steamship Co. Ltd.* v. *McGregor and Co.* (1889) 23 QBD 598; *Temperton* v. *Russell* [1893] 1 QB 715 and a number of US decisions are grouped under 'Malicious Injury to the Plaintiff by Influencing the Conduct of a Third Person'. Ames also has cases on spite fences and wells drained by lowering the water table, including *Leon Rideout* v. *David Knox and Another*.

[140] Peake 270, 170 ER 153.

[141] [1895] AC 587, [1895] 1 ch. 145 (CA), [1894] 3 ch. 53. The case no. is 1892–B–5672. An account of this case was included in a lecture, 'Victorian Law and the Industrial Spirit', which I gave to the Selden Society in 1994, and which is to be published by the Society. The principal sources used were papers in the House of Lords Record Office (Appeal Cases 1895, Vol. 440) which include maps, correspondence, and a transcript of the hearing, 5 boxes of papers connected with the case in the Bradford Record Office (BBD/1/1/68–73), which include affidavits, correspondence, plans, and transcripts, and minute books of the City Waterworks Committee, BBC 1/9/4 (1863) and 12–16 (1889–1911).

it to the Hewenden Beck *below* the reservoir. He could much more easily have returned it above the reservoir. As a mere matter of courtesy he told the corporation of his plans. The corporation and the judge thought Edward Pickles had no intention of working the stone. He wanted to pressure the corporation into buying his land at a handsome price lest Bradford be denied a supply of water. So Edward Pickles was not engaged in disinterested malevolence: doing harm simply for the pleasure of inflicting it. The House of Lords, with what can only be called glee, ruled that his motive was quite irrelevant to the legality of his action. Just as the owner of a box of matches can while away the time by striking them to watch them burn simply to irritate a passing boy scout who has urgent need of two to pass his fire-lighting test, so could Mr Pickles abstract the water just to annoy the Mayor of Bradford. By 1897 he had indeed succeeded in cutting off the supply from the spring to the reservoir completely, but the Bradford Corporation dug in its toes and declined to pay him a single penny; in any event his very success made his land quite useless as a source of water. So Edward Pickles, his money all consumed by lawyers' charges and mining costs, emigrated to Canada in about 1900, hoist by his own petard. Then there was the decision of the House of Lords three years later in *Allen* v. *Flood*, where the issue arose in a labour conflict. The case arose out of a demarcation dispute between two groups of workers, the shipwrights and the boilermakers, and adopted the same idea as to the legal irrelevance of motive, and, by a majority, rejected the suggestion that the common law protected its subjects from 'malicious' interference with their trade or livelihood. All this had cast something of a shadow over the status of *Keeble* v. *Hickeringill* in the legal firmament, though in neither of these two celebrated cases had it been ruled that the decision of Holt's Court of King's Bench had been mistaken.

So *Keeble* v. *Hickeringill*, whatever it was that it actually did decide, lived on to fight another day, and Macnaghten J, confronted with the unhappy silver foxes, reinjected life into its aged carcass by deciding that it was still good law in the type of case he was dealing with, which concerned a nuisance caused by noise, where matters of degree are involved.

Duck decoys are, as we have seen, all but extinct in Britain. It is no doubt only a matter of time before the eating of a wild duck will become politically incorrect, and excite the same sort of moral outrage as wearing an ocelot fur coat, or pursuing a fox with hounds. But there is every reason to suppose that the most celebrated legal decision which duck decoys generated will survive into the next century and beyond. For the fortunes of the case are only loosely linked to the current status of ducks in our society, or to the mechanisms whereby they are persecuted or, today, conserved. Its durability depends on the fact that it addressed issues which possess a timeless quality in legal and moral discourse. Where precisely should the boundary line be drawn between legitimate competition and the wrongful infliction of harm? What precise rights do property owners enjoy in relation to wild creatures whose presence on their property is beneficial to them? Ought the law to prevent people from using their rights in a malicious or evilly motivated way? And what counts as malicious or evil motive anyway? Ought the law to confer on citizens areas of autonomy in which the individual is free and sovereign, and simply accept the fact that some people will misuse this freedom? Or should rights always be limited by considerations of the public welfare? Ought courts, in deciding the boundaries of rights, to pay attention to economic policies, or is that the job of the legislature? To what extent should property owners be allowed to retaliate when their neighbours behave in an unneighbourly way? These are not questions which possess obviously correct answers, or which ever go away. And as a peg on which to base a discussion of them there is a lot to be said for continuing to make use of the entertaining squabble between the decoy man, Samuel Keeble, and the dotty parson, Edmund Hickeringill, albeit that it took place nearly three centuries ago.

4

Legal Science and Legal Absurdity
Jee *v.* Audley *(1787)*

Restraining the Patriarchal Power

One of the deepest mysteries of the common law is a body of doctrine called the modern rule against perpetuities. It emerged in the late seventeenth and eighteenth centuries, and the classic case on the rule for those who enjoy the legal equivalent of the theatre of the absurd is the decision of Sir Lloyd Kenyon, bt. (later Lord Kenyon) in *Jee* v. *Audley* in 1787.[1] The world in which the rule evolved was that of the landed aristocracy and gentry, and its function was to impose limits which seemed reasonable in that world to the degree to which the head of the family, the patriarch for the time being, could make binding dispositions of the family estates which controlled their destination long into the future. Typically, such dispositions would be made by will, but the rule applied to dispositions made between the living, too, and, since there cannot, of course, be one law for the rich, and one for the poor, however sensible that might be, the rule applied to dispositions of property which had no connection with the conventions of upper-class landowning society. That society viewed land ownership as ownership by a family, the family being, ideally at least, a permanent institution, albeit one perpetually threatened by the ravages of death, infertility, and individual folly. Indeed the principal reason a patriarch might wish to tie up the family lands in perpetuity was fear of folly of his descendants, who might, if given the power, fritter away the family patrimony in drink or dissipation, and bring his house to poverty, and his name to dishonour and oblivion.

Plainly if one head of the family is given power to control the destination of family lands after his death, his successor will enjoy less power than he did; there will not be an equality of power between the generations. This was always appreciated. One possible solution would have been to organize the law of property so that each generation possessed an equal power of disposition, just as in the classic theory of Parliamentary sovereignty each Parliament is supposed to enjoy precisely the same legislative power as its predecessor. Given the structure of property law in the seventeenth century, this solution would have required too radical a reorganization of the law by the courts, and nothing of

---

[1] 1 Cox 324, 29 ER 1186, reported by Samuel C. Cox, a Master in Chancery, and first published 1816. A different account, though based on a note by Cox, is given by Sir R. P. Ardern MR in *Routledge* v. *Dorril* (1794) 2 Ves. Jun. 357 at 365, 30 ER 671 at 675.

the sort was ever attempted. Instead, in the *Duke of Norfolk's Case* (1681),[2] the starting point for the modern doctrine, the Chancellor, Lord Nottingham, attempted to make some sense of the very confused state of the law on 'perpetuities' by adopting a notion grounded in natural law, which conformed to the contemporary aristocratic understandings of the way in which a good *paterfamilias* would conduct himself. For a full account of the technicalities concerned readers must go elsewhere, but the essence of the matter is fairly easy to appreciate.

The Earl of Arundel (and fourth Duke of Norfolk) had seven sons, of whom the first, his heir apparent, Thomas, was quite mad. He was kept unmarried lest he should bring ruin to the family by passing the title down to an insane grandchild, for insanity was thought to be inheritable. The Duke, after a family conference, consulted the leading property lawyer of the day, Orlando Bridgman, and then made dispositions to ensure that some of the family property would go to his second son, Henry. But if, as no doubt it was hoped, the earldom were to descend to Henry, then this property was to be used to support the fourth son, Charles, skipping the third son, Phillip, who was a Cardinal in Rome, and no doubt had no intention of ever returning to England. The idea was to make provision by this disposition for the son next in line to the earldom; other property was to be used to make provision for Henry, if he became earl.

Now Lord Nottingham thought that human law should be appropriate to the nature of man, and man, unlike God, possesses only a limited ability to foresee what may happen in the future. Hence a landowner should not be allowed to settle the devolution of family lands too far into a future which he could not possibly foresee. Under this principle the Earl of Arundel's arrangements were quite acceptable—he was merely making prudent provision for people he knew, and for contingencies he could anticipate as likely to occur, such as the earldom descending upon Henry, Thomas having been locked up and prevented from marrying and producing legitimate offspring. The patriarch was doing what a prudent *paterfamilias* could well think best in the interests of preserving the power and honour of his family. But if the Earl had made provision for very remote contingencies, then he would not be behaving like a good *paterfamilias*, but as if he were God, and his dispositions would be bad. But since this did not arise Lord Nottingham thought it unnecessary to say where he would draw the line.

Later judges accepted the idea that dispositions were to be void if they depended upon contingencies which could happen at too remote a time in the future; indeed the rule came to be called a rule against 'remoteness of *vesting*'. A disposition was said to 'vest' when it took effect, so that, for example, a gift of property by will 'to my first grandchild to attain the age of 21' was said to vest when, if ever, such a grandchild did become 21, and thus took an interest in the property. In time—though it took until the nineteenth century—the courts

[2] 3 Ch. Cas. 1, 22 ER 931; 2 Swanston at 454, 36 ER at 690; 2 Ch. Rep. 229, 21 ER 665.

drew the line which Lord Nottingham had refused to draw, and settled on a period of the lifetime of one or more persons in existence at the effective time of the disposition (known as 'lives in being') and a further period of twenty-one years, as the limit for remoteness of vesting.[3] The effective time, in the case of a will, was the date of death of the testator. Thus if a person left his property to his eldest son for life, and then to his first grandson to become 21, this would be good—the contingency, the becoming 21, is inevitably going to happen, if it ever does, within the lifetime of the son (the life in being) and a further period of twenty-one years, and you can be certain of this at the effective time. But the judges, whilst developing Lord Nottingham's idea that dispositions should be policed by a rule against remote vesting, paid insufficient attention to a less precise idea, which underlies his opinion, that it was the function of the courts to favour prudent and sensible dispositions, and, as a corollary, invalidate fool-ish ones. If a disposition, judged by the then state of the highly technical case law, was too remote, the judges were inclined to hold it invalid however ap-propriate it might be to the welfare of the family, and if it was not too remote it was valid, however silly. The validity of the disposition was determined by the logic of the rule, rather than by the purpose it was supposed to serve. Now in the law we often distinguish between the law and its purpose, and allow the purpose, within limits, to police the rule. In perpetuities law this tended not to happen.

Rationalizing the Rule against Perpetuities

As time passed, the underlying purpose of the rule itself came to be uncertain. In law, as in life generally, institutions can exist which do not seem to have any purpose, or whose purpose is unknown, except of course to God, who moves in a mysterious way. One way of thinking about the problem of perpetuities was to conceive of them as arrangements under which a free power of alienation was being taken away from the living by the dead. If the ownership of property is made subject to contingencies, that property cannot be readily alienated; you cannot readily sell property rights when it remains uncertain who has them, or whether they may not suddenly come to an end.

The rule certainly allowed property to be tied up for very long periods; it did not obviously prevent the dead ruling the living, for a life in being and twenty-one years can exceed a century. So the rule against perpetuities was a rule which permitted a great deal; indeed it could be said to give excessive power to the dead. John Tyrrell, in his evidence to the Real Property Commissioners in 1829, pointed this out, and suggested that the rule had become too generous to the

---

[3] To this was added the period of gestation. The lives, it was eventually settled, could be uncon-nected with the family.

dead. In one will, signed in 1818, the testator, Henry Bengough, set up trusts which were to last for 120 years, if—rather hopefully—thirty-eight named persons should live so long, followed by a further period of twenty years, before the inheritance would finally vest in a descendant able to deal freely with the property. These 'lives in being' did not have to be connected in any way with the settlement. Counsel pointed out: 'This is the greatest attempt at a perpetuity that has ever been made . . . For it is admitted that eighty or ninety years hence, and not sooner, will be the time for discussing who the person is in whom the interest is to vest.'[4] But the arrangement did not infringe the rule. So the rule did allow the dead to rule the living, but not for ever. Tyrrell's solution was to limit the number of lives who could be used as lives in being to three, and insist that they must themselves be beneficiaries. He became a commisioner and, in spite of a recommendation for changing the law and limiting the 'lives in being' to persons who 'might be in any manner connected with the objects of the settlement, or the dropping of which might furnish the motive for one of its limitations', the law was not altered.

Its connection with the value of freedom of disposition was not originally established because of some economic theory about the merits of a free market in land; seventeenth-century lawyers had not read Adam Smith. In aristocratic circles freedom of land disposition was valued because it enabled the current head of a family to make appropriate dispositions to perpetuate and aggrandize his family and its power, as by making alliances by marriage. If his hands were tied, he could not do this. But as the theories of the political economists became received, the idea developed that its function was really that of encouraging a free market in land. In the nineteenth century this became a political programme. In so far as the rule restricted the amount of land under strict settlement it no doubt did increase the stock of marketable land.

But, in general, the development and application of the rule was little, if at all, affected by conceptions of what the point of the rule was thought to be. This phenomenon, the rigid application of legal doctrine without regard to purpose or common sense, was classically illustrated by the decision in *Jee* v. *Audley*.

Surgeon Edward Audley and his Family

The dispute, partially reported in the law reports—for it gave rise to two distinct suits in Chancery, only one being reported—arose out of the will of a Birmingham surgeon, Edward Audley.

[4] See J. Tyrrell, *Suggestions Sent to the Commissioners Appointed to Inquire into the Laws of Real Property* (London, 1829), at 51. Tyrrell had in mind the wills of Peter Thelluson (see *Thelluson* v. *Woodford* (1805) 11 Ves. Jun. 112, 13 Ves. Jun. 209, 1 Ves. Jun. Supp. 440, 2 Ves. Jun. Supp. 251, 334, 31 ER 117, 32 ER 1030, 33 ER 273, 34 ER 864, 1080, 1120, as well as Bengough (see *Bengough* v. *Edridge* (1826–7) 1 Sim. 173, 57 ER 544). See also 4 Vesey Jun. 286 on the will of Lady Denison before Lord Kenyon in 1787.

The Audleys, of whom the genealogist Aleyn Lyell Reade identified twenty branches, derive their name from the village of Audley, earlier Aldithel or Alditheley, in Staffordshire. There, in 1130, one Luilph de Audley prudently murdered the local Saxon thane, and thereby established himself as the local potentate.[5] The castle of the Audleys, built in stone about 1215 at Heley or Heighley, survives as their memorial only as an impressively situated ruin north of Madeley. One branch, the Audley Tuchets, has retained a position amongst the top people, with a twenty-fifth baron in the currrent issue of *Who's Who*. The first baron was Nicholas Audley (1289–1316). Another Audley was a founder Knight of the Garter, another an executor of Henry VII, another a bent Lord Chancellor and refounder of Magdalene College, Cambridge, who had done extremely well out of the dissolution of the monasteries. The family took its device on its coat of arms, a fret or fretty or, from its overlords, the Verdons.[6] For those who wish to know, a fret is composed of six pieces, two long ones in saltire, extending as a rule, but not necessarily, to the extremity of the field, and four pieces conjoined in the centre in the form of a masele, interlaced or fretted by those in saltire.

In the course of time the precise relationship between different branches of the Audleys became obscure, but our branch of the family, which came in the seventeenth century or earlier to settle in the parish of Alrewas in Staffordshire, claimed to be armigerous, and to be entitled to the fret of the Verdons; no doubt there was some distant relationship with the Audleys of Audley.

Surgeon Edward, our testator, lived in New Street, Birmingham, in a house leased from the Governors of the Free Grammar School. He was in partnership with John Derington. The will was dated 14 August 1769 and proved on 28 September 1771,[7] for he died in that year and was buried on 23 April at St Phillips, Birmingham, now the Cathedral. Edward was the second son of John Audley, another Birmingham surgeon, of Spiceal Street, Birmingham, who had married Mary Price at St Martin's there on 8 April 1702.[8] Surgeon John died in 1737 and was buried at St Martin's, Birmingham.[9]

Our testator Edward had three sisters, Mary, baptized on 8 December 1703,[10]

---

[5] A. L. Reade, *The Audley Pedigrees* (London, 1929–36) has much detail. It was financed by George Audley of Liverpool (1864–1932), who unhappily expired of a heart attack when dressing, before the pedigrees, which cover 20 families of Audley, were completed. Our particular family is covered in PEDIGREE VIII, AUDLEY OF ALREWAS (CO. STAFFS.) AND OF BIRMINGHAM. I have also used other genealogical records, such as the IGI and parish records with the assistance of Mrs P. Bryars, a professional genealogist. See also W. Beresford, *Memorials of Old Staffordshire* (London, 1909), 32 ff.

[6] B. Burke, *The General Armory of England, Scotland and Ireland* (London, 1884) has at lxxxiii 'Gules, fretty or, a label in chief' as the arms of Sir James Audeley, Knight of the Garter, the hero of Poitiers, and the same device was used by the first Baron.

[7] LJRO.   [8] IGI.

[9] Will PCC Wake 240, dated 9 July 1720, proved 14 Nov. 1737. The Audley Pedigree gives a date of burial as 28 Sep. 1730, but the year must be a slip.

[10] Mary may have become, by marriage, Mary Shenstone. Edward's will refers to his 'sister in law' Mary Shenstone; his brother's will mentions Mrs Mary Shenstone, but as a 'friend'. I suspect she was the sister, but this is not certain.

Elizabeth, baptized on 8 April 1705,[11] and Ann. Ann's date of birth and death are uncertain, but by 1733 or so she had married Roger Hale of St Andrews, Holborn.[12] Ann and Roger appear to have had only one child, Mary, who was baptized on 27 August 1734 at St Martin's in Birmingham. Mary Hale, the niece of our testator, features prominently in our story. Surgeon Edward had two brothers. William, born in 1713, lived for under a month. But John, the eldest brother, was more fortunate. He was born about 1707, and matriculated at Wadham College, Oxford, on 28 March 1724. He migrated to Magdalen, where on 18 January 1743 he became a Doctor of Divinity. He became a fellow of the college in 1736, and its Vice-President in 1747; he also acted as Bursar on a number of occasions. He lived in Birmingham, and became Rector of Brandeston in 1744 and of Boyton in 1763.[13] By the time of his death he had become senior fellow. In 1766 he also became the non-resident Vicar of Curdworth in War-wickshire; he farmed out the living to a local husbandman, and later to the husbandman's wife, who in their turn paid a curate to perform the offices. Relations between the two brothers, surgeon Edward and academic John, appear, from the terms of their wills, to have been particularly close and friendly.

The father of the two brothers, surgeon John senior, would have been born in Alrewas parish, Staffordshire, in the township of Orgreave, where, as we have seen, this branch of the Audleys had settled. He was the son of one Edward Audley of Alrewas. The parish register for the late seventeenth and early eighteenth centuries refers to two Edward Audleys, our man being Edward Audley 'senior'. He first surfaces as an overseer of the poor there in 1677;[14] his wife, who died in January 1690/1, was named Katherine. He was buried on 21 February 1718/19.

Also living in Alrewas in the late seventeenth and early eighteenth century was another Edward Audley, who appears in the records as 'junior'; he was buried on 13 January 1739/40.[15] We may be fairly confident, though there is no definite proof, that the two Edwards were cousins.

On 6 May 1693 Edward Audley junior married Sarah Baggarley.[16] They had a number of children; these children were apparently cousins of our testator Edward Audley and his brother John, the fellow of Magdalen. One son, John, died in infancy,[17] and the name was recycled for another baby boy who was born

[11] Died unmarried between 1720 and 1769.

[12] Ann was unmarried in 1720 and dead before 1744. There may have been some connection between the Audleys of Alrewas and another Audley family of Holborn and Beccles, Suffolk, which might explain this marriage.

[13] *Alumni Oxoniensis*, BA 1727, MA 1730, BD 1739. He was a friend of John Loveday of Caversham; see S. Markhan, *John Loveday of Caversham* (Salisbury, 1984), *passim*. I am indebted to Dr D. J. Ibbetson for information and copies in the college registers by Bloxam and Macray.

[14] Again in 1701, 1703. Churchwarden 1684.

[15] Possibly of the township of Fradley, rather than Orgreave. Fradley was a hamlet in the parish.

[16] LJRO BT. The entry in the Alrewas Register refers to 'Edwardum Audley de Orgreave, pistoreni, & Sarah Baggaly, filia Joannis Baggaly de Fradley'. She was the daughter of John Baggarley of Fradley.

[17] John, born, 10 Feb. 1694 and died the same year.

in about 1700, and survived. He became a surgeon in the Royal Navy, and retired to Alrewas where he was buried in 1763. His headstone there bears these cheerful verses:

> Mourn not for me spectator dear,
> I am not dead but sleeping here,
> My debt is paid my grave you see,
> Wait but awhile you'll follow me.[18]

There were eight daughters, of whom four died in infancy.[19] The four daughters who survived into adulthood were, in order of seniority, Mary,[20] Catherine,[21] Elizabeth, and Sarah.[22]

The Marriage of Elizabeth Audley to John Jee

On 16 May 1740 one of these daughters, Elizabeth, married John Jee, who was a farmer in Alrewas. He, too, is important to the story of *Jee* v. *Audley*.[23] In Alrewas in the seventeenth and eighteenth centuries there was a family of Jees or Gees; thus in the register for 1694 there is a record of the baptism of Ann, daughter of George Gee; in 1699 Thomas, son of George Gee of Lupin,[24] was baptized, and Thomas, son of George Gee of Orgreave, possibly the same child, was buried on 1 November, as was Hannah, wife of George Gee of Fradley on 21 August. There were probably two George Jees in the parish. Our farmer John Jee may have been a son of one of them; if so he would have been born after 1701, the second child of George Jee to be given the name John.[25] There was also a John Gee of Streetham who married Jane Rose in Alrewas in 1672, who could have been our man's father. The baptism of our farmer John Jee is not, however, recorded; all we can say is that he was perhaps born after 1701. It is clear from the provisions of the will of John Audley that the Jees were some sort of distant relatives of the Audley family, but the precise relationship is obscure.

The date of birth and baptism of Elizabeth Audley is also not recorded at Alrewas. The register may be incomplete, or she was baptized elsewhere. It has proved impossible to trace her baptism. However, it is clear that it must have taken place in the period 1705–10; her sister, Catherine Audley, was baptized on 12 February 1703/4, and sister Sarah on 27 December 1711; she was certainly born in the intervening period.

---

[18] Audley Pedigree 94. Died unmarried aged 63 *c*.28 Aug. 1763, will dated 11 Aug. 1763. The son of Edward Audley junior of Alrewas and Sarah (Baggarley).

[19] Elizabeth in 1695, Mary perhaps in 1696, Katherine in 1702, Sarah in 1704. These names were all used for later-born daughters.

[20] Baptized 20 Oct. 1699, died unmarried 1769, buried Sutton Coldfield.

[21] Baptized 12 Feb. 1703/4, married one Rowbotham, died after 19 Apr. 1771.

[22] Baptized 27 Dec. 1711, buried 9 Apr. 1782 Sutton Coldfield.

[23] LJRO BT Cannock.   [24] Lupin survives as a farm name in Fradley.

[25] LJRO BT Alrewas recording the burial on 21 Dec. 1701 of John, the son of George Jee.

John Jee and his wife Elizabeth (Audley) had two sons and three daughters. For three of them we have dates of baptism: John on 31 March 1742,[26] Edward on 20 February 1744/5,[27] and Sarah on 11 October 1747.[28] Elizabeth, whose baptism is not recorded, was born in about 1749, and Mary in about 1753.[29] Sarah married Peter Heathcoate in 1777. Mary married Henry Smith at Alrewas on 20 June 1779, and died on 30 January 1831 aged 78. Elizabeth remained unmarried and died, aged about 61, on 1 November 1810. The mother of all these children, Elizabeth Jee, was, we know, born between 1705 and 1710. We must incline to the later date for her birth, for even that would mean that she bore Mary at the age of 43, which is a little old to be having children in the eighteenth century. But we cannot be sure of this.

Edward and John Audley and their Niece, Mary Hale

Edward Audley, the surgeon and testator, married one Elizabeth; she survived him, dying without issue then living in 1791.[30] In fact, the couple do not seem ever to have had children, or at least any who were alive when Edward came to make his will, which he signed on 14 August 1769. His brother, John, had made his will earlier that same year, on 28 April. Both wills were the outcome of a joint estate-planning exercise, as it might now be called.

Edward made his brother his residuary legatee, and he made other gifts in his favour. He also made extensive provision for 'my loving wife'—thus he gave her a life interest in their home and the silver, and £200 in cash. He also gave her for her life the interest on a sum of £1,000 which 'shall be placed out or continue at interest'. The other principal beneficiary was his niece; the will continues: 'and at her death I give the same thousand pounds unto my niece Mary Hale and the issue of her body lawfully begotten or to be begotten'. Mary Hale must have been something of a favourite, for she was also given a legacy of £200.[31] In papers connected with the chancery suit Mary Hale is said to have been 47 in 1786, which would make her date of birth about 1739.[32] In fact, as we have seen, she was then rather older, about 53, having been baptized on 27 April 1734, and presumably born in that year. Her mother, Anne, was Edward's younger sister, and was no longer alive in 1744; she may well have died in

---

[26] Baptized Alrewas.

[27] Baptized Alrewas. Edward married Emily, daughter of John Wyatt (1700–66), the inventor of the spinning machine.

[28] At Alrewas. In a marriage licence from Lichfield, dated 26 Nov. 1777, she is described as aged 21, but this means 21 or over. The licence is reproduced by A. L. Reade.

[29] Deduced from the age given at her death.

[30] Will dated 6 Jan. 1791, proved 13 Jan. 1792, PCC Fountain 1.

[31] The will also mentions another 'kinsman', Edward Jee of Birmingham, a gunsmith, who was given a legacy of £100. He would be the second son of John and Elizabeth Jee.

[32] PRO C 12/1692/5, confirmed by C 12/1686/35 of 1 Mar. 1785.

childbirth.[33] At the time when Edward and his brother, John, were making their wills she would have been 35. Both brothers may well have thought that it was high time she got married. For, given the fact that Edward had no children, and John was a bachelor, with no plans to marry and lose his fellowship, she was the best hope of perpetuating the line of the Audleys of Alrewas. The risk was that she would leave it too late. Her chances of making a suitable marriage would be considerably enhanced if she were well endowed.

In this event the perpetuation of the Audleys of Alrewas had, of necessity, to become the task of someone else. The other line of the Audleys of Alrewas went back to Edward Audley of Orgreave junior. Only one of his descendants was, in 1769, married with a family—Elizabeth Jee.[34] So Edward's will went on to provide that 'for and in default of such issue [i.e. of Mary Hale] I give the said thousand pounds to be equally divided between the Daughters then living of my Kinsman John Jee and Elizabeth Jee in the parish of Alrewas'. Given this endowment they would be well placed to make suitable marriages, but the arrangement would not, of course, preserve the name of Audley.

John was also fond of his niece, Mary Hale, and was clearly concerned at the situation; she was the best hope. In his will, which had been signed rather earlier the same year, he left £2,000 to his brother, Edward, and expressed the hope that if Edward was childless he would leave this money to 'my beloved niece Mary Hale or to her child or children lawfully begotten'. He also left Edward another £2,000 to provide an annuity of £60 *per annum* for Mary while she remained unmarried. If she found a suitable husband, who would settle £100 a year on her, then brother Edward was empowered to transfer the capital sum to her husband as part of the marriage settlement. He also exhorted his brother Edward, if he came into possession of entailed lands, to break the entail—the reference will be to entails created under the will of his father, John Audley[35]—and leave the property to Mary for life 'and to her child or children if there should be any such lawfully begotten'. But John was aware of the risk that Mary might disappoint his hopes, and fail to produce children. His plan in this event was rather different. He decided to place his hopes on his distant relative, Edward Jee, the younger brother of John Jee, husband of Elizabeth. In 1769 Edward was aged 24 and unmarried.[36] So his will went on to express the wish that his brother should leave the property 'in default of such issue [i.e. of Mary Hale] to Edward Jee and his heirs for ever'. But Edward was a relatively humble Jee, not an armigerous Audley, so he added, 'on condition that the said Edward Jee shall take upon himself and use the surname Audley by Act of Parliament or any other lawful

---

[33] A. L. Reade, n. 5 above, at 97.

[34] Of the other possibles Katherine was an elderly widow and Sarah an elderly spinster. All the others were dead, and none had left families behind them.

[35] See n. 9 above. Conceivably there were hopes of entailed property from more distant branches of the family.

[36] Edward later married Emily, daughter of John Wyatt, and they had a son, John Audley Jee (1778–1864).

method'. The choice of Edward rather than John is reflected in other provisions of the will. John Audley did not dislike Elizabeth Jee—she was to have £20 'as a testimony of my respect'. The favoured Edward was to have £50. But the unfortunate John Jee, who must have for some reason incurred disapproval, was to receive a mere £5. Finally the will made Mary Hale and his brother, Edward, his residuary legatees.[37]

Mary Hale plainly knew how to charm her uncles, but her main source of power was the demographics of the family. The different provisions of the two wills suggest that the brothers were unable to agree entirely on what ought to be done, but they were agreed on Mary Hale.

The Deaths of the Audley Brothers

Of the two brothers, Edward was the first to die, in April 1771; he was buried in St Phillips, Birmingham. On 20 September probate was granted to his brother, John, and his widow, Elizabeth; John alone took possession of the assets.[38] Mary Hale was then unmarried and aged about 46. John and Elizabeth Jee were both still alive, and their three daughters, Sarah, Elizabeth, and Mary, were all unmarried, though, as we have seen, Sarah and Mary were to marry later. The law report incorrectly states that there were four daughters. There were also the two sons, John and Edward; the law report wrongly says there were no sons. Elizabeth Jee was somewhere around 61 or possibly older, and her husband, John, around the same age. He died at Orgreave in November 1777. His wife, Elizabeth, survived him to be buried there on 4 December 1779. Of course, since the will had been made there had been no further children, since Elizabeth was past child-bearing.

On 2 April 1782, brother John died. On 2 May 1782, Mary Hale, still unmarried, was granted administration with the will annexed as being the sole surviving residuary legatee under John's will. The effect of this grant was to give her immediate control of the assets of both of her deceased uncles. Under Edward's will, his widow, Elizabeth, was entitled to the income from the £1,000 fund during her life. The law report states that she was dead in 1787, but this is incorrect; she did not die until 1791.[39] Mary Hale would only become entitled once Elizabeth died. The elaborate provisions of John's will—the annuity of £60 for Mary until her marriage, for example, and the instructions to Edward about a marriage settlement for her—had all been made on the assumption that Edward would survive him, and John had never made a new will adapted to the fact that Edward had died first. Events had overtaken his plans, leaving Mary the residuary legatee with nothing between her and the considerable fortune of her late

[37] PROB 11/1090, 210 at fo. 138.
[38] So asserted by Elizabeth in 1786, C 12/1692/5 of 4 Mar. 1786.   [39] See n. 30 above.

uncle John except a number of specific legacies—£50 to Edward's widow, Elizabeth, £20 each to cousins Elizabeth Jee and Sarah Audley—they amounted in all to £376. The largest such legacy was £100 to Magdalen College Oxford:

on condition they purchase a handsome neat iron rail to fence in the altar or communion table of the inward chapel of the said college and moreover I would have my coat of arms together with the date of the year impressed on four or six places of this rail. My coat of arms is gules a fret or . . .

This proposal, described by J. D. Macray, the historian of the college, as 'hideously mistaken', was not carried out, and Mary Hale agreed that the money might be spent otherwise on beautifying the chapel. Following the Oxford college tradition of always violating trusts if at all possible, the money was in the event spent on a new fireplace in the hall, which was replaced in 1904. The coat of arms was at one time displayed on it, and later on the wainscotting, but is now, so Dr Ibbotson tells me, thought to survive somewhere on the premises in a sort of elephants' graveyard of redundant escutcheons.

Since John's will had dealt in sums of £4,000 we may guess that there was going to be plenty left for Mary as residuary legatee, which may have made her the more willing to agree to the college's proposal.

The Family Dispute and Litigation

The Jees must have felt that Mary had done rather too well out of her uncles; furthermore, John's will had made it clear that it was his wish, if Mary failed to marry and produce children, to provide for her only for her lifetime, and then to perpetuate the name of Audley through Edward Jee, who was to take the name Audley. As time passed, and certainly by the 1780s, it must have been pretty clear that Mary Hale was never going to marry and have children. Precisely what family negotiations or quarrels went on we cannot now tell, but in 1785, when Mary Hale was 50 or 51 and still unmarried, Edward Jee made a somewhat desperate attempt to protect what he saw as his interests through a Chancery suit.[40] Relying upon the terms of John Audley's will, he claimed to be entitled to the fund if Mary Hale were to die 'without child or children lawfully begotten'. His complaint explained: 'apprehending that the said Moneys might be lost and wasted and being desirous of securing his interest therein', he had asked Mary 'to place out the same in the names of proper trustees or in the name of the Accountant General of this Honourable Court'. But the scheming Mary had refused and had 'combined and confederated with divers Persons at present unknown to your Orator'. He could not join them as parties to the suit, since he did not know who they were. So he was asking the court to take steps to prevent

---

[40] *Edward Jee* v. *Mary Hale*, 1 Mar. 1785, C 12/1686/35.

Mary Hale wasting the assets. Mary Hale's reply to this was to say that she had taken advice, and as residuary legatee she was entitled to the assets absolutely. She could do what she wanted with them; furthermore, there had been no combination and conspiracy. Since the terms of the will upon which Edward Jee relied simply expressed John's wishes to his brother, who had in any event died before the will took effect, Mary Hale's contention, or I suppose that of her lawyer, was plainly correct, and the action seems to have been allowed to lapse. So Mary won round one.

The next move by the Jees was taken just a year later, when Elizabeth Jee, Henry and Mary Smith,[41] and Peter and Sarah Heathcote[42] brought a Chancery suit against Elizabeth Audley, surgeon Edward's widow, and Mary Hale.[43] It was this suit, based upon Edward Audley's will, which gave rise to the reported case of *Jee* v. *Audley*. In their affidavits the three daughters of John and Elizabeth Jee explained how John Audley had taken possession of the assets of his brother, Edward, which were amply sufficient to carry out the terms of the will, and how, after John's death, Mary Hale, as his administratrix, had come into possession of them. They claimed to be entitled to a contingent interest in the fund of £1,000 in the event that Mary Hale died 'without issue of her body lawfully begotten'. Since she was still unmarried and, so they thought, aged 47, this looked quite likely to happen; one may guess that Mary Hale may have been a little less than honest about her age, for she was in reality 53 or so. They had asked Elizabeth Audley and Mary Hale to appoint trustees, or put the fund into court, but they, in conspiracy with others, had refused to do this. Again, what was sought was security; the complaint was that the sum of £1,000 'is in danger of being lost unless the same be properly secured'. Mary Hale naturally took legal advice about this suit too, and at this point the rule against perpetuities was introduced as a weapon in the family quarrel. The sisters' affidavit explains that 'the said Elizabeth Audley and Mary Hale pretend that the bequest over of the said sum of One Thousand Pounds . . . to the daughters of his kinsman John Jee and Elizabeth Jee *is too remote*' (my italics). Elizabeth Audley, in her reply, distanced herself a little from the family dispute, explaining that she was not in possession of the assets; the question whether the daughters were entitled, she simply submitted to the judgment of the court. Mary Hale was more forthright; as do some some property law students, she had met and fallen in love with the rule against perpetuities. The sisters, she explained, were not entitled: 'the disposition thereof on failure of Issue of this Defendant being, as this Defendant is advised, void'. It is fairly obvious what must have happened. The Jee sisters, jealous of Mary Hale, pinned their hopes on obtaining some of the Audley wealth once she died. Once it became unlikely she would ever marry and bear children, they, in a moment of folly, allowed lawyers to become involved in the

---

[41] Married 20 June 1779 at Alrewas.   [42] Sarah married him in 1777.
[43] C 12/1692/5 of 4 Mar. 1786.

family quarrel. Those instructed by Mary Hale spotted the fact that, under the rule against perpetuities, there was a problem over the contingent gift in their favour.

So a family quarrel, inspired by jealousy and rivalry between cousins, became transformed into a dispute over the application of the rule against perpetuities to the will of Edward Audley, who had in all probability never heard of its existence.

Lloyd Kenyon's Decision

The case came before Sir Lloyd Kenyon on 14 February 1787. He was later, as Lord Kenyon, Chief Justice of the King's Bench, but at this time was Master of the Rolls. The records of the court briefly explain the outcome: 'since it was admitted that John Jee and Elizabeth his wife in the pleadings named were both living at the time of the death of the said testator Edward Audley', the bill was dismissed, but without costs.[44]

The decision is more fully explained in the law report. This, as we have seen, is very unreliable on the facts of the case: Mary Hale becomes Mary Hall, she is aged about 40 (in reality 53), the Jees have four daughters and no son (they had three daughters and two sons), Elizabeth Audley, Edward's widow, is said to be dead (she was in reality still alive). The report also says both that the Jees were 70 years old when the testator died in 1771 and 'of a very advanced age'; the Chancery records make it clear that the precise age of the Jees was not known, and in reality Elizabeth Jee was considerably younger. Nevertheless, the report is probably fairly trustworthy on the application of the legal dogmas involved, which led to Mary Hale's victory over the Jees.

The starting-point was a peculiar rule of construction, that is a rule as to how the text of the will should be interpreted, ostensibly to conform to the intention of the testator. The gift to the daughters 'then living' of the Jees was to take effect if Mary Hale 'died without issue'. Most people would, by the light of nature, suppose that this refers to the possibility that Mary would have no issue—children, grandchildren, or remoter descendants—at the time of her death. Henry Randell, in his *An Essay on the Law of Perpetuities and on Trusts of Accumulation* (London, 1822), called this the 'vulgar' sense of the expression; the term derives from the opinion of Lord Parker in *Target* v. *Gaunt* (1718), which Randell cited as an example of a court interpreting the expression in this way.[45] But the law eschewed vulgarity; there was also a special legal sense. For, as W. D. Lewis explained in his *A Practical Treatise on the Law of Perpetuities*, 'it must be understood, that the words "dying without issue", and "dying without having issue" mean, in the eyes of the law, death, and the failure of issue,

---

[44] C 33/467, Pt. 1, fo. 170, Hilary Term.
[45] At 139–40. 1 P Wms 432, 24 ER 459; also *Nicholas* v. *Hooper* (1712) 1 P Wms. 198, 24 ER 353; *Pinbury* v. *Elkin* (1719) 1 P Wms. 564, 24 ER 518.

whenever that failure may happen, be the time ever so distant'.[46] This sort of failure of issue was called a 'general' failure. A standard illustration of the notion is that Queen Victoria, though gathered up some years back, has never in the eyes of the law died without issue—she still has living descendants. She may never die without issue.

Since this peculiar interpretative rule could produce results which offended common sense, there was a considerable body of case law on when it applied, and when it did not. John Tyrrell, in his evidence to the Real Property Commissioners in 1829, was very critical of it:

Another absurd and inconvenient rule is that which determines that the words 'die without issue' and 'die without leaving issue' shall not mean, according to the common sense of the expression, if there shall be no issue at the time of the death, but shall mean if there shall be a failure of issue at any distance of time. The effect of the rule is to defeat the intention of the testator, by rendering a gift if another devisee should die without issue as incompatible with the rule against perpetuities and therefore void.[47]

His criticism was accepted, and by an Act of Parliament in 1837,[48] too late to help the Jees, it was abolished as a general presumption.

The interrelation between the interpretative rule and the rule against perpetuities, Lewis explained, was so complex that, 'within the extensive range of property law there is, perhaps, no one subject, which has given rise to so much and so varied discussion'.[49] Obviously if the interpretative rule applied in *Jee* v. *Audley*, the contingency mentioned in Edward Audley's will—Mary Hale's death without issue—*could*, as a matter of logic, happen hundreds of years after Edward's death, and so well outside the period of a life in being and twenty-one years required by the rule against perpetuities. It was too remote a contingency. Now by 1787, and long earlier, it had come to be quite settled law that, in applying the rule against perpetuities, you considered the *logical* possibilities at the time of the testator's death, that is in 1771, and not the practical possibilities. Then, and indeed even at the time the case was decided in 1787, it was still *logically* possible for Mary Hale to have children and start a line, which line might, *logically*, die out centuries later. To be sure the notion of the logical possibility of bearing a child is rather bizarre; having a baby is complicated enough, but having a logically possible baby, or logically having a logically possible baby, is enough to make the imagination boggle.

At the time *Jee* v. *Audley* was decided, there was, however, some authority in the case law for drawing a distinction between gifts of real property and gifts of personal property. In the former case there was certainly a presumption in favour of the absurd 'general failure of issue' interpretation, and this was rationalized as being favourable to heirs at law. Where personal property was involved, as in *Jee* v. *Audley*, the presumption, according to some cases, was reversed, and

---

[46] (London, 1843), 174.   [47] N. 4 above.
[48] I Vict. c.26.   [49] N. 46 above, ch. 15.

favoured the vulgar sense. The origin of this distinction was a case back in 1720, *Forth* v. *Chapman*.[50] Kenyon himself was involved in decisions in which he vacillated somewhat on the matter. The year after *Jee* v. *Audley*, in *Goodtitle d.*, *Peake* v. *Pegden*,[51] he appeared to accept the distinction, in 1789, in *Porter* v. *Bradley*,[52] he cast doubt upon it. He later recanted in *Daintry* v. *Daintry* (1795).[53] The distinction was later approved by Lord Eldon.[54] With some ingenuity, however, Kenyon's decisions could be reconciled. The report of *Jee* v. *Audley* indicates that the point was never raised; how Kenyon would have reacted if it had been is therefore speculative.

Kenyon's somewhat rigorous attitude to artificial legal rules of construction which defied common sense was explained by him in a case in 1786, *Stebbing* v. *Walkey*: 'In construing wills, Courts ought not to indulge in conjecture; it were better that many wills should be defeated; but in this case I am not prepared to control the cases which have been determined.' But he confessed to some unease: 'When rules are laid down, they ought to be such as meet the common sense of mankind. I acknowledge, on the present subject, I yield to the authority of the cases, and not to the reason of them.'[55] There are numerous other examples of judges lamenting the rules of construction they felt bound to apply.[56]

On the fact of things this is rather strange—why develop and apply rules, and yet lament their existence? The advantage of rigidly following rules, however silly the result, was prospective—lawyers who drafted wills would know exactly what construction a court would put upon a will. But, given the fact that wills were often not expertly drafted, the price paid was, as Kenyon realized, to defeat many wills.

If, however, Edward Audley's will had restricted the daughters who could take a share to those living at the testator's *own* death—who would clearly then be 'lives in being'—the gift to them would be logically certain to take effect within a life in being, as required by the rule, that is within the lives of Elizabeth Jee junior, Mary Smith, and Sarah Heathcote. Unhappily the will did not say this—the gift was to the daughters '*then* living', that is living when Mary Hale died without issue, which could, under the general failure of issue doctrine, happen centuries later, at too remote a time.

There was still a possible escape from this demented logic. If the word 'daughters' was interpreted to refer solely to Elizabeth junior, Mary, and Sarah, all 'lives in being' when Edward Audley died, the contingent gift to them would

[50] 1 P Wms. 663, 24 ER 559. See Randell, op. cit., 123 and cases cited in note 41 above.
[51] (1788) 2 TR 720, 100 ER 388.
[52] 3 Term. Rep. 143, 100 ER 500. See also *Roe d.*, *Sheers* v. *Jeffery* (1798) 7 TR 589, 101 ER 1147.
[53] 6 Term. Rep. 307, 101 ER 567.
[54] *Crook* v. *De Vandes* (1803) 9 Ves. Jun. 197, 32 ER 577.   [55] 2 Bro. CC 86, 29 ER 48.
[56] Tyrrell, n. 4 above, cites examples at 323; e.g. Sir James Mansfield in *Doe d.*, *Briscoe* v. *Clarke* (1806) 2 Bos. and Pull. NR 348, 127 ER 659: 'for I have no doubt that our decision will be contrary to the real intention of the testator'.

be good. These were the only daughters the testator knew, so common sense suggested that he meant to refer only to them. A case in 1748, *Ellison* v. *Airey*,[57] had, however, ruled that, where property was left to someone's daughters (or other children) in circumstances similar to *Jee* v. *Audley*, there was no interpretative rule limiting 'daughters' to mean 'daughters existing when I die', or 'daughters existing when I make my will'. Instead the rule was that after-born children could take. So the question now was whether there could be any after-born sisters, who would plainly not be 'lives in being' when Edward Audley died.

Sir Lloyd Kenyon pointed out that it was admitted that John and Elizabeth Jee had both been alive when Edward Audley died; hence they could have further children. He seems to have thought that where there was life there was hope. And so the contingency—a daughter of theirs being around when Mary Hale died without issue could, as a matter of logic, happen outside the required period of a life in being: 'John and Elizabeth Jee might have children born ten years after the testator's death, and then Mary Hall might die without issue [i.e. in the weird sense I have explained] fifty years afterwards.' He should have added, to make his point more clearly, that when the failure of issue occurred, fifty years later, Sarah, Elizabeth junior, and Mary could well, as a matter of logic, be dead. So the gift might take effect outside the perpetuity period; it was therefore invalid as being too remote. The consequence was that the suit failed; Mary Hale was absolutely entitled to the £1,000.

So Mary Hale collected the jackpot under the wills of both Edward and John Audley, and the Jees dramatically lost out. As many have learnt to their cost, they would probably have done much better never to have started legal proceedings in the first place. Once you get lawyers into a family dispute, matters tend to go from bad to worse.

There were a number of common-sensical objections to this result which were, according to the report, put forward by counsel in the case; some have to be deduced from Kenyon's opinion. One was that the interpretation which allowed after-born daughters to qualify was supposed, in the theory of the law, to carry out the intention of the testator. But applying it in this case produced the opposite effect; it was 'never meant to give an effect which would totally defeat such intention'. Another was that 'there was no real possibility of John and Elizabeth Jee having children, they being then 70 years old'. But in 1787 knowledge about the fertility of the old was not what it now is; it was widely believed, for example, that Old Thomas Parr (?1483–1635) had fathered a bastard child at the age of 105. There was clear Biblical warrant for late childbirth in women; Sarah bore Isaac at the age of 90.[58] Hence, perhaps, counsel did not overstate his point, merely claiming, on the basis of a supposed age of 70, that

---

[57] (1748) 1 Ves. Sen. 111, 27 ER 924, distinguished *Leake* v. *Robinson* (1817) 2 Mer. 363, 35 ER 979.

[58] *Gen.* 17: 15. *Co. Litt.* 40b took three score years as the normal upper limit for women.

'there was no real possibility of John and Elizabeth Jee having children after the testator's death'. It was not as strong a point as it now seems, though it was then well known that elderly women did not usually have babies.[59] Kenyon would have none of it: 'if this can be done in one case it may in another, and it is a very dangerous experiment, and introductive of the greatest inconvenience to give a latitude to such sort of conjecture.' More convincing to anyone not a lawyer was the fact, which everyone must have known, though it is not mentioned in the law report and had not at this stage been established in affidavits before the court, that the Jees were both dead, and had not had any further children. Kenyon said in his opinion: 'Another thing pressed upon me, is to decide on the events which have happened; but I cannot do this without over-turning very many cases.' The reference is to the principle which was, by then, well established: the rule against perpetuities was applied in the light of what, logically, might happen, viewing the matter from the date at which a will took effect, and not by reference to what had, in fact, happened. There was no 'wait and see'. So the fact that it was known in 1787 that the contingency would certainly happen within the lives of the three daughters (all 'lives in being' when Edward Audley died) was neither here nor there. That was not logically certain back in 1771, when Edward Audley died.

A decision by the Master of the Rolls was subject to a form of appeal; the case could be argued all over again before the Chancellor himself. It looks as if an appeal was considered, for on 15 July 1787, five months after Kenyon's decision, an affidavit was sworn by one Thomas Gem before A. Mainwairing, a Master Extra in Chancery, to the effect that he had inspected the Church Registers of St Phillips in Birmingham, and Alrewas, and established the dates of burial of Edward Audley, John Jee, and Elizabeth Jee. The fact that the affidavit does not establish the dates of birth of John and Elizabeth Jee indicates that Mr Gem, back in 1787, had the problems that I have met in 1994. No doubt he searched in vain. There is no evidence that the case ever was reheard.

The Original Insignificance of Jee v. Audley

Some later references to *Jee* v. *Audley* are a little puzzling. In *Lord Deerhurst* v. *Duke of Albans* (1820), a case whose progress somewhat resembles *Jarndyce* v. *Jarndyce*,[60] Edward B. Sugden, later Lord St Leonards, said in the course of argument: 'In *Gee* v. *Lord Audley* it was clear upon the gift that it might not take place until twenty-seven years after the death of the testator; on the face of it was bad; and Lord Kenyon held that being void as to some in the class, it was void as to all.' If the testator to whom Sugden was referring was Edward Audley,

---

[59] See below 97.
[60] 5 Madd. 232 at 272, 56 ER 883 at 898. In the House of Lords this case was called *Tollemach* v. *Coventry* (1834) 2 Clark and Finelly 611, 6 ER 1285. The litigation arose out of a will of 1781.

this looks like some mysterious reference to an event which would take place in 1798; as it happens Mary Hale died in 1795, so the reference can hardly be to her death.[61] Probably twenty-seven is simply a typographical slip for twenty-one; if so, the point he was making was that the vesting of the gift was not restrained within a lifetime in being when the will took effect. The rule then was that such a gift must vest within twenty-one years, and he is simply making the point that it was not bound to do so.[62]

Two other references give a significantly different account of what the case was all about. In *Routledge* v. *Dorril* (1794) Sir R. P. Ardern, who was now Master of the Rolls, referred explicitly to the decision, but treated it as a case where a power of appointment was exercised by will. It was not uncommon for a testator to leave property, say, to one person, Smith, for life, and allow that person to determine by his will what was to happen to the property thereafter, by giving him a power of appointment. Such a power might be limited, for example, to Smith's issue, and exercisable by Smith in his will; such a limited power was called a special power. Ardern treats *Jee* v. *Audley* as such a case, where a special power of appointment was exercised by Edward Audley in his will:

That case was on 14 February 1787. There was an appointment by will of £1,000 in default of issue of Mary Hall equally to be divided between the daughters then living of John Gee and Elizabeth his wife; and had that been restrained to the death of the person executing the power [i.e. Edward Audley] it would have been good.[63]

At this date no report of the case had been published, but Ardern relied on a note provided by Master Cox, which was eventually to be turned into the published report. Although there is no direct evidence in either Edward Audley's will itself or in the published law report, it is just possible that the fund of £1,000 which, in Edward's will, was 'to be placed out or continue at interest' had been given to him under an earlier will which gave him a power to appoint who was to get the interest and fund after his death, and that this account is not a mistake. This might explain the reference to the money 'continuing' at interest. If this is correct, then there would have been an earlier will giving the fund of £1,000 to Edward Audley for his life, and giving him the power to nominate by his will who was to enjoy the interest or capital after his death.[64]

Edward Sugden, the leading property lawyer of his time, took this same view of the case in his *A Practical Treatise of Powers*,[65] referring both to *Gee* v. *Audley* and to *Routledge* v. *Dorril*, which in his view followed it, as dealing with the same point. What *Jee* v. *Audley*, in Sugden's view, decided was

---

[61] Will of Mary Hale of Birmingham, spinster, dated 16 Jan. 1795, proved 15 Apr.: PCC Newcastle 258, PROB 11/1259, 258.

[62] The reprinted version in the ER accurately reproduces the original printed text, published in 1816.

[63] (1794) 2 Ves. Jun. 357 at 365, 30 ER 671 at 675.

[64] If he could appoint to whosoever he liked a 'general' power of appointment.

[65] Edn. of 1821, London, at 544–6. The first edn. was in 1808, the second in 1815.

that a gift under a power, embracing objects not within the line of perpetuity [i.e. the possible after born daughter], is wholly void, and the fund cannot be given to those to whom it might be legally appointed [i.e. Elizabeth junior, Mary, and Sarah].

Yet it seems unlikely that the law report would not mention the power if one was involved; on the other hand, Sugden, an outstandingly skilled property lawyer, was unlikely to have misdescribed the case. In *Leake* v. *Robinson* (1817), after Cox's report was in print, Sir William Grant, Master of the Rolls, also treated the case as dealing with a power.[66] If the case really was concerned with the exercise of a power of appointment under an earlier will, the mysterious reference to twenty-seven years in *Lord Deerhurst* v. *the Duke of Albans* could be not a typographical error but a reference to the interval between the date of the first testator's death—in 1744—and that of Edward Audley. But unfortunately I have not been able to find a possible testator who died at the right time, so there is no obvious solution to the mystery.[67]

Some indication as to what counsel engaged in the case supposed it to be about at the time can be deduced from the earlier cases cited as authority in it, of which the law report provides a list of twelve.[68] Of the twelve, four deal with whether children born after the death of a testator could take an interest, and six with the general failures of issue construction. The other two deal with the validity of a contingent gift following a gift of personal property which purports to entail that property, a question which in the event did not arise, since the gift over was held void on other grounds.[69] The cases cited do not throw any light upon whether the litigation concerned the exercise of a power of appointment or not. They do, however, indicate the principal matters which were thought arguable in the case; two were questions regarded as matters of interpretation of the expressions used in the will, rather than questions about the substance of the rule against perpetuities. What, in the eyes of the law, did Edward Audley mean by 'daughters'—did he mean daughter alive when he made his will, or when he died, or any daughters at all? What did he mean by 'in default of such issue' of his favourite, Mary Hale—had he in mind her dying unmarried and childless, or had he in mind more remote possibilities, such as the possibility that she might leave children who in their turn died childless? And Edward was, of course, not around to be consulted.

---

[66] 2 Mer. 363, 36 ER 979.

[67] Edward and John's father, John, the most obvious possibility, died in 1737; see n. 9 above.

[68] *Pleydell* v. *Pleydell* (1721) 1 P Wms. 748, 24 ER 597; *Forth* v. *Chapman* (1720) 1 P Wms. 663, 24 ER 559; *Lamb* v. *Archer* (1693) Salk. 226, 91 ER 200; *Smith* v. *Clever* (1688) 2 Vern. 38, 59, 23 ER 635, 647, and *Rachel's Case* there cited; *Wood* v. *Saunders*, Pollex. 35, 86 ER 503; *Atkinson* v. *Hutchinson* (1734) 3 PW 256, 23 ER 1053; *Hughes* v. *Sayer* (1718) 1 PW 534, 24 ER 504; *Cook* v. *Cook* (1706) 2 Vern. 545, 23 ER 952; *Horsley* v. *Chaloner* (1750) 2 Ves. Sen. 84, 28 ER 55; *Coleman* v. *Seymour* (1748) 1 Ves. Sen. 209, 27 ER 987; *Ellison* v. *Airey* (1724) 1 Ves. Sen. 111, 27 ER 924.

[69] *Rachel's Case* and *Wood* v. *Saunders*, both n. 68 above. The normal rule was that, if personal property, which could not be entailed, was given in terms which purported to entail it, the effect was to make an absolute gift. However, a gift over which was bound to take effect, if at all, within a life in being was valid. The point normally arose where funds were involved.

As to what the early nineteenth century made of *Jee* v. *Audley*, some clue is provided by the use which was made of the case by text writers. H. Randell, whose *Essay on the Law of Perpetuity and on Trusts of Accumulation*, the first monograph on the subject, appeared in 1822, does not mention the case at all, and it is ignored by other writers of the period, though more understandably.[70] As we have seen, Sugden in his treatise on powers viewed *Jee* v. *Audley* as a case on the exercise of special powers of appointment; it was important as the first decision that if a power was exercised in favour of persons some of whom could lawfully be beneficiaries, and some not, even those who could lawfully benefit could not take. The exercise of the power was wholly invalid. This doctrine came, in professional tradition, to be attributed to *Routledge* v. *Dorril* (1794), where, as we have seen, *Jee* v. *Audley* was expressly relied upon;[71] no doubt the reason for this was some doubt whether *Jee* v. *Audley* was concerned with powers at all.

The next writer to notice the case was Thomas Jarman in his *A Treatise on Wills* (1841–4). He used it to illustrate the weird thesis that where a gift is made to a class of persons, and is, under the established and highly technical rules of interpretation, void as to some members, the courts will not fail to apply these rules, 'although it is probable that the testator, if interrogated on the point, would have consented to restrain the class for the purpose of bringing it within the due limits'. Plainly, of course, in *Jee* v. *Audley* Edward Audley, if summoned from the shades before Sir Lloyd Kenyon, or put in touch through an ouija board, would cheerfully have agreed to cut out from his beneficence any after-born daughters of the Jees, more particularly since there had never been any. W. D. Lewis, whose *A Practical Treatise on the Law of Perpetuities*, the first comprehensive treatment of perpetuities, appeared in 1843, follows Sugden, and cites the case for the same doctrine on powers of appointment.[72] He followed Jarman's view, and rather revelled in the perverse absurdity of the doctrine derived from the case:

The courts do not regard the consequences of any rule of construction, which they may have established, as prescribing any objection to its application, when clearly called for: and, therefore, the circumstances that, by the law of remoteness, the effect of applying any particular rule . . . will be to wholly defeat the donor's scheme of disposition, is of no weight in opposition to the application of that rule.[73]

But it is clear that, apart from Sugden, who attributed to the case an important first ruling on powers of appointment, the early writers do not seem to have viewed *Jee* v. *Audley* as a particularly noteworthy decision. It later came to be

---

[70] Of other books of the period, S. Atkinson, *Theory and Practice of Conveyancing, Comprising the Law of Real Property* (London, 1829); W. H. Burton, *Elementary Compendium of the Law of Real Property* (London, 1828); W. Cruise, *Digest of the Laws of England respecting Real Property* (London, 1818); M. Dawes, *Law of Real Estates, and of Remainders Therein Expressed, Implied and Contingent* (London, 1814) do not mention the case.

[71] 2 Ves. Jun. 357, 30 ER 671.   [72] N. 46 above, 493, with a reference to Sugden.

[73] Ibid. 517.

blamed for the rule that a gift to a class of persons could, unlike the curate's egg, not be partly good and partly bad, a dogma slightly different from Sugden's rule as to the exercise of powers, and more usually attributed to *Leake* v. *Robinson*.[74] But it has been argued that *Jee* v. *Audley* was the root of both dogmas; *Routledge* v. *Dorril* followed *Jee* v. *Audley*, and *Leake* v. *Robinson* followed *Routledge* v. *Dorril*.[75]

The Rise to Fame of Jee v. Audley

The case might have come to be more or less forgotten had it not been for the activities of three members of the Harvard Law School. One was Langdell, who, as we have seen, developed the idea of teaching law through the study of leading cases.[76] Once his idea was applied to property law, *Jee* v. *Audley* became a possible leading case on the law of property. But it would only achieve this status if someone thought it worth selecting to illustrate a fundamental legal principle.

Also working at the Harvard Law School in the late nineteenth century was another formidable scholar, John Chipman Gray.[77] Unlike Langdell, whose only systematizing work was his nutshell on contract law, Gray devoted his considerable talents to the writing of legal treatises, works which lived off the theory of legal science. No such work ever expressed Langdell's theory of economy of principles more elegantly than Gray's *The Rule against Perpetuities* (1886). He contrived to reduce the whole body of doctrine, supposedly underlying hundreds of cases, many barely intelligible, to a mere thirty-two words;[78] any cases which were not compatible with his statement of the rule were simply dismissed as wrong. Gray was fascinated with the idea that all perpetuity problems had a discoverable and incontrovertible right answer:

> If the answer to a problem does not square with the multiplication table one may call it wrong, although it be the work of Sir Isaac Newton; and so if a decision conflicts with the Rule against Perpetuities, one may call it wrong however learned and able the court that has pronounced it.[79]

Gray, unlike the modern exponent of the right-answer thesis, Ronald Dworkin,[80] did not think this degree of precision was possible throughout the law, because usually 'there is no exact standard to which appeal can be made'. But perpetuity law was different—in it the ideal of the rule of law was capable of perfect achievement. All the judges had to do was apply the rule to the facts of the case.

---

[74] 2 Mer. 363, 35 ER 979. e.g. by Lewis, n. 46 above, at 456 with no mention of *Jee* v. *Audley*. He purports to explain the dogma as a logical consequence fo the rule that, for perpetuities purposes, possible, not actual, events are considered. Hence if a class is so defined as to include persons not necessarily identified within the perpetuity period, it could, logically, consist only of such persons. Such, for what it is worth, is the argument.

[75] W. Barton Leach, 'The Rule against Perpetuities and Gifts to Classes', 51 *HLR* 1329.

[76] See above 5.   [77] 1839–1915.   [78] (Boston, Mass., 1886), 144.

[79] Ibid. v.   [80] See above 4.

There was, however, a price to be paid for this precision. As I have said,[81] it is usual in legal reasoning to distinguish the law from its supposed purpose. If a rigorous application of the law would produce a result at odds with the purpose, we are inclined to modify the law—for example, by introducing an exception; there are many different ways of putting this approach into words. The thinking involved can be illustrated in the following way.

Suppose we have a family rule ('the law') that the children are to bathe before retiring to bed. But one evening—this was all a long time ago—Jane, Zoë, and Timothy, *en route* to bed, announce that there is a spitting cobra ensconced in the bath—well, that evening we need to introduce the spitting-cobra exception, for the purpose of the rule, always a little vague, was surely to promote cleanliness, sleep, enjoyable games with plastic ducks, a variety of ends, but surely not death by snake bite. But the problem is not solved by the new spitting-cobra exception, now become part of 'the law' (the children are to have a bath before retiring every night on which there is no spitting cobra in the bath), for three nights later a hippopotamus escapes from a travelling circus . . . And then, the rule having been amended, comes the earthquake . . . The purpose of the law can never be encapsulated in the rule. Neither life, nor language, permits it.

Gray was only able to make sense of his theory by persuading his readers that the rule against perpetuities was to be applied, as it is now put, remorselessly, that is to say, however silly the result. He needed a really silly case to illustrate this. Now by 1886 the decision in *Jee* v. *Audley* had come to appear much more silly than it had seemed back in 1787, because it was by now received truth in most circles that women of 70 (as Elizabeth Jee was thought to have been) could not possibly have children.[82] Indeed in a series of cases, beginning with one in 1814, *Fraser* v. *Frasers*,[83] where the woman was aged 55, the courts had accepted the fact that after about this age or even a little younger women were usually past child-bearing. These cases, however, dealt with the distribution of trust funds, and the practice was to hedge bets by requiring recognizances to hand back the money if a child was later born, which was still viewed as possible.[84] As we have seen earlier, writers had not been particularly struck by this aspect of *Jee* v. *Audley* which now seems ridiculous—the silliness they detected and rather admired was the use of a rule of construction, supposed to elicit the intention of a testator, to defeat that intention—a sort of zany fundamental contradiction.

---

[81] See above 40.

[82] J. H. C. Morris and W. Barton Leach in their *The Rule against Perpetuities* (2nd edn., London, 1962), 81, n. 20 mention the case of a lady in Dalkeith, Midlothian, supposed to have had her 23rd child on 29 Nov. 1880 at the age of 62. The case was written up in (1882) 27 *Edinburgh Medical Journal* 1085, but there was no objective evidence of her date of birth.

[83] In notes to *Leng* v. *Hodges* (1822) Jacob 585, 37 ER 971.

[84] Se *Re Widdow's Trust* (1871) LR 11 Eq. 408, a decision of Malins VC where two sisters were aged 53 and 55. The cases are collected in the note to *Edwards* v. *Tuck* (1856) 23 Beavan 268, 53 ER 102.

Gray refers to *Jee* v. *Audley* in six paragraphs of his book—as a source for the formal statement of the rule,[85] as a source, though not the critical one, for the rule that a class gift cannot be partly good and partly bad,[86] and as possibly relevant to special powers of appointment.[87] Most importantly, however, he cites it rather triumphantly as authority for absurdity: that for legal purposes women of any age are deemed to be capable of having children.[88] The decision of Vice-Chancellor Malins in *Cooper* v. *Laroche* (1881),[89] which was not compatible with this, was brushed aside in a lordly but mock deferential way as 'one of the not infrequent blunders of that learned judge'.[90] For Gray, anxious to support his theory of remorseless application, the principle precedential value of *Jee* v. *Audley* just lay in the fact that it seemed so ridiculous. The sillier the case, the better Gray liked it, though he tried to rationalize the case by supposing that there would be indelicacy in investigating the child-bearing capacity of women, an absurd argument. Nobody familiar with nineteenth-century criminal conversation cases would suppose the nineteenth-century courts to be of exceptional delicacy in matters sexual.

Long after Gray's time the Harvard Law Faculty was joined by one W. Barton Leach, a celebrated teacher of property law, also remembered, alas, for male chauvinistic behaviour which has passed into law school legend. He made prominent use of the case in the teaching of the rule, treating it as the source of what he mocked as 'the fertile octogenarian' rule. No doubt he coined the expression to enliven his teaching; it apparently first appears in print in his *Cases and Text on the Law of Wills* in 1947, which contained a chapter entitled 'Perpetuities in a Nutshell'.[91] In his *Cases and Text on Future Interests and Estate Planning* (1961), compiled with Professor J. K. Logan, he provided a poetic version of *Jee* v. *Audley* by R. C. Beresford, entitled 'The Sprightly Septuagenarian'. Beresford was of the class of 1933 at Harvard, which suggests that the comic history of the case was even then under way.[92]

The Oxford Law School now enters the story in the person of Dr J. H. C. Morris of Magdalen College, which had, as we have seen, benefited from the Audley family back in the eighteenth century. He and Barton Leach wrote a treatise on the rule, and the case became the source of the conclusive presumption of fertility:

The outstanding example of the traditional rigour of the Rule against Perpetuities is the rule, derived from ancient cases, that it is conclusively presumed that a person is capable

[85] N. 78, para. 182.
[86] N. 78 para. 373, citing *Leake* v. *Robinson* (1817) 2 Mer. 363, 35 ER 979, however, as the critical decision.
[87] N. 78, para. 573.   [88] N. 78, para. 215.
[89] 17 Ch.D 368. Malins had also decided *Re Widdows Trust* (1871), LR 11 Eq. 408. See above, n. 83.
[90] N. 78, para. 215a. This was still in the edn. of 1942 by Roland Gray.
[91] (Boston, Mass., 1947), 207.
[92] 689, where it is said that this poem was cited to the Supreme Court of Massachusetts.

of having children, no matter what his or her age, and regardless of such physiological facts as change of life, impotence, or surgical removal of reproductive organs.[93]

The case had, of course, nothing whatever to do with impotence or the surgical removal of reproductive organs, much less with their felonious removal by spouses or significant others. Plainly matters had come a long way since *Jee* v. *Audley*, and, if this is the right expression, the waters have been further muddied by the invention of the sperm bank. A. L. Reade, the genealogist who studied the many well-endowed families bearing the name Audley, all perhaps distantly related to the assassin of the Saxon thane back in 1130, pointed out that

for several centuries down to about 1750 the Audleys were well represented in various parts of the country, as landowners, prosperous traders, and professional men. Not a single descendant of any of them in the male line can now be traced; with two exceptions,[94] their families, which for generations had been well represented and even prolific, became extinct, or disappeared into complete obscurity, before the end of the eighteenth century. What is the explanation of this sudden disappearance of the clan, in all its scattered branches?[95]

It would be somehow satisfying if this could all be blamed upon the rule against perpetuities, but it played at most a trivial part; a rival explanation would attribute the general ill fortune of the Audleys to their earlier involvement in despoiling the monasteries. And the rule at least gave to one branch of the family and to their kinsmen, the Jees, a sort of posthumous immortality. Of more practical importance than the rule in *Shelley's Case*, the rule of remorseless application still has its special fans, and the author of a recent book on the whole subject, David Becker's *Perpetuities and Estate Planning*,[96] confesses in his preface to amatory feelings towards a body of doctrine whose charm lies in part simply in the attraction of the utterly absurd. Whether the ghosts of John and Edward Audley are entirely happy about this sort of fame we simply cannot tell.

---

[93] Morris and Leach, n. 82 above, 77.
[94] The Audleys of Liverpool and the Audleys of Inistioge, County Kilkenny, Ireland.
[95] Pamphlet, privately printed, reproducing *Notes and Queries*, 12 Nov. 1927.
[96] I am indebted to Mr Richard Helmholz for this reference.

5

A Case of First Impression
Priestley v. Fowler (1837)

An Accident on the Way to Norman Cross

Throughout the nineteenth century the indexers of *The Times* indulged in gallows humour in listing the more bizarre accidents which the paper had reported. The year 1835 was an average one: 'Mr Eliot, at New Orleans, from his Balloon not being Inflated Enough', 'Mr Brookes, of Tothill, by Falling from the Top of his House while Asleep', 'James Howard, who in Climbing over the Green Park Railings, was by Slipping Impaled'. Captain Humphreys was killed by a tiger; Mr Wilson, the vocalist, fell through a stage trap; and Mr Mansell, the Duke of Rutland's gamekeeper, shot his arm off whilst loading his Grace's gun. Of these accidents, at least two, it will be noticed, occurred at work. Not listed, however, was an unremarkable accident which took place at about midnight on 30 May 1835 between Peterborough and Norman Cross, about a mile south of the city.[1] It involved a van, drawn by four horses, driven by William Beeton. He was an employee of Thomas Fowler, a wholesale butcher of Market Deeping. It was loaded with mutton in 'peds' (hampers). It had set out from Fowler's shop in Church Street, near the Bull Inn, in Market Deeping that same day at about half past nine at night. The ultimate destination was London, but some of the meat was to be sold *en route* at Buckden, twenty miles from Peterborough. Charles Priestley, another of Fowler's employees, was to travel as far as Buckden, and sell this meat. The start was not auspicious; the four-horse team had been unable to move the vehicle at all; the horses 'jibbed'. So some other employees had to push the van to get it moving. Fowler himself was present, and William Beeton complained at the load: 'I told Mr Fowler he ought to be ashamed of himself for sending such a dangerous load he told me I was a "d—— d fool for saying anything of the sort".' Charles Priestley, also present, did not protest; he was not the coachman.

As the van approached Peterborough and passed over some stones, a cracking noise was heard. So at Peterborough Gideon Lucas, landlord of the King's Head Inn in Broad Bridge Street, inspected it by lantern light. He could find nothing amiss. Soon after leaving the city the van toppled over. The immediate cause was the collapse of the front axletree, which had a crack in it for a third of its length. William Beeton was not seriously injured, being pulled forward by the

[1] *Lincolnshire Chronicle and General Advertiser*, 5 June 1835. See n. 5 below.

horses, which broke loose from the vehicle, but some 'peds' of meat weighing about four hundredweight fell on Charles Priestley. Beeton was unable to move them without assistance. Charles' thigh was fractured, his shoulder dislocated, and he suffered other injuries.

He was taken back to the King's Head, a common practice at this period when an accident happened. Initially he was treated by Oliver Sprigge,[2] a Peterborough surgeon, and later by George Mason, another surgeon and bonesetter, who thought that he would never fully recover. The *Lincolnshire Chronicle and General Advertiser* reported, 'he now lies at the King's Head Inn, Peterborough, in a very precarious state'. Charles was to remain there for fourteen, or according to another account nineteen, weeks. Nineteen seems more likely, for Gideon Lucas presented a bill for £19 for his lodging, surely at £1 a week. The medical bills came to £29. So the total cost for treatment and care was £50, a very considerable sum.

Charles Priestley's accident was nothing out of the ordinary, and of course many accidents happen at work. What was remarkable was the aftermath. For at Lincolnshire Summer Assizes in 1836 Charles, through his father, Brown Priestley—for he was a minor aged 19 at the time[3]—sued his employer for damages. So far as we know today, or counsel knew in 1836, nobody had ever previously sought compensation for such an accident from his employer by a tort action. The trial judge, who was Sir James Alan Park of the Common Pleas, thought there might have been an earlier example, but could not say where or when it had occurred. Professor Richard Epstein, in a lecture, dramatized this absence of recorded earlier cases: 'the utter dearth of cases upon the subject indicates, clearer than any judicial opinion could proclaim, an ironclad rule of breathtaking simplicity: no employee could *ever* recover from *any* employer for *any* workplace accident—period.'[4] He offered an explanation for this strange state of affairs:

Silence said it all: an employee should be grateful for the opportunity of gainful employment. That he should receive any special legal protection on top of his good fortune was quite unthinkable. In a society in which disease and injury were rampant, and life itself fragile and short, the result should not come as too much of a surprise. Why should the legal system intervene on behalf of those fortunate enough to gain employment when there were countless others, far worse off, who would gladly trade places with them?

But were matters really as bad as that? Were there perhaps mechanisms other than tort law which addressed the consequences of work-related accidents to wage-earners? These are matters to which I shall return. But I quote Professor Epstein because he is surely right to regard the case as an extraordinary one.

---

[2] In Whellan's 1849 *Directory* as of Church Street. The *Northampton Mercury*, 10 Dec. 1836, records him caring for a drover who became ill and was placed in the White Lion Inn, where he died.

[3] See n. 48 below.

[4] R. A. Epstein, 'The Historical Origins and Economic Structure of Workers' Compensation Law' (1982) 16 *GLR* 775 at 777.

The Trial at the Lincolnshire Summer Assizes

The action was tried on Monday, 18 July 1836.[5] The judge had a reputation for irascibility, though the *Northampton Herald* for 16 July 1836, noting his arrival at Northampton with a large cavalcade of javelin men, generously called him 'the amiable and excellent judge'.[6] He was widely, but incorrectly, thought to be a by-blow of George III, whom he resembled.[7] Priestley was represented by Serjeant Edward Goulbourn[8] and Mr Nathaniel R. Clarke,[9] and Fowler by Serjeant John Adams[10] and Mr Andrew Amos.[11] This galaxy of legal talent cannot have come cheap. It is, however, possible that some sort of contingent fee arrangement was used, but there is no evidence of this.

In the pleadings the claim was presented as based either on wilful negligence in loading the van, or on the existence of a latent defect in it. The declaration alleged that 'the defendant did not take due care that the van was in proper repair, but on the contrary it was in a very insufficient state and much overloaded'.[12] Serjeant Goulbourn concentrated upon the evidence of overloading, rather than on the latent defect, no doubt as a stronger point; as we have seen, it had been drawn to Fowler's attention by his coachman, William Beeton.

The van was second-hand, made by Whitbourne, then the largest manufacturer in London, in 1833. Fowler had bought it in April 1835. According to Whitbourne's superintendent, George Ball, it weighed eighteen hundredweight, and was designed to be drawn by three horses. It was capable, he thought, of carrying four and a half to five tons; indeed, he had seen much heavier loads safely carried. Evidence from employees called by Fowler suggested that the load was about three tons. But Priestley's witnesses disagreed; they thought it was more like four tons, and they thought the vehicle was fit to carry only about two and a half tons. There was also evidence of previous overloading. Fowler had been fined for this on a number of occasions, and had sometimes fraudulently added to the load after the vehicle had been weighed. The reference will

---

[5] Reported at 3 M & W 1, 150 ER 1030; Murphy and Hurlstone 305 (not in ER); 7 LJ Ex. 42, 1 Jur. 987. I have searched for the pleadings in E 13/1310 to 1316 inc. but found nothing. The trial is reported in *Doncaster, Nottingham and Lincoln Gazette*; *Lincoln, Boston and Newark Tuesday's Gazette*; *Gainsborough, Isle of Axholme Louth and Lindsay Advertiser* for 19 July 1836; *Lincoln, Rutland and Stamford Mercury* for 22 July; *Lincolnshire Chronicle and General Advertiser* for 22 July; *Boston, Louth and Spalding Herald* for 19 July. Exchanges during the trial which I quote are based on the newspaper reports, which do not differ significantly. The best modern discussion is by R. W. Costal in *Law and English Railway Capitalism 1825–1875* (Oxford, 1994), 259–72.

[6] 1763–1838. See the *DNB* for irascibility.

[7] M. Gilbert, *The Oxford Book of Legal Anecdotes* (Oxford, 1986), 234.

[8] 1787–1868. Originally a Cornet and Lieutenant in Royal Horse Guards. Resigned after satirical poem, 'The Blueviad'. Author of 3-vol. life of Edward de Montford. Later MP for Ipswich.

[9] 1785–1859. Later a county court judge.

[10] 1786–1856. Wrote on ejectment and mesne profits.

[11] 1791–1860. Prof. of Law, University of London, 4th member of the Council in India 1837–43, Downing Prof. 1848–60. See R. Cocks, *Foundations of the Modern Bar* (London, 1983), ch. 2.

[12] Report in *LCGA*.

be to evasion of tolls on turnpike roads. The van had indeed been weighed *en route* to Peterborough, but since, suspiciously, only two of its four wheels were on the machine, the figure was quite inaccurate. There was also evidence that the defect in the axletree had existed for some time before the accident. No witnesses revealed who actually did load the van. Perhaps suppliers of mutton who were not employees were involved, but this is speculation.

Serjeant Goulbourn also argued that Thomas Fowler had behaved unethically in not voluntarily taking care of his servant:

> he could not but feel much regret that a very opulent tradesman, a man in a very large way of business like the defendant, should have driven this poor lad into court, for he would say that not only in justice, but also in common humanity, he ought to pay the pecuniary damages his client had sustained, and also some remuneration for the suffering he had undergone, and the deprivation under which he was now labouring and would labour for the rest of his days.[13]

As we shall see, this was no mere debating point.

Serjeant Adams, resisting the claim, pointed out that Charles Priestley, having heard the complaint of the coachman, had not hesitated to go on the coach. He also denied any overloading. He also raised a matter of law: a master was simply not liable to his servant in such circumstances. The consequences would be horrific: 'if the defendant was responsible in this case, every master was liable to any accident that might occur to his servant about his work.'[14] There was 'no such case in the books'.[15] He thus relied on two typical legal arguments—the opening of the floodgates, and the absence of any precedent.

Sir James Park could have accepted this and have either stopped the case—called nonsuiting the plaintiff—on this ground, or directed the jury to find for the defendant.[16] He declined to do so. He told Serjeant Adams, 'you may move if you like', meaning, I think, make a formal motion before the full court in London if the verdict went to Priestley. In response Adams invited the judge to give him leave to do so. This is a reference to a procedure, probably invented by Lord Mansfield in the 1760s, designed to isolate a point of law with the consent of both parties for consideration by the full court: 'if the judge felt that the point of law should be decided in the defendant's favour, he would simply nonsuit the plaintiff and give him [i.e. the plaintiff] leave to move the [full] court to enter a verdict in his favour.'[17] But the judge refused either to give leave, or, at first, to indicate his opinion at all.

This exchange took place:

---

[13] *LCGA.*   [14] *LBNTG.*   [15] *LCGA.*

[16] For procedures see M. J. Prichard, 'Nonsuit: A Premature Obituary' [1960] *CLJ* 88. A nonsuit required the consent of the plaintiff. A directed verdict did not.

[17] Prichard at 95 citing as examples *Clay* v. *Willan* (1789) 1 H Bl. 298, *Graff* v. *Greffuhle* (1807) 1 Camp. NP 89.

SERJT. ADAMS. Well if your lordship will neither give us liberty to move, nor the benefit of your opinion . . .

THE JUDGE. I don't think you are right that there is no such case on the books, but I will not give an opinion at present: you may move.

SERJT. ADAMS [to the jury]. I certainly must submit, Gentlemen, as I always do, to the presiding Judge, but I very much regret that an opportunity has not been afforded me of stating why I think the plaintiff is not entitled to recover. I regret it for this reason, that it makes a great difference to the case whether . . .

THE JUDGE. It is not right. I certainly for the few months I have to live[18] do not intend to make a practice of nonsuiting, because the parties are put to tenfold expense. I cannot say that I have such a doubt about it as you seem to have. I think the defendant is liable.

SERJEANT ADAMS. Well now his lordship having stated his opinion I am satisfied . . . The case now stands thus. Here is a master who has a servant, whom he directs to go by a van of his own to a certain place on business; another servant, supposing the van to be overloaded, remonstrates with the master; nevertheless the master sends off the van, and the servants, knowing it to be overloaded, go with it. A crack is heard at Peterborough, which gives them notice that something is wrong, but they still go on until an accident happens. Now if in point of law, under such circumstances, a master is liable for such accidents, it is a very serious thing for every one who keeps a servant of any description; there is not one of you, gentlemen, who may not have a larger load of hay than usual on account of an expected shower of rain, but who will be put to enormous expense on account of every injury.[19]

Adams went on to argue that a master was required to use only 'such ordinary care and diligence as he would use over himself'; if this was the standard to be applied, then it had been satisfied, since Fowler's own property had been involved, and he had plainly taken such care as he thought appropriate to protect his own interests.[20] The judge said that 'he was not prepared to say, that in case, for instance, of an accident by the unavoidable and unforeseen overturning of a carriage, the proprietor was liable for injuries occasioned thereby'. The judge pointed out that the failure of Priestley to remonstrate was a fact the jury could consider.

Serjeant Goulbourn in his speech to the jury played on their sympathies:

His learned friend said the wealthy butcher wished to try the question at law; he (Serjeant Goulbourn) wished he would try it with more wealthy people, for the plaintiff was one of a large family and not at all able to compete in resources with the butcher. He rested his case on the claim that the van was overloaded to the knowledge of the defendant.

This left a simple enough issue to the jury.

The judge, summing up, said that a master would not be liable to his servant for a concealed defect in the vehicle; had this been the only basis of the claim,

---

[18] Park died in Dec. 1838; presumably he thought he already had some terminal illness.

[19] *LCGA*.

[20] The idea of the standard of care which a person shows in his own affairs is taken from Roman law, where it is called *diligentia quam suis rebus*.

he would apparently have given the ruling Serjeant Adams wanted.[21] He went on to explain:

the only question here was,—and it was one of fact—was the van shamelessly overladen; was it laden unsafely and to a dangerous degree; and, if so, was the master acquainted with the fact? . . . if the jury were of opinion that the accident was occasioned by the 'pig-headedness' of the defendant in overloading the van they would find for the plaintiff.[22]

As the case was presented at the trial, nothing whatsoever was made of any possible vicarious liability of Fowler for the acts of whoever it was had loaded the van; as we have seen, no evidence was even called as to who they were.

After retiring for a time variously described as a few minutes, twenty minutes, and half an hour, the jury found for the plaintiff, and awarded the very considerable sum of £100 damages.

The Hearing before the full Court of Exchequer

Any celebrations which took place in the Priestley family were premature. There would have been a stay of execution of the judgment, since the defendant intended to raise the legal issue of employer's liability before the full court; in effect there was an appeal. Serjeant Adams, in Michaelmas Term of 1836, obtained a rule to arrest the judgment on the ground that there was 'nothing in the declaration to throw any liability on the master'.[23]

The proceedings were now complicated by the fact that Fowler's business was in serious trouble; the damages would never be paid in full, if at all. Within six months he was bankrupt; a fiat in bankruptcy was issued on 2 January 1837.[24] The bankruptcy proceedings were reported in local papers.[25] Thomas Fowler, 'butcher, dealer and chapman', was to surrender himself to the Commissioner at Standwell's Hotel in Stamford on 30 January, and again on 28 February. The first meeting was to arrange assignees, and the second to investigate the bankrupt's assets; the assignees were Thomas Newton of Holbeach and Samuel Smeeton of Holland, both farmers.[26] On 17 March the *Lincoln Chronicle and General Advertiser* announced the sale of the assets on 27 March 1837: his premises in Church Street, a 'convenient dwelling house', next door to his butcher's shop and slaughterhouse, stables, granaries, warehouses, and other farm buildings, with a drying kiln. There was also an orchard and a paddock, the whole covering three acres; the key was available for those interested at the Black Horse Inn.

---

[21] The report in *LRSM* is garbled on this point; the point is that Park J did not nonsuit the plaintiff because of the alternative basis for liability set out in the declaration.

[22] *LRSM*.   [23] Murphy and Hurlstone 305.

[24] Ibid. 305. See also the *Jurist* (1837) at 25; *The Times* for 18 Jan. 1837.

[25] e.g. *LCGA*, 24 Jan. 1837.   [26] B 5/101 at fo. 19; the complete papers do not survive.

The creditors would be unwilling to have the assets reduced by Priestley's victory. The appeal was argued on Monday, 16 January 1837, on a motion to set aside the verdict; a motion for a new trial was abandoned on account of the bankruptcy.

Serjeant Adams argued that, since the action was framed in case, and not in assumpsit—we would say as a tort action rather than as a contract action—any liability in the master must exist at common law. For there to be liability at common law

five circumstances must concur. First, that the van was overloaded, by defendant's order. Second, that plaintiff was ignorant of its being overloaded. Third, there must be an order by the defendant, to plaintiff, to go on the van. Fourth, that it was necessary for the plaintiff to do so, in order to perform his duty in respect of the goods. And, fifth, that the order shall be a lawful command which the servant is bound to obey.

The declaration was insufficient because it did not claim that Priestley was ignorant of the overloading (his second requirement), and it failed to allege an order to travel *in* the van, or the necessity of doing so. Charles Priestley could, no doubt, have chosen to walk *alongside* the van. Heavy weather was made of this point, which today seems rather ridiculous. In the event the judges were not impressed by it, and rejected it in the course of the argument. They were, however, impressed by the failure to allege that Priestley was ignorant of the supposed overloading.

Serjeant Goulbourn, arguing for Priestley, contended that a servant should, in such a case, be treated the same as a coach passenger, that is to say, as if there was a contractual relationship: 'If, therefore, a master orders a servant to go on a van which he knows to be overloaded, if the van breaks down, is he not entitled to protection equally with a passenger, each giving a consideration, although of a different kind?' Goulbourn conceded that knowledge by the master, and ignorance by the servant, were necessary to liability. But the defective declaration could be cured 'by intendment' after verdict: 'it will be intended that the master was aware of the danger, and that he denied to the servant that there was any danger, and, in fact, that the servant did not know of the danger.' What was meant was that since the jury had found for the plaintiff it must be assumed that the jury thought that Fowler knew, and Priestley did not. Indeed the form of the direction given by Sir James Park strongly suggested that this must have been so if the jury followed his instructions. Since Sir James was not a member of the Court of Exchequer, there may have been some obscurity about what he had told the jury. The notes of the trial judge were apparently sometimes made available in such circumstances; whether they were on this occasion is obscure.

On the conclusion of the argument the court reserved judgment; the *Lincoln, Rutland and Stamford Mercury* for 20 January explained why: 'The Court would take time to look into the case, as it was a nice one, and involved some important consequences.' Judgment was not delivered until 23 November. The delay of ten months suggests some difficulty in achieving unanimity. Lord Abinger gave the opinion; he was not by disposition sympathetic to the lot of the working classes. As James Scarlett, he had in 1821 and 1822 introduced bills to abolish the poor law entirely.[27]

Abinger's opinion rejected Goulbourn's argument that knowledge in the master, and ignorance in the servant, could be 'intended' after verdict.[28] The question for decision was, therefore, whether, from the mere relationship of master and servant, a duty arose at common law in the master 'to cause the servant to be safely and securely carried'. Abinger then pointed out that, if such a duty existed, it would logically follow, given the normal rules as to the vicarious responsibility of a master, that a master would also be liable for misconduct of fellow servants. This was something which Abinger and his colleagues thought to be quite absurd—it would carry liability 'to an alarming extent'. It would, for example, make the master liable to his servant if his chambermaid put his servant into a damp bed. Hence, the argument went, the court could not recognize a liability in Fowler which would, logically, lead to an absurdity in other cases. This passage came to be treated as the source of what came to be called the 'doctrine of common employment' or 'fellow servant rule': an employer could not be sued by one of his employees for the negligence of another employee in common employment with him, or a fellow servant.

Relying on the argument from absurdity, Abinger thought that whatever duty arose between master and servant at common law, simply from the relationship, it must be more restricted. His solution was the restriction that it could never 'imply an obligation, on the part of the master, to take more care of the servant than he may reasonably be expected to do of himself'. It followed that:

In that sort of employment, especially, which is described in the declaration in this case, the plaintiff must have known, as well as his master, and probably better, whether the van was sufficient, whether it was overloaded, and whether it was likely to carry him safely.

During argument he had given examples which make his idea clear:

Suppose a man put his servant into a bedroom which is infected, and the servant does not know it, and he became diseased, he may have an action against the master; but if

---

[27] See A. Brundage, *The Making of the New Poor Law: The Politics of Inquiry, Enactment and Implementation 1832–9* (London, 1978), 11.

[28] T. Ingham's account in 'The Rise and Fall of the Doctrine of Common Employment' (1978) *Juridical Review* 106 at 108 seems to me to be incorrect. Relying on the report in 3 Murphy and Hurlstone, which is incorrect, he states that the victim complained of overloading; in fact it was the coachman who complained. He claims that Lord Abinger ignored the evidence given at trial that Fowler was aware of the state of the coach; in fact Abinger was not evaluating evidence, but determining as a matter of law whether knowledge could be 'intended' after verdict, there being no averment of knowledge in the pleadings. To be sure it might have been decided differently. Ingham is also incorrect in saying that Abinger treated the case as one of vicarious liability.

the room was exposed to the weather, so that the servant himself could ascertain the state of the room, he could not sue his master for any injury he might suffer from sleeping in the room.[29]

So he concluded that there could be no liability in this particular case.

But Lord Abinger did concede in his formal opinion that a restricted common law duty did arise from the mere relationship of master and servant: 'He is, no doubt, bound to provide for the safety of his servant, in the course of his employment, to the best of *his* judgement, information and belief' (my italics). It will be noted that this implies a subjective standard of care only; that is to say the standard is not fixed by reference to some ideally rational person, the reasonable man of the common law. Oddly enough, the first statement of the objective standard in negligence actions—the duty to behave like a reasonable person—dates from the very same year, 1837, in the case of *Vaughan* v. *Menlove*, decided by the Court of Common Pleas.[30] This was a case in which a farmer, having taken so much care as he thought sensible to protect his own hayrick and property from fire, was nevertheless held liable to a neighbour for a fire which broke out and spread. A reasonable farmer would have taken greater precautions.[31]

Lord Abinger added two further arguments. One was that a servant was entitled to refuse to obey a command which he reasonably anticipates would risk his safety. According to one report the case of *Levison* v. *Kirk* (1610) was cited in support of this; the case does not in fact deal with the point.[32] The argument is somewhat unrealistic, and in some contexts ridiculous; if, for example, every merchant seaman had refused such orders, few voyages could ever have been made. Furthermore, the risk of dismissal would act as a strong deterrent. His other argument was that, if people like Priestley could sue, it would encourage them to neglect to exercise the diligence and caution which they owed to their master, which diligence and caution were also their own best protection. The basic point being made, whether convincing or not, is that both Priestley and Fowler had a common interest in avoiding the accident—which no doubt imposed costs on Fowler as well as on Priestley. The best way to protect their common interest was to do nothing to reduce the servants' incentive to exercise care.

Although Priestley lost his £100 damages, the decision of the Court of Exchequer conceded, for the first time, that there might be circumstances which entitled a servant to sue his master for loss caused through an accident at work; there had, of course, always been liability for deliberately inflicted injuries, subject to possible defences where chastisement was involved. Many later commentators have been hostile to Abinger's opinion, principally because it came

---

[29] 7 LJ Exch. 42.

[30] 3 Bing. NC 468, 132 ER 490, 7 Car. & P 525, 173 ER 232, 1 Jur. 215, 4 Scott 244, 3 Hodges 51.

[31] Ibid. The situations were not quite the same; master and servant are in a relationship which they choose, whereas there is less control over the identity of a neighbour.

[32] 1 Lane 65, 145 ER 303, cited in the LJ Exch. report.

to be treated as the source for the doctrine of common employment, or fellow servant rule.[33] Since most accidents at work are caused by fellow employees, this doctrine virtually excluded employer's liability for such accidents. The decision was not based upon this doctrine, though clearly Lord Abinger thought that an employer ought not to be held liable to one of his servants for the negligence of another. T. Ingman has suggested that the decision was really based upon 'volenti non fit iniuria or rather, scienti non fit iniuria'; the doctrine summed up in the Latin tags excluded recovery for accidents arising out of dangers at work on the theory that an employee had, by implication, agreed when he undertook the job to bear such risks himself.[34] Modern writers in the economic tradition suppose that the pay for dangerous jobs is adjusted by the market to reflect such risks; for methodological reasons it is not at all easy to demonstrate either that this is or is not the case, at least as a general rule. In fact, contractual theory was not Lord Abinger's rationale for denying recovery. His view was based on individualistic notions of fault and responsibility. In a case such as Priestley v. Fowler the employee was as well or even better, placed to avoid the accident as his employee, and this was why recovery should be denied. It was part of the professional skill of employees to protect themselves from the dangers associated with their type of work: the skill of a coachman included skill in avoiding being kicked by horses; the skill of a cook that of avoiding being burnt or scalded; the skill of a sailor that of not falling from the yards. This way of looking at the matter jars with some modern collectivist ideas, but is not in any way unintelligible. It fails, of course, to give weight to another idea—that the skill of an employer included the ability so to organize and manage his enterprise as to produce safe conditions of work for his employees.

The case was specially noted at the time.[35] E. Spike, in his The Law of Master and Servant (1839), a book 'chiefly designed for the use of families', quotes extensively from it and says:

By the relation of master and servant, no contract is implied, and therefore no duty is created, on the part of the master, to make good to the servant any damage arising to him, from any vice or imperfection (unknown to the master) existing in any article or thing used in his service, or from the mode of using the same; nor for the negligence of his other servants.[36]

Thus Spike deduced from the decision the fellow servant doctrine, which appeared in case law in the United States in Murray v. S. Carolina Railroad Co. in 1841

---

[33] Attacks and defences, none of any particular interest to a historian, will be found in F. H. Bohlen, Studies in the Law of Torts (Indianapolis, 1926), 459; R. Pound, Interpretations of Legal History (Cambridge, Mass., 1946), 109–11; R. Pound, 'The Economic Interpretation and the Law of Torts', 53 HLR 365; F. M. Burdick, 'Is Law the Expression of Class Selfishness', 25 HLR 349; J. Gold, 'Common Employment', 1 MLR 225.

[34] 'The Rise and Fall of the Doctrine of Common Employment' [1978] Juridical Review 106.

[35] Ibid. 110–1 to the contrary.   [36] (London, 1839), 43 ff., my italics.

and *Farwell* v. *Boston Railroad Co.* (1842),[37] and in England in *Hutchinson* v. *York, Newcastle and Berwick Ry. Co.* (1850).[38]

Not long after the decision, on 8 December 1837, a notice appeared in the *Lincoln, Rutland and Stamford Mercury* in connection with Thomas Fowler's bankruptcy. A further meeting of creditors was to take place in Standwell's Hotel on 19 December to settle accounts, fix a final dividend, and decide whether to allow one Thomas Horwood his costs for prosecuting certain proceedings—it is not said what they were—against the bankrupt.[39] What became of the unfortunate butcher thereafter I have been unable to discover. However, four Fowler children, Charles (12), John (9), William (8), and Francis (7), are in the Bourne workhouse for the census of 1841, and two of them, Charles and Francis, described as crippled, are still there ten years later.[40] They could well have been his children.

Charles and Brown Priestley

Any investigation of the case must start from the people involved. Although the victim in the accident was Charles Priestley, it was his father, Brown Priestley, who sued. Who was he?

Brown Priestley was baptized in the Anglican faith on 5 April 1772 in Spridlington, a village north of Lincoln. He was the eldest son of Zachariah and Elizabeth Priestley. Her maiden name was Brown.[41] They were married in 1771 at nearby Hackthorn. Zachariah farmed in Spridlington. Spridlington lies immediately north of the larger village of Welton, with Rylands, by Lincoln, next Dunholme.[42] His son Zachariah, as tenant of Earl Brownlow, farmed the 460-acre Faldingworth Grange Farm, east of Spridlington, where Zachariah senior died at the age of 90 in 1827; the farm is still there.[43] He had three other sons, John, William, and George,[44] and one daughter, Elisima (also in the family repertoire of names with other spellings such as Lesimin, Lissiemine, Lissimon, Lisse, Lissey).[45]

Brown and his wife, Anne, were Particular Baptists, associated with the Mint Lane Chapel in Lincoln, built there between 1816 and 1818. Brown does not feature in early lists of the congregation at Mint Lane, but he did contribute £10

---

[37] (1841) 1 McM. 385, with no reference to the English case, (1842) 38 Am. Dec. 339, relying on the English case.

[38] 5 Ex. 343.

[39] A fixing of the first and final dividend was announced in the *London Gazette* for 28 Nov. 1837.

[40] HO 107/615, 2095.

[41] LRO, Spridlington, 1/2. Zachariah was baptized at Hackthorn on 25 February 1738.

[42] Lincolnshire also has Welton le Wold, and Welton in the Marsh.

[43] LRO, Welton by Lincoln, 1/1/6 (MF 03 29 006 01A), LQS/Land Tax/ Lawress/ 1823 and 1830. The son was baptized on 19 Jan. 1777, LRO 1/2 and died 25 Oct. 1865 at Lowfields Farm, Bracebridge. The census return for 1841 shows him with his second wife, Jane (Jubb), and two sons and daughters (HO 107/633) at Faldingworth; in 1851 he was still there with his two sons (HO 107/2106).

[44] LRO, Spridlington, 1/2. Born 1775, 1783, and 1787.   [45] Born 1780.

10s. to the building of the new Chapel.[46] The principal connection may have been through his wife.[47] Its register records the five sons and one daughter of Brown Priestley and his wife, Anne. The first, Brown, was born at Hackthorn. The others were born at Welton between 1813 and 1823. Charles, the victim of the accident, was baptized on 23 January 1816.[48]

In the newspaper reports, Brown Priestley is described as a poor farmer from Welton, with a large family. In Lincolnshire Poll Books for 1818 and 1823 he appears as a freeholder and farmer in Lawress wapentake, in which Welton by Lincoln is situated.[49] Vestry records of Spridlington in 1836–7 have him auditing the accounts of William Sutton, overseer of the poor.[50] Brown Priestley was a small, but not insubstantial, farmer.[51] Sometime before 1823 he had acquired two freehold properties in Welton, and in following years he continued to own one of these, with a rental value of £1 *per annum*; I have been unable to identify it. Lincoln Cathedral had fifty-two prebendaries, canons supported by prebendal estates, engagingly called by the *cognoscenti* the corpses of the prebends from the Latin *corpus*. Six were associated with Welton: Welton Beck-hall, Welton Brink-hall, Welton Pains-hall, Welton Ryve-hall, Welton Gore-hall, and Welton West-hall.[52] In January 1824 he acquired the three leasehold properties of the Prebendary of the Prebend of Welton Ryve-hall. A farmhouse with twelve fields, amounting in all to 114 acres, was 'on the Cliff', the rising ground to the west of Welton; this lay to the north of the road leading from Welton to Ermine Street.[53] There were also forty-five acres at Cow Pasture,

[46] LRO 1, Bapt. 1 (Church Book dating from 1767). 1 Bapt. 4 (Church Book from 1813) contains numerous lists, and 1 Bapt. 5/1 has lists from 1844.

[47] A William Brown, conceivably connected, was a member of the community, which originated at Horncastle, in 1784. There were two Priestleys: Ann, baptized in 1784, and Richard in 1785. Another Anne Priestley, described as of Spridlington, was baptized on 13 July 1817, and became the oldest member, recorded in 1870 as being then of 30 Newport, Lincoln. She was probably Brown Priestley's wife; no other Priestley occurs in the nineteenth-century records.

[48] RG 4/1449, LRO MF 2/75. HO 107/644 (1841, Spridlington), HO 107/2106 (1851, Spridlington), RG 9/2364 (Spridlington), LRO Minton Lane Baptist Records. Brown, 12 May 1813; John, 12 Oct. 1814; Lissey, 28 Sep. 1818; George, 30 Jan. 1820; Zachariah, 19 Jan. 1832. John died in 1824. I am greatly indebted to Mr C. P. C. Johnson, District Archivist, Lincoln and Grimsby Methodist District, for assistance and advice.

[49] In LRO. Some Land Tax Assessments also survive, but not for our Welton.

[50] LRO Spridlington 13, Disbursements of Overseers of the Poor 1808–37.

[51] Information based on LRO CC 133/1505 (Surrender of Lease of Prebend of Welton Ryvall, 12 May 1831; sale advertisement of 1838, LCGA 10 and 24 Aug. 1838; LRO LQS/Land Tax/Lawress for 1823 and 1830 (I have not examined other years); Lindsey Enclosure Award 95 (1773); Welton by Lincoln PAR 9/15 (Map of Prebendal Lands).

[52] Spellings differ; see the Welton Enclosure Act of 1772. W. White's *Directory of Lincolnshire and Hull* (Sheffield, 1826).

[53] To the west of present-day Prebend Lane (formerly Road). North of the road lay four precisely rectangular prebendal properties; is it conceivable that the boundaries are Roman? The properties are still defined by west–east field boundaries, Pains-Hall on the road, then to the north Ryve-hall, Beck-hall, and Brink-hall. A road, formerly called Prebend Lane, ran and still runs from the road northwards through the centre of these properties, leaving the present-day Welton to Ermine Street road by a small wood.

south of present-day Mill Lane,[54] and a farmhouse, yard cottages, and garden amounting to a little over an acre next to the churchyard on its south side—part was called Prebend Yard.[55] The farmhouse still exists as Rivehall House, as do the cottages. His freehold property, a house with associated farm buildings, I have not been able to identify. It could have been the farmhouse of a freehold farm, perhaps Sudbeck Farm, whose land had been sold off earlier.[56] Brown Priestley's prebendal lands, which he would purchase for a lump sum, were held for three lives at a ground rent of £6, the lives originally being those of George Minnitt of Owerby and his sons, Brown and Charles Priestley. Initially the property was mortgaged for £2,500, and by 1831 for £3,000. By then Minnitt had died. In that year Brown Priestley negotiated a surrender and regrant of the prebend from the prebendary, the Revd William Wickam Drake of Malpas in Cheshire, for three lives—those of his sons, Brown, Charles, and Zachariah. By this date the beneficial interest in the mortgage was apparently held on trust for five spinsters of Lincoln, Ann, Mary, Sarah, Esther, and Eleanor Turner, who presumably divided whatever payments Brown was from time to time able to make.

As for Charles, he was not described in contemporary newspaper reports as apprenticed to his employer, Thomas Fowler, but as being 'in his service as a butcher',[57] or as his servant.[58] In the *Lincoln, Rutland and Stamford Mercury* it was said that 'he had been placed with the defendant to learn the trade of butcher'. He would live in as a servant in Fowler's household at Market Deeping, many miles away from Welton. He was baptized on 23 January 1816 at Welton. So, at the time of the accident, he would be 19, and when Lord Abinger gave his opinion in 1837 he had already attained his majority.

Beyond this, nothing seems to be discoverable about either Brown Priestley or his son up to the time of the accident. Numerous Priestleys, who would be relatives, lived in the area; thus the baptismal register of Welton records the baptism of ten children of John and Elizabeth Priestley between 1819 and 1842, and land tax returns refer to a William Priestley, who once farmed lands there. John was Charles's uncle. Census returns for 1841 record that Charles's younger brother, George, was then an agricultural labourer,[59] and brother Zachariah was a baker.[60]

There is slight evidence that Brown was a contentious person, for the Welton St Mary's Vestry Book for 2 April and 30 October 1834 records decisions to take legal proceedings against him to compel him to repair the south fence of the churchyard, and the north fence of Prebend Yard.[61]

---

[54] Described as south of the Market Rasen Road, which then followed Mill Lane.

[55] LRO Welton by Lincoln PAR/15, Prebendal Lands Map 1912–19.

[56] In the 1881 census (RG 11/3246) Sudbeck farm is occupied by Henry Priestley, aged 30, with his wife, Margaret, and son, George. Mr L. W. Capes of Welton, to whom I am indebted, tells me he was still there *c*.1900.

[57] *LRSM.*   [58] *LCGA.*   [59] HO 107/648 (Welton).

[60] HO 107/2106 (1851, Welton), aged 28, a baker.   [61] 1833–78, LRO.

Such meagre information about Charles and his father, as individuals, does virtually nothing to explain the extraordinary suit against Fowler. There is no evidence, so far as I have been able to discover, to suggest that Brown Priestley or his son belonged to some radical organization, one of numerous possibilities which occurred to me, or that the suit was sponsored by a benefactor.[62] Nor did Brown Priestley sue as a pauper—he was, as we have seen, relatively prosperous. It seems, therefore, that we must seek an explanation not so much in the individual circumstances of Brown and Charles Priestley, but in the general state of the law relating to accidents at work, and its administration. For before suits against employers or statutory schemes of workmen's compensation came into vogue, there were other mechanisms for dealing with such accidents. In particular there was the law of master and servant, and the poor law.

Employment Law and the Protection of Disabled Servants

Blackstone divides servants into four categories—menial servants; apprentices; labourers; and stewards, factors, and bailiffs all classed together.[63] As J. B. Bird explains: 'Menial servants are so called, not as a term of degradation, but from them living *intra moenia*, i.e., within the house or walls of their master.'[64] Blackstone calls them domestics, not in the modern sense, but as members of the household or family of the master. In the pre-industrial world, the typical servant was the menial servant in husbandry, retained at the annual hirings for a term of one year.[65] Some other servants, retained for a term of a year or more, might not be menials, but this was a relatively unusual arrangement. What we now call domestic servants were also normally menials. Eventually they became the only servants of this type. Menials received board and lodging as their principal remuneration, and modest money payment, sometimes quarterly, sometimes at the end of the term. It is clear that Charles Priestley was a menial servant.[66]

The old law on such servants gave them an important, if short-term, protection against the consequences of an accident at work. It was explained in Dalton's *Countrey Justice*:

If a servant retained for a yeere, happen within the time of his service to fall sicke, or to be hurt or lamed, or otherwise to become *non potens in corpore*, by act of God, or in doing his Master's businesse, yet it seemeth the Master must not therefore put such servant away, nor abate any part of his wages for such time.[67]

---

[62] See below 128.

[63] *Commentaries*, i. 410 ff. O. Kahn-Freund's 'Blackstone's Neglected Child: The Contract of Employment' 93 *LQR* 508 at 518–9 wrongly supposes 'menial' servants to be servants who perform their service within doors.

[64] *The Law Respecting Masters and Servants: Articled Clerks, Apprentices, Journeymen and Manufacturers* (London, 1795), 1.

[65] See generally A. Kussmaul, *Servants in Husbandry in Early Modern England* (Cambridge, 1981).

[66] See above 112.   [67] Quoted from the 5th (London, edn. 1635). The first ed. was 1618.

This was still the law at the time of Charles Priestley's accident.[68] A. Kussmaul, in *Servants in Husbandry in Early Modern England*, uses the large number of Quarter Sessions orders requiring masters to take back sick and injured servants, and to maintain them to the end of the term, to attest both to the enforceable nature of the obligation, and to the frequency with which it was broken in practice.[69] Working people who were employed for short periods, labourers, and not servants, were hired for the task, the day, or the month. They did not, therefore, enjoy this measure of protection if they fell sick, or were injured. Dalton, going a little beyond his sources, wrote: 'And yet no Reteiner of any servant for lesse then for one whole yeare is good, or according to law. See Fitz 168h[70] Co. Litt. 42b.' There was, in fact, a presumption in favour of retainer for a year, and a retainer for a lesser period was voidable if the individual was later hired for what was viewed as the proper or correct period of a year. By the early nineteenth century, labourers were superseding servants in the agricultural world, though servants in husbandry survived into this century in some parts of the country; I have come across numerous such servants in Lincolnshire census returns, and even known some in the villages where I lived as a child. One reason for the decline of service was that service for a year in a parish gave the servant a settlement in that parish. This made the parish liable to provide support under the poor law, to which employers would normally contribute through the poor rate. In the newer industrial world, labourers, often young children, were the norm. This all meant that the protection afforded to the sick and injured amongst the working population was being reduced by changing employment practices.

There was a considerable case law on the master's duty to his menials. The matter arose indirectly, for example, in connection with the law of settlement under the poor law, which established which parish was liable to provide support. A pauper could be removed by a justices' order back to the parish where he had acquired a settlement, for example, by birth or service for a year there. Illness or incapacity from accident during the year of service did not prevent a settlement being established. In *R. v. Inhabitants of Christchurch*, Elizabeth Maxey was hired for a year on 24 August 1757. On 7 August 1758 she began to have fits, and her master engaged a substitute. The Court ruled that she had still acquired a settlement. Lord Mansfield explained:

If the Servant is taken *ill*, by the Visitation of God, it is a Condition incident to Humanity, and is *implied* in all Contracts. Therefore the Master is *bound* to provide for and take Care of the Servant so taken ill in his Service; and *can not deduct* Wages in Proportion to the Continuance of the Servant's Sickness.[71]

---

[68] R. Burn, *The Justice of the Peace and Parish Officer* (London, 1830), v, 115; E. Bott, *A Collection of Decisions of the Court of King's Bench Upon the Poor's Laws Down to the Present Time* (2nd ed., London, 1773), plea 561 (*R. v. Inhabitants of Islip* 1721), and cases at 308–9. See also J. B. Bird, n. 64 above, at 3.

[69] At 32.   [70] The ref. is to Fitzherbert's *New Natura Brevium* 168H. Coke is similar.

[71] Noted in J. Burrow, *A Series of the Decisions of the Court of King's Bench upon Settlement-Cases* (London, 1768–76), 494. See also E. Bott, n. 68 above, 308–11; *R. v. Inhabitants of Islip*

R. v. *Inhabitants of Sharrington* (1784)[72] illustrates the same principle in a case of accident. The servant, settled in Sharrington, was engaged for a year in Letheringsett to drive a team. Seven weeks into his employment, when drunk, he stood on the shafts, fell off, and broke his thigh. He spent twenty-nine weeks in a hospital in Norwich; his master refused to take him back. Some fourteen weeks later the justices ordered his master to do so, but he refused. The servant retired to the pub in Letheringsett, and after some months was removed to Sharrington. Lord Mansfield and Willes J quashed the order for his removal; he was settled in Letheringsett on the basis of a mere seven weeks' actual service out of a year.

Although the duty to care for a disabled servant until the end of his term was still recognized at the time of *Priestley* v. *Fowler*, and underlies a remark by counsel,[73] it was not clear that it required the master to meet medical bills. Nor was it clear that it was legally enforceable except by a justices' order that the master take the servant back into service. Lord Mansfield and his court considered the matter in *Newby* v. *Wiltshire* (1784).[74] A servant boy, whilst returning to his master's home from Cambridge, and outside his own parish, fell from the shafts of a cart and broke his leg. He could not be moved, and the local overseer provided medical care at a cost of £32. The leg had to be amputated, but the boy recovered and went back to work for his master. The overseer sued his master in assumpsit for money paid, laid out, and expended to the plaintiff's use. The Court held that the action did not lie. Lord Mansfield explained:

I don't applaud the humanity of the master in this case; he does not inquire after his servant for six weeks after the accident; and when he does 'he passes by on the other side'. I think, in general, a master ought to maintain his servants; but the question now is, What is the law? There is in point of law no action against the master to repay the parish for the cure of his servant.

In *Scarman* v. *Castell* (1795)[75] Lord Kenyon upheld at trial an action by an apothecary to recover payment for medicines and attendance on a menial servant. But his view was not followed in *Wennall* v. *Adney* (1802),[76] where a

(7 Geo. I), 1 Strange 433, 93 ER 611. For insanity see *R.* v. *Inhabitants of Sutton*, 5 TR 659; *R.* v. *Inhabitants of Hulcot*, 6 TR 587, cited in Burn, n. 68 above, v, 115. See also *R.* v. *Sudbrooke*, cited in Burn, n. 68 above, iv, 444, 1 Smith's Reports 59. Also *R.* v. *Wintersett* (1783) in T. Caldecott, *Reports of Cases of Settlement 1776–85* 298, 2 Bott 379, assuming master must support in sickness. For apprentices the rule was the same, 'for the master takes him for better and worse, and is to provide for him in sickness and in health'; *R.* v. *Inhabitants of Hales Owen*, *R.* v. *Inhabitants of Sharrington* (1784), 4 Geo I, 1 Strange 100, 93 ER 410. Articles would often specify the provision of medicine in illness.

[72] 4 Doug. 12, 99 ER 742, 2 Bott. 333. Also *R.* v. *Maddington*, Hilary 11, Geo. III (1770), Burr. SC 675—the servant was kicked by a horse 3 weeks before the end of the term whilst on his master's business.

[73] See above 103.

[74] 2 Esp. 739, 170 ER 515, mentioned by the reporter Burrow in *Scarman,* v. *Castell* (1795) 1 Esp. 270, 170 ER 353.

[75] 1 Esp. 270, 170 ER 353.   [76] 3 Bos. and Pul. 247, 127 ER 137.

servant broke his arm when driving his master's team. Wennall, a surgeon who treated him, sued his master, who had provided food but declined to pay the medical bill of £8 18s. 6d. The court ruled that there was no liability. Rooke J said: 'It must be left to the humanity of every master to decide whether he will assist his servant according to his capacity or not.' Although there remained a little uncertainty, the prevailing view was against liability, though if a master did pay he could not deduct the money from the servant's wages.[77]

The practical consequence of all this was that, at the time of the accident to Charles Priestley, a master had an obligation to keep a servant in his employment until his term ended, and an obligation to continue his board and lodging. He had a wider moral duty to care for his servant according to his ability, but there was no compellable obligation to provide medical care. Given Fowler's impending bankruptcy, and the sheer size of the bills for lodging and medical attendance, it is hardly surprising that he declined to pay. As a bankrupt he could not have continued to employ Priestley.

By the 1830s, the master's moral duty may have been weakened by the changes in employment practice I have mentioned. The servant who became a member of the master's family, with a claim to his care and protection, was being superseded by the distanced labourer. Menial servants were coming to be predominantly domestics, in the modern sense, and here the courts, not long before *Priestley* v. *Fowler*, had reduced their protection by decisions allowing them, even if hired for a year or more, to be dismissed with one month's notice, or even just one month's wages. Spike, writing in 1839, noted Blackstone's rule that a general hiring of such a domestic was deemed to be for a year, but adds:

Since this was written . . . another term seems to have been, by usage, introduced into the contract implied on the general hiring of a menial servant, and to be now fully established, viz., that either party shall be at liberty to determine the contract at any moment on giving a month's notice to the other.[78]

The source of the doctrine was *Robinson* v. *Hurdman* (1800),[79] where the servant had misbehaved. But cases such as *Nowlan* v. *Ablett* (1835), where a head gardener living in a house within the grounds of a residence was held to be a menial servant, did not limit the right of dismissal to cases of misconduct.[80] Domestics were coming to resemble mere employees at will.

So it was that, at this period, the protection from the consequences of accidents which, albeit imperfectly, had once existed was being eroded. Priestley's

---

[77] *Sellen and Wife*, v. *Norman* (1829) 4 C & P 80, 172 ER 616, with a note on the subject. See also E. Spike, n. 36 above, 36–42. He mentions the case of *Cooper* v. *Phillips* (1831) 4 C & P 58, 172 ER 834, Taunton J, where counsel assumed there was liability, in Spike's view wrongly.
[78] N. 36 above, 1.   [79] 3 Esp. 235, 2 Selw. NP 1032, 170 ER 599.
[80] *Nowlan* v. *Ablett*, 1 Gale 72, 2 Cr. M & R 54, 150 ER 23, 5 Tyr. 709; cf. *Archard* v. *Hornor*, 3 C & P 349, 172 ER 451. Further decided in Hindman and admitted in 2 Selw. NP 1032; *Fawcett* v. *Cash* (1834) 5 B & A 904, 110 ER 1026; *Beeston* v. *Collyer*, 4 Bing. 309, 130 ER 786 that on payment of one month's wages a servant can be dismissed, even though he thereby loses board.

suit for damages was, in a sense, a move to fill a gap in a protection which had formerly existed by a tort action for damages.

Accidents and the Old Poor Law

Both retained servants, once their term had expired, and labourers, had to rely upon their own resources—for example, savings if they had any, a Friendly Society if they belonged to one, and relatively few did,[81] or family support—until they could get back to work. If they were without such resources they had to seek parish relief under the poor law, unless, of course, they died, in which case their dependants would be in like case. The risk was always that a serious accident would convert an independent wage-earner (or his dependants) into a pauper. So it was that Dalton in *The Countrey Justice* described 'the three sorts or degrees of poore'.[82] First, there were the poor by impotency and defect, who included 'persons naturally disabled, or visited with grievous disease or sicknesse, through casualty, yet thereby for the time being impotent'. The second were the poor by casualty, comprising 'the person casually disabled, or maimed in his body, as the Souldier, or Labourer, maimed in their lawful callings', 'the householder, decayed by casualty of fire, water, robbery, suretyship etc.', and 'the poore man overcharged with children'. The third comprised the 'thriftlesse poore'. The first two categories were to be given relief according to their needs, the third were to be set to work, or sent to the house of correction. Relief was funded by the poor rate, basically chargeable on the occupation of property.[83] In the early nineteenth century and before, it was the poor law which was the principal legal provision for the victims of serious accidents at work, not the law of tort. Given the cost of litigation, and the poverty of the working population, tort law was largely irrelevant.

One form of help for victims of accidents was medical relief. This could be provided on an *ad hoc* basis, by paying a bonesetter or whoever to provide care. But in the south, east, and central parts of England a medical person was retained by yearly contract; such contracts might exclude special cases, such as childbirth, or accidents requiring a surgeon.[84] Thus, F. M. Eden in his *The State of the Poor* (1797) records that in Reading the surgeon is paid £18 18s. *per annum*.[85] Where disablement was long term some parishes provided economic support as 'outdoor'

[81] See P. H. J. H. Gosden, *The Friendly Societies in England 1815–1875* (Manchester, 1961).

[82] N. 67 above, 5th ed. (1635), 100. The poor are considered in ch. 40 from 93.

[83] The law was complex; see W. S. Holdsworth, *A History of English Law* (London, 1922–66), x 287–93.

[84] See D. Marshall, *The English Poor in the Eighteenth Century* (London, 1926), 115 ff.; evidence of G. C. Lewis, a Poor Law Commissioner, 3rd Report of Select Committee on Medical Relief at 10 (PP. 1844 (531), ix, 93).

[85] (London, 1797), ii. 14, 17. In *Extracts from the Information Received by Her Majesty's Commissioners as to the Administration and Operation of the Poor Law* (1833) it is noted that in Lenham, Kent, the annual payment to the surgeon is £70 (3) and see 39 (Stanford Rivers, Essex, £25 p.a.); numerous other examples are given.

relief—that is, relief to persons at their homes. There might be weekly payments to the 'lame', a term used at this period to mean seriously disabled. Thus in Humbershoe in Bedfordshire a 60-year-old labourer was paid 1*s*. 6*d*. a week by the parish.[86] In Cumwhitton in Cumberland T.L., aged 80, and his wife, aged 82, 'have had parochial aid about twenty years. They were formerly employed in agriculture . . . A hurt, which the husband got by a fall, incapacitated him from working, and threw him on the parish.'[87] 'Indoor' relief in the workhouse might also be given; Eden notes that in the Hampshire workhouse in 1796 there were eighty-six men 'from 20 to 90 years of age, consisting of cripples, blind, idiots, lunatics, etc.'. Some cripples would be accident victims. If an accident caused the death of a male married wage-earner, his widow, and any children unable to support themselves, might become paupers, and again the poor law was the provision made for them. Until the Fatal Accidents Act of 1846 there was no possibility of a tort action for a death, and after it was passed little use was made of it by the working population.

Short-term medical relief was not confined to persons who would regularly be viewed as parish paupers, or who were permanently pauperized by illness or accident. It was available to an uncertain degree to the working population in general. Thus, in *The Parish and the Union* (1837),[88] an abridged summary of the *Report of the Select Committee on the New Poor Law Amendment Act*, it is said that under the unreformed poor law—that is before the Poor Law Amendment Act of 1834—'persons in good circumstances, who would have scorned parochial relief in any other shape, did not hesitate to apply to the parish doctor equally with the pauper who received relief in "bread money"'. And when an accident caused death, the parish would cover the cost of burial if the victim's family was unable through poverty to do so, and provide assistance, either in or out of the workhouse, to widows and other dependents.

Thus, the poor law spread the cost of accidents amongst the occupiers of property in the parish, assessable for the poor rate. They would also be the employers. So where servants were injured, the master was supposed to tide the servant over the immediate aftermath of an accident; a wealthy and generous employer might pick up medical bills and the like. But long-term care rested with the parish, whose obligation was enforceable. Heath J defended this system in *Wennall* v. *Adney*:

I am perfectly sure it is more to the advantage of servants that the legal claim for such assistance [i.e. medical care] should be against the parish officers rather than against their masters; for the situation of many masters who are obliged to keep servants, is not such as to enable them to afford sufficient assistance in the case of serious illness.[89]

To be sure the degree of care provided would be subject to much variation.

---

[86] Eden, n. 85 above, ii. 7. Cf. 51 for another example from Caldbeck in Cumberland. In Meopham in Kent accident cases receive 7*s*. a week until they recover; see 290.
[87] Eden, n. 85 above, ii. 72.   [88] See 104 ff.   [89] 3 Bos. & Pul. 247, 127 ER 137.

The Position of the Casual Poor

When a person fell ill, or was disabled from work by an accident outside his own parish, he became one of the casual poor. Originally the term 'casual' was applied—for example, by Dalton—to those who become poor by casualty, by some sudden event. Later it took on the sense I have explained. A person like Charles Priestley, who suffered an accident away from home, thereby needing both board and lodging and medical care beyond the resources of his own pocket, became a casual pauper although he had previously not been in receipt of parish relief. The parish where, by necessity, he lay sick was legally bound to provide for him. Holroyd J at Worcester Assizes in 1820 ruled that an overseer of the poor was indictable for failure to provide medical relief to a pauper suffering a dangerous illness 'though the pauper be not in the workhouse, nor previously in need of parish relief'.[90] Writing in 1828, just before the reform of the poor law, Lewin stated the general principle and added:

if the parish officer stands by, and sees the obligation performed by those who are fit and competent to perform it, and does not object, the law will raise a promise, on his part, to pay for the performance . . . So, if a pauper meets with an accident, which incapacitated him from going to his own place of abode, the parish officers where the accident happens, are liable for the expenses of his cure; for in such a case, the officers are under a moral and a legal obligation to provide assistance for him. And if they improperly remove him to another parish (although it be his own) it does not relieve them of the obligation.[91]

Removal of the Casual Poor

From time to time parishes naturally tried to pass the bill back to the parish of settlement. But the prevailing view was that this could not be done, unless there was an express subsequent promise by the parish officers of the parish of settlement to pay the bill.[92] In the unreported case of *Sneath* v. *Tomkins* (1822) it was even doubted by two judges whether there was liability on an express

[90] Cited G. Lewin, *A Summary of the Laws Relating to the Government and Maintenance of the Poor* (London, 1828), 305.

[91] Lewin, n. 90 above, 200–1. Bott, n. 68 above, app. to edn. of 1773, says 'it has been very lately determined, upon a hearing in the Court of Exchequer, that if a poor person meets with an accident which requires the assistance of a surgeon, the parish officers are obliged to pay the surgeon, although they did not direct him to attend the poor person'. See *Lamb* v. *Bunce* (1805) 4 M & S 275, 105 ER 836. Plaintiff was a surgeon, defendant overseer of poor of Enborne. One Smith, an undercarter to a farmer of West Woodhay was run over and fractured his leg, in Hampstead Marshall. He was moved to a public house in Enborne, half a mile from site of the accident. The plaintiff, who usually attended the poor, treated him; it was obscure who summoned him.

[92] See M. Nolan, *A Treatise on the Laws of Relief and Settlement of the Poor* (London, 1805), citing *Watson* v. *Turner*, Buller *Nisi Prius* (1790 ed.), 129, 147. See also *Atkin and Others* v. *Bonwell and Another* (1802) 2 East 505, 102 ER 462; *Wing* v. *Mill* (1817) 1 B & A 104, 106 ER 1078.

subsequent promise, on the ground that there was no consideration for it.[93] Nor was it lawful for a parish to get rid of liability for a casual pauper who was unfit to be moved by obtaining a removal order and immediately sending him back to his parish of settlement, much less by simply moving him when helpless to resist.

However M. Nolan, writing in 1805, suggested that if a removal order was obtained but suspended, as was done in *R. v. Kynaston* (1800), the bill for treatment could be returned with the pauper once he recovered.[94] This case did not actually address the legality of such removal orders, and in *R. v. St James in Bury St Edmund* (1808)[95] the King's Bench ruled that the only paupers who could be removed were those who came with an intention to settle (*animo morandi* or *manendi*). Accident victims obviously lacked this intent.[96] This was followed in 1821 in *R. v. St Lawrence, Ludlow.*[97] Legislation in 1846 eventually expressly forbade the removal of casual paupers.[98]

The policy behind this was humanitarian; it cannot be explained in any other way. *Tomlinson v. Bental and Another* (1826)[99] tells the sort of horror story which explains it. J. Banister, a poor woman of Malden, was travelling from Witham to Malden in a cart. She was thrown out and her thigh broken in Heybridge. The parish constable, anxious to avoid any cost to the parish, wanted her removed, and she was carted over the bridge which marked the parish boundary with Malden. The carter protested, and so the constable had her brought back to Heybridge. He consulted a magistrate, who said she should be placed in the nearby inn, The Hay, and a doctor summoned. The landlord of The Hay refused to take her in. The carter suggested the poor house; the constable said he did not know where to put her. The woman, having now lain in the cold for some hours, said: 'If you do not know where to put me, for God's sake take me home.' She said she did not want to be treated by the plaintiff, the surgeon and apothecary of Malden (that is on contract), but by one Thorpe, the apothecary of Heybridge. The constable then ordered her taken to Malden, but the carter refused to take her unless given a note that Heybridge would pay the medical bill. The constable said he would obtain one but failed to do so. He accompanied her to Malden, where she arrived at 2 a.m.; apothecary Thorpe then refused to treat her as she was not in his parish, so in the end the plaintiff did. On these

---

[93] See note to *Watling v. Walters* (1822), n. 91 above.

[94] 1 East 117, 102 ER 47. Glover, when in Lexdon on 1 May 1799, driving a wagon, broke both legs; he and family were taken to the workhouse there. On 6 May two justices made an order to remove him and family to Coggeshall in Essex, his parish of settlement, but the order was suspended as it was dangerous to move him. The justices ordered Coggeshall to pay £20-16s-3d; they did not pay and a warrant for distress issued, which had to be endorsed by a Coggeshall magistrate; held they had a duty to endorse, and no power to go into the merits.

[95] 10 East, 103 ER 26.

[96] The power of removal was statutory, and no basis for removal was to be found in 13 and 14 Car. II, c.12, or 35 Geo. III, c.101.

[97] 2 B & Ald. 660, 106 ER 1078.   [98] 9 & 10 Vict. c.66, s. 4.

[99] 5 B & C 738, 108 ER 274.

facts Abbott CJ and Bayley J held that Heybridge was liable to pay him for her medical care; she should have been placed in the poorhouse or some other house if The Hay would not accept her.[100] Bayley J said:

it is highly prejudicial to the *rights of the poor* that, when an accident has happened, the question should be agitated, or even pass the minds of those persons in whose power the sufferer is of necessity placed, whether a burden, which must fall somewhere, must be borne by them, or can, by contrivance, be shifted to others. For, otherwise, the consequence will be, that poor persons, who ought not to be removed from the place where they have met with an accident, will, perhaps at the risk of their life, but certainly at great aggravation of the suffering, be removed to a distance. (my italics)

It will be seen from this that the judiciary of the period were not unmindful of the needs of accident victims.

Yet before the poor law reform of 1834, in spite of its dubious legality, a practice seems to have developed of making suspended removal orders for the casual poor, and, after recovery, returning pauper and bill to the parish of settlement. Possibly the rationale was that if the individual remained in the relieving parish after recovery he was no longer there of necessity, and did show an intention to settle, though I have no evidence for this.

The report of the Poor Law Commissioners for 1834 explains:

The out-door relief of the sick is usually effected by a contract with a surgeon, which, however, in general includes only those who are parishioners. When non-parishioners become chargeable from illness, an order for their removal is obtained, which is suspended until they can perform the journey; in the mean time they are attended by the local surgeon, but at the expense of the parish to which they belong.[101]

The report however goes on to draw attention to a problem which is well illustrated by *Priestley* v. *Fowler*: 'this has been complained of as a source of great speculation, the surgeon charging a far larger sum than he would have received for attending an independent labourer or pauper, in the parish of settlement.' For, as we have seen, the bills for both medical treatment and lodging in the case came to the very large sum of £50.

This problem continued to exercise the Poor Law Commissioners. A circular issued in January 1836[102] criticizes the typical medical contract for being confined to settled paupers:

[100] The court cited *Gent* v. *Tomkins* (1822), reported in notes, before Richard CB at Bucks. Spring Assizes. One Tyrrel, of Newton Longville, had an accident in Winslow; he was taken to a public house. The plaintiff, a surgeon and apothecary, first of all attempted to obtain payment for his bill for £19 10s. from the parish officers of Winslow and, having failed, sued Tomkins as overseer of the poor of Newton Longville. Tomkins had indeed visited Tyrrel, and approved of his treatment, including the provision of wine. The court ruled that Winslow, not Newton Longville, was liable.

[101] *Poor Law Report 1834* (ed. S. G. and E. O. A. Checkland, 1974), 43. In the 1st report of the Poor Law Commissioners at 568 it is aid that in Middlesex, Surrey, and West Sussex the costs of treating the casual poor were usually refunded by the parish of settlement; in these counties the medical contracts covered the casual poor.

[102] Copy in MH 32/28.

on the expressed or implied condition that [the medical officer] should be allowed to make whatever charges he pleased for his attendance and treatment of non-parishioners, under suspended orders or removal, on an order for medical relief by the overseers. When the patient has recovered, he is sent home to a parish with a bill for medical attendance, including charges for medicines, at the highest rates. Against these charges the distant parish to which the pauper belonged had no adequate protection . . . The pauper was exposed to the danger of being supplied with medicines considerably beyond that which was required for his proper treatment.

The grotesque notion of the danger of excessive medical care well illustrates the level of hypocritical self-deception which was typical of Edwin Chadwick and the commissioners at this period. The solution was for the contract to cover treatment of casual paupers as well. An order of the commissioners of 12 March 1842 attempted to lay down a scale of special additional remuneration which included 'cases of urgency, principally those arising from accidents, which cannot be sent to a public hospital with safety and propriety'. Where movement to hospital was not possible, a scale of special fees was provided: £5 for amputations of limbs, operations to reduce strangulated hernias, and compound fractures; £3 for simple fractures; and £1 for dislocation. All apparatus and splints were included; trusses could be charged at cost price. None of these fees was payable unless the victim survived for thirty-six hours, and, except in emergency, an opinion of a Fellow of the Royal College of Surgeons or Physicians must be obtained before an operation. These fees, it will be noted, are dramatically below those charged for the care Charles Priestley was provided.[103]

The Decision in The King v. Oldland (1836)

The practice of returning accident victims with the bill to their parish of settlement, though apparently common, was by implication treated as wholly illegal in *The King* v. *Oldland*, decided on 4 May 1836.[104] Samuel Vox had a settlement in the hamlet of Oldland in the parish of Bilton in Gloucestershire. He resided in Monythusloyne in Monmouthshire, and worked in a colliery there, where he broke his thigh at work on 29 May 1832. He had not before this been chargeable to the parish. The parish officers sent for a surgeon; the bill for his cure and maintenance was £10 2s. 6d. The justices made a suspended removal order; on 31 October, when he had recovered, they removed the suspension. The case was important enough to be elaborately argued by the Attorney-General, Sir John Campbell. He contended that such orders for casual paupers were always illegal. The costs had to be met by the parish where the expense was incurred. The Court of King's Bench upheld the justices. But they did so only because Samuel

---

[103] See 8th *Report of Poor Law Commissioners*, 1842, [389] XIX 1, at 75 and 80.
[104] 4 Ad. & E 929, 111 ER 1033, 5 LJKB 151.

Vox resided in Monythusloyne; he had come there to settle, with *animus manendi.* Had he simply been the victim of an accident when passing through the parish, as was the case with Charles Priestley, the order would have been illegal.

Given this background it is fairly clear what would have happened in the case of Charles Priestley before the Poor Law Amendment Act of 1834. As a casual pauper he would have received immediate care, in much the same way as he did in 1836, and those providing it would have expected to be paid their inflated bills either by his employer, Thomas Fowler, who was conceived to have a moral duty in the matter, or by the local parish officers, who were legally responsible. There was no way in which Thomas Fowler could have been compelled to pay, much less the victim's father, Brown Priestley, unless they had arranged treatment and promised to pay for it. Neither would have been on the scene. So large a sum as £50 could not possibly have been extracted from young Charles Priestley. In due course the parish officers, if they could not persuade Fowler to pay, would have attempted to pass the bills back to the parish in which Charles Priestley had a settlement, Market Deeping, where Fowler would have been contributing to the poor rate. No doubt the parish officers there would do their best to have the bill reduced, and have delayed payment as long as possible. They would not have had so large a sum readily available.

One cannot but suspect that the action for damages might, somehow or other, be connected with the changes in the working of the poor law which were a consequence of the Poor Law Amendment Act of 1834.

The New Poor Law

The Poor Law Amendment Act of 1834 was designed to curb expenditure upon the poor, and to combat the supposed tendency for the system to create the very problem of pauperism it was supposed to alleviate. Its supporters portrayed it as a boon to the working population, discouraging them from degrading themselves by becoming paupers. A central authority, the Poor Law Commission, was empowered, or so it was hoped, to impose a uniform administrative policy. Economical administration was to be made possible by everywhere establishing large unions of parishes, through which the provision of relief could be properly managed. The most important management technique was that of providing relief only in the workhouse, in which conditions would be more disagreeable than those of the poorest independent labourer. The Poor Law Commissioners, dominated at first by Edwin Chadwick, met strong opposition in some areas. In others, Peterborough being one, the new system was adopted with enthusiasm by the propertied.

As for medical relief, no radical changes were made in the legal theory of the matter, nor was it practicable to confine such relief to persons admitted to the workhouse. Section 52 of the Act, for the first time, provided a statutory basis for such relief. But the Poor Law Commission under the influence of Chadwick, that is until 1842, pursued a policy of economy which appears to have severely limited the provision of such relief.

In consequence there was much conflict with the medical profession. The *Lancet*, in particular, printed numerous complaints—over gross underpayment of medical officers, over the new tender system for medical contracts, over the employment of single practitioners for geographically large areas, and over the new policy of encouraging working people to form medical clubs, mutual insurance associations of labourers.[105] In a report of the first anniversary meeting of the British Medical Association the *Lancet* gave figures showing the dramatic reduction in the number of surgeons retained; in twelve unions the number fell from 311 to 107.[106] A Mr Brady quoted from the second report of the Commissioners where Richard Earle, the Assistant Poor Law Commissioner concerned with Peterborough, reported that the cost of medical relief for 21,000 persons in the new Peterborough Union, which had added seventeen parishes to St John's, Peterborough,[107] was likely to come to about £150 *per annum*. Previously, the cost was £80 for the City of Peterborough alone, and just one of the additional parishes had previously expended £80 a year.[108] In Peterborough the medical contract was at a fixed fee per case of 3*s*.[109]

The new economical management was described in evidence presented to the Poor Law Committee of the House of Commons on 19 February 1838.[110] When an independent labourer—that is to say, one not on the list of parish paupers—falls ill, or suffers an accident, application must be made to the magistrates for an order for relief. This would often be refused, or a loan offered.[111] The policy was to confine the provision of outdoor medical relief to persons on the schedule of paupers, and to insist that receipt of medical relief made an individual into a pauper, and thus, for example, liable to removal. As G. C. Lewis insisted to the Select Committee of 1844:

Medical relief is, in fact, parochial relief; the giving of an order for medical relief constitutes the person receiving it a pauper; it is not necessary that he should be in receipt of general relief at the time the medical order is given. An order for removal may be taken out upon the proof of medical relief having been offered by a union.[112]

The loan system was, like the scheme for medical clubs, a mechanism for making the working population carry the cost of its own medical care, whether

---

[105] (1836–7) I, 138; there are quotations from the *Lincoln Journal*.
[106] (1837–8) II, 60.   [107] Previously a select vestry.
[108] 2nd *Report of the Poor Law Commission* PP (595), XXIX Pt. I. I 376 ff. Earle's report was dated 25 June 1836.
[109] NRO PL8/1, 13 Feb. and 5 Mar. Thomas Southam obtained the contract for the first district and was to receive 4*s*. per case outside the City, and 10*s*. 6*d*. for midwifery cases. The *Huntingdon Gazette*, 31 Mar. 1838, notes the same figure per case for the coming year. Rates for other districts, where travel costs would be high, varied and could be as high as 5*s*.
[110] See Question 1874.   [111] See also circular of Jan. 1836 in MH 32/28.
[112] 3rd *Report of Select Committee on Medical Relief* 1844 (531) IX 93, at 10.

occasioned by illness or accident.[113] And Chadwick was, in any event, very sceptical of the claims of doctors to be able to produce cures.[114]

As for the casual poor, Chadwick made it clear in a circular letter that they should be given relief, but there had to be 'actual necessity or destitution'. The degree to which the policy of the commissioners restricted the provision of medical care to victims of accidents would no doubt have differed from place to place. But in Peterborough we may be confident that economy was vigorously pursued.

Economical Management in Peterborough

The inn where Charles Priestley was lodged lay within the Union of St John's, Peterborough, which had its own workhouse and was managed by a Select Vestry, which put the propertied in command. The new expanded Peterborough Union, whose records are in the Public Record Office and the Northamptonshire Record Office,[115] first met on 4 December 1835, Earl Fitzwilliam being appointed Chairman. A dinner given in 1838 in honour of the Earl was devoted to praise of the new system, which had reduced expenditure on the poor by around 30 per cent.[116]

There was an existing medical contract, which was kept going until 25 March of 1836, but the records do not reveal its form, nor the name of the doctor who held it. It would probably not have covered care of the casual poor at all, and certainly not such an accident as Priestley's, for if it had, the bill would have been modest and met by the parish. There is no reference to the Priestley case in such of these records as are available. Only Thomas Fowler makes a cameo appearance: on 25 December 1835 he won the contract to supply meat to the paupers.

We cannot be absolutely certain that, at the time of Priestley's accident, economy prevailed to the same extent as it did once the new union was formed seven months later. But there is good reason to suppose that it did. Richard Earle, the Assistant Poor Law Commissioner with responsibility for Peterborough, was a landowner and barrister; he arrived in the area on 23 September 1835. He wrote, 'I have felt the pulse of few of the Magistrates and Gentry, but I do not fear that their cooperation will be wanting.'[117] It was thought that the City was overburdened with poor relief.[118] Earle was an enthusiast for the new system, for

---

[113] See e.g. app. to 2nd *Report of Poor Law Commissioners*, 384.

[114] See S. E. Finer, *The Life and Times of Sir Edwin Chadwick*, at 157.

[115] MH 32/21, MH 12/6657, the latter currently not available because of problems over asbestos contamination. NRO PL 8/1 and, from 1 Apr. 1837, /2.

[116] *Huntingdon Gazette*, 31 Mar. 1838.

[117] MH 32/21, letters of 23 and 26 Sep. from Earle to John Lefevre.

[118] Material in MH 32/21, especially letter of Earle, 26, Sep. 1835. One of 14 Oct. mentions Earle meeting with 'the great unwashed' to explain the new system. Also MH 12/8828.

economical management, and for medical clubs;[119] he was conscious of the problem of overcharging for relief of casual paupers. His views are to be found in a report of 25 June 1836, appended to the Second Report of the Poor Law Commissioners. He extolled the merits of the order made by the Commissioners 'which directs that the contracts shall include all paupers found within the Union' and goes on to tell a horror story of the evils of the old system:

A man gravely injured on the railway was removed to the workhouse in Coventry, and was there attended by one of four parish surgeons. His case was of a most serious description, and he suffered the amputation of one leg, and the other, being broken, was set.

After some time he was removed to his parish in Cheshire 'with a charge for medical attendance alone, of no less a sum than 40l. I understand that the claim for the amputation of the limb was 10l 10s'. The surgeon's annual payment for his share of work in attending all the outpatients in the town came to a mere £40; hence 'for his cure of one pauper in the workhouse he received a remuneration equal to that which he obtained for his share of all the outpatients for a year, and this only because the man did not happen to be from Coventry'. He goes on to explain how matters are now arranged in the Peterborough Union:

I am informed that the gentleman who has the Peterborough contract [Mr Southam] has expressed his preference for the new plan, only complaining that the guardians do not send many cases to him. This is likely to be true, since they adhere to the rule of never allowing medical relief to any labourer who is in receipt of wages; if the head of the family be the patient, then, in cases of emergency, they supply it on loan.[120]

Once formed, the new Board of Guardians was conscientious and met weekly; it took a firm line with applicants, and the records contain examples of loans for medical relief. The tone is caught when, on 5 February 1836, it was resolved 'that the Relieving Officer refuse relief to any Pauper who keeps a Dog of any description whatsoever'. No example of relief of a casual pauper is mentioned, but figures in the records show that accidents were a very minor cause of relief in Peterborough Union in 1836.

If this was the atmosphere in the period between the accident and the formation of the new Union, it is hardly likely that the massive bills for the care of Charles Priestley—£50 for an institution which we know spent only £80 on medical care in total in the year—would have been viewed with any sympathy by the Select Vestry which managed the poor law in Peterborough. And the final bills cannot have been presented until Charles was able to leave the inn, probably in the first week of October. By the Richard Earle had arrived to preach the gospel of economical management to the converted.

Conceivably the surgeons and innkeeper involved would be familiar with the earlier practice under which their inflated bills would be passed back to the

---

[119] 1st *Report of the Poor Law Commissioners*, PP 1835 (500) XXXV 107 at 181.
[120] 2nd *Report of Poor Law Commissioners* (595) XXIX 1836 Pt. I.I 376 ff., esp. 384.

parish of Charles Priestley's settlement. Market Deeping, where Charles Priestley would be settled, became part of the Bourne Union, which first met on 4 May. Its records are in the Lincoln Record Office; they do not mention the case.[121] We can be quite sure that there was no removal order. Such an order would only have been made if the bill was initially paid out of the poor rate, and we know it was not. The explanation may well have been the spirit of economy which prevailed in Peterborough, and hostility to the practice of making a killing through excessive medical charges for casual paupers. And if any idea of attempting to pass the bill to Market Deeping was mooted, the decision in *The King* v. *Oldland* would have put an end to the idea; the decision was given about the time when steps would be put in hand to sue at the Lincoln Assizes, and although there is no direct evidence this may be significant. One newspaper account indicates that Brown Priestley himself met the bills: 'The present action was brought to recover the amount of the expenses to which the father had been put in consequence of this lamentable occurrence.'[122] Conceivably some discreet arrangement was made by Brown Priestley with the innkeeper and surgeons over financing the litigation. Brown had an obligation to provide necessaries for his son, but this would certainly not have extended to the medical bills.

Tort Law and Accidents at Work

The litigation in *Priestley* v. *Fowler* thus arose at a time when the administration of the poor law was changing, severely limiting the provision made from the poor rates. At the same period the old relationship of master and menial servant was in decline. Although the action failed, and although, no doubt, Brown Priestley was not engaged in some strategic enterprise, it can be seen in retrospect as a first step towards a world in which tort law became a candidate for the job of replacing the older mechanisms of support. Nor was the action a total failure. Lord Abinger had conceded the possibility of an employer being liable; the trial judge had thought that in principle he was. Nobody earlier had said such things.

The next step was taken in 1840. A young woman, Elizabeth Cotterell,[123] whose age is variously given as 16 and 17 (she was probably 19 or 20) by her next friend and guardian, the philanthropist Lord Ashley, later the Earl of Shaftesbury, sued a cotton master, Samuel Stocks, at the Liverpool summer assizes.[124] The action came before Rolfe B on Wednesday, 19 August. Elizabeth

---

[121] LRO PL2/102/1 (Minutes of the Board, 1837–9), PL2/302/1 (Admission and Discharge Books, 1836–7) and PL1/104/1 (General Ledger, 1836–8). Also PRO MH 12/6657, which currently cannot be produced.

[122] *Northampton Mercury*, 23 July 1836.   [123] Also Cottrell, Cotterill.

[124] An account is given in T. J. Howell's Factory Act Report, 1841, Session 1 [294] X 161. See also National Register of Archives, Broadlands MSS, Shaftesbury Diaries SHA/PD/2, 24 Aug., 16 Sep. 1840. See also *The Times*, Friday, 21 Aug. 1840; *Liverpool News*, 25 Aug.; *Manchester Guardian*, 22 Aug.; *Gore's General Advertiser*, 27 Aug.; P. W. J. Bartrip and S. B. Burman, *The Wounded Soldiers of Industry. Industrial Compensation Policy 1833–97* (Oxford, 1983), 27.

worked in the mill of Samuel Stocks and Co. in Heaton Mersey, part of Heaton Norris.[125] An upright unguarded shaft, which revolved some sixty times a minute, caught her clothing; she was spun around 200 to 300 times until the machinery was stopped. She was terribly mangled, but survived, crippled for life. Lord Ashley, hearing of the incident, came forward on her behalf, 'in the hope not only of obtaining for the plaintiff such compensation as money could supply, but also for the purpose of an example, which might lead to measures of precaution, by which such accidents might be prevented in future'. His motives were set out in his diary:

Succeeded in both my suits. I undertook them in a spirit of justice. I constituted myself, no doubt, a defender of the poor and miserable for their rights . . . I stood to lose several hundred pounds, but I have not lost a farthing; I have advanced their cause, done individual justice, anticipated many calamities by this forced prevention, and soothed, I hope, many angry, discontented Chartist spirits by showing them that men of rank and property can, and do, care for the rights and feelings of all their brethren.

The following year, in a speech to working people in Leeds which must rank as a gift to Marxist historians, he told the story of the case and 'impressed on the minds of the operatives the values of law, and proved to them that it was not necessarily opposed to the interests of the working classes'.[126] Ashley could have simply financed the case, leaving the plaintiff, a pauper, liable for costs if she lost, but instead he sued on her behalf and made himself liable. Cresswell Cresswell, for the plaintiff, after saying that he would not describe her injuries (it is said that an arm was torn off), went on: 'It was not generally understood and the defendant was not at first convinced that the law bound him to make compensation for any injury inflicted in consequence of his machinery being left in such a state as to expose his servants to a degree of danger.' In the event liability was conceded and the plaintiff recovered a general sum of £100 and costs, which came to £600; £1,000 was claimed. Counsel for the defendant, Mr Alexander, extolled the virtues of his client, but Cresswell acidly pointed out that an expenditure of ten shillings on fencing the machine would have avoided the accident and the massive bill which Stocks had to pay. At least one other action was settled, apparently out of court.

An Elizabeth Cotterill, with age given as 20, appears as being of no occupation in the census enumerator's book for 1841; the head of the household was Martha Cotterill, also of no occupation, and presumably caring for her daughter. If, as seems very probable, this is the victim of the accident, she died of meningitis

---

[125] Pigot's *Commercial Directory* for 1841 lists the company as of 33 Mosley St Manchester, where its warehouse was located.

[126] E. Hodder, *The Life and Times of the Seventh Earl of Shaftesbury K.G.* (London, 1886), i, 301, quoting the diary for 24 Aug. 1840, but wrongly thinking it relates to chimney climbing boys. See also 347.

in Martha's presence on 7 October 1846 at 3 Water Street, Heaton Norris. Her age was then given as 26.[127]

Accidents and the Political Economists

Lord Ashley's motives combined politics with humanitarianism; he hoped to reduce suffering by deterrence and by securing compensation where it failed. There was another quite different argument for making the employers, whether in industry or agriculture, legally answerable—to reduce the burden accidents imposed on the poor law by reducing their frequency. In the early nineteenth century there was much concern expressed over the general cost of poor relief, but little reference to accidents as a source of cost. Most of the political economists never mention accidents at all. In all probability they were, in comparison with illness and old age, a small factor.

The principal exception was Edwin Chadwick, who was the first to suggest that factory owners should be made liable:[128]

One of the great evils to which people in factories are exposed is the danger of receiving serious and even fatal injuries from the machinery. It does not seem possible, by any precautions which are practicable, to remove the danger altogether. There are factories in which everything is done that it seems practicable to do to reduce the danger to the least possible amount, and with such success that no serious accident happens for years together. By the returns we have received, however, it appears that there are other factories, and that these are by no means few in number, not confined to the smaller mills, in which serious accidents are constantly occurring, and in which, notwithstanding, dangerous parts of the machines are allowed to remain unfenced. The greater the carelessness of the proprietors in neglecting sufficiently to fence the machinery, and the greater the number of accidents, the less the sympathy with the sufferers.[129]

After pointing out that 'whilst some manufacturers liberally contribute to the relief of the sufferers, many other manufacturers leave them to obtain relief from public bounty, or as they may', he argues that in the case of accidents to children under 14 the employer should pay for medical attendance and the expenses of cure, and provide half wages; the same rule for adults where there is no 'culpable temerity'. The principle to be applied was stated thus:

---

[127] HO 107/582; the family, traceable back to the late eighteenth century in the IGI, also had two cotton weavers, Maria and Joseph, with ages of 15 (i.e. between 15 and 19) and two children, John and George. There is no other candidate in the 1841 or 1851 census for Heaton Norris, nor was she then one of the 190 inmates of the Stockport Union Workhouse (HO 107/2156). For her death see Stockport, 19 Dec., 229.

[128] For discussion of his views see Bartrip and Burman, n. 124 above, 68–73.

[129] 1st *Report of the Commissioners of Inquiry into the Labour of Children in Factories*, PP 1833 (450) XX 1 and XXI at 31.

We conceive that it may be stated, as a principle of jurisprudence applicable to the cases of evils from causes which ordinary prudence cannot avert, that responsibility should be concentrated, or, as closely as possible apportioned on those who have the best means of preventing the mischief.

The report also suggests as a possibility a compulsory levy on wages to cover the costs. It will be seen that Chadwick's principle went well beyond mere liability for negligence. It is most unlikely that he had in mind the use of tort actions to recover compensation. Because of their cost they were of little use to the working class. He probably had in mind a combination between penalties of a criminal character and rights to compensation enforceable before justices or perhaps, later, the county courts.[130]

Chadwick returned to the subject, which became something of a hobby horse for him, in his *Report on the Sanitary Condition of the Labouring Population of Great Britain* (1842),[131] and now emphasized the relationship of his ideas to the poor law. He pointed out that 'although the deaths from accidents bear only a small proportion to the deaths from disease, yet they amount to about 12,000 annually'. This caused pauperism by producing widows and orphans; pauperism was also produced by 'injuries which occasion permanent disablement'. Under existing arrangements, manufacturers were 'in a great measure, relieved from responsibility by the charge incurred by the want of care being thrown on other funds raised from persons who have as yet no practicable means of protection or prevention'. So the answer was to make it in the self-interest of manufacturers to prevent accidents, by making them liable. His report quotes with approval a report from John L. Kennedy,[132] a barrister, to the Commissioners for Inquiring into the Labour of Young Persons in Mines and Manufactories, which argued:

The more this question is examined, the more I apprehend will it be found desirable that the full expenses of such accidents should be borne by that branch of industry in which they are created, in which case they will be borne either by those who, as producers, have the chief profits, or they will fall, as I apprehend they ought to fall, on the consumers.

They should be 'a trade charge or form of insurance'.[133]

Chadwick joined the Political Economy Club, formed in 1821, in 1834.[134] In 1847 he raised for discussion the question:

---

[130] For the system of penal compensation under the Factory Acts see R. J. Howells, '*Priestley* v. *Fowler* and the Factory Acts' (1963) 26 *MLR* 367.

[131] Reprinted in the Irish Universities edn. of the Parliamentary Papers in *Health. General*, iii, 109 at 205.

[132] There is correspondence with John Lawson Kennedy of Ardwick Hall, Manchester, in the Chadwick Papers, University College, London, 1141.

[133] See also S. E. Finer, n. 114 above, at 149.

[134] *Political Economy Club. Minutes of Proceedings 1899–1920, Roll of Members and Questions Discussed* (London, 1921), 360. Other members connected with the law included Sir George Bramwell (1855), Henry Thring (1860), Fitzjames Stephen (1862), and J. Fletcher Moulton (1885). Henry Sidgwick (1883) and A. C. Pigou (1906) were also members.

would legitimate enterprise be seriously obstructed by legislative provision, rendering the owner of works, machinery, mines, ships etc. involving danger to life or limb, liable to make good the pecuniary losses for the sufferers and their families from fatal accidents or maiming, incident to their employment as to the operation of such works?

In 1889 he raised the question again, referring to the German system of Workmans' Compensation:

Is the principle of Curative Legislation, by allowances on attaining old age and against accidents from machinery, as adapted for wage classes in Germany, as economical as the principle of Preventive Legislation and the concentration of responsibility on those who have the best means of prevention, after the manner proposed for the regulation of factories in this country?

Chadwick's fullest discussion is in a paper read to the Statistical Society of Manchester in 1846, when the subject was under Parliamentary scrutiny.[135] This paper dealt with the navvies, often migrant Irishmen, engaged in very large numbers in railway construction, and the problems of violence, crime, and disorder associated with major railway works. The problems came to a head over conditions attending the sinking of the Woodhead Tunnel. On accidents, the argument was that at present the costs fell on the parish; by making the undertakers liable they might be prevented. Chadwick's argument was not that compensation would be given where there was none, merely that the number of accidents would be reduced. He thought workmen were too stupid to be in control of working conditions. Hence he favoured making employers liable for accidents, whether caused by fellow workmen or otherwise, except in cases where gross and wilful misconduct by the victim could be proved. The Chadwick Papers contain a pamphlet of his on the subject from 1881, by which time the topic had become a political issue.[136]

Chadwick was an exception amongst the disciples of the new religion. However Nassau Senior, writing about Ireland, argued that:

ample provision be made for the care of persons suffering from disabling diseases and accidents such as blindness, loss of limbs, and what is equivalent to loss of limbs, chronic infirmity, idiocy, and madness in any of its forms. No public fund for the relief of these calamities has any tendency to diminish industry or providence. They are evils too great to allow individuals to make any sufficient provision against them, and too rare to be, in fact, provided against by them at all.[137]

---

[135] *Papers Read Before the Statistical Society of Manchester on the Demoralisation and Injuries Occasioned by the Want of Proper Regulation of Labourers engaged in the Construction and Working of Railways*, The Chadwick Papers (UCL), 79 (Railways 1844–8) contain much other material, including copies of the evidence submitted to the Parliamentary Select Committee on Railway Labourers of 1846.

[136] *Employer's Liability for Accidents to Workpeople*, Chadwick Papers, Pamphlets, Box 1.

[137] In a letter to Lord Howick on the legal provision of the Irish poor (1831). See M. E. A. Bowley, *Nassau Senior and Classical Economics* (London, 1937), 244.

But the solution he had in mind was the introduction of the poor law to Ireland, not an extension of tort liability.[138] Chadwick's only real ally amongst the economists was J. R. McCulloch, though he was a vehement critic of Chadwick's new poor law. He, too, thought that it was idle to expect miners and factory workers to be more careful; he favoured imposing liability on masters to induce them to enforce regulations which would avoid accidents, and thought that the effect on the price of products would be 'trifling'. Although he does not explicitly say so, he was apparently aware that he was merely recommending transferring liability from poor law to employer.[139] Eventually employers did become liable, both under statutory schemes of workmen's compensation and under private tort law, and medical care became universal under the National Health Service, but that is all another story.

The Fates of Charles and Brown Priestley

As for those who started it all back in the 1830s, Charles Priestley, in spite of the severity of his injuries, seems to have prospered. In 1841 he appears as a butcher, living with his brother, George, an agricultural labourer, in Spridlington.[140] By 1851 he is a master butcher still with George, both unmarried, and their housemaid, Eliza Todd.[141] He also appears in directories up to 1856.[142] By 1861 Charles was on his own.[143] On 13 August 1860 George married Jane Chester and moved to Welton as a farmer and cattle dealer.[144] Charles is not at Spridlington for the census of 1871 or 1881, but a Charles Priestley, a labourer, who could be the right person, aged 62, is living at 84 Grantham Street in Lincoln.[145] Possibly he had to abandon his trade as butcher and came down in life. A Charles Priestley, described as a general labourer, who died in 1887 at 9 Yarborough Road Lincoln, could also be him;[146] less likely is one who died in 1892 at Boothby Graffoe, Lincoln, described as a farm labourer aged 77.[147] It is not possible to be sure.

As for Brown Priestley, the loss of the action appears to have been more immediately disastrous. He would have become liable to pay substantial legal

[138] The poor law was introduced into Ireland in 1837–8.
[139] *The Principles of Political Economy*, 307. The passage features in a ch. dealing with the proper limits of government 'interference'.
[140] HO 107/644.   [141] HO 107/2106.
[142] W. White, *The History and Directory of . . . the Country of Lincolnshire* (Sheffield, 1842 and 1856). The brothers also appear in Post Office Directories.
[143] RG 9/2364.
[144] IGI. He appears in a Post Office directory for 1861 and in White for 1876. In the 1871 census, George, married, is a cattle dealer in Rylands with a servant, William Simpson, but no wife or family present; see RG 10/3376. His son, Brown Priestley, died at the age of one month in 1863 (ref. Lincoln 7a 329).
[145] RG 11/3244.   [146] Lincoln, June Quarter 7a, 302, age given as 71.
[147] Lincoln, March Quarter 7a, 361. The census for 1891, RG 12/2587, has him married to one Rebecca, but gives his place of birth as Navenby.

costs, and, given Fowler's bankruptcy, we can be confident that pressure would have been brought on him. He also, as we have seen, probably paid the medical bills. In September 1837 a 170-acre prebendal farm at Welton, held under a lease for three lives, which must have been Welton Rive-hall, was offered for sale, but no sale can have taken place.[148] Brown Priestley was, presumably, already desperate for money.

On 31 December 1837 Brown Priestley was committed to the debtor's prison in Lincoln Castle; the circumstances do not appear.[149] At the Lincolnshire Spring Assizes in 1838 he was sued as a surety on a bond for £1,268 of 20 May 1820, and another for £755. The only issue was the validity of the bonds, which was established before Sir James Park, who had tried *Priestley* v. *Fowler* back in 1836. One Brett Chester, a farmer and grazier of East Torrington, had died on 1 November 1815, and his property, presumably a farm which formed an economic unit, was to be divided between his widow Ann, his daughter Ann, and his two sons, Thomas and Michael.[150] It was arranged that Thomas should keep the property undivided, and give bonds to the others to secure their shares. Brown Priestley, for reasons which do not appear, acted as surety on these bonds.[151] Thomas defaulted, and the actions were brought by Michael Chester, and by Joseph Bownar as executor on behalf of the widow. One newspaper report notes: 'It was pronounced to be a hard case, in which the surety was expectedly called upon.'[152] It was not the intention to press hard for payment; 'the utmost indulgence as to time' would be offered.[153]

This was not to be. On 7 June the *Lincoln, Rutland and Stamford Mercury* reported that a fiat in bankruptcy had been granted against him—in fact on 8 May. He was still in Lincoln Castle, 'late of Welton, and since of Spridlington, farmer, cattle jobber, dealer and chapman'. Also more closely incarcerated in the castle—for the debtors could walk freely in an area of some two acres[154]—was the notorious 14-year-old murderer, Samuel Kirby, who had poisoned his employer, a butcher.

From the keeper's journal we can catch glimpses of Brown Priestley. On 11 February he had been absent from chapel without leave and his allowance of ale was stopped, and on 12 June he was involved in a noisy disturbance and reported to the chairman of the visiting magistrates. Another debtor, Wood Stephenson, had torn his waistcoat and neckerchief, and he had been locked up in his room; it had all been meant as a joke, or so it was said. Meetings of creditors were arranged in the Saracen's Head Inn in Lincoln for 1 June, when he was produced, and for 20 June and 17 July. He was released from prison on the morning of the

---

[148] *LRSM*, 8 Sep. 1837.   [149] LRO CoC5/1/3, *Journal of Keeper William Brockesby.*
[150] Will, LRO LCC Wills 1816/46. There was also a trust for his grandchildren.
[151] The marriage of Jane Chester to George Priestley indicates some sort of connection between the Chesters and the Priestleys.
[152] *LRSM*, 9 Mar. 1838. Fuller reports in *LCGA*, 9 Mar. 1838; LBGN, 6 Mar. 1838.
[153] *LBGNG*, 6 Mar. 1838.
[154] White's *Directory* for 1826, 44 describes the arrangements.

meeting on 20 June. The principal creditors were Michael Chester, John Davey, and Thomas Davey. The assignees were William Seagrave, a farmer and chief constable of Lissington, where Michael Chester lived, and Thomas Davey of Addlethorpe.[155] His properties at Welton, amounting to 170 acres, were sold at the Bull Inn there on 30 August,[156] and a final meeting to settle accounts was held at the Saracen's Head in Lincoln on 2 October.[157]

He was back in Spridlington, no doubt living with his sons when the *Gazette* for 21 June announced a dividend; he was, of course, by now elderly. John Parris, in *Under my Wig*, records the story that Priestley—it is unclear whether he means Charles or his father—spent the next thirty-three years of his life in the Fleet Prison.[158] Brown's incarceration in Lincoln Castle may be the source of this story. Another folk tale is that he died in the Lincoln workhouse, but he was not one of the 173 inhabitants of the Lincoln Union workhouse in 1841 or 1851, though a blind imbecile namesake was then there.[159] He does not feature in the Spridlington census for 1841, or in that of Welton, nor have I found him elsewhere. But he surfaces in 1851 as a lodger in the home of Mary Sharp at 4 Bank Street, in St Swithin's, Lincoln, described as a 79-year-old annuitant.[160] Presumably he or his relatives had contrived to make this provision for his old age. He died on 8 June 1852 at another lodging house run by a blacksmith and his wife, John and Mary Ardern, Mary being present when he died, and reporting his age, wrongly, as 82. The house was at 17 Mint Lane, where his Baptist chapel was.[161] A Brown Priestley of Commercial Road, Spittlegate, Grantham, who died on 8 October 1877, was his son, born on 12 May 1813;[162] he was earlier a butcher and cattle dealer at Wellingore. The infant son of his brother, George, who died in 1863, also bore the same name.[163]

There is, of course, no statue to this village Hampden in Welton, and all local memory of him has passed away; though he was presumably buried at St Martin's in Lincoln, his grave is unmarked. But you can still gaze over his prebendal estate, see his farmhouse, or reflect on his misfortunes over a glass of beer in the Bull Inn where the final degradation of the bankrupt sale took place. You can even meet Priestleys living in the area who may well be his distant relatives. Otherwise his only memorial must be the case of *Priestley* v. *Fowler*.

---

[155] B 5/102. No complete set of records survives.
[156] *LCGA*, 10 and 24 Aug. 1838. The inn still exists.   [157] Issue of 14 Sep.
[158] At 109. Brown Priestley would by then be aged nearly 100.
[159] HO 107/651, 2105.   [160] HO 107/2105.
[161] HO 107/2105 (Census), Lincoln, June Quarter 1852 7a, 307 (death certificate). I am indebted to Mr A. L. Watson, a distant relative, for this reference, having missed the entry in a prolonged search at St Catherine's House.
[162] Grantham, 7a 273, Dec. Quarter.
[163] June Quarter 1863, Lincoln 74 329. A Brown Priestley who turns up in the census for 1881 at 13 Saxon Street, Lincoln St Nicholas (RG 11/3241 fo. 86), born Kirton, Notts., could be related. There were others of the same name.

6
The Beauty of Obscurity
Raffles *v.* Wichelhaus and Busch *(1864)*

An Illuminating Opinion

Cases such as *Shelley* v. *Wolfe* or *Keeble* v. *Hickeringill* were thought to be
important at the time when they were decided. But this is not true of *Raffles* v.
Wichelhaus, the case of the two ships *Peerless*.[1] It was decided by the Court of
Exchequer on 20 January 1864. The judges, Pollock CB and Martin and Pigott
BB, thought that the solution to the problem presented to them was so obvious
that they gave judgment for the defendants without troubling to give any reasons
at all. The opinion reads 'there must be judgement for the defendants.' They did
not even think it necessary to hear the completion of the argument of the defendant's counsel, George Mellish QC and Andrew Cohen. It is hardly surprising
that the case caused no ripples in the contemporary legal world, and, so far as
I have been able to discover, the press showed not the least interest in it. So, if
ever a case did not deserve to become famous, it was *Raffles* v. *Wichelhaus*. Yet
for the last century or so, for reasons which I shall explain, the case has been
under almost continuous examination. Perhaps the best-known modern discussion is in the late Grant Gilmore's maverick book, *The Death of Contract* (1974),
where he argued, with his tongue, I suspect, in his cheek, that contract law, like
God, was dead.[2] Yet, until I published a study of the case in 1989 in the *Cardozo
Law Review*,[3] virtually nothing was known about it as a historical event, and
nobody very much cared: those who held forth on the case did so from positions
of invincible ignorance. Indeed, the fame of *Raffles* v. *Wichelhaus* largely rested
upon the utter obscurity as to what the litigation and its decision was about.

The Course of the Litigation

The action was for damages. It was brought by William Winter Raffles for
failure by the defendants, Daniel Wichelhaus and Gustav Busch, to accept and
pay for 125 bales of Surat cotton 'guaranteed middling fair merchant's Dhollorah'.

This chapter is based upon 'Contracts for Cotton to Arrive: the Case of the Two Ships *Peerless*
(1989) 11 *Cardozo Law Review* 287.
  [1] 2 H & C 906, 159 ER 375, 33 LJNS 160. IND 4375 (Entry Book of Judgments). The pleadings
do not survive, and I have located no useful newspaper account.
  [2] At 35–44.   [3] Vol. 11 at 287.

This had been sold to them at some unspecified date at seventeen and a quarter pence a pound. The cotton was 'to arrive "ex *Peerless*" from Bombay'. This was a Liverpool contract, and it was there that delivery was to be made. *Peerless* was, of course, the name of a ship, and the type of cotton involved was that grown in the Achmedabad district of Bombay. Surat is a port north of Bombay from which cotton was once shipped, and all cottons shipped from Bombay came to be called 'Surats' in the trade. 'Middling fair', an expression still used in Lancashire to refer to the state of one's health, was what was known as a half-grade of cotton. At this time the grades in use in Liverpool for East Indian cotton were 'fine', 'good', 'good fair', 'fair', 'middling', and 'ordinary'. 'Middling fair' was between 'fair' and 'middling'. There was no constant relationship between the prices for different grades and half-grades.

Something of the order of 50,000 lbs. of cotton at a price of £3,593 was involved, so this was a substantial business contract. Raffles said that the cotton had indeed arrived at Liverpool on the *Peerless*; he had been willing to perform his side of the bargain, but the defendants refused to accept and pay for the cotton. The defendants replied to the statement of claim with two pleas, the first of which is now undiscoverable, since it is not given in the law reports and the pleadings have not survived. It probably simply denied that they had refused to accept delivery, without further explanation. The second plea said that in the contract, which was a written one, the defendants intended to refer to a ship called *Peerless* which had left Bombay in October. The cotton which the plaintiff had offered to deliver had arrived at Liverpool on an entirely different ship, which had sailed from Bombay in December. But this ship was, unfortunately, also called *Peerless*. The pleadings do not speculate as to which ship Raffles had in mind, and neither the pleadings nor the law reports reveal the year in which the sailings from Bombay took place, nor the order in which the ships arrived. But they do imply that the October ship, as well as the December ship, had safely reached Liverpool. Absolutely no indication was given about how the misunderstanding, if indeed there was a misunderstanding, had come about.

The plaintiff could have replied to this plea, known as a special plea, by denying the facts which it asserted; then, if the defendants had joined issue on it, the case would have gone to a jury for decision. Instead he objected that, even if this story was true, it provided no answer, as a matter of law, to his claim. A plea of this kind, which did not dispute the factual allegations of the other party, was called a demurrer. The effect of demurring, explained Serjeant Stephen, the high priest of the mysteries of the arcane art of special pleading, was that 'a demurrer admits all such matters of fact as are sufficiently pleaded'.[4] So Raffles was conceding that Wichelhaus and Busch had indeed intended to refer to the October ship. In all probability this was the truth of the matter. Raffles had in mind one ship, and Wichelhaus and Busch another.

[4] H. J. Stephen, *A Treatise on the Principles of Pleading in Civil Actions* (London, 1866), 142.

The demurrer raised a purely legal issue which would be decided by the judges sitting *in banc*, that is as a multi-judge court, in Westminster Hall in London, and there was no occasion for any trial before a jury in Liverpool. There was no dispute over the facts. The case was decided on this demurrer. Essentially the question for decision was whether the defendant's story, as set out in the plea, was *capable* of furnishing a defence to the action. If so, the plaintiff's demurrer must fail. His only hope of success would have been to have joined issue on the plea, raising thereby a question of fact to be submitted to a jury. But it was now too late to do so. Under the old rules of pleading you got only one bite at the cherry; having by demurring raised an issue of law for the judges to decide, Raffles had given up his chance to raise issues of fact before a jury. So there never was, and never could be, a jury trial at which the whole story would have emerged and, no doubt, been covered in Liverpool newspapers.

The gist of Raffles's case was that he had offered to perform exactly and precisely the contract he had made: to deliver Surat cotton of the appropriate type and quality from a ship called *Peerless* sailing from Bombay. The fact that the defendants might have had some other ship of the same name in mind was neither here nor there: 'The contract was for the sale of a number of bales of cotton of a particular description, which the plaintiff was willing to deliver. It is immaterial by what ship the cotton was to arrive, so that [i.e. so long as] it was a ship called the "*Peerless*".' The force of this argument was enhanced by the rule, then much insisted upon, that where a contract had been put in writing, you were not generally allowed to modify or amplify its terms by oral evidence of what you had 'really' meant. This was known as the parol evidence rule, and it was referred to in the case thus: 'The defendant has no right to contradict by parol evidence a written contract good on the face of it.' It was thought that the value of putting contracts in writing would be much weakened unless this policy was generally followed. Since the Victorian period this rule has, for better or for worse, been considerably relaxed. There were, however, some exceptions to the rule even then, as we shall see.

The barrister who argued the case for Raffles was one Clement Milward.[5] He put his case vigorously, but the judges were very much against him. He was in some difficulty in claiming that the identity of the ship—so long, of course, as it was called *Peerless*—was irrelevant since, if the ship foundered at sea, the contract was off, but this could only apply to the relevant ship. The loss would then have been covered by insurance. This was, then, the customary understanding in the Liverpool cotton trade. From this alone it did seem to follow that the contract was for cotton on a unique ship, not just any ship leaving Bombay which happened to have the name *Peerless*. According to one of the two reports Milward made another curious concession: 'If the defendants had said their speculation had fallen through in consequence, it might have been different.'

---

[5] (1821–90), a Middle Temple lawyer who became a QC in 1865. See below 186.

Later we shall see that there is an explanation for this puzzling remark. He went on to assert, correctly enough, that 'the time of sailing of the ship was no part of the contract', meaning that it had not been specified in the written contract, and added, somewhat oddly, 'and, for the purposes of the plea, we must take it that both ships sailed on the same day'. This strange remark indirectly conceded an important point: that the identity of the ship might be relevant because it obliquely indicated the sailing date, and therefore, albeit very indirectly, the date at which the cotton would arrive in Liverpool and become available for sale there in the spot market. Knowledge of the date of sailing, or, if the contract was made after the ship put to sea, knowledge of the vessel's progress, might make it possible to form a useful estimate of the probable date of arrival. Since cotton prices did not remain stable, this might be important commercially. Of this the judges were, of course, well aware. This awareness lay behind a point made by Pollock CB when he intervened in the argument to criticize the claim that the identity of the ship did not matter; he drew attention to the admitted fact that 'one vessel sailed in October and one in December'. For reasons we shall see, everyone at this time knew of the volatility of the cotton market.

The Decision of the Judges

In terms of contract law the judges seem to have thought that, once it appeared there were two ships sailing from Bombay which answered the contractual description, and no way of telling which of the two was intended, the contract was latently ambiguous. Consequently a jury should have been allowed to hear the evidence and decide whether the parties meant the same ship, and if so which, or different ships. As Pollock CB put it: 'whether the same *Peerless* was meant by the plaintiff and the defendants is a matter of evidence for the jury.' Mr Mellish QC put the point in argument: 'there is a latent ambiguity, and parol evidence may be given for the purpose of shewing that the defendant meant one "Peerless" and the plaintiff another.' Cases of 'latent ambiguity' were an exception to the rule that, where a contract was in writing, the law did not allow the parties to rely on oral evidence to modify or explain the written terms. He was no doubt thinking of an earlier case, *Smith* v. *Jeffryes* (1846),[6] in which Alderson B had explained the concept: 'A latent ambiguity is, where you show that the words apply equally to two different things or subject-matters, and then evidence is admissible to shew which was the thing or subject matter intended'. This more or less precisely fitted the facts of the case. So the demurrer failed.

What would have happened if there had been no demurrer, and the case had gone to a jury? Obviously if the jury thought the agreement related to the October ship, the plaintiff would lose; if the December ship was meant, then the

---

[6] 15 M & W 561, 153 ER 972.

plaintiff would win. But what if the jury thought that the parties meant different ships, or that there was just no way of telling to which ship the contract related? The judge would then have the tricky task of directing them as to what consequence followed, as a matter of law, from this. But in *Raffles* v. *Wichelhaus* there was no need for the judges to reach any conclusion on what a suitable direction would have been. It was enough that the pleas, if true, *might* furnish an answer to the claim, for if so the plaintiff's legal objection to it failed. So, 'There must be judgement for the defendant.'

Suppose, however, that the case had gone to a jury, and that it had emerged at a trial that one party meant one ship, and the other the other, and there was just no way of telling which was the ship to which the *contract* related— whatever that means. What then was to be done? This has all the seductive fascination of a conundrum, and it has subsequently captured the imagination of generations of scholars and students of the law of contract. Consequently they have tried, with some desperation, to prise an answer to the conundrum out of the texts of the reports of the case.

Fortunately for the subsequent uses to which the case has been put, there is no clear answer to be found there. Mellish and Cohen certainly argued that, if one party meant one ship and the other party the other, there would be no contract at all; they used the expression *consensus ad idem*, agreement as to the same thing, and their argument was that, without such *consensus*, there would be no contract at all. They would know the story behind the case, and as reputable counsel would not seek to mislead the court; common sense suggests that this was indeed the situation. For some reason, which nobody explained, there had been a complete misunderstanding. Their argument was stopped at this point by the judges, but we cannot conclude from this that the judges all agreed with counsel, and even if the parties did mean different ships there might be some reason for preferring one person's understanding to the other. For example, the misunderstanding could have been the fault of one rather than the other. There was no need for the judges to grapple with this conundrum. So, although they may well have agreed with counsel, there is just no way of being sure of this. There is indeed a limit to what can be deduced from any text, or treated as consistent with it. We can, perhaps, sensibly pore over the text of *Macbeth* to determine the number of Lady Macbeth's children, but it is a waste of time to attempt to discover from it whether Macbeth suffered from athlete's foot.

Raffles v. *Wichelhaus* has both a maritime and a commercial context, and to understand the case it seems obvious that both need to be recreated. When the case first became an object of speculation in the late nineteenth century, the litigants and their lawyers were still alive, and it would have been perfectly easy, by writing a few letters, to have discovered the whole story behind the dispute, the explanation for the misunderstanding, the date of the contract and of the arrival of the ships, and so forth. But nobody troubled to do so, and today it is by no means so easy to discover information on all such matters.

The Maritime Context of the Case

So far as the maritime context is concerned, there is an abundance of information. In the nineteenth century the Registrar General of Shipping and Seamen and the Marine Department of the Board of Trade maintained elaborate records of the voyages of registered merchant vessels, of the articles of agreement between captains and crews, and of the careers of ships' officers. This department had been established in 1850 under the Mercantile Marine Act of that year.[7] Some records, indeed, long predate this legislation. There are registers of seamen from 1835, and agreements and crew lists from the same date, with some dating back to 1747. Records were maintained of the registration of vessels from 1786, and changes in the ownership of the sixty-four shares into which ships were divided. Some of these records have, of course, gone missing, and some returns were never in fact made. The huge mass which has survived is now dispersed between the Public Record Office at Kew, the National Maritime Museum at Greenwich, local record offices, and the Memorial University of St John's, Newfoundland.[8]

Applications by seamen for certificates of competence as mates, masters, and engineers also survive in the National Maritime Museum. Lloyd's of London also kept its own set of records, based on official documents, for the convenience of underwriters. This collection, now in the Guildhall Museum, includes Captains' Registers from 1868 to 1947, which make it easy to trace the careers of master mariners. In the age of sail, seamen, the most rootless and endangered section of the proletariat, moved from ship to ship, in between bouts of drunken relaxation. All sailing ships of the same type worked in the same way, so if you knew the ropes on *Peerless* you would have no difficulty finding them on *Cutty Sark*. But captains, as well as craftsmen, such as carpenters and sailmakers, tended to remain with one ship. The captain's position depended upon a relationship of trust with the owners, and for long periods he was outside their direct control. He would often himself be a part owner. Captains also had to be familiar with the idiosyncratic handling of the particular vessel; sailors merely had to do as they were told.

In addition to official records a mass of information on shipping movements was published in commercial newspapers, and most comprehensively in *Lloyd's List*; an essential manuscript index is available in the National Maritime Museum.

There were at least eleven ships called *Peerless* sailing the seven seas at the time. The *Mercantile Navy List* for 1863 records two American *Peerlesses* and

---

[7] 13 & 14 Vict. c.93.

[8] Anyone attempting to use maritime records should first read C. and M. Watts, 'Unravelling Merchant Seamens' Records' (1979) 19 *Genealogists' Magazine* 313 and Cox, 'Sources for Maritime History', 2 *Maritime History* 168. See also P. Parkhurst, *Ships of Peace: A Record of Some of the Problems which came before the Board of Trade in connection with the British Mercantile Marine, from early days to the year 1885* (New Malden, 1962). The PRO has helpful guides, in particular Family Fact Sheets 6 and 7 and Records Information Number 5.

nine British registered vessels, two of Liverpool. There was nothing unusual in this; popular names were often shared by many ships. Although vessels had a unique registered number, it was not the custom in the shipping press to differentiate them by using it. Instead the practice was to use the name of the captain of the vessel. Possibly this practice was simply traditional, and predated the system of registration. It may also have been convenient for the local agents who sent reports in to Lloyd's. The number was not displayed on a vessel, but the captain's name would be easily discoverable in ports of arrival and departure. There is no difficulty in identifying the ships with which we are concerned. They were the two Liverpool-registered vessels. One was *Peerless* (Major) and the other was *Peerless* (Flavin).

The Voyage of Peerless (Major)

Peerless (Major), number 20279, was the October ship. She was a three-masted sailing vessel of 841 tons register, ship rigged, that is square rigged on all three masts, unlike a barque.[9] She was of wooden construction, carried a female figurehead, and had been built in 1857 at Bridport in Dorset by E. Cox and Company for a number of members of the Prowse family, half the shares being owned by William Prowse. Lloyd's classified her as 'thirteen years A1', 'A' referring to the standard of construction of her hull, and '1' to that of her gear. At the time of her voyage to Bombay she was owned by J. Prowse and Company of Ansdell Street in Liverpool, and she had been registered at Liverpool on 28 October 1857. Her captain, Robert Major, was a Yorkshireman, born in 1817, who had qualified as a master mariner in 1852. He had been her master since she had been built, and she was his second command. Of the papers connected with the voyage which concerns us only one document survives, 'List C', being 'the Account of Crew of Foreign Going Ship'. This records, on a standard form, information about the engagement and discharge of the crew, their conduct, and some other information, such as any deaths on board. As required by law this was delivered to the Shipping Master at Liverpool within forty-eight hours of the conclusion of the voyage on 21 February 1863.

From official documents and reports in *Lloyd's List* we can reconstruct the voyage of *Peerless* (Major) in some detail. After signing off his crew from his previous voyage on 8 September 1861, Robert Major, on 15 November, engaged a new crew comprising two mates, a carpenter, boatswain, steward, and cook, together with thirteen seamen and six apprentices. He put to sea on 19 November; the delay may well have been designed to allow his crew to sober up. The average age of the seamen was 26, and they included two Norwegians, a Swede,

---

[9] Registration details from PRO BT 108/51; details of Captain from Guildhall Library, MS 186567/10; List C from BT 99/49. Ship movements from various issues of *Lloyd's List*.

and a German; only four had been on the earlier voyage. Pay would run from around £6 or even £7 a month for John Judson, the first mate, to around £2 10*s*. for able seamen, and £1 or less for apprentices. The vessel sailed first to Calcutta, and she was 'spoken' on 1 January 1862 at 9N 21W, a position off Liberia. This was reported in London in *Lloyd's List* on 3 February, and in *The Times*, and no doubt in other papers, the following day. She was next reported from Calcutta on 3 April as having reached the port the previous day, after encountering heavy weather off Madagascar on 22 February, and again in the Bay of Bengal on 25 March. In these storms she partially lost her bulwarks, and 100 bales of cargo were damaged by cases containing chloride of lime, which had been wrongly stowed, having been misdescribed as 'General Merchandise'. Five members of the crew were discharged, two being ill; one was the second mate, whose conduct was recorded only as being 'good' rather than the usual 'very good', and which meant 'bad'. His replacement, James T. Prescott of Deal, was even less of a success, and on his eventual discharge received no testimonial whatsoever from his captain. Indeed from the official log of the previous voyage to India, from 17 November 1860 to September 1861, we can surmise that Robert Major was a disciplinarian who did not run a happy ship. Thus, as the vessel lay in the Mersey, one sailor was discharged and an apprentice contrived somehow to abscond. The log also records an unpleasant slanging match between him and a disgruntled sailor on St Patrick's Day in 1861.

On our voyage five replacements were engaged at Calcutta, which she had left by 21 June; she reached Bombay on 13 August 1862, and this was published in London on 22 September. She set sail for Liverpool on 20 October, which is about the time when the north-east monsoon would begin to blow. The mails left Bombay on 27 October, and the Victorian postal service was extraordinarily reliable. Whereas the *Peerless* necessarily sailed to England around the Cape of Good Hope, a voyage of some 11,000 miles, the mails went by steamship, using the much shorter overland route across the isthmus of Suez and, after passing through the Mediterranean, again by steamship, travelled by rail from Marseilles to the Channel for the crossing to England, where they arrived on 20 November. The report of *Peerless*'s departure from Bombay was published on 21 November, and would then be generally known in the commercial world in Liverpool. The information could have been available a little earlier, for Maurice Williams, a cotton broker, noted in his *Cotton Circular* of 19 November that the most recent information available to him from Bombay was of 20 October. He may have relied on information from other ships' captains, or on cables, for since 1857 there had been a telegraph service covering most of the way to India, though it was somewhat unreliable. Amongst other problems was the tendency of indigenous inhabitants to use the cable to make into jewellery and other saleable consumer goods, a practice which explains the preference for using undersea cables in spite of their huge cost. The *Peerless* herself, which had not been publicly reported on passage, took just under four months, which was normal. She arrived in the River Mersey on 14 February. By this period the use of steam tugs for the final stages of a voyage greatly reduced the uncertainty of passage times, and *Peerless* would no doubt have used one if the winds had been unfavourable in the Irish Sea. She would dock and start to unload a few days later.

The Voyage of Peerless (Flavin)

Peerless (Flavin), number 41935, was the December vessel.[10] She was a larger Liverpool-registered wooden sailing vessel of 1005 tons register; she, too, was three-masted, ship rigged, and had a female figurehead. She had been built by P. Brunelle in Quebec in 1858, and first registered there. In 1859, on her maiden voyage, she was wrecked, sold, recovered, and repaired. She was then re-registered at Halifax, Nova Scotia, where presumably the work was done. On 5 May 1862 her registration was transferred to Liverpool, her owners being Messrs Dixon and Wynne of 39 Oldhall Street; the intention would be that she should become a carrier of East Indian cotton for, as we shall see, this trade greatly increased at this time. The voyage with which we are concerned was her first as a Liverpool cotton ship.

Her captain, Thomas Flavin, was an Irishman, born in 1823 in County Waterford; he lived in Liverpool at 53 Bridgewater Street. He became a master mariner in 1857, and took over *Peerless* in 1861 after his previous ship, *Erin-go-brogh*, was lost on 9 December 1860.

For the voyage with which we are concerned only one form, *Agreement and Account of Crew (Foreign Going Ship)*, survives. Of the crew of twenty-five, which included three mates, carpenter, boatswain, sailmaker, and cook, six came from Waterford, and five more were Irishmen; Captain Flavin must have been a man of good repute with Irish sailors. On 7 June 1862 the crew signed or made their marks, for seven were wholly illiterate, to be on board on 10 June by 9 a.m. They put to sea after a prudent interval on 12 June. Pay ranged from £6 a month for the first mate, Evan Evans, down to £1 a month for James Gleven and Patrick Flaherty, whose first voyage it was. The sailors were mainly in their late teens or early twenties. The oldest seaman was Charles Francis from Bordeaux, aged 35, who was to die of tuberculosis in Bombay; this was a relatively common cause of death amongst seamen. Sailors did not last long in Victorian merchant sailing ships.

Peerless (Flavin) sailed direct to Bombay, and entered the port on 10 October 1862. Her arrival was published in England on 5 November where, as we have seen, it had been known since 22 September that the other *Peerless* was also

---

[10] Registration from PRO BT 108/76, 281, 283, 286, information on Captain from Guildhall Library, MS 18567/5; ship's papers from the Memorial University collection at St John's, Newfoundland.

lying there. She remained there until Christmas Eve of 1862, three days before the mails left. Her departure was published in England on 21 January 1863. On 27 March it was reported that she had been sighted off Ascension Island in the South Atlantic, and on 26 February she was spoken by the *Edmund Kay* at 1S 20W, north of Ascension. On 16 April she put into Queenstown (now Cobh) in Cork harbour in Ireland; this was a port of call, where she could receive orders through the telegraph system. Her instructions may have been to sail to Cork for orders, and not necessarily to Liverpool, but there could have been some other reason for her stop in Ireland, for example, to receive instructions on whether to engage a steam tug. She arrived at Liverpool on 19 April 1863, and her papers were handed to the Shipping Master on 23 April.

It was cotton from this vessel, *Peerless* (Flavin), which Raffles offered to deliver to Wichelhaus and Busch; this would be between 23 April and 10 May, when the ship was unloading in Queen's Dock. Raffles had earlier failed to tender delivery from *Peerless* (Major), which had docked in Liverpool almost exactly two months earlier. Clement Milward indicated that Raffles had no cotton on the earlier ship; from his instructions and from gossip in the barristers' mess he would no doubt be well informed about the situation.

The Lancashire Cotton Famine

So much for the maritime background. The commercial background is more complex. Immediately it was the Lancashire cotton famine, created by the blockade of the southern American states during the civil war.[11] The Lancashire cotton industry was, by the time the war began, the largest processing industry in the world, and had long relied primarily on cotton produced in the American south. The blockade cut off this source of supply more or less completely, and the consequent rise in production costs caused many spinners to close their mills, or reduce production. There was heavy unemployment and widespread distress. There were also many bankruptcies; the Liverpool figures rose from 175 in 1861, to 370 in 1862, fell in 1863 to 261, and rose again in 1864 to 387.[12] Spinners turned to other sources of supply, principally to India, and the price of cotton rose dramatically and became extremely volatile. The type of cotton involved in *Raffles* v. *Wichelhaus* more than trebled in value between 1861 and 1864. The sharpest rise was in 1862. In consequence there was much speculative dealing in the cotton market. What were classified by contemporaries as speculative purchases were purchases not made to fulfil specific orders; they were purchases made in the uncertain 'bullish' hope that the cotton could later be sold

---

[11] See R. A. Arnold, *The History of the Cotton Famine* (London, 1864); M. Williams, *Seven Years History of the Cotton Trade* (Liverpool, 1868); T. Ellison, *The Cotton Trade of Great Britain, including a History of the Liverpool Cotton Market* (Liverpool, 1886); D. Farnie, *The English Cotton Industry and the World Market 1815–1896* (Oxford, 1979).

[12] J. Watts, *The Facts of the Cotton Famine* (Manchester, 1866).

more profitably on a rising market, or the rights assigned. The individuals involved in *Raffles* v. *Wichelhaus* were active in this lucrative but hazardous trade. It was widely thought that there remained in the southern states a huge stock of cotton, which would be released onto the market once the war ended and collapse the price; hence any rumour of peace caused sharp falls. In reality most of the cotton in the south had been destroyed, and prices did not collapse immediately when the war ended. The dramatic fall took place later, between March and May of 1865. In this uncertain market it was possible to make or lose a fortune, and at this time techniques for 'bearish' speculation, and for hedging against price fluctuations, were not fully developed.[13] Speculative dealings in cotton long preceded the American Civil War, but the war increased the scale of such operations, and encouraged individuals who were not primarily cotton brokers or merchants, such as Wichelhaus and Busch, to intervene in the market.

The Trade in Cotton

Because of its highly variable character—no two bales of cotton were precisely alike in any respect—purchasing and sampling was regularly left to expert brokers. In the early part of the century the market came to be conducted by cotton merchants who, having purchased and imported cotton from growers abroad, sold through selling brokers to cotton spinners, who employed buying brokers. The trade was conducted under a system of unwritten custom operated in part by members of the Cotton Brokers' Association, originally an association of buying brokers, formed in April 1841. A relatively small number of individuals was involved, and Thomas Ellison, who was both historian of the industry and himself a broker, claimed, rather romantically: 'There was universal trustfulness, all transactions were plain, honest and above board.'[14] The smallness of the community involved, and the continuous interrelationships between brokers and merchants, probably did bring self-interest and probity into line with each other. William Winter Raffles belonged to this community. He appears in Liverpool street directories of the period as a cotton broker in partnership with Samuel Bulley, who was his brother-in-law; they became partners in 1854. He was born in 1830, the son of a noted independent minister, Thomas Raffles, and his wife, Mary, and was the younger brother of a barrister, Thomas Stamford Raffles, who acted as stipendiary magistrate in Liverpool.[15] Daniel Wichelhaus and Gustav Busch were interlopers, neither being a cotton broker or merchant. They were in partnership as general commission merchants, and at one time produced their

---

[13] For a fuller explanation see my 'The Origins of Futures Trading in the Liverpool Cotton Market' in P. Cane and J. Stapleton (eds.), *Essays for Patrick Atiyah* (Oxford, 1991), 179–208.

[14] Ellison, n. 11 above, 273–4.

[15] IGI; T. Ellison, n. 11 above, 254 (1864 is a typographical error for 1854); *DNB* xvi. 603–4; F. Boase, *Modern English Biography* (Truro, 1892–1921), 10–11; *The Times*, 24 Jan. 1891, 7; ILN, 7 Feb. 1891, 171. Raffles lived at 1 Sunnyside, Princes Park; his offices were at 11 Rumford Street; he earlier lived at 29 Mason Street, Edgehill.

own trade journal, *Wichelhaus and Busch's Market Report*, of which copies survive for 1854–5.[16] There were other Buschs in the city, one, E. F. Busch, being Austrian Consul, and the family was of Austrian extraction, as was Wichelhaus, who features with his wife, Clothilde, in the International Genealogical Index as the parents of no fewer than ten children born between 1856 and 1872. Gustav, too, was married to one Louisa, but they seem to have had only one child.

Incomplete records of the Cotton Brokers' Association survive in the Liverpool City Record Office. Originally its main function was to collect statistics on cotton sales and arrivals, from which it was possible to calculate the size of the stock of cotton in Liverpool, which was crucial to the price. The association also worked at improving the system of grading cotton, and encouraged the use of standard contract forms and standard trading rules. It also established a system for arbitrating the disputes which arose from time to time between brokers, and it was this system which explains the striking rarity of reported legal cases on the enormous cotton trade of the nineteenth century.

Most disputes concerned grade and quality; the variable nature of cotton makes it extremely difficult to classify into agreed objective grades; furthermore, individual bales could vary in weight and contain cotton of different grades. The variations are of considerable commercial importance, and the efficient operation of the market required rapid decisions by experts whenever a disagreement arose. The more difficult a commodity is to grade objectively, the more essential becomes the use of trusted experts who simply decide the matter. The ultimate example of the same phenomenon can be seen at dog shows. Up to a certain point, the dogs are ranked according to objective criteria—those that bite the judge, or are missing a leg, or whatever, are excluded, and those which conform to relatively objective breed requirements of deformation prosper. But at the end of the day there is no conceivable rational system for picking the dog of the show. So a judge simply peers at them in an imposing way, engages in a lot of what actors call 'business', and selects according to whim the lucky pit-bull or pekinese, which is then awarded the prize. If there are to be winners at dog shows, such a system is necessary. So it was in Liverpool. In the cotton market all brokers took their turn as arbitrators, and this no doubt produced a degree of confidence in the system which, I am told, is sometimes missing in the world of the dog show.

Speculation in Arrival Cotton

Purchases of cotton in Liverpool might be made on behalf of spinners who needed the material, or for re-export, or to hold the cotton and sell on if the

---

[16] They had offices at 1 Royal Bank Buildings and premises at 10 Dale Street. Daniel lived at 18 Grove Park and Gustav at 18 Church Street, Edgehill.

market moved appropriately. Market reports from as early as 1816 record sales in these three categories. Thus in 1825 Liverpool purchases for consumption totalled 622,106 bales, those 'on speculation' 302,000.[17] Statistics do not indicate the form of these dealings, but most would have been in 'spot' cotton, available for inspection in Liverpool. In the early nineteenth century the variability of the material militated against any considerable trade in cotton sold by description, cotton not on the spot for inspection when the contract was made. The evolution of more refined systems of grading, and the use of standard samples for comparison, increased the objectivity of grading. It became easier to determine whether a specific lot of cotton corresponded to the contractual description. This made it less perilous to buy cotton by description. So, too, did cheap arbitration, with mechanisms whereby prices could be adjusted to reflect minor departures from the contractual specification. But in the first half of the century these mechanisms were still relatively undeveloped. Nevertheless there did exist a trade in cotton *in transitu*, purchased for forward delivery by what were sometimes called 'time contracts', but in the cotton trade more commonly called 'contracts to arrive' or 'arrival contracts'.[18] They do not appear to be at all common until the 1850s; there are references in the *Economist* as early as 1851. By the 1860s, mention of them is standard form in market reports. Such contracts were attractive to speculators, since they avoided warehousing costs, so long as the cotton was promptly sold on once it arrived and, where there was no prepayment, they did not lock up capital.

Technological Change and Contractual Practice

Forward delivery or arrival contracts had long featured in the law; one of the earliest *assumpsit* cases, *Pykeryng* v. *Thurgoode* (1532) involved such a contract, made by a brewer to ensure access to a supply of malt to maintain his trade, and no doubt to guard against any price rise.[19] Their use in the cotton trade was encouraged partly by the development of grading and arbitration systems, but also by technological developments, which enabled information and documents to travel more quickly than bulk cargoes of cotton. J. Todd, writing in 1934, pointed out that the invention of the steamship, and its use in the Atlantic by the Cunard line, enabled news of the American crop size, and samples, to be carried across the Atlantic ahead of the slower sailing vessels transporting cotton in bulk: 'Merchants were advised of cotton coming by certain ships, and transactions took place in cotton "to arrive", which accounts for the fact that in certain

---

[17] Figures from 1811 are given by Ellison, n. 11 above, and E. J. Donnell, *Chronological and Statistical History of Cotton* (New York, 1872) gives figures from 1821.

[18] For legal discussion see J. P. Benjamin, *A Treatise on the Law of Sale or Personal Property* (London, 1868), 497.

[19] J. H. Baker, *The Reports of Sir John Spelman* (London, 1977), 94 SS 247.

offices in Liverpool to-day the futures department is still called the Arrivals Department.'[20] Todd, however, was wrong in thinking that arrival contracts first became common in the Atlantic trade; early references usually relate to the trade in East Indian cotton. As we have seen, in the 1860s mail from Bombay could reach England in three weeks or so; as early as 1849 the time was down to one month.[21] But sailing vessels took around four months, as did the two ships *Peerless*. The Suez Canal opened in 1869, reducing the distance from Bombay from about 11,000 miles to 6,300, but the canal was not practicable for large sailing vessels, and they long remained more economical for the carriage of non-perishable bulk cargoes on routes where suitable wind systems existed. Until the development of the compound engine, steamships consumed very large quantities of coal; bunkers and engines severely limited cargo space, and they required large crews. Indeed they relied on sailing vessels for their supplies of fuel, and catered principally for passengers, mail, and the luxury trade.[22]

In addition to the mails, there were other mechanisms whereby information could travel much faster than cotton. Ports of call such as Cork or Falmouth were in direct touch with Liverpool through the telegraph system—Cork was connected in 1852. International telegraph services enhanced the possibilities. The telegraph between England and India, which passed down the Persian Gulf, was not effectively connected until February 1865, but parts of the distance were served before this. Lines at the European end reached Corfu and Malta in 1857 and Aden by 1859. The Red Sea cable from Suez to Karachi was connected in 1860, though it often failed.[23] In addition the practice of mutual speaking and reporting of ships on passage, and the publication of reports in *Lloyd's List*, made available news on the progress of voyages long before the development of radio communications. In the commercial world there would also be various sources of private information, not reported to Lloyd's.

The Form of Arrival Contracts

One might expect that arrival contracts would specify a time for delivery, since this was of critical importance to the purchaser of the cotton. But, again for technological reasons, this was not the practice; the problem was that, although one could discover, after an interval, when a sailing vessel had left its port of loading or approximately when it proposed to leave, it was uncertain when, if

[20] J. Todd, *The Marketing of Cotton* (London, 1934), 66.

[21] See *The Economist*, 6 Jan. 1849, 16.

[22] Some cotton did come through the canal; *The Times*, 31 May 1870, mentioned instances of cotton carried as part of the cargo of vessels using the canal.

[23] See in particular the article by J. Fleming in *Encyclopedia Britannica* (11th ed., 1911), xxvi, 'Telegraphs'; J. Kieve, *The Electric Telegraph: A Social and Economic History* (Newton Abbott, 1973); F. J. Goldsmid, *Telegraph and Travel: A Narrative of the Formation and Development of Telegraphic Communication between England and India* (London, 1874).

1. The Memorial to Edward and Johan Shelley in the church of the Holy Sepulchre, Warminghurst

2. Warminghurst Place, where Edward Shelley died in 1554, and where William Penn was later to draft the Constitution of Pennsylvania

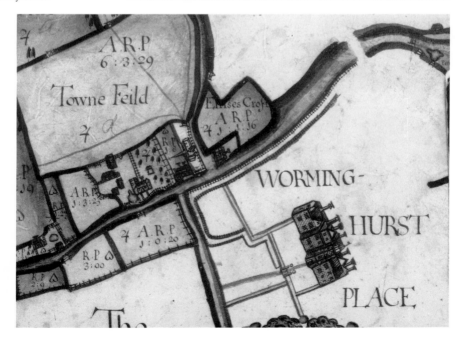

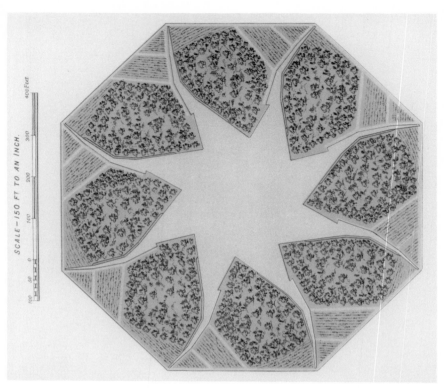

4. Plan of the Lakenheath and Caledon Decoy, Suffolk

3. George Skelton, decoy man of the South Acre Decoy, Norfolk, 1854

9. John E. Rylands (1801–88), the Wellington of Commerce

10. Mrs Carlill, aged 87, holds the hand of the future Admiral Sir Stephen Carlill

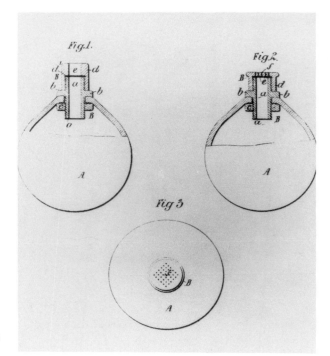

11. The patent drawings of the Smoke Ball

12. Frederick Roe's riposte to the loss of the action

at all, it would arrive. Hence early arrival contracts did not specify the time for delivery even within a fixed period. Instead, they simply identified which shipment of cotton was being sold; presumably the rationale of this was that the buyer, so long as he knew this, could make his own estimate, within the limits of what information was to hand, of the approximate date the shipment would arrive. It is said that at first such arrival contracts were only made when arrival was imminent, the ship having been reported off Point Lynas, some fifty miles from Liverpool, where there was a signal station. This may well have been the common practice, but there must always have been exceptions, with such contracts being made when the vessel was still on the high seas.

No doubt various contractual mechanisms were used in the early days to identify the shipment and, indirectly, the time of arrival. One was to identify the ship by a 'ship-named' contract. Another, which could be combined with it, as in *Raffles* v. *Wichelhaus*, was to name the port as well—'ex *Peerless* Bombay'. A contract could also specify a time of departure, not a day but a period—'ex *Peerless* Bombay guaranteed October shipment'. As for the bales of cotton themselves, more precise identification was achieved by supplying the buyer with the marks on the bales, which would be recorded on the first mate's cargo manifest. So far as I know, the contracts never did this. The marks were declared when the shipping papers or the ship itself arrived. Market reports of contracts, which were published in *The Economist* and the commercial press, show that in mid-1862, in response to the imminent cotton famine, there was much dealing in cotton to arrive from India, some contracts being made for cotton which would not arrive for as much as six months ahead. Contractual practices differed, but naming a month for shipment became more common, probably because contracts were now being made so long in advance. When contracts were usually made only when arrival was imminent, the month of shipment was no longer important, but when arrival was well in the future, it was. Probably it was usual to name the ship, and it would have been very inconvenient not to do this, though later examples of contracts which did not specify the ship are known. In those I have noted the ship was, however, declared before arrival, and the month of shipment named.[24]

The Form of the Contract in Raffles v. *Wichelhaus*

We know that the contract in *Raffles* v. *Wichelhaus* was a 'ship-named' and 'port-named' contract; its failure to specify the month of shipment may simply reflect the conservatism of commercial practice. The full text has not been preserved. However, in June of 1863 a standard form of contract for cotton to arrive was settled by the Liverpool Cotton Brokers' Association; the association had decided

---

[24] *Morgan* v. *Gath* (1865) 13 TLR 96; *Thorburn* v. *Barnes* (1867) 16 TLR 10.

in January of that year to set up a committee to codify the customs of the trade, particularly those governing contracts to arrive, which had given rise to disputes at a time when there was much speculation in cotton.[25] The codification was achieved by incorporating the customary understandings in the contract form itself. The form of contract became the object of controversy in *The Times* in November 1863, and was thus published:[26]

FORM OF CONTRACT FOR COTTON TO ARRIVE

Liverpool, . . . 186

We have this day . . . to arrive, ex . . . from . . . Guaranteed . . .

This is the form employed by Raffles and Wichelhaus; the approved standard form no doubt followed what was already common practice. The document then spelled out the customary understandings in the text. Later, as the trading rules became more elaborate, they were set out in a code to which standard form contracts made reference. The 1863 text continued:

In case of dispute arising out of this contract the matter to be referred to two respectable brokers for settlement, who shall decide as to quality and the allowance, if any, to be made.

The cotton to be taken from the . . .'[27] with customary allowances of tare and draft[28] and the invoice to be dated from the date of delivery of the last bale from the . . . or. . . .[29]

Should, however, the vessel or vessels be lost, the contract to be void; but should the cotton be transhipped to other vessels arriving at the port, the contract for such portion to hold good.

Payment within ten days from date of invoice, or before delivery, if required, equal to cash in ten days and three months.

The contract in *Raffles* v. *Wichelhaus* would have been made on a short printed form, probably supplied by Raffles, which would resemble the standard form of 1863. It may or may not have incorporated the trade customs in the text precisely in the same way as did the standard form. In argument Clement Milward explicitly referred, as we have seen, to the understanding over possible loss of the vessel, and this suggests that the contract did closely resemble the standard form. But traders might use their own forms if they wished. One reported case[30] contains the complete text of a cotton contract to arrive, dated 2 October 1863, which illustrates this point. The contract was for cotton 'per ship or ships from Calcutta, and guaranteed October shipment'. The carrying vessels were declared later. The contract was based on the standard form, but included other terms. These provided that the contract was not to be vitiated by slight discrepancies

---

[25] Ellison, n. 11 above, at 274. The records of the association for this year do not exist. The earliest set of trading rules for arrival contracts I have located is of 1867.

[26] 12 Nov. 1863, 6.   [27] Ship, quay, or warehouse.

[28] The wrappings of bales, and loss in repacking.

[29] Presumably ship, quay, or warehouse.

[30] *Neill* v. *Whitworth*, 18 CB (NS) 435, 1 LRCP 684.

in the marks, that the cotton be merchantable, and that cotton which was damaged and could not be made merchantable might be rejected.

Contracts of this type were called 'shipments', but in the same year we have an early example of a new form of contract, in which the time of arrival was specified in coupled months; a report for 29 November records a sale of 'New Dhollerah to arrive in March and April'.[31] Such contracts came to be called 'deliveries', and in time superseded 'shipments'. They were a response to technological changes which made the duration of voyages increasingly predictable, but although by about 1860 voyages by sailing ships from India had, disasters apart, become predictable within about a month, it took some time for contractual practices to adjust to this new state of affairs. Out of contracts for 'deliveries' evolved the form of contract which was to be used in futures trading, but that is another story.[32]

The Date of the Contract

Although the reports do not give us the date of the contract, it can be deduced with some confidence. The arguments are lengthy and somewhat tedious, and I shall not repeat them here.[33] It is likely that the contract was made at a time when the spot price for 'middling fair' Dhollerah was about $17\frac{1}{4}d.$ per pound, or a little below, the purchasers believing that the price would rise beyond this figure by the time the cotton arrived. This suggests a contract during the week ending 10 January 1863, when spot sales of this type and grade were between $17d.$ and $17\frac{3}{8}d.$

There is evidence that there was massive speculative dealing at this time, and that sales of such cotton for October shipment were being made. As it happens, there is also evidence of sales of Dhollerah for December shipment at the same time,[34] contracts made before it was known in England that the vessel had sailed from Bombay. Raffles must have been one of those who made such contracts, for which the traditional contractual form, which did not uniquely identify the ship, happened to be particularly inappropriate.

If I am right in thinking that the contract was made in the week suggested, only one ship *Peerless, Peerless* (Major), was known in England to be on passage from Bombay to England at that time. But it is also the case that only one ship *Peerless, Peerless* (Flavin), was known in England to be lying in the port of Bombay loading cotton; in fact, the vessel was also at sea, but this was not yet reported in England. In consequence it is not difficult to see why a misunderstanding could have arisen, even if everyone concerned diligently studied the

---

[31] *The Economist*, 29 Nov. 1862, 1333.   [32] See my article cited in n. 13 above.

[33] They are given in my article in the *Cardozo Law Review* at 314–320, and involve an analysis of the system of cotton grading.

[34] *The Economist*, 17 Jan. 1863, 76.

published reports of shipping movements. An additional factor could have been the change in registration for *Peerless* (Flavin) to Liverpool in May of 1862; conceivably Wichelhaus and Busch might have had cotton on *Peerless* (Major) before, and been under the impression when the contract was made that there was only one ship of this name trading between India and Liverpool. For *Peerless* (Major) on her previous voyage, between 17 November 1860 and 12 September 1861, had been to Calcutta, whereas *Peerless* (Flavin) had sailed to Australia and North America, and had not been involved in the cotton trade.

Arrival and Litigation

Peerless (Major), the October ship, arrived at Liverpool on 18 February, and on 26 February *Gore's General Advertiser* reported her unloading in the Albert Dock. She had nearly four thousand bales on board. *The Times* reported on 19 February: 'the cotton market continues peculiarly dull and inanimate, and this days sales do not exceed 1,500 bales—500 on speculation.' *The Economist* quotes the London spot prices for Dhollerah 'middling' on 21 February 1863 as $15\frac{1}{4}d$. and on 28 February as $15d$. So the Liverpool price for 'middling fair' would be well below the contract price at the time the vessel was discharging, for prices continued to fall. Clearly, if Raffles had any cotton of the appropriate type and grade on *Peerless* (Major), he would have happily tendered delivery; the conclusion must be that he did not think his contract related to this vessel. And plainly Wichelhaus and Busch could, at this point, have complained to Raffles about his failure to deliver; they could indeed have sued him. But this they did not do, and it is easy to see why; they had no economic motive for complaining. As matters stood they had made a bad bargain.

The second vessel, *Peerless* (Flavin), arrived on Sunday, 19 April, and was in Queen's Dock by 23 April. Her cargo was more exotic, including eleven tons of buffalo horns, but again it consisted principally of cotton—1,079 bales for designated merchants, and 3,723 and two half bales not so bespoke. By now the Liverpool price of Dhollerah cotton had risen; Dhollerah 'fair' stood at $17\frac{1}{2}d$. on 24 April and fell back to $17\frac{1}{4}d$. in the following week. 'Middling fair' would be fetching around $16\frac{3}{4}d$. So, although the situation was better than it had been when the first *Peerless* arrived, it was still no good for Wichelhaus and Busch, who would have made a substantial loss if they accepted delivery. Of course by now, when the misunderstanding must have come to Raffles's attention, it would have been far too late for him to retrieve the position by tendering cotton off the earlier vessel even if he had owned cotton on it.

So the parties came to litigate. This was very unusual behaviour in the cotton trade. The customary practice was to arbitrate disputes. Disputes over the material itself seem always to have been arbitrated; there was no conceivable reason why anyone would go to court over such a dispute. Quite apart from the delay and cost involved, it would have been ridiculous to accept a jury decision from persons not expert in sampling cotton, necessarily based on expert evidence from those who were, instead of accepting the direct decision of a panel of experts. As we have seen, the standard form contract incorporates this custom of arbitration, but can be read as only relating to disputes over quality. It was not until 1871 that the trading rules required all disputes of whatever kind to be arbitrated, and at the time of *Raffles* v. *Wichelhaus* submission to arbitration was voluntary.[35] The arbitrators at this time for disputes which did not concern quality were the President of the Cotton Brokers' Association, the Vice-President, and an umpire. Why was this particular dispute not arbitrated?

Any answer to this question must be somewhat speculative. We do not know precisely how or when when the misunderstanding came to light, though, since a professional broker would read the commercial press daily, he must have become aware of the existence of two ships *Peerless* from Bombay at the latest when *Peerless* (Major) docked. Relations may have been soured by two factors. The first was that Wichelhaus and Busch were not cotton brokers; they were outside the close-knit world of the members of the Cotton Brokers' Association. They were also foreigners and, given the prejudices of the time, this would perhaps have made them appear to Raffles even more as outsiders.[36] The second is that Raffles appears to have been a somewhat quarrelsome person. He appears in the records of the Cotton Brokers' Association on several occasions involved in disputes, and on one occasion a firm of brokers lodged a complaint against him for what they regarded as aggressive behaviour.[37] In addition his desperate recourse to litigation may have been provoked by the feeling that Wichelhaus and Busch had not themselves behaved with decency in the matter. To appreciate why we need to consider how the matter would probably have been handled by arbitrators.

The Sensible Solution

Assuming that there had been a genuine misunderstanding when the contract was made, what harm had this done to Wichelhaus and Busch? Surely none. Given the way prices had fallen, whichever ship they took delivery from they had made a losing contract, and if cotton had been delivered to them from *Peerless* (Major), the October ship they said they had in mind, they would have suffered a *larger* loss than they would incur by accepting delivery from *Peerless* (Flavin), the December ship. In common sense they had nothing to complain

---

[35] For arbitration in the cotton market see my article n. 13 above, 182–3.

[36] I previously thought they were Jews, and that this might explain prejudice, but I now think this is unlikely.

[37] See Liverpool Record Office, MS COT 1/2 (13 Apr. 1866); 3/1 (1 Mar. 1873); 3/2 (5 Oct. 1874).

about. This must surely be the point of Clement Milward's remark, reported in the *Law Journal* report: 'If the defendants had said their speculation had fallen through in consequence [i.e. of the misunderstanding], it might have been different.' The defendant's speculation had indeed failed, in that it had not been profitable, but the consequence of the misunderstanding, which led to tender of cotton from the second ship, had, if they had accepted the cotton, reduced their loss, not increased it. Hence their speculation had not failed because of the misunderstanding at all, and this must have been the point Raffles's counsel was making.

Had the matter been handled by arbitrators, they might well have decided that the sensible and decent way to handle the problem, the equitable solution, would be to require Wichelhaus and Busch to take delivery from Raffles, and consider themselves lucky not to have lost more. Or the arbitrators might have decided to adopt a solution which courts have always been reluctant to do—split the difference; this would have been rather less favourable to them. What they would surely never have countenanced would be for them to escape all liability on their losing contract. Furthermore, if Wichelhaus and Busch, knowing by the time the first ship docked that another *Peerless* was on passage for Liverpool, had deliberately kept quiet when no cotton was tendered off *Peerless* (Major), in the hope that when the second *Peerless*, *Peerless* (Flavin), arrived, the price would have moved in their favour to something over $17\frac{1}{4}d.$, this might well be viewed as somewhat sharp practice. It would hardly seem fair to allow them both to have their cake and eat it by now refusing to accept the cotton off the second ship when it turned out that their hopes of a price rise had proved vain. Raffles may well have litigated in irritation because of what he would view as conduct bordering on the disreputable; Wichelhaus and Busch should have done the decent thing, either accept the cotton and pay for it, or at least agree to arbitration. And if my suggestions as to the likely consequences of arbitration are correct, then it is easy to see why Wichelhaus and Busch preferred litigation, which they must have been advised they had a reasonable chance of winning.

The Aftermath of the Affair

As for the men of business involved in the case, William Winter Raffles retired in 1868 and died in 1880 or 1881.[38] Daniel Wichelhaus and Gustav Busch remained in partnership until 1883, when Daniel died; Gustav Busch became the partner of one Farrar, remaining in business until the 1890s. Like other prosperous Liverpool businessmen, he acquired a country retreat in the Lake District, now accessible for weekends by train. The house was called Fallbarrow, and is on Lake Windermere; my nephew tells me that it is today in use as an outdoor-pursuits centre. As for the seamen and their ships, the common sailors whose

[38] I have not located a death certificate.

labours brought the Dhollerah cotton to Liverpool disappear from history in the sense that it would require a disproportionate effort to discover what became of them. No doubt some met violent ends, falling from the yards, or from the futtock shrouds, or stabbed in brawls in sailor-towns, or died of the illnesses which flourished in the dripping fo'c' sles of the days of sail. Others would end their days in the workhouse, the common lot of sailors. As for the master mariners, Lloyd's *Captains' Registers* record that, for both Thomas Flavin and Robert Major, *Peerless* was their last command. Thomas Flavin remained master of his vessel until 1870; she then passed into the ownership of John Hall of Newcastle, who changed her registration to that port, from which she probably operated as a collier, for which a leaky elderly vessel remained suitable. In 1881, by which time she was owned by the Peerless Ship Company of Limerick, though managed from Newcastle, she was sold French, and her register was closed in December 1881. Her last English captain was Joseph Noble, and under him she sailed to Marseilles on two occasions, and on the second voyage was sold there. I have been unable, in spite of correspondence with French maritime museums, to discover what became of her thereafter, or what new name she sailed under for her final voyages, for it is unlikely that she would retain the name *Peerless*. She continues, however, to appear in Lloyd's register as *Peerless* until 1885.

Robert Major kept command of his *Peerless* until 1867. She later met an end which is, for a sailing ship, entirely appropriate and suitably dramatic. On 9 December 1870 she was abandoned in a sinking condition seventy miles north-north-west of Cape Horn. She was, at the time, on a voyage from Newport in Wales to Callao. Her crew survived, and were landed at Coquimbo; they had been rescued by the Norwegian barque, *Elise Mathilde*. The articles for this voyage survive. Attached to them is a letter from her Captain, Alfred Millidge, dated 3 March 1871, and it somehow contrives to give a reality to the terrible final scene:

I have to inform you that the official Log Book of the Ship *Peerless* was lost at the time we were being transferred to the Barque Elise Mathilde in the night of the 9th. December last when we had to abandon the Ship of [*sic*] Cape Horn on her voyage from Newport to Callao.

> Your obedient servant,
> Alfred Millidge.
> Late Master of the Ship Peerless.

It had indeed not been a happy voyage. One apprentice drowned when the ship called at Rio, and six of the crew of thirty-two deserted there. It is fairly obvious why. As an elderly wooden vessel she would be leaking badly, and require continuous pumping, work carried out with no mechanical help by the crew. This explains the size of the crew, the desertions, and the eventual abandonment when the exhausted and reduced crew could hold back the water no longer. I am reminded of the lines in the well known sea shanty, *Leave Her Johnnie, Leave Her*:

> Its pump or drown,
> The Old Man said,
> Or else damn soon,
> Ye'll all be dead.[39]

But fate was, at least on this occasion, kinder to the crew of the *Peerless*.

The Factors Behind the Rise to Fame of Raffles v. Wichelhaus

Both vessels were to enjoy a posthumous fame greater than they had enjoyed in life. For this the explanation lies partly in the general history of the law of contract, and partly in the history of legal education, particularly a form of it which developed in the Harvard Law School in the late nineteenth century.

From about 1800 there took place a very considerable elaboration of the Anglo-American law of contract.[40] Lawyers came to believe that contractual disputes should be analysed and resolved by reference to general principles of law of a highly abstract nature. These principles, in their turn, were thought to elaborate the fundamental notion that contractual obligations all derived from the voluntary agreement of the parties to the contract, from what some called the 'meeting of the minds' of the contractors. In working out this idea the common lawyers, to a considerable extent, borrowed principles and categories from the stock of ideas employed by continental legal writers. They, in their turn, had borrowed conceptions used, and to a very limited extent developed, by the Roman jurists of antiquity, who had conceived the idea that certain forms of contract were consensual. In consensual contracts the obligations of the parties derived not from the use of some special formality or ceremony, nor from some action, but simply from the metaphysical fact of agreement, from the *consensus ad idem*, agreement as to the same thing. Such fragmentary texts of the Roman lawyers as had survived in the Emperor Justinian's sixth-century restatement of the law, the *Digest*, became an object of study in European universities from the twelfth century onwards, and in the nineteenth century the ideas developed in their exegesis began to permeate the common law, hitherto a somewhat impoverished intellectual system.

Contractual obligations, the theorists supposed, all derived from the joint wills of the contractors, which became one will through the mysterious phenomenon of agreement. Given this organizing myth, whose centrality and capacity to

---

[39] Text from S. Hugill, *Shanties of the Seven Seas* (Oxford, 1966), 297.

[40] See my 'Innovation in Nineteenth Century Contract Law' (1975) 91 *LQR* 247 reprinted in *Legal Theory and Legal History. Essays on the Common Law* (London, 1987), 171; and P. S. Atiyah, *The Rise and Fall of Freedom of Contract* (Oxford, 1979).

encourage the suspension of disbelief rather resembles the myth of the free market in the thinking of economists, situations in which the contractors have misunderstood each other, or reached an apparent agreement under some mistake or misapprehension presented a special problem. Centuries earlier the Roman jurist, Ulpian, writing about the contract of sale, which jurists classified as a consensual contract, had put the point bluntly:

It is obvious that agreement is of the essence in sale and purchase; the purchase is not valid if there be disagreement over the contract itself, the price, or any other element of the sale. Hence, if I thought that I was buying the Cornelian farm and you that you were selling the Sempronian, the sale is void because we were not agreed upon the thing sold . . . Of course, if we are merely in disagreement over the name but at one on the actual thing there is no doubt that the contract is good.[41]

Ideas of this character, sometimes categorized as dealing with the effect of *mistake* (the latin *error*) in contract, came to be received into English law, and thereby into American law, which at this time did little more than reflect English law, and they posed a special difficulty when the parties appeared to have agreed. Was apparent agreement sufficient, or must there be a true agreement, a real meeting of the minds?

The nineteenth century also saw great developments in legal education; here America led the way, for in England such legal education as there was amounted to little. But in America there were thriving law schools. In 1870 Langdell, as we have seen, decided to embark on a new experiment in legal education through the use of leading cases, using the law of contract as his vehicle. The reason for this choice was that legal thinkers of the time thought that contract law possessed a pre-eminent social significance. It was through the formation of contracts that free and independent individuals could arrange their mutual affairs to suit their own preferences and choices. Contract law was indeed the legal instrument of progress and social improvement. Again there is a close similarity between this legal theory and the economic theory which extols the benefits to society of free trade and free markets.

In common with many intellectually minded lawyers of the time, Langdell believed that the case law both was, and ought to be, based upon a finite set of legal principles. These principles lurked beneath the apparently disorderly farrago of case reports, and invited discovery. So law was a science, in the sense that it possessed a deep rational structure, of which knowledge of a systematic kind could be had. The function of the legal scientist was to identify, formulate, organize, and expound this structure.[42] He married this theory to an educational technique. His students were to be given the opportunity, under his guidance,

---

[41] *Digest*, xviii, 9.
[42] See above 4. I have elaborated accounts of legal science in 'The Rise and Fall of the Legal Treatise. Legal Principles and the Forms of Legal Literature', 48 *UCLR* 632, and in a more light-hearted form in 'Legal Iconoclasm and Legal Ideals', 58 *UCINLR* 819.

to become legal scientists. To assist them he published in 1871 a selection of suitable cases: *A Selection of Cases on the Law of Contracts*, with a preface explaining the theory.

This idea of a case book was, as I have explained, derivative.[43] What Langdell did was to marry such a collection to a particular system of teaching, the case class, and to abandon the use of formal lectures. In the case class, in theory at least, the teacher does not lecture to the students but, by questions and critical comments on the answers given, persuades them to work out for themselves what the principles of the law are. In reality what happened, and still happens, is that a fair amount of the time in a class is occupied by disorderly dogmatic exposition by the teacher, and that the function which had, before Langdell, been performed by formal lectures came to be performed by books. Langdell, presumably exasperated by the failure of the students to get the answers right, himself, as we have seen, published *A Summary of the Law of Contract* in 1879. It was in effect a 'nutshell'.

But although Langdell's ideal and the reality were always fairly far apart, the case class continues to thrive in American laws schools, and has even been celebrated in the film *Paper Chase*. There are other published accounts of the excitement or horror it has generated in law students.

Judah Benjamin and the Rise of Raffles v. Wichelhaus

The first edition of Langdell's case book did not include *Raffles* v. *Wichelhaus*, which still languished in well-deserved obscurity. Its rise to fame really began in 1875, when it was discussed by a barrister who practised on the Northern Circuit, the American exile to the English bar, Judah P. Benjamin. He had been called in 1866, but in spite of his great ability he had not prospered on circuit. His treatise on the law of sale established his reputation; in it he discussed the case. He may well have heard stories about the case from fellow barristers, and a few years after it he acted as legal adviser to the Liverpool Cotton Brokers' Association.[44] His treatise was much the fullest treatment of the law of sale which had yet appeared in the common law world. The case is mentioned in Book I, which deals with the formation of contract, when Benjamin is discussing the need for 'mutual assent'. From this requirement he deduces that 'where, through some mistake of fact, each was assenting to a different contract, there is no real valid agreement, notwithstanding the apparent mutual assent'.[45] On the following page appears *Raffles* v. *Wichelhaus* and, after summarizing the report, he adds, 'on demurrer, held that on this state of facts there was no *consensus ad idem*, no contract at all between the parties'. In reality, as we have seen, there was no such holding; Benjamin is attributing this view to the judges. Later on, however, he hedges his bets by saying that when the mistake is by one party only:

---

[43] See above 5.   [44] See MS COT 3/1 (1872).   [45] N. 18 above, 51 in ch. 3.

It must be borne in mind that the general rule of law is, that whatever a man's *real* intention may be, if he *manifests* an intention to another party, so as to induce the latter to act upon it in making a contract, he will be estopped from denying that the intention was manifested was his real intention.

How this affected *Raffles* v. *Wichelhaus* he does not say; the two principles seem, if not to contradict each other, to pull in different directions. It was part of the tradition of legal science in which Benjamin was writing, however, that the law was conceived as based on principles which were all mutually compatible. Thus they provided one right answer to any legal problem.

In the second English edition of his book, published in 1873, Benjamin amplified his discussion, perhaps because he saw that in the earlier edition he seemed almost to contradict himself.[46] If there are two ships *Peerless*, as in *Raffles* v. *Wichelhaus*, and the parties are referring to different ships, there is no contract. But if there had been only one *Peerless*, and one party meant to refer to another ship called *Peeress*, then there would be a good contract:

Men can only bargain by mutual communication, and if A's proposal were unmistakable, as if it were made in writing, and B's answer was an unequivocal and unconditional acceptance, B would be bound, however clearly he might afterwards make it appear that he was *thinking* of a different vessel.

There was indeed at the time a ship called *Peeress*, which worked on the Atlantic run to the United States; perhaps Benjamin knew the ship or had even travelled on it. Later in his treatise, the case is used to illustrate an exception to the rule that you cannot use parol evidence to modify the terms of a written contract. We are now told that:

Where a bargain was made for the sale of cotton, 'to arrive *ex Peerless* from Bombay', parol evidence was held admissible to show that there were two ships *Peerless* from Bombay, and that the ship *Peerless* intended by the vendor was a different ship *Peerless* from that intended by the buyer, so as to establish a mistake defeating the contract for want of a *consensus ad idem*.

In reality no parol evidence had been admitted; the case never went to a jury at all. Benjamin was embroidering the laconic report. His discussion of the decision, with the attribution of reasoning to the judges for which there is no direct evidence, must have done much to launch it on its subsequent career.

True Consent and Contract Theory

When in 1876 the English writer, Sir Frederick Pollock, published his *Principles of Contract at Law and in Equity*, he must have been familiar with Benjamin's

---

[46] N. 18 above, 347–8.

work. Now Pollock firmly believed that unless there was true consent there could be no contract. In setting out the basic elements of a contract he said: 'the next thing is that these persons [i.e. the contractors] have a distinct intention, and the intention of both or all of them is the same. Without this one obviously cannot say there is an agreement.'[47] Awareness of each other's intention, he explained, was a quite distinct contractual requirement. Later he discusses 'mistake as excluding true consent', and, following the Roman jurists, one sort of mistake he discusses was mistake as to the specific thing—commentators on Roman law call this *error in corpore* (mistake as to the subject-matter). For Pollock, *Raffles* v. *Wichelhaus* was a godsend, for it was very difficult to find any cases which could be used to illustrate and support his true consent theory:

A striking modern case of this kind is *Raffles* v. *Wichelhaus* . . . the plea was held good, for 'the defendant only bought that cotton which was to arrive by a particular ship' and to hold that he bought cotton to arrive in any ship of that name would have been 'imposing on the defendant a contract different from that which he entered into'.[48]

Pollock's view of the case appears to involve the idea that Wichelhaus and Busch had indeed made a contract to purchase some cotton, but not the cotton tendered by Raffles; this differed from Benjamin's view, which was that there was no contract at all. Pollock's analysis was attributed in a footnote to Pollock CB and Martin B. In reality neither had said anything about mistake, or about the need for true consent, though the remark last quoted was uttered by Martin B in the course of the argument. What Pollock CB had in fact said was: 'it is like a contract for the purchase of wine coming from a particular estate in France or Spain, where there are two estates of that name.' The point he was making was that the identity of the thing sold might be commercially relevant, though of course the example goes to quality, not to time.

Pollock's theory of contract was derived from the German jurist, Friedrich Karl von Savigny's *System des Heutigen römischen Rechts* (1840). Pollock adopted Savigny's definition of contract.[49] Sir William Anson, another true-consent man, included the case in his very successful treatise on contract, published in 1879.[50] So it was that, in the same year, Langdell included the case in the second edition of his case book, no doubt influenced by Benjamin and Pollock. In his summary of the law, a dogmatic statement of the principles of contract, he explained that normally the intentions of the parties had to be discovered from what they did, so that if they appeared to agree it would normally be presumed that their minds were at one. But, in conformity with the true-consent theory, he added: 'the performance of the acts will avail nothing, if mutual consent is found to be lacking.' *Raffles* v. *Wichelhaus* was made to serve as an illustration of this dogma. In 1880 it was used to illustrate 'mistake arising out of the name of the

---

[47] 2.   [48] See 472 (ref. is to edn. of 1888).   [49] At para. 140.
[50] W. Anson, *Principles of the English Law of Contract* (Oxford, 1879), 130.

object' by Sir Thomas Erskine Holland in his *Elements of Jurisprudence*, now a forgotten work, but in its time a very successful book.[51]

The case was on its way to join the immortals. Its fame was further enhanced in 1881 when Oliver Wendell Holmes Junior, in *The Common Law*, attacked the interpretation placed upon the case by Pollock, Anson, Langdell, and Holland. His attack was part of the development of his own theory, which was that 'the law has nothing to do with the actual state of the parties' minds'. Holmes applied this theory generally in the law; though the contrary is often assumed, he, too, like Langdell and others of the period, believed in legal science, and in *The Common Law* he argued, with desperate ingenuity, that the common law was based on a single finite set of ultimate principles. Nothing so establishes a young writer as a radical attack on the establishment, and Holmes argued that the contractual establishment of his time had got *Raffles* v. *Wichelhaus* entirely wrong. Holmes soon acquired converts to the new faith. In 1886 Holland recanted in the third edition of his *Elements of Jurisprudence*, attributing his conversion to Rudolf Leonhard's *Der Irrtum bei nichtigen Vertragen*, though the credit, it has been argued, should really belong to Holmes.[52] A letter by Holland to Holmes, dated 21 March 1888, refers to the dispute, noting that A. V. Dicey had been persuaded, but that 'Anson and Pollock are still obdurate'.[53] *Raffles* v. *Wichelhaus* had now been cast as the focus of a high theoretical debate on the basis of contractual obligation, a debate of considerable intellectual interest but of virtually no practical importance.

In time, news of Harvard's exciting new system of legal education filtered back across the Atlantic, and in 1886 Gerard B. Finch, who taught law at Queen's College, Cambridge, and who is today an obscure figure, published his *A Selection of Cases on the English Law of Contract*, designed to be 'a Text-Book for Law Students in the Universities'. In the introduction he extolled the virtues of the Langdellian system, which he attempted to introduce into Britain. He had absolutely no success; the sturdy individualism of English law students, or, if you like, their innate idleness, made it impossible to introduce so authoritarian and disciplined a system.[54] Finch inevitably included *Raffles* v. *Wichelhaus* in his fifth chapter on 'Reality of Consent'.

---

[51] T. E. Holland, *The Elements of Jurisprudence* at 176. Holland cites Justinian's *Institutes*, iii, 19.23.

[52] T. E. Holland, *The Elements of Jurisprudence* (3rd edn., Oxford, 1886), 194–5, 213, and 216; cf. the 2nd edn. (Oxford, 1882), 199. For discussion see M. de W. Howe, *Justice Oliver Holmes: The Proving Years 1870–1882* (Cambridge, Mass., 1963), 144–6.

[53] O. W. Holmes Jr., Papers, Harvard Law School Library, MS Box 44, folder 6. The letter in question accompanied a copy of Holland's 4th ed. of 1 Dec. 1887.

[54] Gerard B. Finch (1853–1913) was a graduate of Queen's College and a barrister of Lincoln's Inn, where he practised as an equity draftsman and conveyancer. He returned to teach at Cambridge, and in 1885 published an inaugural lecture, 'Legal Education. Its Aims and Methods'. His casebook (Cambridge) was edited by R. S. Wright and W. E. Buckland in 1896, and later, in 1922, was reborn as C. S. Kenny, *A Selection of Cases Illustrative of the Law of Contract* (Cambridge, 1922). Finch appears to have had some connection with Francis Miles Finch (1827–1907), a New York judge who

In the American case books, and in the classes based upon them, it became a set piece, and in the English treatises, too, it continues to flourish. And from time to time academics add some new twist to the discussions of the decision. The most entertaining in modern times has been Grant Gilmore's treatment in *The Death of Contract*, published in 1974, a book which made a remarkable impression on the world of academic law. Gilmore, who never felt inhibited by mere ignorance from writing legal history, ridiculed the judges who heard the case, claiming that they stupidly failed to grasp the fact that the identity of the carrying ship was, from a commercial point of view, wholly immaterial. Absolutely everything Gilmore said about the case is wrong, but I am by no means sure that this matters very much. It certainly should not discourage anyone from reading his entertaining and enlightening book, which merely needs to be treated with extreme caution on matters historical.

Indeed the real beauty of *Raffles* v. *Wichelhaus* lies in the utter obscurity surrounding both the dispute itself and the legal decision which that dispute generated. In a sense, the less one knows about the case the more fun can be extracted from it. The absence of any reasoned judicial opinion makes the case into an empty vessel, into which theories of contract law can be poured as desired. Its very function is to provoke ill-informed yet illuminating speculation. Those whose pleasures lie in the intricacies of legal doctrine are commonly quite uninterested in empirical reality.

became Dean at Cornell in 1896. Finch gave Cornell a copy of his book; it was the first gift to the law school library. I am indebted to Mr D. Hutchinson for this information.

7

Victorian Judges and the Problem of Social Cost: Tipping v. St Helen's Smelting Company (1865)

A Dismal Event

Had you, on the morning of 13 March 1889, been suitably positioned outside New Bold Hall, an imposing Palladian mansion near the prosperous but squalid town of St Helens, you would have first been struck by the neglected appearance of the entire property: 'even the gates were fastened with pieces of string, the fences repaired in a most primitive fashion, and altogether in the surrounding scenery there is nothing in keeping with the previous history of the place.' Soon, about 10 a.m., you would have been witness to an even more depressing spectacle. A funeral procession of a peculiar character, bearing a polished oaken coffin with brass furniture, was leaving the house. The coffin contained its recent occupant, struck down at the age of 69 by apoplexy, now to be transported unlamented fifteen miles to the family vault at Horwich:

The scene was a melancholy one; the noble mansion standing in the middle of a broad expanse of land, from which the late owner was being borne by the hand of strangers; the total absence of the tenantry; and no near relatives to take a last look, or accompany the remains to the grave.[1]

The funeral was boycotted by the family, and sparsely attended by anyone else. It was that of William Whitacre Tipping, a wealthy former cotton spinner from Wigan, whose attempts at gentrification had dismally failed. His claim to immortality in legal history rests upon the great case of *Tipping* v. *St Helen's Smelting Company* (1865),[2] which presented the courts with an opportunity to settle, so far as tort law was concerned, the response of the classical common law to what has come to be called the problem of social cost.

---

[1] See *Liverpool Daily Post*, 14 and 16 Mar.; *St Helen's Reporter*, 15 Mar. 1889, *St Helen's Newspaper and Advertiser*, 12, 16 Mar.; *Wigan Examiner*, 13 Mar., and *Prescott Reporter*, 16 Mar. all give accounts; the quotations come from the *St Helen's Newspaper and Advertiser* and the *Liverpool Daily Post*.

[2] 4 B & S 608, 616, 122 ER 588, 591, XI HLC 642, 11 ER 1483, 1 Ch. App. Cas. 66. See nn. 49 and 114 below.

The Problem of Social Cost

A remarkable article, 'The Problem of Social Cost',[3] first appeared in 1960. It was the work of Professor Ronald H. Coase, the only member of a Faculty of Law ever to win a Nobel Prize. The problem he discussed is easy enough to grasp: what ought to be done about 'those actions of business firms which have harmful effects on others. The standard example is that of a factory, the smoke of which has harmful effects on those occupying neigbouring properties.'[4] And since few uses of property have no effects on neigbours whatever, the problem is ubiquitous. In a sense it is plainly a legal problem—what ought the law to do about such cases? But it can also be seen in other ways—as an ethical problem, for example—which raises questions of justice or fairness. To Coase, however, it is an economic problem—what solution is best economically? And, as we shall see, an economist's view of how the problem ought to be handled is very different from that of common lawyers.

Coase, in this article, attacked certain views on social policy which he attributed to the late Professor Arthur C. Pigou, who has in recent times acquired a certain notoriety by featuring in J. Costello's *Mask of Treachery* as a sublimated homosexual who enjoyed taking handsome undergraduates mountaineering (and why not?), and even as a communist sympathizer with sinister Russian contacts. For good measure Costello gives him a knighthood, too.[5] To judge from his writings, Pigou's left-wing sympathies were in reality of a very mild nature; those attacked by Coase are to be found in his *The Economics of Welfare*.[6] Pigou 'set out to investigate the full conditions for maximum satisfaction, the conditions in which private and social net product (as he called them) might diverge, and the measures which could be taken to bring them into equality, and maximise satisfaction'.[7] He confined himself to satisfactions which could readily be related to monetary value.

Pigou's idea too is easy enough to grasp. There are situations in which the pursuit of private self-interest, and the needs of public welfare, might diverge, both in relation to benefits and harms. Some actions—for example, putting a light over one's front door—may produce public benefit, as by lighting the highway. But, as the common law now stands, the householder, who has to pay for the

---

[3] 3 *JLE* 1–44, reprinted in R. H. Coase, *The Firm, the Market and the Law* (Chicago, Ill., 1988), 95, developing ideas set out the previous year in the same journal in 'The Federal Communications Commission'. All references hereafter are to this reprint.

[4] Coase, n. 3 above, 95.   [5] (New York, 1988), 149, 176, 181.

[6] Coase gives references to the 4th ed. of 1932 (London). There was a 5th ed. in 1952, elsewhere used by Coase. Pigou's views developed out of his earlier *Wealth and Welfare* (London, 1912).

[7] In ch. 7 of his 1912 book (n. 6 above), Pigou gives numerous examples of situations in which there can be divergences. Some arise out of the form of contracts, e.g. in leases which provide no incentive for the tenant to maintain the fertility of the land or improve it. Examples are given of uncompensated services (see 158–69), and these are followed by cases where the social net product falls short of the private net product, as where motor cars wear out roads without having to pay for this (162 ff.).

light, is not entitled to be paid for these benefits by members of the public who enjoy them. The advantage he obtains may be less than the cost of the light to him. Consequently he may not install the light at all. But if he did so society would be better off.

Coase was predominantly concerned with the harmful effects of actions, with social costs, not with benefits. For example, a factory producing useful chemicals may, by emitting smoke, cause a great deal of harm to neighbours. If the factory owner does not have to pay for this harm, it may be in his self-interest to operate the factory. It can be operated profitably so long as these effects on neighbours ('externalities', in the language of economists) do not have to be taken into consideration. But, if these effects entered the equation, it might not be in the general interest that the factory be operated at all; it might do more harm than good. Pigou considered the possibility of using bounties, or taxes, to correct the divergence between private self-interest and public welfare; the householder who installed a light could be given a grant, or the factory owner made to pay a pollution tax. Thus could individuals be given incentives to behave in ways which furthered public welfare.

Coase took Pigou as his target, and presented the Pigovian theory—what he calls his 'basic position' or 'central tendency', as this: 'when defects were found in the working of the economic system, the way to put things right was through some form of government action.'[8] Coase's criticism expresses an attitude which runs through all his writings—a deep distrust of 'public intervention',[9] 'government action',[10] 'governmental intervention',[11] 'governmental regulation';[12]— the expressions vary but the thought is the same. Coase suggests that the ubiquity of externalities, and the experience of regulation in the United States, suggests that there is 'a *prima facie* case against intervention'.[13] The implication is that it will, more often than not, make matters worse. Coase does not demonstrate by evidence that this is true, nor is it easy to see how he could do so in any rigorous way. His view seems more like a political position than a proposition of economics. He does, however, present a general thesis as to how to consider possible government intervention in cases of social cost. What is needed, from an economist's point of view, is a cost benefit analysis of the total situation without intervention, and the total situation with such intervention. We can then compare the two and see which is, economically, best.

The chemical produced by the factory (for example, an anti-malarial drug) may produce great social benefits. But if the owner of the factory has to pay damages, or a heavy tax, for pollution caused in its production, he may be unable to remain in business—the factory may have to close down. Yet society, saved from malaria, would be better off if it remained in operation even though it causes pollution. Hence, the mere fact that an activity produces harm to

---

[8] N. 3 above, 20.   [9] Ibid. 22.   [10] Ibid. 20.
[11] Ibid. 26.   [12] Ibid. 28.   [13] Ibid. 26.

neighbours does not provide an argument in favour of state intervention. Of course, if the factory owner also got a bounty to pay for the benefits, then he could continue in production, but Coase does not consider this possibility. Another way of presenting his thesis is to say that state intervention (for example, imposing a pollution tax, or imposing liability to pay damages) can also impose its own social costs, and these need to be taken into account. If this is done it will sometimes (or even usually) turn out that intervention causes more harm than good to society generally.

Coase produces an even more radical argument. So far we have assumed that it is the factory which *causes* the harm. But, from the viewpoint of an economist, this is a mistake. The question in cases of social cost is really a reciprocal one—who is to be allowed to harm whom? If the factory can emit smoke and not pay for the damage to the laundry next door, then the factory is harming the launderer. If the launderer, who chooses to hang out washing on a line, can recover compensation, then the laundry is harming the factory owner. Since someone is bound to be harmed (which Coase treats as the same thing as bearing a cost), then the real question is how to minimize the harm.[14] Coase sometimes writes as if he finds the whole notion of causing harm unintelligible. Since the smoke only harms the laundry if the launderer hangs it out, both parties cause the harm.[15] Had President Kennedy not been in Dallas, he would never have been shot by Oswald or whoever; he and Oswald both caused the death. But Coase is really merely emphasizing the reciprocal nature of the problem of incompatible forms of land use. I suppose the same theory might, at the risk of seeming offensive, be applied to attempts to reclaim the night.

This point is linked to a further one—the factory owner and launderer, or whoever, can, whatever the state of the law on pollution, sort out their problems by making a contract. The launderer might, for example, pay the factory to relocate. Indeed, so Coase argues, if we lived in a world in which everyone behaved with economic rationality, and there were no costs or difficulties in making a bargain ('transaction costs', in the language of economists), the parties would reach an economically efficient solution.[16] The law, or at least the law of tort, would have no function. This is true by definition. In the real world, in which hardly anyone behaves with economic rationality, and there are transaction costs, nothing whatever follows from this. But the idea has got around that Coase's observation, originally intended merely to highlight the importance of transaction costs in the real world, demonstrates that it is best to leave conflicts to be sorted out by the market rather than by government regulation. Of course it is possible to resolve conflicts of land use by private bargains, and legal proceedings may merely function as steps in a process of bargaining. This is well illustrated in nineteenth-century case law, and was fully understood by the

---

[14] Ibid. 96.   [15] Ibid. 112.
[16] This came to be called the Coase theorem, on which there is a huge literature.

judges of the period.[17] The trouble was, however, that the weakness of legal remedies provided little incentive on the part of polluters to enter into bargains. They did better by continuing to pollute.

The Ghost of Pigou and State Intervention

In fact, Pigou nowhere says that whenever one of his divergences exists there should be government action. Since virtually anything anyone ever does has third-party effects of the sort we are considering—unpaid benefits, uncompensated harms—only a demented eccentric could think that. Indeed Coase conceded that Pigou expressed his supposed enthusiasm for government action with 'numerous qualifications'. Though I do not propose to argue the point in detail here, Pigou's views on the merits of state action or intervention through taxes, bounties, or regulatory agencies—he had no interest in tort law, and, so far as I can tell, virtually no knowledge of it—were not very different from those of Coase. He started from a less jaundiced view of the possibilities, and in this his political faith differed from that of Coase. He wrote:

The issue about which popular writers argue—the principle of *laissez-faire versus* the principle of State action—is not an issue at all. There is no principle involved on either side. Each particular case must be considered on its merits in all the detail of its concrete circumstances.[18]

Coase is better conceived as attacking a Pigovian tradition of support for intervention, current perhaps in economic circles in Britain in the 1930s, which was not based upon any careful reading of what the unfortunate Pigou had ever written. At a biographical level Coase, in lectures delivered on the fiftieth anniversary of the publication of his article, 'The Nature of the Firm', has explained that he began life as a socialist, and that it was only after he went to the London School of Economics to study for his Bachelor of Commerce degree that he began to lose his socialist beliefs, after he had come under the influence of Professor Arnold Plant—'he made me aware of the benefits which flow from an economy directed by the pricing system.'[19]

Can the state wash its hands of the problem of social cost? Those who, like Coase, favour *laissez-faire* commonly do not, of course, think that relations

---

[17] Good examples are provided by *Broadbent* v. *Imperial Gas Co.* (1857) 7 De GM & G 436, 44 ER 170, where a market gardener located next to a large gas utility was attempting to force the company to purchase his land, polluted by the utility; and *Wood* v. *Sutcliffe* (1851) 2 Sim. NS 163, 61 ER 303 where Sir Richard Kindersley V-C, refers to the use of actions at law 'to apply to the defendants a certain pressure in order to bring them to terms'.

[18] See his *Economics in Practice. Six Lectures on Current Issues* (London, 1935), Lecture V, 'State Action and *Laissez-Faire*', 127–8.

[19] The original article and the conference papers are in O. E. Williamson and S. G. Winter (eds.), *The Nature of the Firm. Origins, Evolution and Development* (Oxford, 1993). The biographical material is in ch. 3.

between neighbours should be left in a lawless state of nature, the parties settling the matter with their fists. They pin their faith on private contract and the free market. Their existence entails the intervention of the state through contract law, as well as through criminal law. What of tort law? If *laissez-faire* is understood in a more absolute sense, in which the law (itself an aspect of government) washes its hands of the problem of social cost entirely, this is simply not an option. If a factory pollutes adjacent property by emitting smoke, the courts, presented with a suit by the property owner, just have to take a position on the matter one way or the other. Someone wins and someone loses, and what is involved is the allocation of power and the imposition of costs. *Laissez-faire*, non-intervention by government, as understood by economists such as Pigou and Coase, has to mean *legislative* intervention of some form or other through the political process, rather than judicial intervention. Coase's hostility to government intervention is confined to legislative intervention, and nowhere directed against the regulation of the matter through the common law process of judicial decision. Why remains obscure, but the explanation may lie in the notion that judicial decision is apolitical. Politics are the evil. Those of the political right have a tendency to fall in love with the classical common law.

Sparks from Railway Engines

In the nineteenth century and long before, the courts were, inevitably, presented with Coase's problem. The legislature largely left the matter to the judges for solution. One nineteenth-century example of the problem, mentioned *en passant* by Pigou, and much discussed by Coase, is that of fire damage caused by the escape of sparks from railway steam engines. In the first edition of *The Economics of Welfare* (1920) Pigou used this example merely to show how one person might profit at the cost of harm to others: 'it might happen, for example, as will be explained more fully in a later chapter, that costs are thrown upon people not directly concerned, through, say, uncompensated damage done to surrounding woods by sparks from railway engines.'[20] Pigou nowhere gives any indication of what, if anything, ought to be done about this. When he wrote this passage, in about 1919, he was perhaps thinking about the tort law of the time. Someone operating steam locomotives under statutory authorization was not then *strictly* liable for such damage, but only for negligence. The Railway Fires Acts of 1905 and 1923 introduced some exceptions.[21] Such railways enjoyed a *partial* immunity from liability, for the general rule which applied when the

---

[20] N. 6 above (London, 1932), 115. The passage occurs in all later eds., but the terminology used in the first ed. is a little different. Coase quotes from the fourth ed. The example is not used in *Wealth and Welfare*, n. 6 above.

[21] The Railway (Fires) Act 1905 imposed strict liability for some fire damage (basically damage to agricultural land or crops) caused by railways, up to a limit of £100, subject to certain procedural requirements. The Railway (Fires) Amendment Act of 1923 put the limit up to £200. Damage outside the scope of these Acts could only be claimed by showing negligence.

locomotive was not operated under statutory authority was that of strict liability—liability even without negligence.

In *The Problem of Social Cost*,[22] and again in the introduction to *The Firm, the Market and the Law*,[23] Coase discusses the illustration in detail, and, amongst other points, claims that the partial immunity to which Pigou referred, which in Pigou's view, so Coase quite wrongly claims, amounted to an imperfection in the working of the economic system which should be remedied by government action, was in reality itself the consequence of government action: 'in the real world Pigou's example could only exist as a result of a deliberate choice of the legislature.'[24] So Pigou had dramatically got the wrong end of the stick. What the example really showed was the evil consequences of governmental meddling. In fact, the example shows nothing of the kind, for Coase misunderstood the legal history of the matter. There was no statute passed in the nineteenth century conferring a partial immunity upon statutorily authorized railway undertakings for the escape of fire. The immunity was instead the product of court decisions, taken by judges who had to settle a rule on the matter one way or the other.

The basic tort law rule imposing strict liability for the escape of fire was not established until 1868, in *Jones* v. *Festiniog Railway*.[25] Earlier it was not settled whether liability had to be based on negligence or not. The doctrine that negligence must be shown to impose liability for damage arising from a statutorily authorized undertaking can be traced back to a criminal case, *Rex* v. *Pease* (1832), where the operators of the Darlington and Stockton Railway were indicted for public nuisance.[26] Later decisions transferred the same notion to civil cases.[27] When the general rule of strict liability for fire was settled in 1868, this doctrine came to represent a partial immunity from what was now the norm—strict liability. The courts, not the legislature, were responsible; the local and personal statutes and general legislation which governed railway undertakings had left the matter for decision by the judges. There was no deliberate choice of the legislature; the choice was that of the Victorian judges.

In any event, even if there had been a legislative provision, the illustration does not show that the results were undesirable. They might or might not be desirable—it all depends upon questions of empirical fact.

Social Cost and the Bates Motel

The judges were also confronted with what may be called the problem of the Bates Motel. In Alfred Hitchcock's film, *Psycho*, the depressed state of the

---

[22] 135–42.   [23] N. 3 above, 138.   [24] Ibid. 138.
[25] (1868) LR 3 QB 733, relying upon the decision of the Exchequer Chamber in *Rylands* v. *Fletcher* (1866) LR 1 Ex. 265.
[26] 4 B & Ad. 30, 110 ER 366. See also *Rex* v. *Russell* (1827) 6 B & C 566, 108 ER 560.
[27] In particular *Aldridge* v. *Great Western Railway Co.*, 3 Man. & Gr. 515, 133 ER 1246; *Pigott* v. *Eastern Counties Railway Co.* (1846) 3 CB 229, 136 ER 92; *Vaughan* v. *Taff Vale Railway* (1860) 3 H & N 743, 157 ER 667, 5 H & N 679, 157 ER 1351.

motel, which sets the lonely scene in which the murder occurs, is explained by Bates to his victim as the consequence of the highway having gone away. In the nineteenth century many undertakings—roads, harbours, markets, railways— were authorized by local and personal Acts of Parliament, conferring on the undertakers powers of entry onto private property, and powers to acquire property compulsorily if agreement could not be reached.[28] Either under individual Acts, or under general legislation such as the Land Clauses and Railway Clauses (Consolidation) Acts of 1845, compensation had to be paid. But the legislation left the scope of compensation uncertain. Could Bates recover compensation for loss of future custom? For loss of amenity through the noise inevitably associated with a nearby modern highway? In the case of a railway could a property owner whose land was not taken, or used in the work of construction, recover compensation for the reduction in value of his property, at least for residential purposes, brought about by the smoke, noise, sparks, and risk of damage which were an inevitable consequence of the operation of the railway, however carefully operated?

Such issues caused differences of judicial opinion in the many cases in which they were raised. Controversy came to a head in two cases which reached the House of Lords in mid-century: *Rickett* v. *Directors of the Metropolitan Railway* (1864–7),[29] and *The Hammersmith and City Railway Company* v. *Brand* (1864–9), which I shall discuss more fully later in this book.[30] The courts were not, of course, left with the comfortable option of pure *laissez-faire*—they had to settle the scope of the right to compensation one way or the other. To be sure, there is a sense in which the courts could leave the relations between the parties to the market, letting them settle their differences by negotiation. But until the rights of the parties were defined, the basis for a market transaction was unsure, and the power of the parties uncertain. When they litigated, this normally meant that attempts to settle the matter by negotiation—the usual way in which compensation was managed—had failed.

The Law of Private Nuisance

The pure common law mechanism for dealing with the problem of social cost was the action for nuisance. In nuisance law we might expect the common law to take its stand on the problem of social cost.

Since the sixteenth century it had been possible to recover damages for nuisance when a neighbour's activities which, whilst not involving any physical entry onto your property, interfered with its use and enjoyment.[31] An early suit for such a nuisance was brought by John Jeffreys, a barrister, later the Chief Baron,

---

[28] See below, Ch. 8.   [29] 5 B & S 149, 156, 122 ER 787, 790, (1867) II HL 175.
[30] LR 1 QB 130, 2 QB 223, 4 HL 171. See below, Ch. 8.
[31] See J. H. Baker, *An Introduction to English Legal History* (3rd ed., London, 1990), 487–9.

in around 1560. He complained that *le jabber de boys* in a schoolroom near his study prevented him working there, but lost.[32]

Early in the history of such actions it was appreciated that there had to be a degree of live and let live between neighbours if life was to go on at all. As Dodderidge put it in a case in 1629, *Jones* v. *Powell*,[33] which concerned smoke, 'if a man is so tender-nosed that he cannot endure sea coal he ought to leave his house'. In the same case a quite different point was made: that actions for nuisance did not simply involve the interests of the parties to the litigation, but also the public interest. What was involved in *Jones* v. *Powell* was a brewhouse, and the very British argument was made that a brewhouse was 'a thing necessary for the commonwealth inasmuch as man cannot live without drink. And in whatsoever case a thing is necessary for the public good a person shall not have an action for particular damage done to himself.' This involved an attitude to the problem of social cost of which an economist like Coase might well approve. But in the nineteenth century the force of this argument, which suggests that the common law should be prepared to sacrifice individual interests to public welfare, became very controversial.

On the one hand, there was a traditional disposition in the common law not to require such sacrifices; it favoured individualism and freedom. Its high priest, Sir William Blackstone, had waxed lyrical on the matter:

So great moreover is the regard of the law for private property, that it will not authorize the least violation of it: no, not even for the general good of the whole community . . . In vain may it be urged, that the good of the individual ought to yield to that of the community; for it would be dangerous to allow any private man, or even any public tribunal, to be the judge of this common good, and to decide whether it be expedient or not.[34]

But Blackstone, who in this passage had in mind the taking of property, rather than interference with its use, went on the explain that, in fact, Parliament could and did authorize the taking of property for public purposes: 'Not by stripping the subject of his property in an arbitrary manner; but by giving him a full indemnification and equivalent for the injury thereby sustained.' This Blackstonian approach, applied to nuisance law, would suggest that considerations of public utility should not stand in the way of providing compensation for nuisances simply because the activity causing the nuisance produced public benefits.

On the other hand, an opposing idea could be found in the reports, both in cases on liability for private nuisance, and in cases on the liability of statutorily authorized utilities to pay either damages or statutory compensation: if there was to be economic progress, the interests of private individuals just had to be subordinated to the general public good which development furthered. In so far

[32] Text in J. H. Baker and S. F. C. Milsom, *Sources of English Legal History Private Law to 1750* (London, 1986), 592.
[33] Baker and Milsom, n. 32 above, 601.   [34] Blackstone, *Commentaries*, i. 35.

as individuals lost out, they would, as members of the public, be compensated by the advantages which economic progress conferred on all. The public-good argument goes further than the idea that there must be some give and take. The neighbour, denied recovery in the name of the public good, suffers disproportionately, but obtains no more in return than other members of the public. That is on the assumption that the value of his property is reduced either absolutely or for the purpose for which he wishes to use it.

The Doctrinal Context of Tipping v. St Helen's Smelting Company

Tipping's suit against the St Helens Smelting Company was contrived to settle the relevance of public benefit to liability for private nuisance. Leading cases commonly have a doctrinal context, and this was provided by two conflicting earlier reported decisions which took opposite sides in the matter. As we shall see, there were also unreported directions in important trials; these were well known in the profession, and could be influential.[35]

In *Hole* v. *Barlow*, in 1858, a landowner had sued over a nuisance caused by brick burning.[36] The action was tried before Sir John Byles. He directed a jury that: 'If you are satisfied . . . that the enjoyment of the plaintiff's house is rendered uncomfortable through the instrument of the defendant that is sufficient to entitle the plaintiff to maintain the action.' But he went on:

> that is subject to this observation, that it is not everybody whose enjoyment of life and property is rendered uncomfortable by the carrying on of an offensive or noxious trade in the neighbourhood, that can bring an action. If that was so . . . the neighbourhoods of Birmingham or Wolverhampton and of other great manufacturing towns of England would be full of persons bringing actions for nuisances arising from the carrying on of noxious and offensive trades in the vicinity, to the great injury of the manufacturing and social interests of the community. I apprehend the law to be this, that no action lies for the use, the reasonable use, of a lawful trade in a convenient and proper place, even though some one may suffer annoyance from its being carried on.

The Court of Common Pleas *in banc* approved this direction, and added that it would also exonerate the defendant from liability if the business was reasonably conducted. Willes J drew an analogy with the law of defamation, in which some statements are, in the public interest, privileged even though they cause damage, and with the rule allowing private property to be entered in defence of the realm: 'In these and such like cases private convenience must yield to public necessity.' The direction may well have merely reflected what middle-class propertied jurymen commonly assumed, but the matter was now becoming transmuted into

---

[35] For discussion see J. F. Brenner, 'Nuisance Law and the Industrial Revolution' (1974) 3 *JLS* 403; J. P. S. McLaren, 'Nuisance Law and the Industrial Revolution. Some Lessons from Social History' (1983) 3 *OJLS* 155.

[36] The direction to the jury on 5 May 1858 is in LJCP 207; see also 4 CB (NS) 334, 140 ER 1113.

a matter of law for the judiciary to settle. In effect, the case introduced a special defence to actions for private nuisance. Taken to its logical conclusion, the rule was that, so long as a business seemed to the jury to be appropriately located and operated in the normal way for such a business, it did not matter how much damage or inconvenience it caused to adjacent landowners.

Why Sir John Byles laid down the law thus is a little puzzling. He, like any lawyer of the period, would have been aware of the conflicts between landowners and industrialists over pollution, and felt that their resolution ought not to be simply left to jury discretion. What was needed was a legal rule, but what rule? He was familiar with the writings of the political economists, and had written two books attacking the theory of *laissez-faire: Observations on the Usury Laws* (1845), and *Sophisms of Free Trade and Popular Political Economy Examined* (1849), the second of which, originally published anonymously, went into numerous editions.[37] But as P. S. Atiyah points out, it is not easy to relate Byles's legal opinions to his economic views. His direction in *Hole* v. *Barlow* seems surprising for a critic of *laissez-faire*.[38] The explanation is that neither distrust of *laissez-faire* nor enthusiasm for it provides any guidance at all on the issue. Deciding what you leave to the market is logically prior to questions of the form of legal regulation.

The implications of *Hole* v. *Barlow* were worrying not simply for landowners who used their property for agricultural or residential purposes; they were also a problem for some other entrepreneurs, and particularly serious for waterworks companies. So an attempt was made to challenge the decision in *Stockport Waterworks Co.* v. *Potter and Another* (1861).[39] A waterworks company, which drew its supply from the Mersey, sued for pollution caused by a cotton printing works. The issue was raised before the full court after a trial designed to raise it but, although some reservations were expressed, the earlier case was merely distinguished. In *Bamford* v. *Turley* (1863) the issue arose again and *Hole* v. *Barlow* was rejected by the Court of Exchequer, and by the Exchequer Chamber, with Pollock CB dissenting.[40] The majority opinion was delivered by Williams J, and contained no reference to economic theory. But the idiosyncratic Sir George Bramwell B, who was an enthusiast for *laissez-faire*, delivered a separate opinion in which he set out what looks like an economic theory, and attacked the thesis that private rights must be sacrificed without compensation:

I think this consideration misapplied in this and in many other cases. The public consists of all the individuals in it, and a thing is only to the public benefit when it is productive of good to those individuals, on the balance of loss and gain to all. So that if all the loss

---

[37] There was a 9th ed. by 1870, and a new ed. with notes by W. S. Lilly and C. S. Deves. There was a reply by E. A. Bowring and Lord Hobart (2nd ed. 1850). Byles also wrote *Foundations of Religion in the Mind and Hearts of Men* (1875), as well as a well-known work on bills of exchange.
[38] P. S. Atiyah, *The Rise and Fall of Freedom of Contract* (Oxford, 1979), 380–3. Byles (1801–84) was a Justice of the Common Pleas 1858–73; his reputation was as a strong conservative.
[39] 7 H & N 160, 158 ER 433, 31 LJ NS 9.   [40] 3 B & S 62, 66, 122 ER 25.

and all the gain were borne and received by one individual he, on the whole, would be the gainer. But whenever this is the case—whenever a thing is for the public benefit, properly understood—the loss to the individuals of the public who lose will bear compensating out of the gains of those who gain. It is for the public benefit that there should be railways; but it would not be unless the gain of having the railway was sufficient to compensate the loss occasioned by the use of the land required for the site; accordingly, no one thinks it would be right to take an individual's land without compensation to make a railway. It is for the public benefit that trains should be run, but not unless they pay their expenses. If one of these expenses is the burning down of a wood of such value that the railway would not run the train and burn down the wood if it were their own, neither is it for the public benefit that they should if the wood is not their own.

In modern economic jargon Bramwell is arguing that industry should 'internalize' its costs.

Though Coase discusses a number of common law nuisance cases in his famous article to which I have referred—'The Problem of Social Cost'—he nowhere, so far as I know, refers to Bramwell's argument.[41] Nevertheless, as I can attest, the idea has got around that Bramwell's views were in some sense an anticipation of Coase's ideas on the proper relationship between law and economic theory.[42] Indeed, at a colloqium at which Coase was present, Professor Kitch said:

Ronald suggested, though it was not the focus of his article, that judges had an instinctive grasp of the economic issues in these cases. I think he quoted some passages from Justice Bramwell, who was a nineteenth century English judge who obviously had an instinctive understanding of economic principle.

Bramwell expressed similar views in *Hammersmith and City Railway Co.* v. *Brand* (1867).[43]

Bramwell was certainly interested in political economy, so the idea that he was applying economic theory to law is not intrinsically implausible.[44] In 1855 he joined the Political Economy Club, formed in 1821, and regularly attended meetings. He read two papers to the Club, one in 1859 on the question 'Is there any sufficient foundation for the provision that all contracts, involving value of more than Ten Pounds, should be in writing?', and another in 1880 on 'How should the liability to workmen, in consequence of accidents arising from the negligence of fellow workmen, be regulated according to economic principles?'.[45]

---

[41] Coase does, at 109 quote a passage from Bramwell's opinion in *Bryant* v. *Lefever* (1878–9) 4 CPD 172, but this deals with a different matter.

[42] E. W. Kitch, 'The Fire of Truth: A Reminiscence of Law and Economics at Chicago 1932–1970', XXVI *JLE* 163.

[43] 2 QB 223, 36 LJQB 139. See Ch. 8.

[44] On Bramwell, see below 215 in Ch. 8; C. Fairfield, *Some Account of George William Wilshere, Baron Bramwell of Hever and His Opinions* (London, 1898); P. S. Atiyah, n. 38 above, 374–80; J. P. S. McClaren, n. 35 above.

[45] See *Political Economy Club. Minutes of Proceedings 1899–1920, Roll of Members and Questions Discussed* (London, 1921), 76, 104, 361, and 328. Unhappily, no text of Bramwell's papers appears to survive, so we only have the titles.

In 1880 he published a pamphlet, *Letter from Lord Justice Bramwell to Sir Henry Jackson Bart. O. C., M. P.*,[46] opposing changes to the common law proposed in the Employers Liability Bill.[47]

Bramwell certainly shared Coase's deep misgivings about government intervention, or, as he would have called it, grandmotherly government. He was a prominent member of the Liberty and Property Defence League, evolved out of the earlier State Resistance Union, which held its inaugural meeting on 5 July 1882: 'The objects of the League are to uphold the principle of liberty and guard the rights of labour and property of all kinds against undue interference by the State; and to encourage Self-help versus State-help.' Bramwell gave a speech on liberty at its first general meeting on 29 November 1882, and, drawing attention to the prosperity of the times, assured his audience: 'To whom are you indebted for this prosperity? Not to the Government, or the State . . . Everything that has been done for this country has been done by that new subject of persecution—the capitalist.'[48] Yet he came out against the entrepreneur over internalization.

In part, Bramwell's views were plainly based not on theories of political economy, but on an ethical notion of fairness—an enterprise which did not pay for the harm it did was being unjustly enriched. He stood in the Blackstonian tradition. In part, his argument seems, at first sight, like an economist's argument. If an enterprise which did cover 'its' costs could not continue to operate profitably, it was in the general economic interest of society that it should close down; you have, of course, to allocate losses and gains to a particular enterprise by some conventional scheme or other. But, from an economic viewpoint, you have to put incidental benefits to third parties into the equation, and Bramwell firmly resisted this. My conclusion is that he was not engaged in economic analysis at all. His real concern was ethical—the injustice of someone profiting through depriving another of property rights without compensation. Again he stood in the Blackstonian tradition.

The conflict between *Hole* v. *Barlow* and *Bamford* v. *Turley*, or, if one likes, between Byles and Bramwell, came to a head in *Tipping* v. *St Helens Smelting Company*, decided by the House of Lords in July 1865.[49] The appeal to the Lords was designed to determine the matter. The rejection of *Hole* v. *Barlow* in *Bamford* v. *Turley* seemed to pose a serious threat to some forms of industry; it was therefore bound to be challenged in litigation sooner or later.

[46] Copy in CUL LO 47 8.

[47] This became the Employers Liability Act of that year. See P. W. J. Bartrip and S. B. Burman, *The Wounded Soldiers of Industry. Industrial Compensation Policy 1833–1897* (Oxford, 1983), 152. His evidence to the Select Committee on Employers' Liability in 1876 are in BPP (1876) IX 669 and (1877) X 551, 628.

[48] See *Self-Help* v. *State-Help. The Liberty and Property Defence League. Its Origin, Objects and Inaugural Meeting.* (Pamphlet, 1882); *Lord Bramwell on Liberty and Other Speeches Delivered at the General Meeting of the Liberty and Property Defence League 1882* (pamphlet, 1883).

[49] 4 B & S 608, 616, 122 ER 588, 591, XI HLC 642, 11 ER 1483, 1 Ch. App. Cas. 66. For the trial see the Liverpool *Albion*, 31 Aug. 1863; *Daily Post* and *Daily Courier* for 28 Aug. Full documentation in the House of Lords Records Office, Vol. 216 for 1865, and material in Vol. III of the VCH Lancashire 402 ff. For the Chancery case see n. 114 below.

The Battle against the Alkali Works

The doctrinal background to the case was also affected by unreported litigation in the industrial north-east, in which the lawyer principally involved was Sir Cresswell Cresswell, who had taken the same view as Bramwell, particularly in litigation at the Liverpool assizes involving Sir John Gerard Bt. of Garswood New Hall,[50] lord of the manor of Windle. As we shall see, his view was influential in Tipping's case, and would be well known to lawyers practising on the northern circuit. He sued a number of alkali manufacturers for damage caused to his gardens and estate, which lay about five miles north-east of St Helens. The gardens had originally been laid out in 1796 by the landscape gardener, Humphrey Repton, who deserves to be remembered for his enthusiasm for the use of what he called the humane man trap, which merely broke rather than crushed the leg of intruders into private property.[51] Sir John, his wealth increased by coal deposits, had spent some £30,000 on their improvement, and in 1826 had reconstructed the house, which dated from 1692.[52]

The legal proceedings took place between 1838 and 1850. In 1838 a number of indictments for public nuisance were preferred, but a settlement was reached with a reference to arbitration to determine whether the nuisances had been abated.[53] In 1839 there was also an action for damages against Crosfields; this was settled for £1,000, the costs being variously stated as £1,500 and £500.[54] In 1840 two actions were brought by Gerard and Samuel Taylor. Taylor came from a commercial family and had rebuilt Eccleston Hall in 1825.[55] Gerard and Taylor sued two firms; these actions were also settled, Gerard receiving £1,000 and Taylor £250; undertakings were given to reduce the nuisance.[56] In 1846 four more civil actions were begun. The most significant was against James Muspratt, who had pioneered the development of the alkali industry in Britain.[57]

The process he used, originally invented in the late eighteenth century in France, involved making sulphuric acid; this was then combined with common salt to make Leblanc soda. This replaced alkali formerly produced from kelp, or imported barilla. The process produced hydrochloric (muriatic) acid gas, emitted as a pungent and corrosive white smoke.[58] The process greatly reduced the price

---

[50] (1804–54).

[51] (1752–1818). His views were quoted recently in *Country Life* from a work of his I have not been able to trace. Man traps became illegal in 1827.

[52] See J. M. Robertson, *A Guide to the Country Houses of the North West* (London, 1991) 184. The house was demolished in 1921.

[53] See T. C. Barker and J. R. Harris, *A Merseyside Town in the Industrial Revolution. St Helen's 1750–1900* (London, 1959), 236; *Wigan Gazette*, 9 Nov. 1838; *Liverpool Times*, 18 Aug. 1840.

[54] Barker and Harris, n. 53 above, 235–9, relying on L. R. O. Cross Papers and *Wigan Gazette*, 9 Nov. 1838; speech of Lord Derby, *Hansard* 1862, 166 at col. 1462; evidence of Adolphus Moubert, agent to the Gerard family, SCNV 60.

[55] See Barker and Harris, n. 53 above, 181, n. 2.

[56] See *Liverpool Mercury*, 10 May 1840, cited in Barker and Harris, n. 53 above, 239.

[57] *Liverpool Mercury Supplement*, 4 Sep. 1846. See the article in the *DNB*.

[58] See Barker and Harris, n. 53 above, ch. 17; XXIV DNB; G. Chandler, *Liverpool* (London, 1957), 214 has a picture of the Liverpool works at 214.

of soda, which between 1823 and 1862 fell to a fourteenth of its previous price. The soda was used in the production of soap, reducing the cost of cleanliness and promoting hygiene. The soda was also used in the production of glass, paper, cotton, linen, and woollens, and indeed in all branches of the chemical industry. William Gossage invented a technique which condensed out the acid in towers. But this raised the cost of production.

What should be done about alkali works, viewed in the nineteenth century as the most polluting of all industries, classically raised Coase's problem of social cost. Ought the state to insist on the use of Gossage towers? At the time of Gerard's tort actions there was no significant state regulation. But in the early nineteenth century matters were regulated by the common law, either through an action for nuisance or a criminal indictment for public nuisance.

Muspratt's original alkali works in Vauxhall Road, Liverpool, escaped condemnation in public nuisance proceedings in 1831, when it was even argued that the gas purified the air and contributed to health, a notion later parodied in verse.[59] But in 1838 a special jury at the Lent Assizes convicted Muspratt. The proceedings were brought by the corporation.[60] It was at this point that Cresswell Cresswell, the conservative member of Parliament for Liverpool, entered the picture, for he led the prosecution, and squarely faced the problem of social cost:

To a certain extent the comfort of the citizens must be sacrificed to the general interest of the state; but to say that, because an individual introduced a new and extensive branch of trade, he was to be justified in destroying the comfort and injuring the property of all around him, was a system of ethics which could not be tolerated. If it were a part of the science of political economy that any person, for the sake of increasing the trade of the country, might injure the trade, and destroys the comfort of all his neighbours, it was a most mischievous doctrine, and ought not to be encouraged.

Neither opposing counsel nor Coleridge J dissented from this, and the judge, in his direction, said:

If they were of opinion that the effect of a verdict against the defendant would be to remove a growing and beneficial branch of trade, and to remove it to a foreign shore, they had nothing to do with that; nor would it be any defence at all that Mr Muspratt caused great benefit to accrue to many individuals, and that he was making a large and honourable fortune.

He went on to say that to constitute a public nuisance the nuisance must be 'generally and widely diffused' and 'substantial': 'it must not be something which a person of delicate imagination or fancy took offence at, but something they could lay hold of, something tangible and substantial. It must be an injury

---

[59] *Gore's General Advertiser*, 12 May 1831. In 1828 Muspratt had been fined a nominal 1*s.* for public nuisance; see G. E. Diggle, *A History of Widnes* (Widnes, 1961), 17. See Barker and Harris, n. 53 above, 225–30. For the verse see *Liverpool Mercury*, 13 Apr. 1838.

[60] See *Liverpool Mercury*, 6 Apr. 1838 for a full report. There is an account in S. Warren, *Miscellaneous Critical, Imaginative and Juridical Contributions to Blackwood's Magazine* (London, 1855), 73–9.

to the health, comfort or property.' A criminal conviction for public nuisance did not of itself necessarily lead to the abatement of a nuisance. In the 1850s a number of landowners put up some £2,000 to proceed against one Peter Spence's alum ammonia works; he was convicted at the Liverpool Summer Assizes, the total costs of the hearing amounting to £6,000, but continued production until he was forced to move in late 1858 under a clause in his lease under which he was not to commit any nuisance.[61] But Muspratt decided to move his operations away from Liverpool. It was this decision which brought him into conflict with Sir John Gerard.

Gerard's four actions in 1846 were successful. Sir Cresswell Cresswell, now a judge, presided.[62] £2,000 in damages were recovered, but at considerable expense, six counsel being engaged. The costs—it is not clear whether these were costs not recovered—came to £900, and Gerard spent very considerable sums on 'watchers', who monitored emissions. He sued again in 1849 since the nuisance continued, and recovered £450 by agreement. Gerard did not attempt to obtain an injunction; either the complexity of Chancery proceedings, or the belief that such injunctions were unlikely to be granted, must explain this. Even as late as 1862 Lord Chelmsford, who at the bar had been counsel for Peter Spence, informed Lord Derby that such an injunction would not be granted, though he may have merely meant that an injunction ordering works to close was not possible.[63]

Gerard also started proceedings against other manufacturers in 1852, but not long after this he became unwell, and after his death they were not continued by his brother, Sir Robert Tover Gerard, who abandoned the use of common law actions because of the difficulty of proving causation, which became worse as polluting plants multiplied in the area. In 1862 he encouraged Lord Derby to move for the appointment of the Select Committee on Noxious Vapours.[64] This recommended state regulation, a proposal largely accepted by the industry. The Act of 1863, An Act for the More Effectual Condensation of Muriatic Acid Gas in Alkali Works, required 95 per cent of the acid to be condensed, and set up a corps of inspectors under the Board of Trade to enforce the requirement by penalties recoverable in the local County Court.[65]

Gerard was not, however, the only wealthy landowner to take proceedings, and persistence could be effective. Thomas Legh, the enormously wealthy owner

[61] The case is discussed in the SCNV.

[62] See *Liverpool Mercury* and *Supplement*, 4 Sep. 1846; *The Times*, 3 and 4 Sep. 1846. Only *Gerard* v. *Muspratt* and *Gerard* v. *Crosfield and Another (Gamble)* came before the court.

[63] *Parliamentary Debates*, HC (1862), 166 at col. 1463. As a barrister he had represented the defendant, Peter Spence, in the public nuisance proceedings in 1857.

[64] In addition to Barker and Harris (n. 53 above), see R. M. Macleod, 'The Alkali Acts Administration 1863–84: The Emergence of the Civil Scientist' (1965) 9 *Victorian Studies* 85.

[65] 26 & 27 Vict. c.124. The inspectors published annual reports, and there was amending legislation in the Alkali Act of 1874 (26 & 27 Vict. c.124). This made the control more stringent, and extended it to sulphate of soda produced in the treatment of copper ores with common salt. The legislation did not provide for compensation, and made no changes to the common law of nuisance.

of Lyme Park in Cheshire, owned extensive properties in the area: Newton Park at Newton le Willows, Haydock Lodge, and Goldborne Lodge.[66] He also sued Muspratt (who was his lessee) in 1845 or 1846, and recovered damages, as did the Revd J. Hornby, Rector of Winwick.[67] Legh commenced four further actions against Muspratt in 1851. One of Legh's actions, claiming damages amounting to £17,000, was also tried before Sir Cresswell Cresswell, but compromised before verdict, Muspratt paying £2,000 and undertaking to move his works. In the end, he moved to Widnes, and retired from business in 1857. At some point his chimney, a celebrated brick structure 393 feet high, was demolished.

During the course of all this litigation Sir Cresswell Cresswell, as we shall see, maintained the view of the law he had presented to the jury in prosecuting Muspratt back in 1838.

William Whitacre Tipping's Gentrification

We must return to Mr Tipping. William Whitacre Tipping was a self-made cotton spinner from Wigan, where he lived with his mother at Henhurst Bridge House; they were cared for by Elizabeth Pilkington, a cook, and Jane Glover, a housemaid.[68] Born on 2 March 1820, he was the only one of three children to survive infancy. Apprenticed at 17 to a cotton spinner, Richard Pennington, he went into business on his own account at the age of 21 in the Henhurst Mill, in Wigan, and later at the Poolstock Mill; the other reported case in which he was involved, *Tipping v. Eckersley* (1855),[69] involved a dispute over the water supply to this mill. Tipping won.

Whether to acquire gentility, or because of a genuine desire to take up farming—he eventually gave up his business as a cotton spinner—he sought a landed estate. South-east of St Helens lay the extensive Bold Hall Estates, in the townships of Bold, Burtonwood, and Sutton in the parish of Prescot. These, since the early Middle Ages and possibly since the time of Edward the Confessor, had been the property of the venerable Bold family, represented at such events as the battle of Agincourt, who held them until the death of Peter Bold, MP, in 1762. There, Peter and Ann Bold had built an imposing three-storey Palladian mansion, New Bold Hall, a princely residence. The date on a tablet which once existed there indicates that the house was completed in 1731.[70] Richard Almond, an estate

---

[66] (1793–1857), MP for Newtown 1814–32. He also owned land at Ashton.

[67] The Revd F. G. Hopwood of Winwick gave evidence to the Select Committee of 1869 on the St Helen's Improvement Bill. See Barker and Harris, n. 53 above, 353, n. 3.

[68] RG 9/2774 (Census of 1861). In what follows I have used articles at the time of his death in 1889 in the *Wigan Examiner*, 13 and 15 Mar.; *Prescott Reporter*, 16 Mar.; *St Helens Newspaper and Advertiser*, 12 Mar.; *Liverpool Daily Post*, 16 Mar.; and *St Helen's Reporter*, 15 Mar.

[69] 2 K & J 264, 69 ER 779. He had a reputation for being litigious, but I have not traced other cases.

[70] E. Baines, *History, Directory and Gazetteer of the County Palatine of Lancaster*, ii. 467; F. Twycross, *The Mansions of England and Wales* (London, 1848–50), iii. 27 has the completion as 1730.

agent, described the house as possessing 'on the Ground Floor a Noble Hall, Grand staircase, Ante Room, Breakfast Room, Lofty Drawing Room fifty seven feet by thirty, Dining Room forty feet by twenty three, Library, Gentleman's Room, Justices Room, Tenants' Waiting Room', with eighteen lofty bedchambers and, in the basement, extensive domestic offices.[71] This gentleman's residence replaced the moated older home of the family, which had been built in 1616 on the site of an earlier house. The architect of New Bold Hall was the Venetian, Giacomo Leoni (1686–1746), who had settled in Britain in about 1714 and, between 1716 and 1720, published the influential *The Architecture of A. Palladio, Revis'd, Design'd and Publish'd by Giacomo Leoni, A Venetian, Architect to his Most Serene Highness the Elector Palatine*. Leoni's most notable surviving house is Lyme Park in Cheshire, now owned by the National Trust, a property whose owner has already featured in our story.[72] There were extensive grounds, the largest in Lancashire apart from those of the Earls of Derby at Knowsley, and 'extensive Ranges of Vineries, Peach House, Conservatory, Melon Pits . . . and a Reservoir or Fish Preserve'.[73] In the park there were exceptionally fine trees: 'The plantations surrounding the house are very fine, and at the south side a cluster of oaks of great size cover lands to the extent of forty acres.'[74] These oaks, said to be 800 years old, had somehow escaped the demands of the British Navy, and survived into the 1860s; they had mostly been felled by the time of Tipping's death in 1889.

After Peter Bold's death in 1762 the estates went to his daughter, Anna Maria, who died, aged 82, in 1803, and then to her sister and her husband, Peter Patten. He assumed the name and arms of Bold, and soon thereafter died, in 1819. His daughter, Mary, succeeded him, and married a Polish nobleman, His Serene Highness Prince Eustace Sapieha, of Dereczym in the Duchy of Lithuania. After she died in Rome in 1824, her sister, Dorothea, who was married to one Henry Hoghton, owner of the decayed sixteenth-century baronial Hoghton Tower, near Preston, inherited the estate. Henry succeeded to the second most ancient baronetcy in existence, purchased from James I in 1616. He became Sir Henry Hoghton-Bold. On the death of his wife he acquired the estate.[75] For recreation

---

[71] Affidavit 1308; see n. 114. The St Helen's Archives have sale particulars of 1860, which give a slightly different description and a ground floor plan, not dated.

[72] J. M. Robertson, n. 52 above, provides much information. There is a picture and account in K. Downes (ed.), *The Architectural Outsiders* (London, 1985), 38–9, an engraving in F. Twycross, n. 70 above, 26–7, and photographs in Robertson, n. 52 above, at 163–4, and in the *VCH Lancashire*, lii, 394. Other houses with which he was concerned include Lathom House in Lancashire (engraving in J. P. Neale, *Views of the Seats of Noblemen and Gentlemen* (2nd. Ser., London, 1824–9), i); *Moor Park*, Hertfordshire; *Clandon Park*, Surrey; *Cliveden House*, Bucks.; Burton Park, Sussex; *Alkrington Hall* near Middleton (Robertson, n. 52 above, 151); and Moulsham Hall in Essex (demolished 1816); those italicized still exist. See also *DNB*.

[73] Sale of 1860.   [74] Twycross, n. 70 above, 27.

[75] Born at Walton Hall near Preston, 3 Jan. 1799, died Anglesey, Nr. Gosport, 19 July 1862. See *Gentleman's Magazine*, 1862, 2, 360–2, cited F. Boase, *Modern English Biography* (Truro, 1892–1921); E. Baines, n. 70 above, v, 23 ff.

he devoted himself to cock-fighting, which, though legislated against in 1835 and 1849,[76] continued to flourish in Lancashire, as it still does; he kept some 500 fighting cocks. He was succeeded on 9 July 1862 by his son, Henry, the ninth baronet, who, inspired by a love of antiquity, returned to the Catholic faith of his ancestors, joined the world of Victorian chivalry, and, by Royal licence, promptly took back the ancient name de Hoghton.[77] Sir Henry set about restoring Hoghton Tower, abandoned by the family in the eighteenth century, to its former glory, and had little interest in the relatively modern Palladian mansion at Bold.

Sir Henry Hoghton, the eighth baronet, probably with his son's agreement, had earlier decided to sell the Bold Hall Estates, and in 1858 instructed his agent, Richard J. Flowerdew.[78] The mansion had long been unoccupied; Sir Henry preferred to live at Walton Hall, and for six years or so the occupant of the house was John D. James, the Under Steward of the Bold Estates.[79] But Sir Henry's library and pictures and furniture remained there.

At auction in 1858 there was no bidder for the Bold Estates as a single lot. In 1859 some 5,798 acres were put up for auction at the Lion Hotel in Warrington, but much of the property failed to reach its reserve.[80] Soon after, a Mr Walter R. Critchley bought another lot at a price of £2,306 9*s.* 1*d.*, well above its value for agriculture; it fronted on a railway. On it he and his partners, who included Lord Alfred Henry Paget,[81] set about completing the building of a copper-smelting plant. This was known to be the reason for the purchase. The building of the works had begun in 1849 or so; the land would then have been leased from the Bold Estates. During the 1850s construction was discontinued for some considerable period. The works were largely finished by 14 March 1860, when the conveyance of this lot took place.

The lots put up for sale in 1859 included the mansion and its associated woods and gardens, amounting to five and sixty-seven acres, together with the lordship of the manor. The bidding reached £29,500; the reserve of £37,050 was not reached. Some lots were sold off privately in 1860. On 5 July 1860 another attempt was made at the Clarence Hotel, Manchester, to sell Bold Hall and the remaining 3,066 acres of land by auction in forty-six lots.[82] Lot one comprised the Hall together with 343 acres; it was described as:

admirably arranged for comfort and convenience, with all the requisite appendages for a family of fortune, without being too large or necessarily entailing a very extensive

[76] 5 & 6 Will. IV c.59 and 12 & 13 Vict. c.92.
[77] 2 Aug. 1821–2 Dec. 1876. See *ILN* for 16 Dec. 1876 at 590; J. B. Burke, *A Visitation of Seats and Arms of the Noblemen and Gentlemen of Great Britain* (London, 1852), ii. 23; Boase, n. 75 above; Robertson, n. 52 above, 199.
[78] Chancery deposition.   [79] Affidavit 1352.
[80] St Helen's Archives Library has a press cutting, undated.
[81] 1816–88, liberal MP for Lichfield 1837–65, equerry and clerk marshal of the Royal Household, later General Paget. Son of the Marquis of Anglesey. See *DNB* under Henry William Paget.
[82] Sale particulars in St Helen's Archives.

establishment; while its situation, within little more than half an hour from either Liverpool or Manchester, renders it peculiarly adapted for the residence of any gentleman moving in the upper walks of commercial life.

There was no bid for the Hall, though some lots seem to have been then sold. There is some uncertainty about the dates, but it was probably in August 1860 and early the next year that Tipping bought most of what remained in two transactions. He himself was anxious to place the date of the two contracts as early as possible, and claimed that the first contract was signed in July or August 1859, but his agent put the contract dates later, in 1860 and 1861. The transactions were formally completed early in 1861. He bought the mansion, 400 acres of park, 140 of plantations, sixteen of pleasure grounds, and two of gardens; with the farmlands the total amounted to 1,300 acres. Tipping at the trial said the price had been between £60 and £70 an acre for the whole property, that is around £78,000–£91,000. It produced an income of between £1,400 and £1,500 *per annum*, principally farm rents on around 740 acres at about £2 an acre, together with sales of timber and sales of the produce of the home farm.

Local rumour had it that the price paid had been much larger, around £120,000.[83] The discrepancy may be partly explained by the fact that other items were included. Tipping bought paintings, together with an extensive library, the books, which he had no intention of reading, being purchased by weight. The price may, through negotiation, have been reduced because of the copper works. Tipping was well aware of their existence when he bought the property. His accounts of the negotiations at the trial and the later Chancery suit seem somewhat evasive.

In April 1861 Tipping moved in with his 74-year-old mother. After Tipping's father had died in his infancy she had married a brewer, Henry Robinson, by whom she had a son, Walter Robinson. He continued the brewing business in Wigan. She was now a widow. From 1862 Tipping ceased to use his Wigan home. The move was all too much for his mother, who died in the early summer of 1862.[84] So Tipping became the solitary proprietor of the mansion, where he lived as a recluse. At first his wants were attended to by Samuel McDouall, an agricultural labourer, with his wife, Agnes, and one maidservant,[85] but after his mother's death he acquired her cook and one maidservant, a tiny establishment for so large a mansion.[86] He never married, and developed a reputation for extreme eccentricity:

he lived in about four rooms, and generally neglected the whole place. He was an eccentric character, rough in manner and dress, uneducated and without taste. Like Bold-Hoghton before him . . . Tipping's chief pleasures lay in the barbarous sport of cock-fighting, in card playing, and in visits to the Tipping Arms on the Warrington Road. He

[83] E. Baines, n. 70 above, v, 23.   [84] Her will reference is Prescot 8b, 341, June 1862.
[85] RG 9/2743 (Census of 1861, which counts Tipping twice).
[86] RG 10/3857 (1871) and RG 11/3723 (1881).

preserved the hall, however, in which there were two Vandyck full-length portraits of Charles I and his Queen, a Royal gift to one of the Bold family; two Claudes, and a Holy Family by Rubens.[87] The stories of Tipping's eccentricities are legion. He appeared to hoard up money in the shape of buckets of sovereigns . . . and he also had a fancy for going down to the Tipping Arms with a thousand pounds or so in his pocket.[88]

His neglect of the property was such that the front door collapsed, and Tipping would come and go through a window. Local tradition has it that he buried much of his money, and many attempts to locate it have failed. He was a notoriously heavy gambler.[89] A photograph of the eremitical bearded Tipping, standing grimly in his library before the two Royal portraits, has been published.[90] Another photograph, dating from 1888, exists in the St Helen's Archives.

Tipping said at the trial that he bought the property as an agricultural investment. This is not implausible; farm land near an industrial town tended to rise in value as farm land, however polluted. But it was hinted by opposing lawyers that he really bought it for use or sale for industrial purposes. He certainly did become a farmer, and a successful one, and he never sold the property for industrial development.

Tipping's Action for Nuisance

St Helens by the mid-nineteenth century was a notoriously dirty industrial town.[91] There were collieries, alkali works, and copper smelting works, both in St Helens and in nearby Sutton. Industry brought work, prosperity, and serious air pollution. Alkali works were the worst offenders. Copper smelting plants, which emitted sulphuric acid, came next; the effects, though more localized, could be more severe. There were at least six smelting plants in the St Helen's area; they emitted about 6,000 tons of sulphuric acid annually.[92] Land not taken over by industry, or for urban dwellings, was mainly used for farming, but the area also had a number of notable gentlemen's residences—to the north, Windle and Rainford Halls; to the west, Eccleston Hall; and, further away, Knowsley, which survives, the seat of the Stanleys, Earls of Derby. To the north-east was Garswood Hall, demolished in 1921, the seat of the very wealthy and ancient family of the Gerards of Bryn who, as we have seen, battled against pollution; and nearer to the east Blackbrook Hall, which survives.[93] And to the south was Sherdley House,

---

[87] For which he paid £6,000.
[88] Quoted *VCH Lancashire*, iii. 402 n. 7, from an unidentified newspaper account.
[89] Information from Mrs Victoria M. Tipping.   [90] Reproduced Robertson, n. 52 above, 164.
[91] See generally Barker and Harris, n. 53 above. Also the report and evidence before the Select Committee of the House of Lords on Noxious Vapours of 1862, BPP 1862 (486) XIV 1, also available in the IUP reprint in *Health: General Public Health 1854–62*, hereafter cited as SCNV, the speech of Lord Derby on 9 May 1862, *Hansard* 1862, 166 col. 1452 ff.; the Royal Commission on Noxious Vapours of 1878, BPP 1878 [C.2159] [C.2159.I] XLIV. 1, 43., hereafter RCNV.
[92] SCNV 1821, evidence of David Gamble.   [93] The home of the Orrell family.

built by the industrialist Michael Hughes between 1802 and 1807, and torn down in about 1950.[94]

At the time of the purchase the copper works at St Helen's Junction, on land purchased from Sir Henry Hoghton in 1859, was still under construction. But its 200-foot chimney, which lay a mile from the Hall to the north-west and half a mile from the boundary of Tipping's property, was already built. Tipping conceded that its mere existence reduced the value of his property as a gentleman's residence. But the works were then not in continuous production. Between September and December 1860, and again between February and July 1861, there had been some smelting operations under Critchley and his partners. In August 1862 the defendant company, formed in 1861 and incorporated in June 1862, acquired the works and greatly increased the scale of operations.[95]

Litigants always lie, and it is therefore not easy to unravel the story of the litigation and how it came about. That the Bold Estate had long to some degree suffered from pollution from copper smelting is clear from the fact that, for some ten years, one William Croft had arbitrated claims presented by farmer tenants against the copper works company, and a similar arrangement had been operated by a Mr Rothwell up to 1860 for claims against William Keates.[96] Tipping's story was that, when he bought the property, it was not adversely affected by pollution from the numerous works in St Helen's, which were sufficiently distant. In May 1861 he was sent a prospectus from the Commercial Copper Smelting Company, then the name of the business, the chief promoter being the same Lord Paget. Tipping instructed his solicitor to write protesting about the damage recently caused to his timber and ornamental trees by emissions from the chimney. Though reluctant to do so, he indicated that he would, if need be, litigate unless the company found some way of making the emissions harmless. However, at this time there was no economically feasible technique for condensing out the sulphuric acid produced by copper smelting; hence the company could satisfy Tipping only by ceasing production—at least when the wind was blowing from the west, as it usually did.

In June 1861 he protested again; production was reduced, and for a while little harm was caused. In the spring of 1863 production was greatly increased and there were further protests and threats of litigation. Since all these communications were ignored, Tipping, on 25 May 1863, started an action for damages for nuisance against the company. But he still tried to avoid legal action. On 2 June his lawyers wrote:

Although quite determined to maintain his rights Mr Tipping is desirous to do so with courtesy and propriety, and if possible he will concur in avoiding litigation. If therefore

[94] See Barker and Harris, n. 53 above, ch. 12.

[95] There is again some confusion and conflict about the precise dates.

[96] SCNV 216. It is not clear when this system ended in the case of Mr Croft, or which copper company was involved.

Lord Alfred Paget will meet Mr Tipping at Bold Hall they can look and talk over matters together without prejudice to either side to see what can be done for present compensation and future prevention.

Lord Paget expressed surprise over the damage and offered to meet Tipping, but there was a failure of communication and no meeting ever took place; Lord Paget was a grandee, unlikely to defer to his social inferior, Tipping. On 19 June counsel were instructed to press on with the action, in which Tipping claimed £5,000 for damage caused to his property by 'noxious gases, vapours and other noxious matter'. His declaration specified damage to trees and crops, and unhealthy cattle—these would be Tipping's cattle on the home farm. Tipping was later to claim that at one point 120 of his cattle were actually blinded.[97] He also complained of illness to himself and his servants, and went on to claim that the mansion and property were 'rendered less comfortable and wholesome and fit for habitation, and that the Plaintiff has been prevented from having so beneficial and healthy a use' of the land and premises as he would otherwise have enjoyed. He also claimed that his reversionary interest in leased farms was permanently depreciated in value.

The timing of the action is surely significant. On 9 May the Earl of Derby, whose seat at Knowsley Hall was in the same general area, moved in the House of Lords for the appointment of a committee on noxious vapours, encouraged, as we have seen, by the Gerard family. The proposal was unopposed. He explained that:

He was the last person who would desire to interfere with the increase of our manufacturing prosperity, if only for the reason that half of his property was situated in the manufacturing district, and its prosperity or deterioration depended on the prosperity or depression of the manufacturing interest.

The outcome was the the Alkali Act of 1863, which received the Royal assent on 28 July.[98] So in 1863 pollution by noxious gases was very much in the news. But this Act, following the recommendations of the committee, did not regulate copper smelting plants:

but as, unhappily, no means have yet been devised of neutralising those effects (though they may be mitigated) consistent with the carrying on of this important branch of industry, the Committee cannot advise that it be classed, for purposes of regulation, with the works [i.e. Alkali Works] to which we have already adverted.[99]

So Tipping had, perforce, to make use of the common law, there having been no state interference by the legislature with the copper industry. If there were to be interference, the task was that of the judges.

[97] RCNV 1817–74.   [98] See above 178, below 191.   [99] SCNV 6–8.

The Trial of the Action

The judge was Mellor J, himself a Lancashire man from a commercial back-ground.[100] The evidence was mainly of extensive damage to trees and herbage, and the unpleasant effects of the smoke, which caused irritation and even vom-iting. Dispute centred upon whether the problem was caused by the Bold copper works, or by the other works in the area, and upon whether the damage had arisen since Tipping bought the estate; many of the ancient oak trees were dead by 1861, though Tipping attributed this to old age. Tipping's witnesses, who included William Hill, gardener for thirty years at Bold Hall, thought the prob-lem recent. Professor Frederick C. Calvert FRS, Professor of Chemistry at the Manchester Royal Institution, gave expert evidence on the emission of sulphuric acid from chimneys; he used kites to take samples. Witnesses for the company emphasized the general state of pollution locally. William Keates, who ran a smelting works at Sutton, and whose company Tipping was also suing,[101] frankly admitted that between the Bold Estate and St Helens 'you cannot find a living thing'. So, as is so typical in leading cases dealing with nuisance law, the litigation arose because a frontier created by the practice of local land use was being crossed, or, if you will, was moving.

William Keates, and other witnesses, made a critical point, which was not disputed: 'I am not aware of any better mode of conducting the works. I should be happy to avail myself of it if there were any. If the trade is to go on in this district, I cannot think it can be conducted in any other manner.' He also explained:

I have paid compensation, and have been glad to get off without the nuisance of coming into Courts of Law . . . and I may say here on my oath that the great bulk of the money I paid was not paid for injury done by me; but it is like many other things in this world, it is a sort of compromise as to what is desirable for a man to do under particular circumstances.

Although there was dispute over the severity of the effects, and over causation, there was no doubt that serious damage had occurred.

The tricky question was how the jury ought to be directed. Arguments were presented by the impressive array of legal talent engaged—for Tipping, two Queen's counsel, William B. Brett and George Mellish, with Mr Clement Milward; and for the defendants the Attorney-General himself, Mr Edward James QC, and Mr William Hindmarch QC, with Mr Thomas Webster. The judge decided to adopt the direction employed by Sir Cresswell Cresswell[102] 'in the celebrated case of *Gerard* v. *Muspratt*'.

---

[100] He was born in Oldham, and his father belonged to the firm of Gee, Mellor, Kershaw and Co.
[101] See below 191.   [102] (1794–1863).

The Cresswell Cresswell Theory of Nuisance Law

For Sir Cresswell Cresswell there was no question of a public good defence. In *Gerard* v. *Muspratt* he said:

The law affecting the question was exceedingly simple. If the defendant's works had done damage to the plaintiff's property, the plaintiff was entitled to maintain an action against him, and have full compensation in damages for the actual injury to his property and estate, as well as his comfort and convenience, as the jury thought proper to award him. The law did not tolerate that any person should erect works and carry them on to the injury of the health and property of another. The legislature occasionally, for special reasons, made exceptions, but in such case compensation was always given to the injured parties.[103]

He presumably left it to the common sense of the special jury not to treat trivial inconvenience as a nuisance. Mr Justice Mellor's direction was rather more elaborate:

I tell you that if a man by an act—either by the erection of a lime kiln, or brick-kiln, or copper works, or any works of that description—sends over his neighbour's land that which is noxious and hurtful to an extent which sensibly diminished the comfort and value of the property, and the comfort of existence on the property, that is an actionable injury.

He softened the test by saying that the jury—'when you are coming to the facts'—must consider 'the place, the circumstances, and the whole nature of the thing'. The jurymen must remember that 'the law does not regard trifling and small inconveniences, but only regards sensible inconveniences, injuries which sensibly[104] diminish the comfort, enjoyment, or value of the property'. Otherwise business could not go on, especially in Lancashire. But as a matter of law there was no public good defence; his direction rejects *Hole* v. *Barlow*.

The Appeal and its Outcome

It is clear that counsel from the start viewed the case as a test case, bound, whatever the decision at the trial, to go on appeal. The judge had done what was expected of him. But it was desirable to settle what the facts of the case actually were. Counsel for the defendants therefore asked the judge to put three questions to the jury before they reached a verdict. There is some difficulty in discovering what these three questions were, but Thomas Webster put them thus:[105]

---

[103] *Liverpool Mercury Supplement*, 4 Sep. 1846.

[104] 'Sensible' here means 'appreciable'. The word is used in the first edition of C. J. Gale and T. D. Whately, *A Treatise on the Law of Easements* (London, 1839), 284 and 285; *Parker* v. *Smith and Others* (1833) 5 C and P 438, 172 ER 1043, where Tindal CJ uses the expression 'sensible degree' in an action for interference with light which is cited.

[105] William Hindmarch QC expressed them slightly differently.

I should put it in this way:
   [1] whether it was not a necessary trade,
   [2] and a suitable place for carrying on the trade,
   [3] and whether the trade was not carried on in a regular and proper way.[106]

The judge himself said that if he did put questions, he would ask 'the four questions that were put by my brother Channell'. The reference is to some of the questions put by Channell B in *Stockport Waterworks* v. *Potter and Another:*[107]

   [1] Was the discharge from the defendant's works of noxious matter (such noxious matter causing damage to the plaintiffs) necessary and unavoidable, or might the same have been avoided by their using reasonable care in the conduct and management of the business?[108]
   [2] Was the defendant's trade a lawful trade, carried on for purposes necessary or useful to the community,
   [3] and carried on in a reasonable and proper manner,
   [4] and in a proper place?.[109]

But the questions could only be put before verdict by consent, and since the plaintiff's counsel did not consent the questions were not put at this stage.[110]

After the verdict, in which the jury awarded £361 18s. 4½d. damages,[111] Mellor J did put three slightly different questions to the jury: '[1] Was the enjoyment of the Plaintiff's property sensibly diminished?' To this the foreman replied: 'We think so.' '[2] Do you consider the business there carried on to be an ordinary business for smelting copper?' The foreman replied: 'We consider it an ordinary business, and conducted in a proper manner, in as good a manner as possible.' This answer made Channell's question three otiose. '[3] And do you consider, supposing that makes any difference, that it was carried on in a proper place?' The foreman replied: 'Well, no, we do not.'

This last reply was somewhat awkward; to raise the issue which the lawyers wanted to have settled the ideal reply would have been 'yes'. Hence, when the case went to the Court of Exchequer Chamber, one of the grounds of appeal tried to get around the difficulty posed by this answer by asserting: 'The suitability of the locality is matter of law, on which the learned Judge should have directed the Jury.' The statement of the grounds of appeal included a neat formulation of the central issue in the case, the validity of the claim: 'that sensible discomfort from the carrying on of a necessary trade, in a reasonable manner and in a suitable locality, is not an actionable injury.'[112]

---

[106] I have added the numbers.
[107] 7 H & N 160, 158 ER 433. The questions were originally set out as two questions.
[108] Originally question 8 by Channell. The text given in 7 H N 160, 158 ER 433 adds after 'care' the words 'that is not by any extravagant outlay, but in the ordinary course of this business with such an outlay as such a business requires'. The version used by Mellor comes from 31 LJNS 9 at 12.
[109] Mellor's [2]–[4] are Channell's question 10.   [110] Reports leave it a little uncertain.
[111] Tipping's lawyers viewed this as compensation for damage caused over a period of four weeks from 24 Apr. 1863 to 25 May; opposing lawyers did not concede this.
[112] This is the first reason stated.

If this was indeed the law, it seemed to be a manufacturers' charter to pollute both an industrial area and its non-industrialized surroundings. In reply Clement Milward for Tipping asserted: 'That no person has a right of carrying on an injurious business to injure another person or his property' and 'that no person has a right, to the damage of his neighbour, to carry on in an improper place, *or at all*, any noxious trade, however conducted that trade may be' (my italics).

After the Court of Queen's Bench, in a short opinion from Cockburn CJ, had upheld the direction of Mellor J as being correct and, if anything, too favourable to the defendants, the case went to the Exchequer Chamber, which affirmed the decision. Since it was known that this was a test case on its way to the House of Lords, and that the House would consult the judges, no elaborate opinions were delivered: 'We think that the Judgement ought to be affirmed, and that there is no misdirection.' Pollock CB agreed, thinking the court bound by *Bamford* v. *Turley*, though he did not himself agree with that decision. And so the case went to the House of Lords. There the judges were consulted, and unanimously advised that the direction was correct. The House accepted this advice.[113] So it was that the claim that in nuisance cases the private rights of individuals must be subordinated to the public interest in economic development was rejected. A properly conducted business in an appropriate location was not, as a matter of law, immune from nuisance liability. But a jury might take into account all the circumstances when considering 'the facts'; this, and the *de minimis* principle, considerably weakened the rejection of *Hole* v. *Barlow*.

The waters were further muddied by the three sloppy opinions delivered by the Law Lords. The Lord Chancellor, Lord Westbury, suggested that there was, in spite of his approval of the rejection of *Hole* v. *Barlow* in the case before the House, a different rule covering other sorts of nuisance cases, where the nuisance involved 'sensible personal discomfort', something which merely affected the 'senses' or 'nerves', whereas Tipping's case involved what he variously called 'material injury to property' and 'sensible injury to the value of the property'. Where only the senses or nerves were offended, individuals had to put up with the discomfort produced by trades carried on in the location. These remarks were strictly *obiter*—that is, not directly relevant—since he did not think Tipping's case was of this type. Lord Cranworth indicated that the location in which the nuisance arose was indeed relevant, and Lord Wensleydale emphasized that a nuisance, to be actionable, must 'sensibly diminish the comfort, enjoyment and value of the property'. The writer of the headnote, attempting, against the odds, to make some sense of these remarks, set out a principle which, though not justified by the decision, neverthless came to be received as correct:

There is a distinction between an action for nuisance in respect of an act producing a material injury to property, and one brought in respect of an act causing personal discomfort. As to the latter a person must, in the interest of the public generally, submit to the

---

[113] The judges were Blackburn, Shee, Willes, Martin, and Pigott JJ.

discomfort of the circumstances of the place, and the trades carried on around him; as to the former the same rule does not apply.

'Material' here is quite ambiguous between meaning either 'physical', or alternatively 'non-trivial'. So it was that the ghost of *Hole* v. *Barlow* was not laid, and it has continued to haunt the law to this day.

In effect the judicial system just could not make up its mind as to what ought to be done about the problem of social cost, and this inability was intimately connected to a problem which plagued Victorian law—was it best to leave these difficulties to juries, to resolve with little guidance from the judge as matters of mere fact, which here means matters for jury discretion, or ought the judges to spell out in precise detail how they should be resolved. Can the law of nuisance be encapsulated in precise rules? Ought it to be so encapsulated?

Tipping's Chancery Suit

William Tipping had won his common law action on 5 July 1865, no doubt at very considerable expense, though the costs would have been paid by the defendant company, but he was now little better off than he had been at the outset. For the company, which had thousands of tons of copper ore on the site, and contracts to fulfil, continued to operate as before. There was some evidence that conditions became even worse. Tipping could have brought a further action for damages, and hoped, by a succession of such actions, to induce the defendants to close down. Instead, his lawyers on 10 July filed a bill for an injunction, requiring the company to abate the nuisance. This was granted *pro tempore*, pending the hearing.[114] The company appears to have paid no attention to it, and tried to have it discharged before the case was heard. The principal argument was that Sir Henry Hoghton had sold the land to the defendants for the very purpose of using it as the site for a copper smelting works; he surely could not have prevented its being used for this purpose just because it polluted his retained land. Tipping, having bought the land from Sir Henry, ought not to be in a better position *vis-à-vis* the defendants than Sir Henry had been. But this and other arguments were rejected by Wood V-C, and by the Court of Appeal.[115] Tipping again employed Professor Calvert, who collected more samples of the smoke from the chimney without entering the property by using kites; matters, he thought, were getting worse.[116] Affidavits put in for the defendants attempted to reopen issues already ventilated at the trial; thus a veterinary surgeon thought that Tipping's cattle had suffered from pneumonia, not copper fumes. More constructively, James Andrew, the general manager, claimed to be engaged in promising experiments whereby the need for a high chimney would cease, and

---

[114] For the Chancery case, see PRO C 16/306/T97 (1865) for complaint and depositions; C 31/1955, 1956 Nos. 1304–9, 1347–52, 1582, 1595–6, 1601, 1603–4, 1664, 1723 for affidavits and C 33/1115 at 2055, 1123 at 1119, 1133 at 993 for orders of the court.

[115] *Tipping* v. *St Helen's Smelting Co.* (1865) 1 Ch. App. 66.   [116] Affidavit 1306.

harmful gases would be condensed; he was doing his best to conform to the injunction. But in the end the Company conceded defeat, and on 29 May 1866 Tipping obtained a perpetual injunction restraining the defendants 'from using or causing or permitting to be used the Copper Smelting Works . . . in such manner as that any vapour or smoke may be emitted therefrom to the injury or damage of the Timber, plantations, gardens, pleasure grounds and crops upon the Bold Hall Estate'.

An enquiry into damages suffered since 27 August 1863 was instituted, and on 25 April 1867 a sum of £681 13s. held in court was transferred to Tipping, and the defendants were given until 6 May 1867 to pay whatever else was owing. The costs and expenses by now must have been enormous; Tipping later said that it had cost him several thousand pounds to sue, though he thought the expenditure worth it since otherwise his estate would have become worthless.[117] So it was that Tipping actually succeeded in closing down the copper works, and the company moved its operations to the Ravenhead works, some three miles away, from where it could continue to pollute the Bold Hall Estate, albeit much less severely.[118] Tipping was less succesful over the smelting works of Newton Keates and Co., which were also located there. He recovered a mere £27 and did not try for an injunction. But this company did attempt to control emissions as techniques which made this practicable were slowly developed. By 1878 they were annually condensing some 1,300 to 1,400 tons of vitriol each year, all of which had previously gone into the atmosphere.[119]

Legislative regulation of copper smelting began in 1874 when what was known as the 'wet' process was controlled,[120] but not the more usual 'dry' process. The Royal Commission of 1878, though set up in part because of concern over sulphuric acid pollution, also thought it not practicable to regulate the 'dry' process. The problem largely solved itself when it became normal to smelt copper ore where it was produced, and British production of copper ore in any event declined.

Tipping's Memorial and Economic Rationality

Whatever his original intention may have been when he purchased Bold Hall, old Tipping never sold the estate for commercial development. He lived there until his death at the age of 69 in 1889, devoting himself to eccentric behaviour, litigation, and farming, at which he was apparently successful; by 1881 he was employing ten farm labourers. Amongst his other pursuits, so local gossip claimed,

[117] RCNV 1817–24.

[118] See Barker and Harris, n. 53 above, citing St Helen's News, 2 Sep. 1863; St Helen's Standard, 25 Nov. 1865; evidence of J. F. Allen to RCNV 11,699; St Helen's News, 5 Dec. 1868.

[119] Evidence of Tipping, 1878. William Keates gave evidence to the SCNV of 1862 and to RCNV of 1878.

[120] 37 & 38 Vict. c.43.

was the making of wills, of which three, it was said, were made and revoked. He apparently planned to leave his assets, which at his death were said in the press to amount to some £400,000,[121] to persons who were already wealthy, rather than to relatives like his half-brother, Walter Robinson, who needed the money. A fourth will, though planned, was never executed, and after his death on Sunday, 10 March, Walter ransacked the mansion in the hope of finding a will, but with no success. What was found was a will dated 24 January 1843, leaving all his property to his long-dead mother. His property therefore went to his first cousin as next of kin, the daughter of his father's brother, John W. Tipping, a Mrs Harriet Wyatt. On 9 July 1856 she had married a wealthy landowning parson, the Revd John Ingram Penfold Wyatt, formerly Penfold, Perpetual Curate of Hawley Parsonage, near Farnborough.[122] Tipping's intestacy was one reason for his sparsely attended funeral, at which the principal and no doubt cheerful mourners were the Perpetual Curate's two barrister sons, Arthur and Hugh; the latter, indeed, was present when old Tipping passed away.

Old Bold Hall, replaced by Leoni's mansion, had become the home farm, and survives to this day under its original name, being more fortunate than New Bold Hall, of which only the gates and stables survive. A chimney piece and bookstack is in Meols Hall near Southport, which also incorporates some fragments of another Leoni mansion, Lathom Hall. After Tipping's death the estate long remained unsold, but in about 1899 a consortium known as the Bold Hall Estates Ltd. purchased it. A colliery was sunk there; the derelict mansion was demolished in about 1901 or a little earlier, and a new home farm was built on the site. The colliery has long since been abandoned. Eventually the old disused copper works were used by Messrs Keates and Rawlinson for the manufacture of patent manure, not, I suspect, a salubrious trade.[123] The M62 motorway now passes hideously through what was once the parklands of New Bold Hall, and is crossed by a footbridge to preserve what was once the Ladies' Walk in the park. Apart from the approach to the mansion, preserved as Hall Lane, the ha-ha, some coach houses, and three cottages from the old laundry, there is little to remind a visitor that this was the site of the most notable triumph of nineteenth-century nuisance law. But the site of the cock pit was still visible in 1975, and the Tipping Arms still flourishes in Poolstock, Wigan.

William Tipping and Thomas Legh, whose activities never generated a leading case, were the only two private litigants in the area who actually succeeded in closing down a polluting plant. The decision of the House of Lords seems, on its face, to represent a severe reverse for the manufacturing interest, but its

---

[121] His personal estate was valued for the grant of administration at £235,406 gross.

[122] (1817–1901). He assumed the name Wyatt in 1837, and his two sons became barristers. Hugh Richard Penfold was a graduate of Christ Church Oxford, Arthur Penfold went to Trinity Hall; both were Inner Temple. He had two unmarried daughters, Mary and Alice, as well. Administration was first granted to Harriet, and later, with consent, to her eldest son John Arthur.

[123] Barker and Harris, n. 53 above, citing *St Helen's Record*, 29 June 1894.

practical effect was minimal. Nuisance actions against manufacturers were extremely expensive. The fact that Mellor J's direction, which the House of Lords approved, had invited the jury to consider 'the place, the circumstances, and the whole nature of the thing' gave juries, whose members would be well aware of the northern adage, 'Where there's muck, there's brass', considerable discretion. There is no reason to suppose that Tipping's success imposed any serious impediment on the expansion of British industry. J. P. S. McLaren, in a notable study, 'Nuisance Law and the Industrial Revolution. Some Lessons from Social History',[124] has shown how the common law of nuisance played a relatively unimportant part in controlling pollution, not primarily because of its doctrinal form, but because other social and institutional factors diminished its utility. And it is noticeable that the two triumphant litigants, Tipping and Legh, were very wealthy individuals. They could cope with the transaction costs; in a sense they and their lawyers were transaction costs.

But was Tipping's vindication of the right of private property, his ability, derived from his wealth, to insist that he was entitled to choose to use his land as a gentleman's residence and farm, and to prevent his neighbour engaging in any incompatible land use, a triumph for rationality? Or some sort of economic disaster? Or simply an example of the fact that those who have a great deal of money often get whatever they want? How ought a case such as *Tipping* v. *St Helens Smelting Company* be decided? Were the judges right to give Tipping such power? That is what such legal decisions do. Unhappily, Coase does not discuss it; hence it is not possible to be entirely certain what view he would take of its rejection of the public-good defence, though the general tenor of his argument suggests that he would not view this favourably. In 'The Problem of Social Cost' he is at pains to argue against the view that the mere fact that an industrial enterprise causes damage to third parties is a reason for imposing liability. Coase argues that, if this closes down the enterprise, more may be lost, overall, than gained. For all I know, or indeed anyone else knows, this may have been what happened in St Helens, if you take into account all third-party effects—unemployment caused by shutting the works, moving costs, loss to local pubs, etc. And into the equation would, of course, have to be put the litigation costs, and the costs involved in Tipping moving elsewhere, and so forth. There was no shortage of alternative gentlemen's residences—or, for that matter, sites for smelting works.

It may well be that in some ideal world the Coasean way of approaching the problem of social cost is correct, and one which rationality dictates. But courts do not, of course, engage in any such cost benefit analysis, and a moment's consideration would suggest that, if they did, the case of *Tipping* v. *St Helen's Smelting Company* would have occupied the trial court for months, if not years, or at least until the money ran out. There is simply no limit to the amount of

[124] (1983) 3 OJLS 155.

information which would be of potential relevance. Furthermore, a cost benefit analysis, applied to the circumstances of a particular case, will generate no general rule; it inevitably follows from Coase's economic theory that imposing liability will sometimes make the situation better, and sometimes worse. His thesis leads to the conclusion that, from an economist's point of view, general rules of tort liability are a mistake. This bleak conclusion must have occurred to him and, in one passage, the significance of which seems to have been over-looked, he tries to escape his own logic and propose a way of generating a general rule, using the example of sparks from railway engines: 'The question at issue is whether it is desirable to have a *system* in which the railway has to compensate those who suffer damage from the fires which it causes or one in which the railway does not have to compensate them.'[125] How one can compare two *systems* is nowhere explained, and the idea seems to be wholly fanciful; furthermore, there is a problem of deciding what systems to compare—a system for sparks from engines, another for straying cattle? Or, more generally, a system covering all damage to neighbours?

The Coasean approach suggests that, in deciding the respective rights of Tipping and his neighbour, the court should investigate the economic consequences of a decision one way or the other, either at a particular level or at the level of a system, and go for the allocation which would best promote the national wealth. Courts neither do nor can do this; the idea is wholly at odds with the sort of system of private property we have, in which idiots can be the beneficiaries of gifts, nincompoops can inherit, and chinless wonders can acquire title to pheasants by shooting them. In allocating property rights, private law treats economic efficiency as quite irrelevant.

Coase has also argued that efficient solutions to problems of competing land use can, in principle, be achieved by private contract between the parties. If escaping the pollution was worth more to Tipping than to the St Helen's Smelting Company, then he would, if rational, pay the company an appropriate sum to abate the nuisance; conversely, the company might, if it was more profitable to continue production, have paid Tipping money to discharge the injunction. In ideal circumstances all we need is the market. No doubt in principle such things are possible, but in the real world people rarely behave with economic ration-ality, even if they have the the the least idea of what such rationality dictates; there are, in any event, powerful social limits to the market, and those who offer money to resolve quarrels run a serious risk of aggravating the situation. The story of the negotiations between Tipping and his neighbour illustrates both points. Quarrelling neighbours and common lawyers, engaged in the process of dispute resolution at the margins of a largely traditional system of property law, inhabit one world, which is real and very untidy. Economists inhabit another world. Between them a gulf seems to be fixed.

[125] N. 3 above, 141–2.

8

Bursting Reservoirs and Victorian Tort Law: Rylands and Horrocks v. Fletcher (1868)

Rival Principles of Tort Liability

A book could be written on the general influence of disasters upon legal history; recently, indeed, Professor Robert C. Palmer, in his *English Law in the Age of the Black Death 1348–1381*,[1] has argued that a particular disaster had extremely wide-ranging effects upon English law and government. The case with which this chapter is concerned, *Rylands* v. *Fletcher*,[2] did not itself arise out of a disaster, but out of a run-of-the-mill mining accident which involved no loss of life. Yet its outcome was, I shall argue, much affected by one.

The starting-point for the enquiry is a curious feature of the tort law built up by the Victorian judges: the espousal of two apparently antithetical principles of liability.[3] One makes liability depend upon proof of negligence or fault and, in the absence of such proof, leaves the injured party without a remedy. Negligence or fault is defined as failure to conform to an objective standard of prudent behaviour. The other principle, that of strict liability, differs in permitting the injured party to recover compensation for loss arising from the defendant's conduct or activities even though negligence cannot be proved. What is rather surprising is the adoption, albeit in different contexts, of both principles in one body of tort law, and this seems to call for an explanation. No doubt in many situations a plaintiff can recover under either principle, and there are legal doctrines which may reduce the sharpness of the distinction between the two, or reduce its practical importance. For example, the doctrine of *res ipsa loquitur* ('the facts speak for themselves') permits a court to presume negligence in some situations; there can also be defences to strict liability which, in effect, exonerate the defendant if there has been no negligence. But they are, nevertheless, in an important sense in opposition to each other, and in some cases will lead to a

---

This originally appeared in a slightly different form as 'Legal Liability for Bursting Reservoirs: the Historical Context of *Rylands* v. *Fletcher*' in (1984) 13 *JLS* 209.

[1] (Chapel Hill, 1993).

[2] More fully, *Rylands and Horrocks* v. *Fletcher* (1865) 11 Jur. NS 714, 34 Ex. 177, 3 H & C 774, 159 ER 737 (Court of Exchequer); (1866) 12 Jur. NS 603, LR 1 Ex. 265, 35 LJ Ex. 154 (Exchequer Chamber); (1868) LR HL 330 (House of Lords).

[3] The first writer to address this peculiarity was O. W. Holmes in *The Common Law* (1881), Lectures II and IV.

different result, or significantly affect the way in which a case has to be presented to a court. *Rylands* v. *Fletcher* is the leading Victorian case adopting a theory of strict liability in tort law, and its continued fame rests upon this fact.

The apparent inconsistency in Victorian tort law may be illustrated by contrasting *Rylands* v. *Fletcher* with the case of *Vaughan* v. *Menlove*,[4] decided by the Court of Common Pleas in 1837, some thirty-one years earlier. The litigation arose out of an incident in 1835, just a quarter of a century before the mining accident which generated *Rylands* v. *Fletcher*. The plaintiff, Robert Chambre Vaughan, was a wealthy man of property, who lived at Burlton in Shropshire. The defendant, Thomas Menlove, was described as a respectable farmer. He lived at Petton, a mile or more away, and possessed a freehold property at Burlton, on which there were farm buildings. Across a carriageway lay the plaintiff's property, on which there were two cottages, occupied by Thomas Ruscoe and Thomas Bickley. Both were employed by Vaughan, the former as a domestic servant, the latter as a labourer. Menlove had stacked hay on his property, starting in July. On the morning of Friday, 4 September, at about 4 a.m., the rick burst into flames, and the fire was spread across the carriageway by a strong westerly wind, and burnt down the two cottages. They were uninsured, a policy having lapsed, and the estimated cost of rebuilding them was £147. Menlove's own losses were considerable, estimates varying wildly between £100 and £600. Vaughan sued for negligence, and won both at the trial before Patteson J and a special jury on 30 July 1836, and before the full Court of Common Pleas sitting in London on 23 January 1837.

At no point in the proceedings was it ever suggested that liability for the escape of fire should be strict; it was assumed that either no liability existed at all or that it must be based upon fault. The opinion of the Court of Common Pleas explicitly relied upon the maxim of the common law *sic utere tuout alieno non laedas*—'so use your own as not to harm another's'—and what the judges thought this entailed was liability for negligence, not strict liability. This was not an unconsidered view; the case throughout was regarded as one 'of first impression', posing special difficulties and requiring a considered judicial response. One set of difficulties concerned the proper standard of care to be applied. The debate covered not only the difference between an objective standard of care and a subjective standard which would exonerate Menlove if he had taken the care which he personally thought sensible (as he had), but also the relevance of the many standards of care which had been developed in the Roman law of bailments, and which, it could be argued, the common law had adopted.[5] There were also tricky questions of causation—earlier cases had dealt with fires deliberately kindled, whilst this fire arose from spontaneous combustion. The decision has

---

[4] 3 Bing. NC 468, 132 ER 490, 7 C & P 525, 173 ER 232, 1 Jur. 215, 4 Scott 244, 3 Hodges 51. I have also used the *Salopian Journal and Courier of Wales* and the *Shrewsbury Chronicle and Advertiser for Wales* for 3 and 5 Aug. 1836, and ASSI 1/43.

[5] See *Coggs* v. *Bernard* (1703) 2 Ld. Raym. 909, 92 ER 107.

come to be treated as important because it first clearly applied the notion of an objective standard of care—later the reasonable man standard—in negligence actions, and when Sir Frederick Pollock published his treatise on tort law in 1887, at a time when there was much interest in the theory of tort law, it featured as a leading case.[6]

Some twenty-five years later, on 11 December 1860, a newly excavated reservoir in Lancashire burst downward as it was being filled for the first time, and the escaping water flooded the adjacent Red House Colliery; this event gave rise to the litigation in *Rylands* v. *Fletcher*, which ran from 1861 to 1868. There were three points of similarity with *Vaughan* v. *Menlove*. First, the plaintiff's claim for £5,000 damages was based squarely on allegations of negligence. Thus, the first count in the declaration alleged that the reservoir had been 'carelessly and negligently constructed'; the second was similar but did not allege negligent construction, whilst the third did in slightly different language. Yet the final decision in the case espoused the theory of strict liability, and became the *locus classicus* of that theory. Somehow or other, an action for negligence turned into an action for strict liability. Secondly, the case was, like *Vaughan* v. *Menlove*, treated as a case of first impression, not covered by earlier authority, itself a surprising fact. Thirdly, the decision in *Rylands* v. *Fletcher* relied upon the selfsame maxim as did *Vaughan* v. *Menlove*, but deduced an entirely different principle of liability from that maxim—liability without fault, strict liability. Why should liability for escape of fire in 1837 depend upon proof of negligence, and escape of water in 1868 involve strict liability?

Writers on the law of tort have long regarded *Rylands* v. *Fletcher* as an anomalous decision. Back in the nineteenth century Pollock criticized it in his treatise on the law of torts; Holmes had considerable difficulty in fitting it into his general theory of tort law.[7] A commonly held view used to be that the original common law proceeded on the basis that a man acted at his peril, but this harsh doctrine was progressively relaxed in the nineteenth century with the reception of the principle of liability only for negligent conduct. The law was thus moralized, and *Rylands* v. *Fletcher* can only be explained as an atavistic decision, a throwback to or a survival of more primitive times. This picture of legal development would today not be accepted by serious legal historians, but the alternative story still leaves much to be explained. It goes like this. Before the nineteenth century, questions of fault, contributory fault, assumption of risk, standards of appropriate behaviour, causation, and so forth, certainly arose in litigation. But there was virtually no law about them. They were treated as jury questions, to be handled in the main by lay common sense. The trial judge might

[6] *The Law of Torts* (London, 1887), 357–8.
[7] Pollock, n. 6 above, 398; O. W. Holmes, *The Common Law* (Boston, Mass., 1881), Lect. 3 and 4. See also J. B. Ames, 'Law and Morals' (1908) 22 *HLR* 97; F. H. Bohlen, *Studies in the Law of Torts* (Indianapolis, 1926); R. Pound, *Interpretations of Legal History* (Cambridge, Mass., 1946), 105–9; C. H. S. Fifoot, *Judge and Jurist in the Reign of Victoria* (London, 1959), ch. 2.

well give the jury some guidance, but what he said was not subject to review and did not feature in law reports or legal treatises. What happened in the nineteenth century was the creation of law on issues where there had been none before. But on this view *Rylands* v. *Fletcher* still appears puzzling, for it was decided at the end of a period during which the negligence principle had been steadily gaining ground through the extension of the tort of negligence.

The numerous judges who were involved in the case must have been aware that, if tort law was to incorporate two different principles of liability, there was a need to explain the relationship between them. Only two of them attempted to do so. One was Bramwell B, who favoured strict liability in his dissenting opinion in the Court of Exchequer, and the other was Blackburn J, speaking for his colleagues in the Court of Exchequer Chamber. By the 1860s it was quite clear that fault liability reigned in some areas, typically in collision cases. Bramwell B dealt with the problem very briefly, but thought that in collision cases the negligence principle had to apply as a matter of logic, and this because of a problem over causation: 'where two carriages come into collision, if there is no negligence in either it is as much the act of the one driver as of the other that they meet.'[8] Only by deciding who was at fault could you decide who collided with whom. Blackburn J, the judge most closely identified with the so-called rule in *Rylands* v. *Fletcher*, offered a much more radical theory. It was that the *primary* principle of tort law was that of strict liability. The negligence principle applied only as an exception in situations in which people had, by implication, agreed that it should—the theory of assumption of risk:

Traffic on the highways, whether by land or sea, cannot be conducted without exposing those whose persons or property are near to it to some inevitable risk; and that being so, those who go on the highway, or have their property adjacent to it, may well be held to do so subject to their taking on themselves the risk of injury from that inevitable danger.[9]

Blackburn's theory was not very convincing, but his contention that strict liability was the norm was stated in an opinion agreed by Willes, Keating, Mellor, Montague Smith, and Lush JJ. It is a curious fact that three of these judges, Willes, Keating, and Montague Smith JJ, had, only three months earlier, been concerned in the leading case of *Indermaur* v. *Dames*,[10] which applied the negligence principle to an action for personal injuries arising not on a highway but on private premises to which the plaintiff had lawful access; the case is noted for the opinion of Willes J, commonly viewed as the outstanding common lawyer of his time. It seems as if Willes and his colleagues were persuaded in *Rylands* v. *Fletcher* that strict liability was the basic common law principle, and fault liability the exception. This, viewed at least from a modern perspective, seems to reverse the natural order of things, and certainly nothing of the sort had ever been said in the nineteenth century before this.

---

[8] 3 H & C 774 at 790, 159 ER 737 at 744.   [9] LR 1 Ex. 286.
[10] (1866) LR 1 CP 274, affirmed (1867) LR 2 CP 311.

The Need for Explanation

Since *Rylands* v. *Fletcher* appears to be such a peculiar or anomalous decision, scholars have attempted to explain it. F. H. Newark, in 'The Boundaries of Nuisance',[11] offered a purely doctrinal explanation, and Blackburn J, both in his opinion in the case and later in *Ross* v. *Fedden*,[12] claimed that the endorsement of strict liability in the case merely stated what had always been the law, an explanation which signally fails to make sense of the case's status as a leading case. F. H. Bohlen, back in 1911, tried to explain the case in terms of a conflict of interest between the conservative landowners on the one hand and the innovative industrial and commercial class, who produced the reservoir builders, on the other, the judges favouring the former.[13] His argument, uninformed by even the sketchiest historical knowledge, was totally demolished by R. J. Molloy in 1942. Other attempts have been perfunctory.[14]

In what follows I shall pursue a different approach, starting from a new working hypothesis as to what the case was all about. In a perfectly valid sense, the case was about the theory of tort liability, but it was also about bursting reservoirs and what, if anything, the common law should do about them, and this is the basis of my investigation into the case.

Dam Failures and the Holmfirth Disaster of 1852

Dams and reservoirs have a long history in Britain.[15] You can still see today at Alresford a massive earth dam, still retaining water, though leaking badly, built in the twelfth century at the instance of Bishop Godfrey de Lucy of Winchester as part of a scheme to make the River Itchen navigable between Alresford and Southampton Water. Most early dams were relatively modest affairs, designed to canalize rivers for navigation, as in this case, or designed to generate a modest head of water to provide power for mills. Innumerable examples survive. In the eighteenth century increased industrialization led to the construction of many new mill dams, water power being eventually, however, superseded by steam; some were substantial constructions, but most were fairly small. In one village where I lived as a child, Lothersdale in Yorkshire, four separate reservoirs were constructed to power the largest mill wheel which has survived from this period. In the canal era, much larger reservoirs were constructed to provide high-level

---

[11] 65 *LQR* 480.   [12] (1872) 26 LT 966.

[13] 'The Rule in *Rylands* v. *Fletcher*' (1911) 59 *U Pa. LR* 298, 373, 423, reprinted in his *Studies in the Law of Torts*, n. 7 above. For R. J. Molloy see '*Fletcher* v. *Rylands*—A Reexamination of Juristic Origins' (1942) 9 *Univ. Chicago LR* 266.

[14] e.g. G. H. L. Fridman, 'The Rise and Fall of *Rylands* v. *Fletcher*' (1956) 34 *Can. Bar Rev.* 810 with correspondence at 1225.

[15] See in particular N. Smith, *A History of Dams* (London, 1971), and G. M. Binnie, *Early Victorian Water Engineers* (London, 1981).

water supplies. Thus the Todd Brook Dam, which was built in about 1794 and apparently still exists, was built to service the Peak Forest Canal; it is seventy feet in height, 200 or more feet broad at the base, and 700 feet long.[16] The fashion for landscape gardening also led to the construction of dams and artificial lakes, such as the well-known example at Blenheim Palace in Oxfordshire. Another village where I once lived, Clapham in Yorkshire, has one constructed for the Farrer family in about 1820. In the nineteenth century the need to provide adequate supplies of water for the rapidly growing industrial towns gave a new impetus to the construction of massive dams and reservoirs, and towards the end of the century the development of the water turbine led to the construction of reservoirs to generate hydro-electric power. The Clapham Lake, originally purely ornamental in function, was used from around the 1890s to provide the Farrer mansion, Ingleborough Hall, with electric light, and Clapham itself with the first ever village electric street lights; in the 1940s it was still producing lighting for the village church. One has only to look at a map to see that Britain, especially industrial Britain, is dotted with innumerable artificial reservoirs, some still in use or holding water but many now derelict and empty.

Until the construction of the Vyrnwy Dam between 1881 and 1892—its function was to provide water for Liverpool—all large dams in Britain were earth gravity dams. Their strength depended upon their sheer mass, and their structural integrity on their impermeability, and the protection of their external surfaces from erosion. They were made impermeable by having a core of puddled clay, sometimes incorporating a binding agent—local tradition has it that the Clapham Dam used sheep's wool. The core had to rest on an impermeable foundation. Until the late nineteenth century there was no adequate theoretical knowledge about the behaviour of earth dams and their cores under stress. Civil engineers relied on common sense and experience, slowly augmented by theoretical knowledge. Dams not infrequently failed. This might be because of inherent instability—for example, through a defective foundation, or because water permeated through or under the dam and eroded the structure. They might also fail through rapid erosion, which would occur if the water level rose uncontrollably and overtopped the dam. Well-designed structures had spillways adequate to control the level even in exceptional storms, and dams might be provided with low-level sluices so that the water level could be reduced in a controlled manner when disaster threatened. But some dams possessed no adequate arrangements for regulating the level. If a small dam failed the damage might be trivial, but the failure of a large dam situated above a centre of population could produce a catastrophe.

In the nineteenth century, major catastrophes or disasters typically arose from accidents involving ships, mines, railways, explosives, and reservoirs. In their ability to kill large numbers of people at the same time, ships were in a class of their own, the nineteenth-century record being held by the *Bywell Castle*, which,

---

[16] Smith at 171 gives an account of this massive structure.

in 1870, bisected the pleasure steamer, *Princess Alice*, in the Thames and killed at least 640 people.[17] Shipwrecks also caused massive property losses, normally, of course, covered by insurance. Mining accidents ranked next; where there were many deaths they caused acute social dislocation by removing the adult working males on whom the rest of the population, concentrated in a small area, relied. The worst incident was the Oaks Colliery disaster on 12 and 13 December 1866, with a death toll of 361; the worst ever was the Senghenydd disaster on 14 October 1913.[18] Disastrous incidents involving explosives were fairly uncommon; they were rather like boiler explosions in causing steady loss of life rather than major calamities. The most spectacular nineteenth-century explosion took place in London on the Regent's Park canal in October 1874, proximity to the zoo adding to the alarm—what if the venomous reptiles had escaped?[19] The incident did, however, lead to government regulation—the Explosives Act of 1875.[20] Railways certainly killed considerable numbers of people, but in the nineteenth century they never caused a major disaster.

Reservoirs, in spite of their immense potential for causing havoc, enjoyed in Britain a relatively good record. No British dam failure can compete with that of the South Fork or Johnstown Dam in Pennsylvania. Originally built as a canal feeder, it had been reconstructed in 1854 with cheerful incompetence to impound a lake for an exclusive club, the South Fork Fishing and Hunting Club, whose members included Andrew Carnegie and Andrew Mellon. It failed on 31 May 1889, killing more than 2,000 people.[21] Nor did reservoirs produce the steady loss of life caused by ships, mines, and railways. But there were two sensational reservoir disasters in nineteenth-century Britain and, to appreciate the significance of these incidents, it is important to appreciate the menacing character of a large dam once anxiety as to its security develops. Those who live or work in the area thought to be endangered can conceive of themselves as permanently and continuously threatened. Depending on the state of the law, they may also think of themselves as being impotent in the facing of the ever-present threat. Nuclear power stations possess this menacing character for many people today, and it is not a product of the frequency of accidents at all. Major killers such as ships and railways lacked this quality; they seemed to be essentially benevolent artefacts, though contemporaries viewed a ship voyage in particular as a hazardous undertaking. But what was feared was the sea, not the ship.

The first major failure occurred in 1852, and involved the Bilberry Dam above the village of Holmfirth in Yorkshire.[22] Construction of this ill-designed

---

[17] G. Thurston, *The Great Thames Disaster* (London, 1965). See also *The Bywell Castle* (1879) 4 PD 219.

[18] See H. Duckam and B. Duckam, *Great Pit Disasters* (Newton Abbott, 1973).

[19] See *The Times* 3–20 Oct. 1874.

[20] See J. Pellew, 'The Home Office and the Explosives Act of 1875', 18 *Victorian Studies* 175–94.

[21] See D. G. McCullough, *The Johnstown Flood* (London, 1968).

[22] For discussion, see Binnie n. 15 above, ch. 4. The Kirklees District Archives in the Huddersfield Central Library has papers of the Holme Reservoir Commissioners and other documents concerned

and ill-maintained structure had begun in 1839, and its collapse at 1 a.m. on Thursday, 5 February 1852, came as no surprise; fifty or more people were nearby at the time, confidently expecting it to go. Others, more optimistic or fatalistic, had retired to bed below it. The dam had been constructed under the Holme Township Reservoir Act 1837[23] to provide water for the numerous woollen mills in the valley, on which the local population depended for employment. The Act conferred power on 105 named commissioners to raise capital and construct eight reservoirs, charging water rates to consumers. The project was under-capitalized and only three reservoirs were ever built, the Bilberry, the Home Stye, and the Bosham Wham.

The Bilberry Dam, designed by George Leather, was for the period a very ambitious undertaking, ninety-three feet high and 340 long. It was defectively sited over a spring, which eroded the clay core and caused the embankment to subside. Leather adopted an extremely casual attitude; in the first two years of construction he never even visited the site. The original contractors were dismissed, and between 1840 and 1845 continual attempts were made to repair defects in the dam. The commissioners ran out of money and became involved in Chancery litigation; at the time of the disaster, they were heavily in debt; an attempt to solve their problems by a new Act failed in 1846.

In 1852 it was known that the dam was in a deplorable condition and dangerous, as was the Holme Stye. Both the valve gear provided for lowering the water level and the waste pit provided to provide automatic control were inoperative. The designed safe depth was fifty-nine feet, and the defective dam was thought to be safe only to forty; the water level was normally kept down only by excessive leakage, which in its turn made the reservoir even more dangerous. When very heavy rain began to raise the water level to a dangerous height, Charles Batty, the drawer of water, prudently sent his family away from its home beneath the dam, but could do nothing else about the problem, and at a level of sixty feet the dam failed catastrophically, releasing an enormous volume of water. This swept down the valley, killed seventy-eight people, caused extensive property damage, and put out of work 4,986 adults and 2,142 children, who were threatened with destitution or the workhouse.

The Aftermath of the Holmfirth Disaster

A coroner's inquest was held on one victim, Elizabeth Marsden, and George Leather was able to avoid personal blame; the Commissioners had not followed

---

with the incident, including a typescript account by the Holmfirth Local History Group (1972). For pictures see ILN 1852 at 144–6 *The Times* (issues from 6 Feb.–1 Mar.), *Huddersfield and Holmfirth Examiner*, and *Huddersfield Chronicle* have full coverage. HO 45/4210 includes drawings and plans. There is also material in the House of Lords Record Office, 6 HL Evidence (1853).

[23] 30 Will, IV c.54.

his advice on safety, as they could have done by modifying the automatic system of control at a price of a mere £12 10*s*. On the advice of a barrister, Anthony Cleasby, the commissioners' clerk, William Jacomb, gave a frank account of the deplorable history of the undertaking.[24] The jury, encouraged by the coroner, George Dyson, found the commissioners guilty of 'wilful and culpable negligence', and expressed regret that it was not legally possible to bring in a verdict of manslaughter against them. The verdict went on:

We also hope that the legislature will take into its most serious consideration the propriety of making provision for the protection of the lives and property of Her Majesty's subjects exposed to dangers from reservoirs which should be placed by corporations in situations similar to those under the charge of the Holme Reservoir Commissioners.

The Holmfirth magistrates requested the help of the Home Office, and the Home Secretary, Sir George Grey, arranged for Captain Moody of the Royal Engineers to inspect the remains of the dam and the other reservoirs. As well as giving evidence at the inquest, he reported on the Holme Stye Dam, where the spillway had been deliberately blocked; he expressed doubt as to the sanity of the Commissioners. The Home Office, never anxious to assume new responsibilities for which the parsimonious Treasury was unlikely to provide extra staff, took no further action, nor was there any Parliamentary pressure for general legislation.

The possible civil liability of the commissioners, who were in any event without means, seems never to have been considered, and under clause 11 of their Act they enjoyed limited liability; as a matter of law they would in all probability have been immune from any action for damages.

This did not mean, however, that the victims went uncompensated. As happened after virtually all major Victorian disasters, a public charitable appeal was organized to relieve the distress.[25] For, as the *Huddersfield and Holmfirth Examiner* put it on 7 February: 'suffering not infrequently elicits those holy feelings and generous emotions which continued prosperity fail to produce.' Orgies of pious sympathy were arranged, and the press, reinforced by bad poetry, ensured that everyone knew about the plight of the sufferers. One piece by B. Stanley noted that even the dead had not escaped:

> Its onward sweep spared not the coffin'd dead,
> These scattered tombs bear witness to its power.
> While chapless skulls, torn from their silent bed,
> Darkened the gloom of that appalling hour.[26]

Special railway excursion trips were organized and much enjoyed: 'The levity of the people strangely contrasted with the mournful scenes they had come to

[24] Details in Kirklees MSS B/KM/HRC/1 and 31.
[25] The Kirklees Archives (T/H/F/1–76) has complete papers on the appeal, which is the best documented I have come across.
[26] Published in the same paper on 7 Jan. The BL Crampton Collection (1876 e 6) has a ballad.

witness.' Some 40,000 people visited the valley, causing a local food shortage. The appeal raised £69,000, paid out £31,000 in compensation, and gave £6,000 to trustees to rebuild the dam and thus restore the water supply essential to the prosperity of the area. At the end of it all 8s. 8d. in the pound was returned to subscribers. So it was charity, not the law of torts, which coped with the distress and helped to restore the local economy. The legislative response was a new Act.[27] It reorganized the commissioners, enabled them to raise new capital, and empowered them to reconstruct the Bilberry Dam and repair the other two dams. The Act did incorporate safety provisions—a requirement for annual inspection, and a power in local magistrates to order reduction in the water level on complaint of danger; the same power was conferred on local magistrates in other private Acts passed after 1853. In 1863 the Waterworks Clauses Act incorporated this power (but not the requirement of annual inspection) in all subsequent Waterworks Acts. In bad cases it was unworkable, and I have not discovered any occasion upon which the power was ever used. The main consequence was, as we shall see, the influence of the disaster on provisions for compensation in other private Acts authorizing the construction of reservoirs.

The Sheffield Inundation of 1864

The other major dam failure occurred in 1863, that is during the litigation arising out of the accident which gave rise to *Rylands* v. *Fletcher*; the chronology is, as I shall later show, significant. The dam involved was the Dale Dyke, which impounded the Bradfield Reservoir of the Sheffield Waterworks Company.[28] It was constructed under statutory powers originating in an Act of 1830, enlarged by Acts of 1845 and 1853.[29] It will be noticed that the last of these Acts was passed after the Holmfirth disaster; again the chronology is important.

The Bradfield Reservoir was situated some eight miles to the west of Sheffield; when full it would be a mile and a quarter long, and the earth gravity dam was ninety-five feet high and 1,250 long. On 11 March 1864 the new reservoir was almost full, and during the evening a crack was noticed in the face of the dam by a labourer, who informed the resident engineer, Mr Gunson. He and the contractor inspected it, and at first were not alarmed. When it began to widen,

---

[27] 16 & 17 Vict. c.138. There are papers in the House of Lords Record Office, 40 HC Evidence (1852–3) and 6 HL Evidence (1853).

[28] See G. Amey, *The Collapse of the Dale Dyke Dam, 1864* (London, 1974); S. Harrison, *A Complete History of the Great Flood at Sheffield* (Sheffield, 1864), is a near contemporary account. Pictures ILN (1864) 261, 288, 292, 300, 304, 325, 328. The Sheffield City Libraries have much material; the Home Office file is HO 45/7656. There was extensive coverage in newspapers, such as the *Sheffield Times* and *Sheffield Daily Telegraph*. Fuller references to the sources are provided in the original version of this article. The novel, C. Reade, *Put Yourself in his Place* (London, 1870), is based on the incident.

[29] 11 Geo. IV c.155 (1830), 8 & 9 Vict. c.175 (1845), and 16 & 17 Vict. c.22 (1853).

desperate attempts were made to reduce the water level, but before anything could be achieved the dam failed catastrophically, for reasons which are still not entirely clear. The breach was 100 yards wide.[30] Some 200 million gallons of water poured down the Loxley valley at around eighteen miles an hour, arriving in Sheffield just after midnight. Immense devastation was caused; some villages in the valley virtually ceased to exist and parts of Sheffield were flooded to a depth of nine feet. The precise loss of life was never established, but there were 238 known deaths. Very large numbers were reduced to destitution; the relief committee, chaired by the Mayor, Thomas Jessop, later reported giving assistance to 20,537 individuals.

In late March a coroner's inquest was held on one victim, Thomas Ellston.[31] It was not possible to determine with any certainty why the failure had occurred, though there was criticism of both the design and the methods of construction; the jury exonerated the engineer, John Towlerton Leather, of personal criminal fault, but added:

that in our opinion there has not been that engineering skill and that attention to the construction of the works which their magnitude and importance demanded: that in our opinion the legislature ought to take such action as will result in a government inspection of all works of this character, and that such inspection ought to be frequent, regular and sufficient.

Naturally enough there was widespread alarm over the possible failure of other dams, and the Home Office employed two civil engineers, Robert Rawlinson and Nathaniel Beardmore, to report on the failure; Rawlinson was then employed to inspect numerous other suspect reservoirs—the Doe Park Reservoir of the Bradford Corporation, the Dunford Reservoir, the Pickthorn and the Varty in Ireland, for example. A considerable body of correspondence and various reports were published as Parliamentary Papers,[32] and pressure was brought on the government to introduce legislation. What was envisaged was the establishment of a permanent inspectorate, such as those which had been or were to be set up for mines, factories, prisons, constabularies, industrial and reformatory schools, burial grounds, anatomy schools, and salmon fisheries.[33] The government bowed to pressure and the matter became the responsibility of the Board of Trade. A bill was introduced and referred to a House of Commons Select Committee, which recommended establishing an inspectorate; it also recommended that there should be strict liability imposed on those responsible for reservoirs.[34] A new bill was introduced but ran out of time, and on 18 February 1867 the new President of the Board of Trade, Sir Stafford Northcote, announced

---

[30] For discussion see Binnie, n. 15 above ch. 13. [31] *The Times*, 24 and 25 Mar. 1864.
[32] BPP 1864 (290) L 363; 1865 (95) XLVII 481, 493; 1865 (179) XLVII 497; 1866 (66) LX 337, (136) LX 351.
[33] J. Pellew, *The Home Office 1848–1914: From Clerks to Bureaucrats* (London, 1982), ch. 6.
[34] See BPP 1865 (112) IV 625, (401) XII 455.

that there was no intention to reintroduce it. Alarm had now died down, and there was no further attempt to introduce state regulation until a serious failure in 1925 in Wales, and a less serious one in Scotland, rekindled anxiety.

The Legal Liability of the Sheffield Waterworks Company

Although the Home Office contrived to head off any risk of becoming responsible, if only politically, for the safety of reservoirs, it was not concerned to come to the aid of the Sheffield Waterworks Company. The private bill, authorizing the construction of the Dale Dyke embankment, had been promoted in 1853, just after the Holmfirth Bilberry Dam had failed, and had drawn everyone's attention to the disastrous consequences of such a failure. Hence the Sheffield mill owners had secured the inclusion in the Sheffield Waterworks Act 1853, as it became, in clause 68, of what came to be called a Holmfirth clause:

The said Company shall . . . pay and make good to the Owners, Lessees and Occupiers of all Mills, Manufactories, Buildings, Lands and Grounds, and to every Person whomsoever, all Loss [etc.] . . . of what Nature and Kind soever, as well immediate as consequential, which such Owners . . . or other Person may suffer . . . by reason or in consequence of the Failure or giving way of the Reservoirs, Embankments, Watercourses or other Works of the said Company.

Such clauses became standard form, but this was the first example. Soon after the disaster local solicitors organized a meeting in Sheffield at the Victoria Hotel, and it was decided to take the opinion of Sir Hugh Cairns QC and a Mr Brown. They advised

that the Company are liable to make compensation to every person without distinction of class, who has sustained any legal damage or injury by the flood in question; and the learned counsel think it clear that section 68 of the Act of 1853 imposes this liability upon the Company without proof of negligence on their part and though there should have been no negligence.[35]

The Company also consulted lawyers—the Attorney-General, Sir Roundell Palmer, and Messrs Quain, Crompton, and Mellish, who do not appear to have dissented from this view. It was clear that the damages must be enormous; an estimate by the company, excluding death and personal injuries, was £327,000. The principal assets of the Company were its waterworks, including the derelict Dale Dyke Dam and the unfinished Agden Reservoir; they were virtually unsaleable. As Mr Ferrand, MP for Bradford, put it, 'of what value is a right of action against a bankrupt Company?'[36]

The directors nevertheless came up with a scheme. A new Act should be promoted, enabling £400,000 to be raised, out of which all legitimate claims would be met; adjudication upon them should be taken out of the hands of the courts and entrusted to special commissioners. Ultimately the money had to come from somewhere, and the plan involved acquiring under the new Act a right to raise water rates by a moderate amount—in fact a rise of 25 per cent in perpetuity was envisaged. The publication of this plan restored the value of the shares in the Company, but caused fury when it was realized that the Company proposed to make the inhabitants of Sheffield pay for the disaster, and might in the end even profit from its hazardous activities. But in spite of opposition from the Sheffield Corporation, the scheme was embodied in a new Act which became law on 29 July 1864.[37] The rise in rates was, however, limited to a term of twenty-five years, and an attempt by the Company to make it possible to require those claiming for death or personal injury to prove negligence failed. Proof of negligence, never admitted by the Company, would have been extremely expensive, and probably impossible; five engineers consulted by the company favoured landslip as an explanation, and the other eleven experts consulted at the time had other explanations. In modern times, G. M. Binnie has suggested a new explanation, according to which the core fractured under stresses caused by uneven support from its bedrock foundation, but the precise sequence of events remains to this day uncertain.[38]

William Overend QC became the chairman of the Sheffield Inundation Commissioners, sitting with J. J. Smith, a local magistrate and manufacturer, and M. F. Mills, a real estate agent. The number of claims received was 7,200, aggregating £455,000; the massive register of claims and their outcome survives in the Sheffield Central Library. A tricky question, on which the commissioners spent two days hearing arguments from George Mellish QC and Henry Manisty QC, was whether compensation was to be paid for purely economic consequential loss, for which there were many claims, or whether recovery was limited to damages which would be recoverable at common law, which, it was thought, did not allow such recovery. The commissioners ruled against any such liability, thereby substantially reducing the total bill. In the event, the commissioners completed their work in 1865, awarding a total of £276,000 compensation. This was far and away the largest sum recovered by way of damages in the nineteenth century. The total cost incurred was £332,242. Only 650 claims were actually determined by the commission, the others being settled or withdrawn. The vast majority were for loss of property, but not by the wealthy, though there were, of course, some large awards; in a poor society, loss of what little property is owned is peculiarly grave. There were seventy-nine awards for loss of life, claims by dependants being governed by the Fatal Accidents Act 1846. The average award was £115, with a range from £1,000 to a widow, down to £3 1s.

---

[37] 27 & 28 Vict. c.324.

[38] See BPP 1865 (232) XLVII 455, and W. Taylor, *Analysis of Evidence before the Sheffield Jury on the Cause of the Failure of the Bradfield Reservoir* (Sheffield, 1864). See G. M. Binnie, *Early Victorian Water Engineers* (London, 1981), ch. 13 and personal correspondence.

to the parents of a child. There were 269 for personal injury, averaging just under £19.

A charitable appeal fund was also established, run by Mayor Jessop of Sheffield, who was anxious that charity should not in any way reduce the liabilities of the company, but merely offer speedy interim relief. This policy led to acrimonious disputes and Chancery litigation but, broadly speaking, the Mayor avoided a situation in which charity picked up the bill, as had happened after the Holmfirth disaster.

The Sheffield inundation and its aftermath can hardly have failed to draw the attention of lawyers, and the public generally, to reservoir safety and the problem of the social cost of development. Incidental litigation, in *In re the Sheffield Waterworks Company*,[39] brought the procedures of the commission before Pollock CB and Bramwell, Channell, and Pigott BB in November 1865. The incident also provided the Sheffield Corporation with an argument for municipal ownership of the Waterworks Company, which came about in 1888; if the City had to pay for the disaster, it might as well reap the rewards. But after around a century fashions changed, and private ownership took over once again.

The Failure of the Ainsworth Mill Lodge in 1860

The reservoir involved in *Rylands* v. *Fletcher*, or Number 2 Lodge, to use the Lancashire term, still exists, and, when I visited it in 1983, was still leaking and half-empty. It remains in this state at the time of writing. In comparison with the Bilberry Dam or Bradfield Reservoir, it is a modest piece of engineering, having a maximum capacity of a mere 4,350,000 gallons, and covering 1.51 acres. It was formed not by damming a valley, but by excavating a gently sloping site and piling the spoil around the excavation. The water originally came from another lodge, Number 3, higher up the hill side, and was fed to Number 1 Lodge, now filled in, close to the mill. Today the supply comes in part from a deep bore-hole. Legally, Number 2 Lodge was quite different from the Bilberry or Dale Dyke Reservoirs. It was not constructed under statutory powers, but as an exercise of a private landowner's right to do as he wished with his property. It is still in constant use, providing water for the Ainsworth Finishing Company, working the Ainsworth Mill. This was built in the early nineteenth century, and was originally a calico mill.[40] The mill stood on land owned by the Earl of Wilton's settled estates, and at the time of my visit was held under a 999-year lease granted on 4 February 1911 to the predecessors in title of the Ainsworth Finishing Company. Back in the 1860s it was held on a similar lease.

[39] (1865) LR 1 Ex. 54.
[40] E. Baines, *The History of the County Palatine and Duchy of Lancaster* (Manchester, 1888–93), ii, 684.

In 1839 the mill was acquired by the firm of John Rylands and Son.[41] John
E. Rylands (1801–88), 'the Wellington of Commerce', 'the Cotton King', was
an enormously successful entrepreneur who, with his two elder brothers and
father, operated the family business of Rylands and Sons (1819–42); he became
a partner in 1821. The partnership was dissolved in 1842, before his father died
in 1847, and thereafter the firm, which retained the same name, was under his
sole control. John Rylands became the leading textile merchant in the land, and
by 1865 was employing 6,500 people, more than any other firm in the cotton
industry. By 1873 the figure was just under 12,000. He became the biggest
employer of labour in the country, and when he died at Longford Hall on 11
December 1888 his personal estate was worth £2,574,922, then the largest fortune yet acquired by a cotton manufacturer. He is today remembered principally
because his third wife and widow, Enriqueta A. Tennant, in 1892 bought the
library of Earl Spencer of Althorp, Northamptonshire, and established the John
Rylands Library at a cost of around a million as his memorial. It is now administered by the University of Manchester.

The Ainsworth mill was steam powered, and in 1865 was running 600 looms;
it was managed by Jehu Horrocks, who appears in the census returns for 1851
living on the Bury to Bolton Road where the mill is situated, with his wife,
Maria, and their six children.[42] Construction of the new lodge would begin in
1859 or early 1860, and was presumably intended to provide a reliable source
of water for steam power, perhaps because the number of looms was being
increased.[43] The site was selected by the engineer and contractors employed by
Rylands and Horrocks; I have been unable to identify them.

The land upon which the reservoir was constructed was also owned by the
then second Earl of Wilton, Thomas Grosvenor, and Viscount Grey de Wilton
(1799–1882), a celebrated and enthusiastic fox hunter, organist, yachtsman,
composer of psalm tunes, and lover. The *New Sporting Magazine* depicted him
in a poem in 1838:

> Whilst on his switch tail'd bay, with wandering eye,
> Attenuated W——n canters by,
> His character how difficult to know,
> A compound of psalm tunes, and Tallo-ho!

The reservoir was constructed under either a licence or a lease, probably the
latter, with a short right of way to provide access across the agricultural land
which surrounds it.

[41] On Rylands see in particular D. A. Farnie, *John Rylands of Manchester* (Manchester, 1993),
also 56 *Bulletin of the John Rylands Library* 93–129 (1973). Dr Farnie, on whom my brief account
is based, gives full references which supplant those provided in the original version of this article.
[42] HO 107/2215. He was probably related to James Horrocks (1832) who became Chairman of
the firm after John Ryland's death.
[43] My account of the case is based on the reports cited in n. 3 above and on material in the House
of Lords Record Office (242 Appeal Cases, Item 36, 1867–8), and E 13/1427, also *Liverpool Daily
Post* and *Liverpool Courier*, 6 Sep. 1862.

Construction was completed in 1860, and in the course of the work five old blocked vertical shafts were discovered in the bed of the excavation, filled with marl or soil similar to the surrounding soil. On 11 December, when the new reservoir was partially full, one of these burst downwards, emptying it. The shafts connected with old abandoned coal workings lying under the lands of the Earl of Wilton, and these were connected with the active underground workings of the nearby Red House Colliery to the east of the mill, so called because they were adjacent to a red-roofed house, now demolished but replaced with a modern red-roofed house. When I visited the area, the site was derelict and dangerous, the location of the mine shaft concealed by undergrowth.

Thomas Fletcher operated this mine and a number of others in the area, and he was the plaintiff in the action; his mine may well have been the source of the coal used at the mill.[44] His mine was inundated, and work had to stop. It is nowhere made absolutely clear in the finding of facts arising out of the litigation whether the critical connection between his mine and the disused passages under the reservoir was made before the reservoir burst, or after, but it is likely that the connection existed before the reservoir was filled and burst. Had it been made after, one would expect the finding to be that the inundation was Fletcher's own fault for not following good practice. Inundations, often caused by encounters with disused workings, were a common source of accidents in the nineteenth century, and the mining inspector for the area, John Dickinson, may have even had the incident at the Red House pit in mind when he wrote in his report for 1861:

The maps and plans of the underground workings are now, I find, in nearly every case kept in the best styles . . . Of many old workings, however, there is no plan, and when workings are going on near to them, great care requires to be exercised in keeping bore holes in advance, and on the sides, to prevent inundations.[45]

As we shall see, counsel at one stage in the litigation did try to suggest that Fletcher was himself to blame.[46]

Fletcher had, in 1849, been granted by Lord Wilton the coal-mining rights under land which lay to the south-east of the reservoir site. His lease expired in 1855. Also in 1849 he had been given an agreement for a sixteen-year lease, to commence in 1855, both of the same rights, and of rights under other land belonging to Lord Wilton. But the exploitation of some of this coal proved uneconomic and, in 1850, with Lord Wilton's permission, he sank a new pit, the Red House pit, on Lord Wilton's land. From this he began to get the coal under the other lands of Lord wilton. These coal deposits lay closer to the reservoir site

---

[44] (1805–93). Other mines included the Stopes and Bents Colliery at Little Lever, the Brightmet at Bolton, the Stopes at Radcliffe, and Clough Side at Outwood. His home came to be Lever House at Little Lever. I am told that other members of this family ran collieries up to the date of nationalization of the industry in 1947.

[45] BPP (1862) 312 [3050] XXII 293.　　　　[46] See below 214.

and to the Ainsworth mill. From 1855 he also worked the Radcliffe (or Wilton) Colliery, which was somewhat further away.

No lease was ever granted of the coal levels worked from the Red House pit. There was a verbal understanding that this colliery was a substitute for such of the coal levels demised in the original lease of 1849, and referred to in the agreement for a lease of the same year, as had proved uneconomic, and that a lease would in due course be granted of both the Red House Colliery and the Radcliffe Colliery. At the time of the incident Fletcher was either operating the Red House pit under an agreement for a lease, or was a tenant from year to year, and the case was eventually determined on the latter basis.

Between the Red House pit and the site of the reservoir lay lands belonging to Walter Hutton and John Whitehead. Fletcher obtained permission to extend the workings under Whitehead's land, and began to do so in 1851. He came across some old abandoned workings, which apparently connected with other abandoned workings under Hutton's land, which lay nearer the site of the reservoir, though this may not have been appreciated at the time. Since the dip of the coal seam was downwards between the reservoir site and the Red House pit, the water which entered the old workings on 11 December 1860 flowed inexorably into the Red House Colliery.

Thomas Fletcher, confronted with an everyday mining problem, set about pumping the water out and repairing the workings. This took until March 1861, and apparently cleared the mine; the flow of water must have been at a controllable rate. But life in the mining business never was simple, and on 17 April the boiler of his pumping engine burst. Fragments were blown southwards for 100 yards, *en passant* hitting a horse and cart, and injuring the unfortunate carter, James Butterworth. The engine tender, Thomas Segas, and his banksman, Ralph Makin, were badly injured, buildings were demolished, and even Fletcher's book-keeper was hurt. Nobody was safe in the nineteenth-century industrial world.[47] So the Red House pit again began to flood. At this point John Dickinson, the inspector of coal mines, visited the mine, and warned Fletcher 'of the danger and responsibility he would incur if he employed men in the Red House Colliery for the purpose of working the same whilst the said reservoir was used for storing the water'.[48] He must have feared a more violent inruption. On his advice Fletcher abandoned the mine, though at the time the reservoir was empty.

Dickinson's caution proved to be justified; the reservoir was repaired and refilled, and then burst downwards a second time in August 1861. The mine was later acquired by the Ainsworth mill and used as a source of water; maps show the Red House pumping station on the site, and as late as the 1940s there was a scheme to draw water from it. Water is still leaking into the underground workings, but sufficient remains in the reservoir for it to be used for fishing.

---

[47] Accounts in the *Bury Guardian and General Advertiser* and the *Bury Times*, 20 Apr. 1861.
[48] Quotation from the arbitrator's report.

Dickinson did not record the incident in his annual report; it was a minor affair, and local newspapers did not mention it.[49] Locally all memory of it has long passed away, and when I visited the mill nobody knew of the leading case associated with it.

A Suit for Negligence and its Transmutation

Deprived of his mine, and presumably defeated in whatever negotiations took place, Thomas Fletcher, on 4 November 1861, commenced an action for £5,000 damages, suing Rylands and Horrocks rather than the engineer and contractors. They are nowhere named; conceivably they became insolvent and were not worth suing. As later itemized, Fletcher's losses were £348 for equipment left in the mine, £331 for pumping expenses, £56 loss of profit up to abandonment, and £202 loss of interest as tenant from year to year (or £670 as he was a sixteen-year lessee). The action, which was framed wholly as an action for negligence, came on for trial at the Liverpool Summer Assizes before Mellor J and a special jury on 3 September 1862. At the judge's suggestion a verdict was entered with consent in favour of the plaintiff for £5,000 and £2 costs, subject to a reference to a barrister arbitrator, James Kemplay.[50] The function of the fictitious verdict was to give the arbitrator's award the status of a court judgment. The judge suggested that Kemplay should be given power to call in a mining engineer, and if need be to state a case—that is, formulate a question of law for the opinion of the court if need be. But this power was apparently not expressly set out in the order.

Nothing more is heard about the case until 31 December 1864, when Channell B ordered that, instead of making an award, the arbitrator should have power to state a special case for the opinion of the Exchequer of Pleas, if he thought fit, and that the parties should be allowed to bring error on the judgment of the Court. No report of the proceedings before Channell B has been traced. But it seems that what had started life as a simple action for damages for negligence, referred for inexpensive determination to an arbitrator, had come to be viewed as an important case, fit to be taken up the hierarchy of courts on a writ of error. Given the chronology—the Sheffield disaster occurred in March 1864—it seems a reasonable inference that the Dale Dyke disaster and its legal aftermath had suggested to the lawyers concerned that *Rylands* v. *Fletcher* was, potentially, a leading case.

James Kemplay stated a special case on 4 January 1865. This set out what had happened, and in particular found that, although there had been negligence by the contractors, there had been no negligence by the defendants. The case

---

[49] Dickinson's report (BPP (1862) 312 [3050] XXII 293) does mention the boiler explosion.
[50] (1810–82), Middle Temple, QC 1872.

concluded: 'The Question for the opinion of the court is whether the plaintiff is entitled to recover any and if so what damages from the defendants by reason of the matters hereinbefore stated.'

The case came before Pollock CB and Bramwell, Martin, and Channell BB on 3, 4, and 5 May 1865. By then a fault-based claim had been transmuted into a strict liability claim. We can be perfectly sure that the judges were very familiar with the story of the recent Sheffield inundation and the earlier Holmfirth disaster. The two incidents, occurring in a country liberally endowed with reservoirs of all shapes, sizes, and ages, must surely have brought home to them, as to the public generally, the menacing power of these bodies of water, capable at any moment of unleashing death and destruction on an enormous scale. The counsel involved were Henry Manisty QC and John A. Russell for the plaintiff, and George Mellish QC with Thomas Jones for the defendants. Both leading counsel had appeared before the Overend Commission to argue the question of consequential loss, and had been briefed in *In re the Sheffield Waterworks Act*; Mellish had been earlier engaged by the Sheffield Waterworks Company in connection with the disaster.

The judges would also know of the Board of Trade's proposed legislation. Most large reservoirs were, as we have seen, constructed under statutory powers, and liability was primarily determined, as in the Sheffield case, by the legislature. The reservoir in *Rylands* v. *Fletcher* was a private venture; the special case provided the judges with an opportunity, if they wished to take it, to pronounce generally upon what the common law had to say about bursting reservoirs; the matter was primarily their responsibility, not that of Parliament, at least until the outcome of the proposed legislation was known.

According to the one theory of judicial decision, the orthodox theory, courts are never concerned to determine wide issues of policy. Their job is simply to determine the case in hand, saying what rights the parties have under the law. In modern times this theory has been elaborately developed by Ronald Dworkin.[51] His theory, wholly devoid of empirical basis, reflects a convention of legal reasoning, long established in the common law, and in conformity with it there is no explicit reference in the arguments or opinions of the Court of Exchequer to either of the two major disasters. But when Henry Manisty, arguing for the plaintiff, opened with the remark: 'A large collection of water is a thing pregnant with dangers, and it behoves anyone who makes a collection for his profit, to beware how he may prejudice his neighbours by mismanaging it,'[52] the court could hardly fail to catch the reference. George Mellish's argument for the defendants seems to have been strongly influenced by the context, in which those whose reservoirs failed could expect little sympathy. Thus, he did not attempt to argue that his clients would not have been liable in an ordinary case

---

[51] See generally his *Law's Empire* (London, 1986) and *A Matter of Principle* (Harvard, 1985).
[52] (1865) 11 Jur. (NS) 714.

of the failure of a reservoir, which would plainly cause damage if it failed. Instead he emphasized that it was Fletcher's secret mining operations, of which his clients had no knowledge, which gave rise to the danger; the drift of his argument was that the accident was all Fletcher's own fault. But for this, as we have seen, there was no firm factual basis in the arbitrator's finding to which he could point. Mellish also relied on the fact that this was not a typical embanked reservoir at all; there was no reason to suppose that any damage would arise if it failed, which came about only through the unknown underground passages.

The three judges who took part in the decision disagreed. Pollock CB and Martin B ruled for the defendants; both opinions attempt to distinguish the facts of the case not so much from some earlier decision, for there was none directly in point, but from the Dale Dyke disaster, which legal convention forbade them from mentioning. Pollock stressed the existence of the underground passages, and reserved his opinion on liability for water escaping on the surface. Martin B made the same point, adding:

It does not appear that there was any embankment or that the water in the reservoir was ever above the level of the natural surface of the land, and the water escaped from the bottom of the reservoir, and in the ordinary course would descend by gravitation into the defendant's own land, and they did not know of the old workings.[53]

He employed other arguments—the case was determined by authority (Pollock said it was not, and Martin indeed said the same in one passage)—and 'to hold the defendant liable without negligence would be to constitute him an insurer, which in my opinion would be contrary to legal analogy and principle'.[54] He clearly thought that fault liability was the norm in tort law, and that in the absence of knowledge of the underground workings there was no duty of care at all. But conceivably he would have regarded an embanked dangerous reservoir as a nuisance, and actionable as such. In fact the piling-up of the spoil meant that there was an embankment on the downhill side, but the judges would not have realized this.

Bramwell B dissented, strongly favouring strict liability. Part of his opinion was devoted to reconciling his view with authority, claiming that the defendants had committed either a trespass, relying on *Gregory* v. *Piper* (1829),[55] or a nuisance. As to trespass, his colleague Pollock CB had expressed no opinion, and Martin B thought there was no trespass. In principle, however, Bramwell B argued that 'the general law in matters wholly independent of contract' imposed liability 'on the plain ground that the defendants have caused water to flow into the plaintiff's mines, which but for the defendants' act would not have gone there'.[56] Later he added: 'the defendant's innocence, whatever may be its moral bearing on the case, is immaterial in point of law.' His reasoning, applied to the Dale Dyke disaster, would have made the company liable at common law without

---

[53] 159 ER 737 at 745.   [54] Ibid. 747.
[55] 9 B & C 591, 109 ER 220.   [56] 159 ER 744.

proof of negligence, the result which had been brought about by the Holmfirth clause in its private Act.

Bramwell's commitment in this case to strict liability is in line with other decisions of his in which he favoured industry internalizing its own costs.[57] But, as we shall see, his later decision in *Nichols* v. *Marsland* (1876)[58] seems almost contradictory. Bramwell was an opinionated man with an interest in political economy, as we have seen; he expressed his views vigorously, both on and off the bench, in speeches, letters to the press, and pamphlets. He was an exponent of rugged individualism, deeply suspicious of collectivist or paternalist legislation, or indeed any form of intermeddling by the State. His commitment to freedom of contract was absolute; he placed a high value on individual responsibility and this, in the criminal law, brought him into bitter conflict with the alienists who saw the irresponsible mad when Bramwell could see only the bad.[59] In tort law he consequently enthused over the defence of contributory negligence, and over the notion of assumption of risk, and the fellow servant rule, which he viewed as contractually based. And whenever a plaintiff could, in some sense, have adjusted his conduct so as to avoid the accident, there was a risk that Bramwell would forget about the internalization of costs and find against him.[60]

The most striking example is *Mangan* v. *Atherton* (1866).[61] The defendant exposed in the street a machine for crushing oil cake, unfenced and unsupervised. The plaintiff, aged 4, was returning home from school in the company of his 7-year-old brother and some other children. Encouraged by his brother, he put his hand in the cogs, and his fingers were all crushed and had to be amputated. At trial in the Staffordshire County Court he recovered £10. This was reversed, Bramwell saying:

the defendant is no more liable than if he had exposed goods covered with poisonous paint and the child had sucked it. It may seem a harsh way of putting it, but suppose this machine had been of delicate construction, and had been injured by the child's fingers, would not the child, in spite of his tender years, have been liable to an action as a tortfeasor?

As J. P. S. McClaren has pointed out,[62] Bramwell's erratic decisions turned upon how he characterized the facts. Given the distances involved, obvious enough

[57] See above 173; *Bamford* v. *Turley* (1863) 3 B & S 62, 122 ER 25 (where he again differed from Pollock CB); *Hammersmith and City Railway Co.* v. *Brand* (1867) LR 2 QB 223, 36 LJQB 139 (EC).

[58] 2 Ex. D 1.

[59] S. Staples, Supplement to the DNB; R. Smith, *Trial by Medicine: Insanity and Responsibility in Victorian Trials* (Edinburgh, 1981); N. Walker, *Crime and Insanity in England* (Edinburgh, 1968), 106, 128–9.

[60] In addition to cases discussed above at 173 and below 221 Bramwell's views can also be followed in *Blyth* v. *Birmingham Waterworks Co.* (1856) 11 Ex. 781, 156 ER 1047; *Cooke* v. *Waring* (1863) 2 H & C 332, 159 ER 138; *Byrne* v. *Boadle* (1863) 2 H & C 722, 159 ER 299; *Stubley* v. *London and North Western Railway Co.* (1865) LR 1 Ex. 13; *Powell* v. *Fall* (1880) 5 QBD 597.

[61] LR 1 Ex. 239.

[62] 'Nuisance Law and the Industrial Revolution—Some Lessons from Social History', 3 *OJLS* 155 at 192 and generally.

from the plan used in court, Fletcher must have known of the construction work, and he, too, could have taken precautions (as by blocking off connections with the disused workings) and so avoided the accident, or so at least it could have been argued.

Rylands v. Fletcher in the Higher Courts

Having lost in the Court of Exchequer, Fletcher pressed on to the next tribunal, the Exchequer Chamber, where he won on 14 May 1866; the costs by now amounted to £1,500, considerably more than the sum agreed in damages, which was £937.[63] Sir Colin Blackburn delivered the sole opinion, which was agreed by Willes, Keating, Mellor (the trial judge), Montague Smith, and Lush JJ. There is again no specific reference to the Dale Dyke disaster in the arguments or opinion, but the court surely had the matter well in mind. Henry Manisty QC opened his argument thus:

The principle of law which governs this case is, that he who does upon his own lands acts which, though lawful in themselves, may become sources of mischief to his neighbours, is bound to prevent the mischief from occurring. This will be peculiarly the case when the act done consists in the construction and use of artificial works, for the purpose of collecting and impounding vast quantities of an element which will certainly cause mischief if it escapes.[64]

Of course, on the facts no 'vast quantities' were involved: Manisty was talking about the Dale Dyke Reservoir. Later, Blackburn referred in general terms to the case of damage done by the bursting of waterworks companies' reservoirs, and Manisty pointed out that 'such cases usually arise under a clause in the special act of the company, imposing on them a liability to make compensation'.[65] He went on to argue that even at common law there would be liability, relying upon *Bagnall* v. *London and North West Railway Co.* (1861–2),[66] but though he won the case he failed to convince either Blackburn or Willes, who had delivered the opinion in the earlier case, that this case supported him. George Mellish for the defendants argued that there was only liability for negligence, as in personal injury cases, and as he argued there are indications that the Dale Dyke disaster was in everyone's mind. Thus Lush took up the point that this was an excavated, not an embanked reservoir: 'Suppose the banks of the reservoir had burst and the water had flowed over the surface and down the pit's mouth.' Later the same judge returned to the theme of catastrophes: 'Suppose the case of a gunpowder magazine bursting, what liability do you say its owners would incur?' Eventually, in the slightly mocking words of the *Times* reporter, Blackburn delivered his opinion 'at very great length'. His well-known opinion, with its elaborate

[63] (1866) LR 1 Ex. 265, 12 Jur. (NS) 603, E 13/1427.   [64] LR 1 Ex. 265 at 269.
[65] LR 1 Ex. 265 at 270–1.   [66] (1861) 7 H & N 423, 158 ER 538.

display of historical learning, conforms to the judicial convention that judges decide the case before them, not other cases, real or imagined. But the mask falls when, with one slip of the pen, he made a curious oblique reference to the Dale Dyke disaster. The slip occurs in a passage in which he referred to actions brought some years earlier through the escape of chlorine fumes from Liverpool alkali works: 'There is no difference in this respect between chlorine and water; both will, if they escape, do damage, the one by scorching, and the other by *drowning*, and he who brings them there must at his peril see that they do not escape and do that mischief.'[67] Nobody was drowned by the inundation which the court was supposed to be considering; Blackburn was surely thinking about what the common law should say about a catastrophe like the Dale Dyke disaster, which did drown many people.

Two days later, Thomas Jones entered 'a suggestion of error':

1. That there was no duty on the Defendants to take any precautions to prevent the water entering the Plaintiff's mine.
2. That the negligence found in this case is not negligence of any precautions the Defendants were bound to take.
3. That the damage to the mine arose from the Plaintiff's own Acts and Defaults.
4. That the negligence found by the arbitrator was the negligence of skilled persons (viz.) the engineer and contractor for which the Defendants are not responsible.
5. That the Plaintiff has no interest in the mine.

To this the plaintiff's reply was:

1. That the Defendants have for their own purposes collected and impounded a vast quantity of water in a Reservoir made by them on their own land, and the water having without any fault or default of the Plaintiff, escaped out of the Reservoir and flowed into and damaged the Plaintiff's Mine, they, the Defendants, are liable to compensate the Plaintiff for such damage.
2. That under the circumstances stated in the Special Case, the Action was maintainable against the Defendants.[68]

About this time George Mellish dropped out and was replaced as counsel by Sir Roundell Palmer, who, as we have seen, had been the principal adviser to the Sheffield Waterworks Company back in 1864.

The case was argued before the Lords on 6 and 7 July 1868, and the decision in favour of the plaintiff of 17 July was approved by an oddly constituted House of Lords comprising, so far as is revealed in the law report, only Lords Cairns and Cranworth.[69] The third Law Lord who should have been there was Lord Colonsay, but for some reason he failed to turn up, and it has been suggested that the Archbishop of Armagh was pressed into service to make up the quorum.[70]

---

[67] N. 65 above, at 285–6, my italics. The reference is to the cases discussed above at 176–9; chlorine is a slip for muriatic acid.
[68] E 13/1427.   [69] (1868) 3 HL 330.
[70] R. F. V. Heuston, 'Who Was the Third Lord in Rylands v. Fletcher', 86 *LQR* 160.

The two opinions are perfunctory; the impression they give, combined with the failure to raise objections over the lack of a third law lord, is that the answer to the question posed by the appeal was thought obvious. Lord Cairns expressly agreed with Blackburn's statement of the law; it will be recalled that he had been the legal adviser to the Sheffield mill owners. Whether Lord Cairns, by referring in his opinion to 'non-natural' use of property, whatever that meant, intended to modify Blackburn's formulation of the law, and restrict in some obscure way the scope of strict liability, has been much discussed as a matter of legal dogmatics.[71] As a matter of history it is fairly clear that he did not have this intention.

The Aftermath of Rylands v. Fletcher

The apparent outcome of the House of Lords decision was that the common law imposed strict liability without proof of negligence on those who operated private reservoirs which failed and caused property damage to neighbours. The position over personal injuries was left a little uncertain. The common law thus coincided with the state of the law imposed by Parliament in the Acts of 1853 and 1864 relating to the Sheffield Waterworks Company, a privately owned utility company. The coincidence, I should suggest, was not accidental. The judges may well have felt that the Acts expressed a prevailing legislative policy, to which they should conform; perhaps they thought that, by backing strict liability at common law, they might encourage Parliament to pass general legislation imposing such liability on all water undertakings.

Be that as it may, no general rule of strict liability now applied to all reservoirs. There were in 1868 hundreds of other reservoirs constructed under private Acts; some were governed by Holmfirth clauses, others were not. The legal position of those not so covered remained uncertain; the essential question was whether the rule in *Rylands* v. *Fletcher* applied to them or not. The litigation presented the judges with an opportunity to impose a uniform principle of liability upon all such works, a uniformity which in 1868 did not exist; private legislation left very considerable freedom of interpretation to the courts.

Local and Personal Acts and Legal Liability

The absence of any uniform scheme of legal liability calls for explanation. The industrial and agricultural revolutions of the eighteenth and nineteenth centuries were accompanied by the evolution of new legal regimes; the typical instrument

---

[71] He presents the expression as reflecting the ruling in the earlier case of *Smith* v. *Kendrick* (1849) 7 CB 515, 137 ER 205, which does not use it. See F. H. Newark 'Non-natural User and *Rylands* v. *Fletcher*' (1961) 24 *MLR* 557.

employed was the private or special Act, technically called a local and personal Act, passed by Parliament, and promoted by the advocates of change and development who hoped to profit by it. The judicial role in interpreting such legislation, and filling in the gaps, was important but peripheral. The number of special Acts passed was very considerable, reaching a peak in 1846 during the railway boom, when 402 were passed. In the same year only 170 public Acts were passed. In the 1860s the annual figure for special Acts fluctuated between 159 in 1869 and 372 in 1865. In the first fifty years of Victoria's reign, as Frederick Clifford pointed out in dedicating his *History of Private Bill Legislation* to her, 'nearly Eleven thousand Local and Personal Statutes have been passed by the Parliament, and received your Majesty's assent'. He argued that this legislative activity coincided with a 'period of social and industrial Progress throughout the United Kingdom of which History affords hardly any other example'.[72] In addition to railways, agricultural inclosures, tramways, river tunnels, gas and later electricity utilities, improvements in the navigability of rivers, canals, harbours, docks, town improvements, policing and sanitation, turnpike roads, burial grounds—the list is endless—were all authorized by special Acts, which were the typical instrument of the agricultural and industrial revolutions.

There were two principal reasons for the use of special Acts. One was the need to override private property rights, which are not compatible with rapid economic development. The other was the wish of the entrepreneurs to escape from the limitations of the free market and produce conditions of monopoly and often to acquire what amounted to legislative powers themselves. The price paid in return by the developers was some degree of state regulation of the enterprise—for example, a limit on profits and charges, or an obligation, for example, in the case of a canal company, to accept all custom. The promoters of a particular scheme could and did devise their own Bills, adapted to their own needs and interests. Depending on the level of objection and their success in Parliament, the end-product on the statute book differed from scheme to scheme. Amongst the entrepreneurial class there was absolutely no hostility to legislative interference in the economy. It was through such interference that they were enabled to prosper. I do not know how modern theorists who oppose state interference in the economy would categorize privately promoted special Acts, whose effect depends upon the doctrine of Parliamentary sovereignty. Plainly they cannot be regarded as products of the market.[73]

There was, however, a move towards uniformity, which gathered momentum during the nineteenth century; the critical agricultural and industrial developments, however, long predate it. The starting-point was in 1829, when there was published a set of sixteen specimen Bills, approved by the relevant committee

---

[72] F. Clifford, *A History of Private Bill Legislation* (London, 1885 and 1887).
[73] See the views of Coase discussed above in Ch. 7.

of the House of Lords, including one for a waterworks. The sixth Earl of Shaftesbury was chairman of committees from 1814 to 1851, and he encouraged uniformity, as in the 1840s, by circulating model Bills to Parliamentary agents, and by insisting on the inclusion of standard clauses in particular types of Acts, these being known as 'Shaftesbury clauses'.[74] This led in 1845 to the passing of general legislation, promoted by the Board of Trade, which automatically incorporated certain provisions in particular special Acts. The general Acts were called 'clauses' or 'consolidation' Acts, those of 1845 being the Companies Clauses, Land Clauses, and Railways Clauses Consolidation Acts.[75]

So far as waterworks and reservoirs were concerned, it was not entirely clear whether they were the concern of the Board of Trade or the Home Office. No uniform scheme of legal liability had been established, as we have seen, by 1868. There was a Waterworks Clauses Act in 1847, which contains no general provision on liability, though section 27 preserves, in favour of mine owners, any rights to compensation for flooding they might have at common law.[76] The Waterworks Clauses Act of 1863 was similar; it did, as we have seen, respond to the Holmfirth disaster by setting up a somewhat futile safety procedure for lowering the level of dangerous reservoirs. It is against this background that the courts possessed an opportunity after the decision in *Rylands* v. *Fletcher* to impose what was now the common law theory of strict liability for bursting private reservoirs to reservoirs generally, and indeed to develop a coherent and consistent scheme of civil liability to all dangerous public and private works. But no sooner had the decision been taken than the opportunity was lost, and the law governing bursting reservoirs was reduced to a state of schizophrenic uncertainty by the House of Lords itself in *The Directors of the Hammersmith and City Railway Company* v. *Brand* (1869).[77] Confusion was further confounded by two later decisions, both in 1876, *River Wear Commissioners* v. *Adamson* in the House of Lords[78] and *Nichols* v. *Marsland* in the newly established Court of Appeal.[79]

The *Hammersmith Railway* case, to which I have already briefly referred,[80] had begun back in 1864, and was the culmination of a long line of cases dealing with the scope of compensation for statutorily authorized works. These cases had generated considerable judicial disagreement; the most recent example was *Rickett* v. *Directors of the Metropolitan Railway* in 1867.[81] It was argued in the Lords on 3 and 6 July 1868 before Lords Cairns, Chelmsford, and Colonsay;

---

[74] See D. L. Rydz, *The Parliamentary Agents: A History* (London, 1979), 52–5.

[75] 8 Vict. cc.16, 18, 20. See Clifford, n. 72 above, i, 103, 221–3, 250, and ii, ch. 15.; O. Williams, *The Historical Development of Private Bill Procedure and Standing Orders in the House of Commons* (1948), 107–11, and on Shaftesbury clauses see Lord Blackburn in *River Wear Commissioners* v. *Adamson* (1877) 2 App. Cas. 743 at 765.

[76] 10 & 11 Vict. c.17; the provision had to be expressly incorporated in a special Act.

[77] (1869) LR 4 HL 171; in the lower courts (1865) LR 1 QB 130 (Mellor and Lush JJ) and (1867) 2 QB 223 (Bramwell, Keating, Montague Smith BB, with Channell B dissenting).

[78] (1877) 2 App. Cas. 743 and (1876) 1 QBD 546 (Court of Appeal).

[79] (1876) 2 Ex. D 1.   [80] See above 174.

[81] 5 B & S 149, 156, 122 ER 787, 790, (1867) II HL 175.

argument in *Rylands* v. *Fletcher* took place on 6 July, too. The Lords, after argument, put a question to the judges, which was answered after a long delay, no doubt caused by disagreements, on 22 April 1869. The question at issue in the case was regarded as being of very great difficulty and importance, and a decision was not given until 23 July 1869.

The plaintiff's wife owned a house by a railway built by the appellants under a special act of 1861, into which were incorporated the provisions of the Land Clauses and Railway Clauses Consolidation Acts of 1845. The operation of the railway, without negligence, caused damage by vibration to the house; no property of the plaintiff was taken or used in the construction of the railway. A jury, under section 68 of the Land Clauses Act, assessed compensation payable as £272. This was *compensation* under the statutory scheme, not *damages* for common law nuisance. Usually such compensation was settled by negotiation, but in this instance it became the focus of controversy. The case turned on whether the right to compensation was limited to loss caused through the activity of constructing the railway, or whether it extended to provide compensation for loss caused later through its normal operation without negligence. The critical legislative provision was section 6 of the Railway Clauses Consolidation Act of 1845: 'In exercising the power given to the company . . . the company shall make to the owners and occupiers of . . . any lands . . . injuriously affected by the Construction thereof, full compensation for all damage sustained', but this appeared in a part of the Act introduced by the words: 'And with respect to the construction of the railway and the works connected therewith . . .'.[82] The case could be viewed simply as raising a tricky point of interpretation. Viewed more broadly, it gave the judges a chance to address themselves generally to the problem of social cost, to formulating principles to govern compensation for the losses inevitably resulting from the multifarious privately operated public utilities of Victorian England, most of them authorized by special Acts. A question of general policy was involved.

In the Queen's Bench before Mellor and Lush JJ it was argued for the defendants on the basis that the special Act took away any common law right of action for nuisance[83] and that compensation under the Act was limited to compensation for damage which would have been actionable at common law in the absence of statutory authorization; in the event, the decision was for the defendants. This was reversed by the Exchequer Chamber, comprising Bramwell B, and Keating and Montague Smith JJ, with Channell B dissenting. Erle CJ would also have dissented, but resigned before judgment was given. Bramwell strenuously argued that utilities should, as a matter of general policy, be made to internalize the costs they imposed: 'it is said that the railway and the working of it are for the public benefit, and therefore the damage must be done and *be*

---

[82] 8 & 9 Vict. c.20, para. 6.

[83] A view derived from *R.* v. *Pease* (1832) 4 B & Ad. 30, 110 ER 366; *Vaughan* v. *Taff Vale Railway Co.* (1860) 5 H & N 679, 157 ER 1351. See above 169.

uncompensated. Admitting the damage must be done for the public benefit, that is no reason why no *compensation* should be given.' Bramwell went on to argue that in his view the common law remedy for nuisance was not taken away, as had been held, in his view wrongly, in *Vaughan* v. *Taff Vale Railway*, but he conceded that he was bound by the decision. Since it was unthinkable that there should be no remedy, he concluded by arguing that the legislation must be interpreted so as to give a right to statutory compensation.[84]

The judges, consulted by the Lords, gave their opinions on 22 April 1869. Reasoned opinions in favour of liability to pay compensation were delivered. Willes J (with Keating, Lush, and Pigott JJ) thought that the common law remedy was taken away, but there must be compensation. Lush J, who had changed his mind, gave his own opinion for liability, following the same general line. Bramwell repeated his earlier expressed views. The only judge to oppose liability was, astonishingly, Blackburn, the apostle of strict liability in *Rylands* v. *Fletcher*. He thought that the normal non-negligent operation of a statutorily authorized railway could not be regarded as a common law nuisance, and that the legislation gave no right to compensation.

Blackburn's view was adopted by a bare majority of the Lords, in the persons of Lords Chelmsford and Colonsay. Lord Cairns dissented—he agreed there was no common law liability for nuisance but there must be statutory compensation.

The broad implication of this decision was that the common law doctrine enunciated in *Rylands* v. *Fletcher* did not apply to the vast majority of large reservoirs—it would not, therefore, apply to such a disaster as the Holmfirth flood or the Sheffield inundation. It seems, however, to have been assumed that, if there was negligence in the execution or management of statutorily authorized works, there would be liability.[85] So liability would depend either upon proof of negligence, a very expensive and difficult requirement, or on the terms of the particular special Act, and there seemed to be no general settled policy favouring claimants, of the type Bramwell seemed to think appropriate. The case law suggests that the judiciary of the period, if we include members of the Lords, were hopelessly divided in their attitude to the construction of relevant legislation, some leaning to compensation, others not. And the ultimate source of the disagreements seems to have been that some were disposed to welcome strict liability, whilst others were disposed to reject it.

It might be supposed that at least there would be strict liability to compensate when the legislation expressly said so, as had been accepted in relation to the Sheffield Waterworks Act of 1853. Any such assumption was rudely shattered

---

[84] Keating agreed; Montague Smith agreed with the conclusion but did not himself disapprove of the *Vaughan* decision.

[85] This was explicitly applied to the rule in *Rylands* v. *Fletcher* in *Green* v. *The Chelsea Waterworks Co.* (1894) 70 LT 547, 10 TLR 259. Generally see *Geddis* v. *Proprietors of the Bann Reservoir* (1878) 3 App. Cas. 430; *Caledonian Ry. Co.* v. *Walker's Trustees* (1882) 7 App. Cas. 259; *Mersey Docks Trustees* v. *Gibbs* (1866) LR 11 HLC 686, 11 ER 1500; *London & Brighton Ry. Co.* v. *Truman* (1885) 11 App. Cas. 45.

by the extraordinary decision in *River Wear Commissioners* v. *Adamson* in 1876.[86]

The steamship, *Natalian*, attempting to make the port of Sunderland in a storm, was driven on shore and the crew rescued; the derelict was refloated by the tide and driven by the elements against a pier, which it damaged. Section 74 of the Harbours, Docks and Piers Clauses Act of 1847 provided that 'the owner of every vessel . . . shall be answerable to the undertakers for any damage done by such vessel . . . to the harbour, dock or pier.' Nothing was said about needing to prove fault. At trial in 1873 a verdict was entered for the plaintiffs; this was upheld by the Queen's Bench. Blackburn was sitting and thought the court bound by an earlier case, *Dennis* v. *Tovell*,[87] in which he and his colleagues had favoured strict liability. But he now began to have second thoughts, hoping that this decision would be overruled, as it was when the case reached the Court of Appeal. In 1877 the case went to the Lords, which by now included Lord Blackburn. He, and a majority, held the defendants not to be liable. The reasoning varies from judge to judge—there might be no liability for 'act of God', or in the absence of wilful or negligent conduct, or if there was nobody on the ship at the time. What Lord Blackburn thought was and must remain obscure, for his opinion is quite incoherent. The decision, though it involved liability to a utility, suggested that even if a Waterworks Act included a Holmfirth clause the judges might still interpret this to exclude liability for 'act of God', or '*vis major*', or for an accident happening without negligence; it was not very clear at this time what difference there was between various formulae.

Whilst *River Wear Commissioners* v. *Adamson* was proceeding slowly through the courts, *Nichols* v. *Marsland* was also being litigated. Jane Marsland was the widow of Major Edward Marsland of the Cheshire Yeomanry, who had died in 1867. She occupied Henbury Hall, a Georgian mansion situated to the west of Macclesfield in Cheshire.[88] The census returns of 1871 show her, aged 57, in residence with her lady companion, attended by eight living-in servants, no doubt afforced by numerous gardeners, grooms, and the like.[89] Through the grounds of the hall ran a stream, the Bagbrook, and at some point before she came to live there, and perhaps even before her father-in-law had acquired the property back in 1842, this stream had been dammed to form three ornamental pools; I have not visited the site but current maps suggest that two are still in

---

[86] (1876) 1 QBD 546, 2 App. Cas. 743.   [87] (1872) 8 QB 10.

[88] For the property see G. Ormerod, *The History of the County Palatine and City of Chester*, (London, 1882), iii. 706; J. P. Earwaker, *East Cheshire Past and Present, or, a History of the Hundred of Macclesfield in the County Palatine of Chester* (London, 1880), 420, 422. The property was acquired by T. U. Brocklehurst in 1874, and was the place where the American grey squirrel was first released in Britain. After acquisition by Sir Vincent de Ferranti in 1957 the Hall was demolished, but the cellars and stables apparently survive. A new Palladian villa was built on the site in the 1980s; see J. M. Robertson, *A Guide to the Country Houses of the North West* (London, 1991), 42, for pictures of the old hall and its replacement.

[89] RG 10/3678.

existence. They had been constructed with paddles to control the water level, but for some years these had been out of order. On 18–19 June 1872 there was a very violent thunderstorm in the area—'greater and more violent than any within the memory of the witnesses'; this was fully described in local newspapers of the time.[90] All three dams failed, apparently in succession, and the flood carried away three county bridges, for whose destruction the plaintiff, suing as representative, claimed damages against Jane Marsland as nominal owner, for the legal title was in trustees, amounting to £4,092.[91] The action was a test case, other claims awaiting its outcome. At the trial four civil engineers gave evidence for the plaintiff to the effect that the design of the upper pool, whose failure precipitated the disaster, was defective in that the weir was much too small. This evidence was not challenged, and it was pointed out that similar pools in the area did not fail. The ordnance survey six-inch-to-the-mile map of the area, surveyed in 1871–2, shows that the adjacent Thornecroft Hall and Capelthorne Hall had numerous large artificial pools which survived the storm.

The special jury, in defiance of the evidence, indicated that the accident was caused by *vis major*, and told the judge, Cockburn CJ, that in their view 'there was no negligence in the construction or maintenance of the works, and that the rain was most excessive'. But he ruled that the rainfall, though 'extraordinary and unprecedented', did not amount to *vis major* or excuse the defendant, and entered judgment for the plaintiff, subject to the view of the full court in London. The court could draw inferences of fact and order a new trial if the view of the jury was against the weight of the evidence. But the court ruled in favour of the defendant, and refused to order a new trial. Cleasby B, whose involvement in bursting reservoirs went back to the time when he had, as counsel, advised the Holmfirth Commissioners' clerk back in 1852,[92] thought the case differed from *Rylands* v. *Fletcher* on the ridiculous ground that 'there the defendant brought the water onto his land, not so here'.[93] Bramwell B, most surprisingly, was against liability, even though he had recently in *Smith* v. *Fletcher and Another*[94] poured scorn on the idea that exceptional rainfall should exonerate a defendant from liability under *Rylands* v. *Fletcher*. He was even reduced to arguing that the magnitude of the precautions necessary to ensure safety were too great, essentially an argument relevant only to a claim based on negligence:

Had the banks been twice as strong, or if that would not do, ten times, and ten times as high, and the weir ten times as wide, the mischief might not have happened. But these are not practical conditions, they are such that to enforce them would prevent the reasonable use of the property in the way most beneficial to the community.

---

[90] *Macclesfield Courier and Herald*, 22 June, 29 June 1872; *Chester Chronicle*, 22 June.
[91] For the trial, see local papers for 15 Aug. 1874.
[92] See above 203.   [93] LR 10 Ex. 255 at 258.
[94] (1872) LR 7 Ex. 305. For the trial see *Carlisle Journal*, 27 Feb. 1872.

This rhetoric simply defied the uncontradicted evidence. Bramwell also made the implausible claim that in *Rylands* v. *Fletcher* the defendants 'poured the water into the plaintiff's mine' whereas here 'the defendant merely brought it to a place where another agent let it loose'. It is as though Bramwell had come to repent his earlier beliefs. The decision was upheld by the newly established Court of Appeal; 'act of God' became a defence to strict liability. The opinion was delivered by Mellish LJ, who had been losing counsel in *Rylands* v. *Fletcher*. Time has its revenges.

Although the law was now confused, many years were to pass before there was another serious dam failure in Britain. There were disasters abroad, as that of the Lake Fork in Pennsylvania in 1889, and that of the Bouzey Dam near Épinal in France in 1895, to remind everyone of the terrible consequences which might follow.[95] The worst was that of the Eigiau in North Wales on 2 November, when the higher of two dams designed to provide hydro-electric power for the supply of the aluminium company collapsed. Defective construction had allowed seepage to undermine its foundations, and the escaping water caused the lower Coity Dam to fail in sequence. There were sixteen deaths, but no problems arose over legal liability, which was accepted. The coroner's jury recommended government inspection once again and, although there had been gross neglect, no individual was indicted. But this disaster, and the less serious failure of the Skelmorie Dam in Scotland, and the recollection of the near failure of the Colwyd Dam, also owned by the aluminium company, drove the government at last into action.[96] The outcome was the Reservoirs (Safety Provisions) Act of 1930, the child of an interdepartmental conference chaired by Sir John Anderson, then Permanent Under Secretary of State at the Home Office; this reported in 1926. It recommended that the same law should apply to reservoirs authorized by statute as applied to private reservoirs under *Rylands* v. *Fletcher*; there should be liability without proof of negligence. But it did not recommend abolishing the defence of *vis major*, thought a long memorandum pointed out the difficulties caused by *Nichols* v. *Marsland*.[97] After some delay, this recommendation was implemented in the Act of 1930, but it applied only to reservoirs constructed under powers granted after the Act came into force, thereby excluding older and potentially more dangerous structures. The Act also set up, for the first time, a scheme of supervision and inspection for the larger reservoirs, defined as those holding more than 5,000,000 gallons of water; modified, this remains in force.[98]

Since 1930 there have been no serious reservoir failures in Britain. The

[95] See Smith for accounts.
[96] See *The Times*, 4, 5, 6, 9 Nov., 2, 3, 22 Dec. 1925; Parl. Deb. H. C. 189 cc.1976, 1996; 218 c.647; 220 c.329; 231 c.333; 234 c.330; 236 c.221; 237 cc.1284, 2297–315; 242 cc.278–9, 654, 902, 1014.
[97] HO 45/13762, 14754.
[98] The Reservoirs Act of 1875 repealed the Act of 1930 but preserved the basic provision. See also now the Water Act of 1981.

Keppelcove Dam in the Lake District failed on 27 October 1927, was rebuilt, and failed again on 30 August 1931, but there was no loss of life.[99] The rebuilt Bilberry Dam came within an ace of failing a second time on 29 May 1944, and it must be a relief to those who live in the area to know that, although the embankment still exists, it is largely submerged beneath a new reservoir, and serves only as a silt trap.[100] So, although Britain has many ancient dams, some ill-maintained, the only person who ever seems to have benefited directly from the rule in *Rylands* v. *Fletcher* in litigation was Thomas Fletcher himself. But the principle of strict liability, having acquired an assured status in the law in the special context of reservoir disasters, has survived to flourish in other areas of modern law, and continues to compete for dominance in the law of tort with the idea of limiting liability to cases of negligence.

[99] HO 45/13762, 14754.
[100] G. M. Binnie, n. 15 above, at 169–71, has an account with photographs.

9

The Ideal of the Rule of Law Regina v. Keyn (1876)

Victorian Legal Idealism

For English lawyers at least, the concept of the rule of law is particularly associated with the writings of Professor Albert Venn Dicey, and the controversies to which his analysis of the English constitution gave rise. His *Law of the Constitution* was first published in 1885. In it he claimed that the rule, or, as he also called it, the supremacy, of law, together with the absolute supremacy of Parliament, constituted the leading characteristics of the Victorian constitution. He continued to maintain his view into the present century, the last edition of *Law of the Constitution* from his own hand being published in 1914.[1] His book is divided into three parts, and Part II, which provides a detailed analysis of the rule of law, is much the largest. He claimed that it involved three elements.[2] The first was the exclusion of wide governmental power over persons or goods. The second was the equal subjection of all to the ordinary law of the land. The third—and this seems very curious—is that the constitutional system, including the system of individual rights, stemmed not from some body of fundamental law, but was deduced from judicial decisions 'determining the rights of private persons in particular cases brought before the courts'. The rule of law, to Dicey, was the rule of the common law. As an account of British constitutional arrangements, Dicey's analysis has been heavily criticized, and, being no philosopher, he never attempted to address the iconoclastic arguments which have induced many thinkers to doubt whether the ideal of the rule of law, for an ideal is what it really is rather than a description of reality, can ever in principle be realizable, a matter upon which there is a huge literature.[3] Legal philosophy is about very little else. It has been plausibly argued that Dicey's views were, at least in part, immediately derived from W. E. Hearn, the first Dean of the Faculty of Law at Melbourne, whose *The Government of England* appeared in 1867.[4] But the love-affair with the government of laws and not of men has a very long history, going back to the Greeks, and of course since Dicey's time

---

[1] 9th ed., London, 1952 by E. C. S. Wade.   [2] Ibid. 187–98.
[3] For legal idealism see my 'Legal Iconoclasts and Legal Ideals' (1990) 58 *UCINLR* 819.
[4] H. W. Arndt, 'The Origins of Dicey's Concept of the "Rule of Law"' (1957) 31 *Australian LJ* 117.

it has continued to inspire both legal thinkers and some practitioners of the law, too.

I have used the term ideal of the conception, but it can also be taken to refer to a certain attitude of mind, one which Dicey, in one passage in his book, called 'the predominance of the legal spirit', and in another 'the predominance of rigid legality throughout our institutions'.[5] Today the conception, as understood and valued in the Victorian period, has come under vigorous attack. Some regard it as essentially a mechanism for legitimizing oppression and exploitation. Others, operating at a more practical level, as politicians, officials, and sometimes as judges too, are not enamoured by the constraints which, they feel, respect for the rule of law places upon the activity of government. Yet the ideal remains an influential one, and is central to the self-esteem of the legal profession. It is difficult to see how the legal protection of human rights can be advanced except by lawyers who are committed to the notion.

It is no accident that it was in the Victorian period that Dicey's analysis appeared, for at that time the ideal was perhaps more powerfully influential than it has since become. Although there were always doubters, the more powerful theoretical attacks, particularly those associated with the American realist movement, lay in the future. In any event, they have only ever flourished in legal academia, which, in Victorian Britain, hardly existed. In private law the pursuit of the ideal led to the progressive erosion of jury discretion, the institution of the uncontrolled jury being of course at odds with the notion; hence the right to jury trial is not treated by Dicey as a major feature of English constitutional arrangements, and is fitted into his scheme of thought as respectable only because jurors regularly do as they are told by judges.[6] In legal theory and legal education it found expression in belief in the existence of legal science. In the heyday of the British Empire many believed that the extension of the benefits of the rule of law to lesser breeds both legitimized imperialism, and provided a practical goal for those involved in the administration of subject peoples.

In the world of practical politics, where the rule of law always had its enemies, the best illustration of its power is provided by the acrimonious disputes which arose in the 1860s within the intelligentsia over the actions of Edward Eyre in Jamaica. The story has been explored in a number of books, most notably in Bernard Semmel's *Jamaican Blood and the Victorian Conscience: The Governor Eyre Controversy*.[7] Governor Eyre, after making his name as an explorer as the first of the overlanders, became, successively, Governor of New Zealand, of St Vincent, of the Leeward Islands, and, in 1864, of Jamaica. In 1865 he was faced with what he thought a serious disturbance in Morant Bay. This induced him to

---

[5] N. 1 above, 195 and 406.   [6] N. 1 above, 394–5.

[7] See also G. Dutton, *The Hero as Murderer: The Life of Edward John Eyre* (London, 1986), and for other effects of the affair my *In the Highest Degree Odious. Detention without Trial in Wartime Britain* (Oxford, 1992), 6.

issue a local declaration of martial law, the very idea of which seems wholly at odds with the ideal. The insurrection, if indeed there ever actually was one, was put down with ferocious brutality. In a month some 608 persons were killed or summarily executed, and about the same number savagely flogged. George William Gordon, a black member of the legislature, was suspected by Eyre of being the instigator of a general rising; he was arrested, moved into the area where martial law had been put in force, summarily tried, and hanged. Eyre's handling of the matter was at once the subject of official criticism and, after a commission of enquiry, he was dismissed. But mere dismissal did not satisfy the devotees of the rule of law. They wanted Eyre and others involved, particularly Lieutenant H. C. Brand, who had sentenced Gordon to death, and Colonel Sir Alexander A. Nelson, who had confirmed the sentence, brought to trial for crimes against regular law. Hence, between 1865 and 1870, a body calling itself the Jamaica Committee made continuous attempts to bring the persons involved to trial. The chairman was John Stuart Mill, and the members included Herbert Spencer, John Bright, Charles Darwin, Thomas Huxley, and even Tom Hughes, author of *Tom Brown's Schooldays*. In all there were around 800 members. For a while James Fitzjames Stephen acted as the lawyer for the Jamaica Committee.

Other intellectuals, however, also committed to the rule of law, were more impressed by the need to preserve law and order, and this, a little paradoxically (for we commonly do not emphasize the rather embarrassing fact that the rule of law everywhere relies upon the use of coercive violence), made them oppose the Jamaica Committee. Their organization was chaired by Thomas Carlyle, and included amongst its members Charles Dickens, Lord Tennyson, Charles Kingsley, Sir Richard Murchison, and, though no intellectual, the awful but heroic Earl of Cardigan, who had led the charge of the Light Brigade with such conspicuous gallantry and then returned to his yacht for a relaxing dinner. In addition, there were seventy-two peers, six bishops, forty generals, and twenty-six admirals. The controversy gave rise to numerous legal cases, some of which feature in Dicey's book; Dicey's curious treatment of the subject, and his account of the rule of law, are in part a product of this controversy, behind which lay some unease about the brutal suppression of the Indian Mutiny back in 1857.[8] It also generated a remarkable public quarrel between Cockburn CJ and Blackburn J; nothing of the sort was to happen again until Lord Maugham fell to quarrelling in public with Lord Atkin, again about the rule of law, after the decision in the wartime detention case of *Liversidge* v. *Anderson* in 1941.[9] In the event, Eyre escaped trial and, after being awarded a pension by Disraeli, lived quietly in retirement, dying in 1901.[10]

---

[8] Ch. 8.

[9] [1942] AC 206. For accounts of the incident see my *In the Highest Degree Odious*, n. 7 above, 362 and references provided, G. Lewis, *Lord Atkin* (London, 1983), 132 ff.

[10] Obituary in *The Times*, 1, Dec. 1901.

A Ghastly Hint to the Home Secretary

My own preferred illustration of the 'predominance of the legal spirit' in Victorian government is the curious case of what was known as the Home Office Baby, which occurred in November 1884.[11] Partly as a result of the cholera epidemic of 1849, there developed during the nineteenth century state regulation of the burial of the dead. The threat to health was most severe in towns; the moving spirit was Edwin Chadwick, who favoured what he rather grimly called Extramural Sepulture, a solution anticipated by the Romans many centuries before. Under legislation of 1850, the General Board of Health was empowered to close burial grounds, and in 1852 this power was conferred on the Home Secretary, and extended by later legislation. In 1855 an inspectorate was established.[12] The Revd John Mirehouse was the Rector of Colsterworth in Lincolnshire, and was one of that legion of dotty clerics who find their natural home in the Church of England, where they continue to flourish. He thought that the Home Office had behaved in a dilatory way in closing his burial ground and failing to approve its replacement. He no longer had anywhere to inter his parishioners. To emphasize and dramatize his predicament, he dispatched a still-born infant, given him for burial by its unfortunate parents, to the Home Secretary of the day, Sir Vernon Harcourt, marking the parcel 'perishable' and 'carriage paid'. The duty clerk, John Horton, who unwrapped the parcel on Sunday, 2 November 1884, thinking it might be a gift of game, was naturally upset. The conduct of the Rector of Colsterworth enraged the Home Secretary. In some societies at some times no doubt the parson would have ended up in the Bastille, or been subjected to the knout, or whatever, for such insolence, but not in Victorian England. In conformity with the rule of law, Sir Vernon took the learned opinion of the ecclesiastical lawyer, Mr Walter G. F. Phillimore, who was Chancellor of the Diocese of Lincoln. He, after consulting his books, gave it as his opinion that the Rector had committed no ecclesiastical offence and could, therefore, not be disciplined, much less deprived of his cure of souls, in which he enjoyed a freehold. There was no breach of regulations; as those who have visited the Powell-Cotton Museum in Quex House, Kent, will know, the Victorian postal and railway services transported more or less anything, including the decomposing skins of dead elephants, on payment of the appropriate charges. One display there includes the largest elephant ever stuffed; it is emerging from a cave, the skin of the hindquarters having arrived in a bad condition. At the inquest the jury 'severely censured the reverend gentleman' and the coroner disallowed his expenses. And that was the end of the matter.

---

[11] See the journal of Lewis Harcourt and Harcourt Papers MS 256 (Bodleian Library) at fo. 83; *Lincoln Gazette*, 15 Nov.; *Lincolnshire Chronicle*, 14 Nov. (from which I have taken a headline); *The Times*, 7 and 13 Nov.; *Daily Telegraph*, 13 Nov. I have not traced papers in the PRO.

[12] See J. Pellew, *The Home Office 1848–1914. From Clerks to Bureaucrats* (London, 1982), 138–40.

Popular Clamour and the Rule of Law

Now the message of this book is that legal decisions have a historical context, and that sometimes the decision may be influenced by factors which, in legal theory, ought not to influence the court, though it is commonly not easy to demonstrate their influence. Convention forbids reference to them in judicial opinions. Although Dicey does not develop the point, one reason for the incompatibility between the rule of law and extensive discretionary power is just the fact that the exercise of such power may be so influenced by improper motives. One of the functions of regulating power by law is to exclude certain considerations from influencing the exercise of power. Dedication to the rule of law will mean that judicial decisions will not be influenced by such factors as popular clamour and prejudice, witch hunts, and searches for scapegoats and sacrificial victims after disasters; indeed by a whole range of factors which may have to be taken into consideration in taking political decisions, particularly in a democracy, but by general agreement ought to play absolutely no part in judicial decisions. Merely, however, to entrust a decision to the courts will not, of course, guarantee that the ideal will actually be achieved; there are many examples of legal decisions which fall short of this. That is the nature of ideals. There are, however, counter-examples, and these, too, can be appreciated if only the context of the decision is understood; only thus can we understand the pressures which were resisted.

A Collision off Dover

The classic Victorian illustration is *Regina* v. *Keyn*, often called the case of the *Franconia*.[13] At a technical level it involved a question of criminal jurisdiction, the right of an English court to try a foreigner for an offence committed on the high seas, but within British territorial waters, which, at this time, were taken to extend three miles out to sea. This issue arose out of a collision which took place on 17 February 1876 between the British steamship *Strathclyde* of Glasgow (Captain John Dodd Eaton), and the German steamship *Franconia* of Hamburg (Captain Ferdinand Keyn[14]).

The *Franconia* was a two-masted crew steamer which had been built in 1874 by Cairds at Greenock on the Clyde in 1874. She was 350 feet long, and her gross tonnage was 3,098. She was registered at Hamburg, and was operated by the Hamburg American Packet Boat Company. Her Captain, Ferdinand Keyn, had been in charge of her since 1874, having previously been master of the

---

[13] (1876) 2 Ex. D 63, 13 Cox Crim. Cas. 403, 47 LJMC 17.

[14] Keyn's name is spelled Kuhn or Kühn in some reports (for example in *The Times*), but Keyn appears to be correct.

Bavaria from 1871 to 1873.[15] She was on passage from Hamburg to St Thomas in the West Indies. She was primarily carrying cargo, but there were also four passengers on board. The crew numbered seventy-three. She had called at Grimsby to take on pilots. One was James Porter. His duty was to take the vessel into the Channel and through the Downs past the Goodwin Sands as far as the South Sand Light Vessel.[16] At the time of the accident his work was finished, and Captain Keyn had resumed control, so there was no question of the pilot being in any way to blame. The plan was to land him at Le Havre; in order to enter the port the *Franconia* also had on board a French pilot. The somewhat peculiar plan followed by the *Franconia*, for both Grimsby and Le Havre lie off any direct track, was never explained, but presumably there was some other reason for calling at Le Havre.

The *Strathclyde*, of Glasgow, was also an iron steamer, somewhat smaller than the *Franconia*, with an engine of 180 horsepower; she was 300 feet long and her gross tonnage was 1,953.[17] She was owned by Burrell and Sons. Her Captain was John Dodd Eaton, who had been born in Liverpool in 1841. He had obtained his master's certificate there in 1866, and had served on the *Strathclyde* since 1874, becoming her master on 18 June 1875. She was his first command.[18] She was carrying mixed cargo and twenty-three first-class passengers, together with two servants, to Bombay. Twelve of the first-class passengers were women, and there were in all fifteen women on board.[19] Her voyage began at 5.30 a.m. the same day, when she left the Victoria Dock in London. She, too, had taken a pilot; once she had passed through the Downs, she had no need for his services; the vessel dropped him off close to the Admiralty Pier, Dover, at 3.45 p.m. She then headed out again into the Channel on a course of south-west by south, a magnetic course of 227 degrees, which would bring her close to Dungeness.

The *Franconia*, having passed through the Downs, was also heading towards Dungeness, and was moving a little faster than the *Strathclyde*. There was dispute over the respective speeds of the two ships, but the *Franconia* was probably moving at just under nine knots. Since visibility was excellent, and the seas in the area uncrowded with shipping at the time, it is by no means easy to understand why the accident happened at all, and Captain Keyn never gave his side of the story.[20] When first sighted at a distance of around four miles from the *Strathclyde*, the *Franconia*, which was also heading for Dungeness, appears to have been on a slightly more westerly course than the *Strathclyde*; Captain Eaton thought she was on about west-south-west. Being a faster vessel, she

[15] Formerly *Petropolis*. Information from Dr B. Meyer Friese of the Altonauer Museum, Hamburg.
[16] Now the South Goodwin Light.   [17] Registered no. 63841.
[18] Details from Guildhall MS 18567/18 (Captain's Register). Master's certificate number 01657.
[19] List published in *Dover Chronicle*, 26 Feb., omitting the two servants. The official passenger list went down with the vessel.
[20] What follows is based upon evidence given at the two inquests (transcripts in DPP 4/9–10), the trial at the Central Criminal Court (transcript DPP 4/11), and in the civil litigation (n. 21 below), as well as newspaper accounts.

came up on the port quarter of the *Strathclyde*. It is not at all clear whether those in charge of the *Franconia* anticipated passing across the bows of the *Strathclyde* or across her stern, but it seems probable that the idea in Captain Keyn's mind initially was to cross her bows. If his vessel was faster than the *Strathclyde*, this would have been a possible course of action, though a slightly hazardous one. Evidence from the German side, however, suggested that the plan was always to pass astern of her.

The British rules for the prevention of collisions, brought into force in 1863 under the Merchant Shipping Act of the previous year, were supposed to provide guidance in all circumstances, but the trouble was that it was not always very clear which rule applied, and in any event it usually takes two to produce a collision at sea. Was the *Franconia* an *overtaking* or a *crossing* vessel? Whether as an overtaking vessel—the view of the matter taken by the *Strathclyde*—or as a crossing vessel—the view taken by the first officer of the *Franconia* and probably by her Captain—the *Franconia* was under an obligation to keep clear. A crossing vessel had to keep clear of a vessel to her starboard side. In the subsequent civil litigation,[21] Sir Robert Phillimore took the view that the *Franconia* (and the *Strathclyde*) were *crossing* vessels, but on appeal was told he was wrong about this, and that the *Franconia* was an *overtaking* vessel, on the somewhat peculiar ground that, had it been dark at the time, which of course it was not, the angle of approach was such that the side port light of the *Strathclyde* would not have been visible from the *Franconia*, an original idea born after the accident took place. But this did not conclude the matter. Possibly both vessels, since they were getting closer to each other, were both to be regarded as *approaching* vessels, governed by rule 16, in which case both ships should have taken positive action to avoid the collision. It was also the duty of the *Strathclyde* to maintain a steady course whilst being overtaken or crossed.

As the *Franconia* gained on the *Strathclyde*, Captain Eaton thought she was getting too close to his port quarter, though he denied thinking there was at this stage a risk of collision. Probably assuming that it was the intention of the *Franconia*, which he believed to be moving faster than in fact she was, to overtake him on his port side and cross his bows, he made a small alteration of course to starboard, which would bring his vessel's heading more towards the shore. On the assumption that the *Franconia* intended to overtake him to port, this alteration would increase the distance separating him from the *Franconia*. Since, however, the *Franconia* either had always intended to pass across his stern, or at about the same time decided to do so, this alteration probably increased the risk of collision.[22] Captain Keyn now thought a collision imminent and ordered his engine astern; his first mate, probably on his captain's instruction, ordered the helm put hard to port, turning the vessel to starboard before the reversal of

---

[21] *The Franconia* (1876) 2 PD 8 (9 May, 8 Dec.).

[22] This is compatible with the evidence of the first officer of the *Franconia*, Edward H. Meyer, given at the Poplar inquest.

the engine had slowed the vessel. According to the evidence given from those on the *Strathclyde*, the *Franconia* was already overlapping the *Strathclyde* when it altered course to starboard. In consequence, the bow of the *Franconia* struck the port side of the *Strathclyde* some fifty feet from her stern, penetrating to a depth of four feet. Had the helm not been ported until the vessel had slowed, the accident would not have happened, and it is at least arguable that it was caused both by the *Franconia* and by the Captain of the *Strathclyde*, who had failed to maintain his course. Another possible explanation is that Captain Keyn, without due deliberation, changed his mind; having originally planned on crossing the bows of the *Strathclyde*, he precipitately decided to pass across her stern. In the legal proceedings the impression was given that Captain Keyn, by altering to starboard, in effect rammed the *Strathclyde*. Since an experienced ship's master would not wantonly ram another vessel, it seems probable that the cause of the accident was a mutual misunderstanding between the two captains. Captain Keyn did not give evidence either at the inquests held after the disaster or, of course, at his trial, since the evidence of the accused was not admissible.

The British rules had never been agreed by Germany, but it was the law that they applied in any civil case before an English court, and it seems to have been assumed that they also applied in the criminal case if the *Franconia* was within British jurisdiction at the time, the question which was in issue in the legal proceedings. Even if they did not, they nevertheless embodied the regular maritime practice of the period.[23]

The *Franconia* backed off or rebounded, and then struck the *Strathclyde* a second time nearer the stern. The *Franconia*, with helm hard to port, would be swinging to starboard at the time of impact. The *Strathclyde* began to sink rapidly. After checking the damage, Captain Eaton told his passengers that there was no cause for alarm, since there was ample time to get the boats out and save them all. The vessel had four boats in davits, and the Captain put all the fifteen female passengers and the stewardess into the port boat, which was capable of holding forty persons. It was then rushed by most of the male passengers, and a number of members of the crew, with the consequence that it could not be lowered. The Captain appealed to them to get out of it; some did so and four ladies also left the boat, which was then lowered. The delay was disastrous; before the boat got clear a wave caused by the sinking of the stern capsized it and threw everyone in it into the water; one of the tackles may not have been unhooked in time to allow the boat to ride the wave. The second officer, Robert Bird, lowered another boat, the gig, on the starboard quarter and with four sailors got clear and went to the assistance of those in the water. A third boat, containing the ladies who had left the swamped boat, was cleared but does not seem to have been actually launched. The *Strathclyde* went under at 4.22 p.m. Some of her crew, including the first mate, John Bevan, the pantry steward,

---

[23] The relevant rules were 14, 16, 17, and 18.

James Chescoe, and three other sailors, jumped onto the *Franconia*. Those who did not, and who were not in the gig, were thrown into the water; Captain Eaton, in conformity with maritime tradition, was the last to be swept off his sinking ship.

A number of vessels came to the assistance of those who were struggling in the water. They did not include the *Franconia*. The Deal lugger, *Early Morn* (Captain Edward Hanger), rescued twenty-four persons, including Captain Eaton. One, a passenger, Thomas Quinlan, died after rescue. The lugger, *Brave Nelson* (Captain William Cuchney), picked up three, all alive, but one, the bosun, James Sullivan, died after he was taken ashore. The barque, *Queen of Nations*, hove to off Dover, lowered a boat, and picked up the body of one women, Jessie Dorcas Young, and two men who were then alive, but who died after rescue. The *Strathclyde*'s gig took nineteen bodies from the water. In due course some other vessels arrived, but too late to save anyone. Eventually the death toll was thirty-nine lives out of the eighty-two persons aboard.

The collision took place only two miles off Dover beach, and a little nearer to Admiralty pier, and was clearly visible from the shore. There was naturally much recrimination over the failure of local boatmen, and of the Dover lifeboat, to render more effective assistance. The local papers were full of letters on the matter. But the main target of criticism was Captain Keyn of the *Franconia*, who had done nothing to assist those struggling in the water.

The bow of his vessel had been severely damaged, but her collision bulkhead held, though it was in a precarious state. She was taking on very little water, though this would not have been immediately apparent until the carpenter sounded the wells. Members of her crew began to lower a boat, but it was not possible to launch it whilst she was under way, and no boat was ever lowered; the point of preparing the boat may have been fear that she was about to sink. She headed away from the scene towards Dover at about five knots, and was fairly soon in contact with a steam tug, the *Palmerston*, which accompanied her to Dover harbour, which she was unable to enter because of her draught.[24] She therefore later anchored north of Dover in the Downs. First officer John Bevan, a very excitable person, who had jumped onto the *Franconia*, suggested that she should return to the sinking *Strathclyde*, and seems to have caused considerable confusion by attempting to take charge; the French pilot on board said that the *Franconia* was sinking, and the English pilot, James[25] Porter, also thought the vessel was in danger and might have to be beached. In fact the *Franconia* was not in danger, and in due course reached London for repairs. No doubt Captain Keyn thought his first duty was to his own ship and those on board her, and it was not at once apparent that he could safely have stood by the sinking *Strathclyde*. But his conduct could be viewed as showing a callous disregard for the drowning passengers and crew of the *Strathclyde*.

[24] Letter from her master, Captain G. Manser, in *Dover Chronicle*, 26 Feb. The *ILN*, 26 Feb. 1876, 213 has a picture of the *Franconia* backing off after the collision.
[25] Some sources give him as Samuel.

The legal position at the time was that, under the Merchant Shipping Amendment Act of 1862,[26] a master of a British ship, and of a foreign ship within British jurisdiction, was bound to stand by and render assistance after a collision, but only 'if and so far as he can do so without danger to his own ship and crew'.

The Inquests and the Decision to Charge Captain Keyn

Two inquests were held. One, held at Deal before Coroner George Mercer on the deaths of two pasengers, William Bussell and Thomas Quinlan, and James Sullivan, the bosun, opened on Friday, 18 February. It was resumed the following Tuesday, with the assistance of Captain Harris RN, a Board of Trade assessor; the foreman of the jury was a Royal Navy Commander, and there were a number of nautical men on it.[27] The coroner told the jury that if the collision was the result of a miscalculation, or error of judgement, or some mistake, the deaths would be accidental, but if they had come about through 'such negligence, want of seamanship or want of proper knowledge of what was needing to be done' the position would be different. On Thursday, 24 February, the jury found that

the sinking of the said steamer was caused by negligence and reckless navigation on the part of the person in charge of the steamer *Franconia*, and we find the person so in charge, Ferdinand Kuhn, guilty of manslaughter. The Jury express their strongest condemnation of the person so in charge, Ferdinand Kuhn, for steaming away from the scene of the occurrence, and leaving the crew and passengers of the *Strathclyde* to their fate, apparently without rendering them any assistance.

The jury also made the same criticism of the tug *Palmerston*. The coroner did not suggest that Captain Keyn might be guilty of failing to give assistance.

A second inquest was held at Poplar before John Humphreys, opening on Monday, 21 February, and concluding on 8 March, on the three bodies landed there.[28] One was that of Jessie Dorcas Young. She was an 18-year-old passenger, whose body had been recovered by the barque, *Queen of Nations*, and landed at London. The coroner's jury found that the deaths were the result of culpable negligence; although they thought Captain Keyn should have stood by, they thought his conduct had been influenced by the advice of the pilot, James Porter. This amounted to a finding of manslaughter against Captain Keyn. But it was uncertain, as a matter of law, whether Captain Keyn, the foreign captain of a foreign merchant vessel, *en passant* down the Channel and not bound for an English port, could in these circumstances be tried in an English court for manslaughter. Was he, as he passed through British territorial waters off Dover, amenable to English criminal law?

---

[26] 25 & 26 Vict. c.63, ss. 33, 57, and 58.   [27] Transcript in DPP 4/9.
[28] Transcript in DPP 4/9 and 10.

After complicated proceedings, which have been very fully explored by G. Marston,[29] Ferdinand Keyn was placed on trial, not at the Kent assizes but at the Central Criminal Court in London. The trial opened on 5 April 1876, Keyn being charged with the manslaughter of Jessie Dorcas Young. The selection of Jessie Young, rather than a male victim, was no doubt motivated by a desire to exploit the sympathies of the all-male jury. Women and children were supposed to be saved in cases of shipwreck.

The Home Office naturally became involved, as the department concerned with the administration of the criminal law within the country;[30] the Board of Trade as the department concerned with merchant shipping;[31] and the Foreign Office as the department concerned with foreign countries.[32] It was appreciated from the outset that there was a tricky question of law involved—whether Captain Keyn, a German citizen in charge of a German ship, could be tried by an English criminal court at all. It was not simply a question of English law. The incident took place within the three-mile or one-sea-league limit and, consequently, in the British view, was definitely within territorial waters.[33] But it also took place upon the high seas, and it was by no means clear that in international law Captain Keyn was subject to English criminal jurisdiction. It was all thought probably to depend upon whether the old jurisdiction of the Admiralty extended to such a case. It could be argued that jurisdiction over territorial waters was limited to what was necessary for defence against attack, the protection of the revenue, and the regulation of fisheries, but did not entail any right to apply criminal law to mere transients. The Foreign Office official, G. E. March, who was head of the treaty department, looked into the matter. He could trace no precedent of any kind for such a trial, though he thought that there might have been cases arising out of the Foreign Enlistment Act.[34] He nevertheless took the view that an English court did have jurisdiction, though a German court might also have jurisdiction, since the *Franconia* was a German ship. He thought it was inexpedient, and possibly illegal, to waive this jurisdiction.[35] The Foreign Office seems to have been quite happy with this view. Back in 1874 the Foreign Office had reacted to a Spanish claim to a six-mile limit on its territorial waters by sending an enquiry to the principal maritime nations to see what their response

[29] G. Marston, 'The Centenary of the Franconia Case—the Prosecution of Ferdinand Keyn' (1976) 92 *LQR* 93.

[30] HO 45/9402/53058 contains papers.

[31] The Board of Trade wreck inquiry file has apparently been destroyed.

[32] FO 64/873 is the basic file; papers also exist in FO 83/732, which is concerned more generally with the extent of territorial waters and the investigation of collisions at sea.

[33] T. L. Futton, *The Sovereignty of the Sea* (Edinburgh, 1911), 576 ff. gives the history. Some countries made more extensive claims.

[34] The Foreign Enlistment Act 1870 (33 & 34 Vict. c.90) applied by s. 2 to territorial waters. Since the Act dealt with defence, where British jurisdiction might extend further, cases under the Act were distinguishable.

[35] FO 64/873 has the opinion. The illegality would arise because of the indictment by the coroner's jury, which perhaps obliged the authorities to put Keyn on trial.

was to the Spanish claim.[36] Germany had replied to the effect that there did not appear to be any clear rule on the extent of territorial waters:

The only principle established is that each State must be considered as entitled to extend its defensive arrangements and preventive measures for the security and its system of trade, custom and intercourse as far over the waters of its coast as is necessary and sufficient to protect itself against hostilities and disturbances from the sea side.

This general view, though not, of course, directed to the enforcement of criminal law, was compatible with the assumption of criminal jurisdiction over Captain Keyn, without being conclusive on the matter. But the waters were muddied when Henry C. Rothery, the learned and experienced Registrar of the High Court of Admiralty,[37] gave his opinion that the English court would have no jurisdiction. He also thought it would be most unwise to try Captain Keyn. This was the view taken by T. H. Farrer, the official head of the Board of Trade, the department of state responsible for merchant shipping. In a letter of 18 March 1876 to H. K. Stephenson, the Director of Public Prosecutions, which accompanied a copy of Rothery's opinion, he said:

I quite agree with him that it would be most injudicious for the Government to try the Master on a criminal charge. You can never succeed in convicting the Master of a British Ship for the offence; and it would have a most invidious appearance if we were 'to convict a German'.[38]

He was also influenced by the fact that other countries might reciprocate by trying masters of British ships, which was surely not in Britain's best interests. The problem was dramatized in a later newspaper article:

For instance the law of Spain forbids, or a short time since forbade, any public service other than that of the Roman Catholic Church. Could it be pretended that if an English vessel, on its way from Plymouth to Gibraltar, skirted the Spanish coast on a Sunday, and if the Captain celebrated divine service in accordance with the Anglican ritual, it would be lawful for the Spanish authorities to arrest him . . . ?[39]

Confronted with this conflicting advice, the Home Office presented all the relevant papers and the problem to the Law Officers for their opinion.[40] The Attorney-General, Sir John Holker, and the Solicitor-General, Sir Hardinge Giffard, later Lord Halsbury, took the view both that the English courts did have jurisdiction and that it was expedient to put Captain Keyn on trial; the opinion was also signed by Treasury Counsel in the persons of Henry B. Poland and Douglas S. Straight.[41] The proceedings were moved to the Central Criminal Court, the Law Officers' view being that the territorial waters in which the accident occurred were not part of the County of Kent, so that a trial at the Kent

---

[36] Papers in FO 64/837.   [37] See below 252.   [38] Letter in HO 45/9402/53058.
[39] *Post*, 14 Nov.   [40] HO 34/36 and 37 has the letters.
[41] Mr Marston notes that the original Law Officers' Opinion remained with the Treasury Solicitor and may have been destroyed during the war.

Assizes was not appropriate; the location was, however, within the jurisdiction of the Admiralty, and had been passed by statute to the Central Criminal Court.[42]

Another good reason for moving the trial to London would have been to provide Captain Keyn with a fair trial, which he and his legal advisers claimed he could not receive in Kent. By the time he landed at Dover he had already been cast as a villain, and he was seriously frightened by the hostility shown to him there. He swore an affidavit on 6 March requesting that his case be moved to London, and stated:

The said collision and great and lamentable loss of life had occasioned the greatest possible feeling and excitement throughout the County of Kent partly I believe in consequence of my being a foreigner and a German and partly in consequence of no witnesses on my behalf or who were on board my ship having been heard.

He was even afraid to enter into bail there; it was safer to remain in custody. He instanced attacks upon him in local newspapers, the *Kent Argus* of 26 February, the *Deal, Walmer and Kentish Telegram* and *Dover Standard* of the same date, the *Kent Court Times* of 24 February. An associated affidavit sworn by his solicitors described the hostile atmosphere at the Deal inquest, and referred expressly to the affair of the *Deutschland*, which, as we shall see, played its part in the affair.

So, even if the law officers had not seen a technical difficulty about a trial in Kent, the trial would in all probability have been moved to London.

The Trial of Captain Keyn and the Appeal

Captain Keyn was indicted for that on the 17 February he 'feloniously did kill and slay Jessie Dorcas Young against the peace of our Lady the Queen, her Crown and Dignity'. There were two variant counts in the indictment, the first alleging that the crime took place 'upon the high seas within the jurisdiction of the Admiralty of England, and within the jurisdiction of the Central Criminal Court'. The second omitted the reference to the Admiralty. The judge, Pollock B, formally ruled that the court had jurisdiction to try the case, and reserved the point of law for consideration by the Court for Crown Cases Reserved, which at this period served as a Court of Appeal in criminal cases, but only on questions of law with the consent of the trial judge. At the trial, which occupied three days, opening on 5 April, the Crown was represented by the Attorney-General, with H. B. Poland, C. S. C. Bowen, and D. S. Straight. Captain Keyn had two Queen's Counsel, Serjeant J. H. Parry and Arthur Cohen, with M. S. Williams, W. G. F. Phillimore, and A. Stubbs. In spite of their efforts, he was convicted

---

[42] This view was repeated by the Solicitor-General at the trial. See DPP 4/11. 4 & 5 Will. IV c.36 by s. 22 gave the Central Criminal Court the jurisdiction previously exercised by the Admiralty.

of manslaughter.[43] It is not very clear why. There were essentially two distinct criticisms which could be levelled against Captain Keyn. One was that he had made a grave navigational error, and thereby indirectly killed Jessie Young through culpable negligence in navigation. The other was that, having collided with the *Strathclyde*, and knowing that there was grave danger to her crew and passengers, he had sailed off, and not stood by after the collision and rendered assistance. Both ways of presenting the case are to be found in the transcript of the trial; thus the Attorney-General, after claiming that Captain Keyn could have rendered assistance, said: 'Instead of doing that, or taking any steps whatever to save human life, the prisoner steamed away to Dover, in order that he might save the wood and iron of which the vessel was composed, and which he appeared to consider of greater value than human life.' In directing the jury, the judge said that they could convict of manslaughter on the basis of negligence in navigation, giving no indication of what degree of negligence would suffice. He also said that, although in general there could be no criminal liability for failure to assist another person in peril, there might be criminal liability if Captain Keyn had, through negligence, brought that peril about, though not if his first duty was to his own crew and passengers. On what basis the jury convicted must remain obscure. At the hearing before the higher court, it seems, however, to have been assumed that his conviction rested on his negligent navigation. So far as I am aware, no other ship's master was ever convicted of manslaughter arising out of a maritime casualty in the whole of the nineteenth century. Pending the hearing of the case before the Court for Crown Cases Reserved, Captain Keyn was released on bail, no sentence being passed.

On 6 May a hearing began before five judges in Westminster Hall; argument extended over four days.[44] The Solicitor-General argued the case for the Crown, and Captain Keyn was represented by Judah Benjamin, the former Confederate statesman who, in exile in Britain, had been called to the English bar 1866; we have already met him in connection with the case of *Raffles* v. *Wichelhaus* and, after a slow start, he was at this time the leading appellate barrister.[45] After hearing argument the judges were unable to agree, two favouring the view that the Court did have jurisdiction, whilst four were on the side of Captain Keyn. At this period it was not the convention that the problem of lack of unanimity could be solved by voting, though there was a convention that, if the junior judge alone in a five-judge court disagreed, he would alter his opinion to conform to the majority.[46] The case had to go before a full court, comprising all the judges of the three common law divisions—the Queen's Bench, Common Pleas, and

[43] Transcript in DPP 4/11. Also in OBSP (1876) at 475–513.

[44] Kelly CB, Pollock B, Lush, Field, and Lindley JJ, and Sir Robert Phillimore. The last was the Judge in Admiralty. Transcript in DPP 4/12.

[45] 1811–84. He was elected to the US Senate in 1852, and refused the offer of a seat on the Supreme Court. He became AG, Secretary of War, and then Secretary of State for the Confederate Government. Biographies by P. Butler (1907) and R. D. Meade (1943), and E. Evans (1988).

[46] I have unhappily lost the reference.

Exchequer, or at least as substantial a proportion of them as could be got together. Thus the notable case of *Regina* v. *Prince* (1875) was argued before fifteen judges, as was *Regina* v. *Ward* (1872).[47] The Judicature Act had transferred the jurisdiction of the Court for Crown Cases Reserved to the High Court; it was arguable that all the judges of the High Court, twenty-eight in number, were entitled to sit. Before the transfer the only judges who sat were those who administered the criminal law, belonging to the three common law courts, the total normally being eighteen. In the event the case was re-argued before a somewhat strangely constituted court of fourteen judges, probably selected by the Lord Chancellor, who at first proposed to sit himself.[48] The case was again argued on behalf of Captain Keyn by Judah Benjamin QC, and the Solicitor-General again represented the Crown; the arguments took five days. The handwritten transcript runs to over 1,200 pages.[49] The opinions were delivered over two days after a delay of five months, one of the judges, Sir Thomas Archibald, having died in the intervening period.[50] By a majority of seven to six the court ruled in favour of Captain Keyn. So the conviction was quashed; there was no further appeal possible. Judah Benjamin thought this to have been his greatest legal triumph; the majority would have been eight to six in his favour had not Archibald died.

The occasion was marked by an extraordinary display of recondite legal learning, a sort of orgy of doctrinalism—in addition to such run-of-the-mill legal authorities as English reported cases, there were references to American jurists, such as Story, Kent, Marshall, and Bishop; and to continentals Azuni, Bluntschli, Bynkershoek, Calvo, Casaregi, Galiani, Hautefeuille, Hefftner, Huber, Loccenius, Martens, Massé Merlin, Ortolan, Fiore, Rayneval, Vattel, Holtzendorff, Wolff—the list could be continued. The opinions run to the size of a substantial book. There really never had been an earlier English decision quite like it, and there has never been a rival since.

It is obvious enough that Captain Keyn was some sort of scapegoat, and that the quashing of his conviction deprived the public of the pleasure of casting him in this role. But without a little more information than is provided by the law report of the context in which the case was decided, its connection with the ideal of the rule of law is not fully apparent. A clue to this context is provided by a curious feature of contemporary attitudes to the case. Thus on 20 May the Attorney-General in a letter to Lord Tenderden called it 'a case of such vast importance'.[51] Kelly CB went further; it was 'of transcendental importance'. Nearly fifty years later an anonymous writer, a legal correspondent to the *Morning*

---

[47] 12 Cox Crim. Cas. 123, 13 at 138.
[48] See G. Marston, n. 29 above, 103–4, relying on PRO 30/51, Bundle 10 (Cairns Papers).
[49] 15–17, 21, and 23 June; transcript in DPP 4/13. The transcript is bound up in five books in the wrong order.
[50] 11 and 13 Nov. Archibald died on 18 Oct.
[51] FO 64/873, quoted Marston, n. 29 above, 103.

Post, gave an account of the passion and solemnity which accompanied the delivery of Cockburn CJ's opinion.[52] *The Times*, in a leader on 15 November 1876, said: 'On all accounts, the case will be remembered as one of the greatest ever argued on a point of law, and the arguments and judgements which it has elicited will, we believe, more than sustain the reputation of the English Bar and Bench.' On the face of things it is a little difficult to see why. There was no regular practice of indicting ships' masters, whether British or foreign, for manslaughter, notwithstanding the annual carnage on the high seas. So far as foreign masters were concerned, there was no precedent for such a prosecution. In any event the German government was perfectly willing to investigate the matter and, if need be, try Captain Keyn in his own country. No doubt the sheer learning displayed in the arguments and opinions was in part the explanation. Thus the *Shipping and Mercantile Gazette*, in a leader published on 15 November, although it found the decision 'difficult to reconcile with reason and common sense' nevertheless felt bound to concede: 'Never, perhaps, in our time has any case been argued before a court in this country with more consummate ability on both sides, and never has a judgement been arrived at after more careful, enlightened and mature consideration.'

The Politics of the Case

I suspect, however, that there were other reasons. As it was put at the time by Cockburn CJ himself, some of the judges felt that 'the present case involved a question of a quasi political character'. Consequently it was Cockburn's view that the Lord Chancellor, Lord Cairns, who was proposing to sit in the Court for Crown Cases Reserved, should carefully consider the wisdom of this, since he was a member of the government and might be suspected of bias.[53] The political character no doubt arose from the fact that the decision in the case might affect relations between Britain and Germany, and indeed with other foreign powers. Clearly Cockburn CJ was anxious to maintain the distinction, so critical to the ideal of the rule of law, between a legal decision and a political decision. During the argument on 23 June he said:

I have no hesitation in saying that it would be desirable if we could make him amenable here and punish him here according to our law, but I say we must not arrogate to ourselves a law we do not possess . . . We shall not allow ourselves to be biased by a desire to possess the jurisdiction if we cannot see our way clear to saying that we do possess it'.[54]

In his opinion he returned to this theme in terms or reproof which bordered on the discourteous to such of his fellow judges as disagreed with him:

[52] *Morning Post*, 21 May 1923, quoted Marston, n. 29 above, 106.
[53] PRO 30/51 Bundle 10, quoted Marston, n. 29 above, 104.
[54] DPP 4/13, Book 1 at 4 and 6.

The question is, whether legislative action shall be applied to meet the exigency of the case, or judicial authority shall be strained and misapplied in order to overcome the difficulty. Every such usurped exercise of judicial power is, in my opinion, a violation of fundamental principles, and in the highest degree unconstitutional. The responsibility is with the legislature, and there it must rest.

To appreciate the climate of thought in which such anxieties arose, one needs to be aware, as all contemporaries were aware, of two earlier maritime disasters which had inflamed public opinion, and given to the affair of the *Franconia* something of the emotive quality of the Lockerbie disaster to the Pan American airliner. Inevitably, given the conventions of legal argument and reasoning, no mention of them is to be found in the purely legal sources.

The Disaster to the Northfleet

The first of these took place in 1873, and involved a sailing vessel, the 877-ton *Northfleet*.[55] She had originally been built in 1853, of teak planking on English oak frames, as a clipper ship for the China trade, but the opening of the Suez canal in 1869, and the development of the steamship had already begun to end the days of the tea clippers, and in any event the *Northfleet* was now nearly 20 years old and well past her prime. Owned by John Patton Jnr. and Co., she had been chartered to carry a cargo of railway lines to Hobart in Tasmania, together with navvies and their families. They were to build the Tasmanian railway, and then settle as emigrants there. There were 417 passengers aboard, of whom ninety-two were women (forty-six travelling with their husbands), forty-five were children,[56] and nine or possibly nineteen infants;[57] a number of the women were in an advanced state of pregnancy. The *Northfleet*, defying maritime tradition, commenced her voyage from the Port of London on Monday, 13 January, and on Friday, 17 January, after a delay caused by trouble with a condensing engine, left Gravesend, under tow by the steam tug, *Middlesex*. The *Northfleet* dropped her tow off the bleak headland of Dungeness. Her crew scrambled up the ratlines and over the futtock shrouds, cast off the gaskets and made sail, and she made a number of attempts to beat down Channel and reach the open Atlantic. She was defeated by a south-westerly gale; by Wednesday, 22 January, she was back off Dungeness where she had started. There she lay at anchor in company with 200 or 300 other sailing vessels, all in the same predicament.

The *Northfleet*'s regular master was Thomas Oates, who had been in charge of her since August 1868, but he had been required by *subpoena* to give evidence

---

[55] See MT 9/109/M5279/75, MT 9/69/M1379/73. Registered number 11167. Another vessel of the same name was still at sea, having been built in 1789. I have made use of reports in local papers, particularly the *Deal, Walmer and Sandwich Mercury*, and the *Dover Chronicle and Kent and Sussex Advertiser*, and in the London *Times* for various dates up to 19 Dec.

[56] i.e. between 2 and 12.   [57] Under 2.

in the *Tichborne* case; he was the last person to have seen Sir Roger Tichborne alive in Rio de Janeiro. In consequence, on 13 January he had relinquished command to Edward Knowles, who had, since 1868, served as first mate on the vessel, and who had his master's certificate.[58] Six weeks earlier Edward Knowles had married; now that he was master he was able to take his wife, Frederica, on the voyage to Tasmania, and he decided to do so. It must all have seemed an auspicious start to their married life together.

The night of 22 January was very squally and dirty; the barque lay to her main anchor with sixty fathoms of chain veered, with her second anchor ready to be let go, between two and three miles off the lighthouse at Dungeness. She had a strong riding light exhibited in the fore rigging, and an anchor watch set. At ten minutes to eleven she was struck by a steamer, which promptly backed off and vanished into the night. She was severely holed; appalling scenes took place as she rapidly sank. She went under at twenty-five minutes past eleven; since she was in relatively shallow water, her masts stood up high above the surface of the sea. Although there were many other vessels in the area, and distress signals were fired, the disaster escaped general notice; the blue rocket signals were mistaken for requests for a pilot, it being a common practice to fire distress signals for this purpose. Thus the master of the Australian clipper ship *Corona*, anchored only 300 yards away, was quite unaware of the accident, though the watch had heard the screams of the drowning passengers and taken no action. Only three vessels—the pilot cutter *Princess*, the lugger *Mary*, and the tug *City of London*—immediately realized that she had been sunk.

The *Northfleet* carried six boats, with capacity for 142 persons. Emigrant sailing vessels never carried sufficient boats for all the passengers; given the design of such vessels, the need to keep the decks clear enough to work the ship, and the fact that the decks were regularly swept by the sea in heavy weather, it was quite out of the question to do so. Such boats as were carried had to be inverted and lashed down, and in the event only two boats were ever launched. No doubt matters were not helped by the mass of panicking, screaming passengers, fully aware of the danger in which they were placed. Captain Knowles was familiar with the moral folk myth of the period according to which women and children were entitled to priority. But the crew and the male passengers had other ideas. He ordered the men to stand back, adding, 'if I had a revolver I should make you obey me.' Mr Frederick S. Brand, a cabin passenger and engineer travelling out to manage some of the construction of the railway, had been concerned that amongst the navvies there were 'some rough fellows' in a mutinous mood. He had acquired a revolver shortly before sailing just in case there was any trouble with them. It was loaded; he gave it to the Captain, who called out: 'The women first—I'll blow the man's brains out that dares get into a boat.' One of the navvies, Thomas Biddies (or Biddles), defied him and

---

[58] No. 1889.

clambered into the second of the two boats. His Captain ordered him out, and when he refused to move set about the task of killing him. His first shot, aimed to kill, missed; the second hit Biddies in the knee, and he remained in the boat, which also now contained a sailor, nicknamed Billy Ducks. The Captain's attempts to kill Billy failed when the revolver misfired, and no further shots were required to maintain some level of control over the situation, a task in which the Captain was assisted by Herman Kunde, the doctor, and the pilot, George Brack, who survived the disaster.[59] Captain Knowles had ensured that his wife got into one of the two boats. He placed the bosun, John Easter, in command of it, and, adopting the formal style which appears to have been thought appropriate for nineteenth-century ships' officers on these melancholy occasions, called out: 'Here is a charge for you, bosun; take care of her and the rest, and God bless you!' Wringing his wife's hand, he bade her goodbye with what must surely have been a profession of faith, for he can have had few illusions over his own chances: 'I shall see you again. Shove off! God bless you. Mind your charge!' Captain Knowles did not survive; nor did Frederick Brand. Of the entire complement of 449 persons, eighty-five in all were saved, including only three women, one being Frederica,[60] and two children. One child, aged 10, was Maria Taplin; she was promptly adopted. The other was Harriet Stargeon (or Sturgeon), aged 6 months, whose mother and father survived. Both children were thrown down into the boat.[61] Thomas Biddies survived and the bullet was removed from his leg by the house surgeon in the Dover hospital. The officers and crew numbered thirty-three; ten were saved, including 'Billy Duck'.[62] The first and second mates perished; the only officer to survive was the bosun. A pilot cutter, *Princess* (Captain James Pilcher), lowered two boats, which managed, in very difficult conditions, to rescue four persons clinging to an upturned boat, ten persons from the mizzen rigging, five from the main, and six from the foremast, an operation which took until two in the morning or later. Another unidentified boat was in the area, but did not apparently rescue anyone. Those who had got off in the boats were rescued by the *City of London* (Captain Samuel Kingston), a steam tug, and by the Deal lugger *Mary* (Captain George Pont).

All in all, it was a very typical maritime disaster, with women and children last. Nor was it the only one to take place that night off Dungeness, for by morning two barques and one steamship were hard aground on the shingle.

A Victorian Hero

Given the romantic tradition of the period, together with the morbid fascination with death, the 'Captain's farewell' to his young wife was bound to be a winner;

[59] Statement of Thomas Biddies in *Dover Express*, 24 Jan.
[60] The others were Eliza Huggett, and Lucy Stargeon.
[61] Accounts as to the number of lives lost vary trivially.
[62] 13 were British, 3 German, 1 Chinese, 9 Swedes, 4 Norwegians, 1 American, and 2 Jamaican.

the *Illustrated London News* published a splendid picture of the event, possibly based upon an oil painting, though I have not been able to trace one.[63] The tragedy was celebrated in the mournful ballad of the *Northfleet*, with its lugubrious chorus:

> God bless those widows and those orphans,
> Comfort them where'er they be.
> May God in heaven above protect them,
> From all the perils of the sea.

It begins:

> Come listen all ye feeling people,
> While this sad story I relate,
> About a vessel called the *Northfleet*,
> Which met with such a dreadful fate.
> Five hundred souls she had aboard her,
> Lay anchored there off Dungeness.
> Bound for Australia was the vessel,
> They'd bid farewell with fond caress.

The ballad somewhat improved upon reality over the incident with the revolver:

> The Captain stood up on the poop deck,
> 'Stand back, you men, the women first.
> I'll shoot the first man disobeys me!'
> They did not heed, but madly rushed.
> He fired! The shot alas proved fatal,
> And one poor fellow's life was laid.
> While those, still back on board the *Northfleet*,
> Went down upon their knees and prayed.[64]

The popular response was matched by that of Queen Victoria herself, whose concern was reported in the local press.[65] She communicated with Mr John Patton, the owner of the *Northfleet*, and was told that 'Mrs Knowles is as well as can be expected, but still in great mental distress.' Arrangements were made with one of the diving vessels from Whistable, the *Star* (Captain W. H. Bell), hired to salvage the valuable cargo, to search the private cabin and recover the letters and trinkets which her husband had given her. Frederica eventually received a grace and favour residence at Windsor, and a civil list pension of £50 *per annum*. She also received £1,000 from the Mansion House relief fund. The Queen's personal interest is confirmed by the fact that an anonymous citizen of Dover, who wrote an account of the tragedy, dedicated it to her with her gracious permission. The proceeds were to be devoted to raising a national memorial to

---

[63] *ILN* 1873, vol. 62 117–18. At 93 is a picture of a rescue from the rigging; at 109 pictures of the *Northfleet* and Captain Knowles; at 173 the *Murillo*.

[64] Slightly different text and music in R. Palmer, *The Oxford Book of Sea Songs* (Oxford, 1986), no. 126.

[65] Also documented in MT 9/69/M1379/73.

Captain Knowles and to Mr Brand, who had assisted him in his efforts to protect the women and children. Mr Brand's body was recovered, together with his revolver, and he was buried in the graveyard of New Romney, near Lydd, where a memorial was erected. There was also a charitable appeal, to which the Queen contributed £200 and the Prince of Wales £100; Disraeli added a handsome sum. By 1 February over £4,000 had been collected.

The Hunt for the Culprit

There was much recrimination over the failure of other vessels anchored in the area to render assistance; to those unfamiliar with the sea it seemed extraordinary that so many people had perished so close to the shore when the *Northfleet* was surrounded with hundreds of other ships, one anchored only 300 yards away. Naturally, attempts were made to identify the colliding vessel, apparently guilty both of criminally negligent navigation, and of callous indifference to the fate of those on board the *Northfleet*. A reward of £200 was offered by the Board of Trade and the railway contractors for her identification; 1,000 posters were ordered and distributed around European ports. The hunt for the culprit, made possible by the telegraph system, is fully documented in a surviving Board of Trade file.[66] By 24 January *The Times* reported suspicions that a Spanish steamer had been involved: 'the one thing now to be done is to lay hands on the delinquent steamer, and, with the help of the telegraph, this ought to be effected without difficulty.' Suspicion centred upon either the *Pelayo* or the *Murillo*. The *Murillo* had dropped her pilot, George Swainson, at Dover, and he was interviewed by the press. The master of the *Avoca* reported that he had seen a vessel off Dungeness which appeared to be using a light to examine its bows. James Moore, first mate of the *Marshal Pelissier*, reported from Falmouth that he had seen a steamer in the vicinity, and described it. The Foreign Office, operating through the consular system, collaborated. By the end of January it was being publicly stated that it was the *Murillo* which had caused the disaster.[67] Interest in the tragedy was maintained by press reports of inquests, held in Lydd, Deal, and Poplar, and by the opening, on 4 February, of the official Board of Trade inquiry into the loss. This was adjourned to await further evidence.

The *Murillo* was reported by Consul Brackenbury as having entered the River Tagus on 29 January. The press was fed with information by the Board of Trade.[68] Her bows, it was said, were newly painted. She was then located in Cadiz, from where Consul Thomas Reade telegraphed the Foreign Office: '*Murillo* arrived. Positively caused *Northfleet* disaster. No apparent damage. Authorities take depositions tomorrow after pratique . . . Circumstances have come to my

[66] MT 9/69/M1379/73.
[67] e.g. in the *Dover Express and East Kent Intelligencer* for 31 Jan.
[68] Documents were later published as Parliamentary Papers; see BPP HC 1874, LXI, 555.

attention which leave no doubt that the *Murillo* is the steamer that ran down the *Northfleet*.' She was inspected three times. The Spanish authorities found no marks of collision; representatives of Lloyd's agent did, and officers of HMS *Pheasant* agreed with the Spanish authorities. How could a vessel sink a large sailing ship and escape unscathed? Experts told the Board of Trade that this might well happen, and that a vessel the size of the *Murillo* would, at around three knots, exert a force sufficient to pierce the twenty inches of teak and oak of the side of the *Northfleet*.

It transpired that at the time of the incident the *Murillo* had been under the command of her mate, Don Felipi Berutti; Reade discovered that he had on board as a passenger an English engineer, Samuel Bell, and that the first and second engineers were also English—Giles Bethell and William Goodeve. The latter had been on deck at the moment of collision, and did not think that it had been severe. He had, however, heard cries for help, and expressed surprise that the *Murillo* had sailed on and not stood by; so, too, did Giles Bell. The logs of the *Murillo* were obtained and published. The steam log grimly read: 'Full speed 8.30 p.m. Half Speed at 10.15 p.m. Easy at 10.30. Stopped engines at 10.45. Put engine astern. Struck a ship at anchor. Put engines ahead easy. Full speed at 11.30 p.m.' Her navigational log, which reads as if it was written up sometime after the incident, explained the accident itself fairly plausibly. Given the course of the *Murillo*, the lighthouse at Dungeness was in line with the riding light of the *Northfleet*. It continued:

We struck her slightly, and at the moment of separating from her, the engine was stopped to see if her crew were anyway in danger, which was supposed not to be the case from the slight blow we struck her and because a boat immediately left the said ship and examined the damage and presuming nothing of moment had happened as the crew of the boat returned on board again we proceeded on our course.

This all sounds a little disingenuous, but in the conditions which obtained there could conceivably have been a mistaken interpretation of the situation.

The Spanish authorities set an enquiry in hand, over which disputes arose with Consul Reade; national pride became involved. He wished to interrogate the Spanish sailors himself; this was naturally resisted. He was refused copies of their depositions; under Spanish law the first stage in the legal proceedings was confidential. Depositions taken in Britain were dispatched to Cadiz to assist the authorities there. Eventually the rather implausible story told by the Spanish sailors was accepted by the authorities. It was that there had indeed been a collision, but only a slight blow was involved, and in any event the injured vessel had not been the *Northfleet*, but some other vessel, which was never identified. The acting Captain of the *Murillo* lost his certificate for a year, and the vessel herself put to sea from Cadiz on 27 July. By then local feelings ran high; there was fear of a riot if she were not allowed to sail. The Captain of HMS *Triumph*, which was standing off the port of Cadiz, suggested arresting her on the high seas. But the Law Officers, whose opinion was taken, opposed any such action as being quite illegal. So for the moment the rule of law triumphed and the *Murillo* escaped.

Many of the documents connected with the attempt to bring the *Murillo* and her master to justice were published in Britain, and widely commented upon. The tone may be illustrated from the *Dover Chronicle*, which, in January, described the master, then unidentified, as 'a rascally foreigner'; it called for 'condign punishment for his cruel and dastardly conduct'. The violent chauvinistic animosity of the time was well expressed in a sermon on the general theme of the need for repentance all round preached by the Revd W. Yates of St John's Mariners' Church in Dover. He spoke of;

those fiends in human shape, the officers and crew of that 'hell on earth', the steamer which ran down the *Northfleet* . . . Found out they will be at last, and let them be execrated by every human being they meet, and fled from as one would fly from the presence of a lion or tiger. If they escape human justice a whip should be placed in the hand of every honest man to whip them around the world.

There was much more in the same vein, and few dry eyes when he had finished his tirade.

Although Don Felipi Berutti had in a sense escaped, the *Murillo* did not. An action had been commenced against her owners, claiming some £14,000 in damages. She turned up off Dover, and was arrested; apparently her surrender was quite deliberate. *The Times*, reporting this curious incident, expatiated on the inhumanity of her captain.[69] In the civil litigation, which was largely uncontested, the vessel was condemned to be sold and fetched £7,000; the claims amounted to £14,000. The judge, Sir Robert Phillimore, exceeded his judicial duties by flinging some more abuse at her captain:

I find it difficult to express in adequate terms the indignation which the brutality and meanness of those in charge of the *Murillo* must excite in the bosom of every man not void of the ordinary feelings of humanity. This case indeed represents the cruelty, without any of the courage, of the pirate.

But slowly some degree of dispassion returned. In December the Board of Trade enquiry was concluded. It decided that in all probability there had been no deliberate indifference on the part of the master, who might well have been unaware of the seriousness of the accident. He was, however, severely criticized for failing to check more carefully.[70] And so, for the moment, the affair rested. As for the unhappy clipper *Northfleet* herself, you can in a sense still see her, for her remains still lie off Dungeness where she sank on that terrible night over a century ago; they form an attraction for the local sub-aqua club. If you go down to Dungeness, you can also see the old lighthouse which confused the captain of the *Murillo*. And on the bleak pebbly shore, close to the nuclear

[69] Issue of 24 Sept.   [70] *The Times*, 19 Dec.

power station, you may meet with relics of the old seafaring community of inshore fishermen; until recently it was their custom to sing the ballad of the *Northfleet* each year at Christmas by way of a memorial. A daughter of one of them told me how 'they did sing that awful old song when they get rather drunk', and, for all I know, this may still be the practice. But at the time of the case of the *Franconia*, memories of the disaster were very fresh.

The Wrecks of the Schiller and Deutschland

The second incident took place in 1875 and it, too, has been immortalized in verse. It involved a German vessel, the *Deutschland*.

The year opened badly for German shipping when another vessel, the *Schiller* of Hamburg, a large transatlantic liner, struck the Retarrier ledges near the Bishop Rock lighthouse on the Scillies.[71] She was on passage from New York to Plymouth, Cherbourg, and then to Hamburg. Her Captain was George Thomas, an Englishman, but born at Frankfurt am Main, and a former first officer with the Peninsular and Oriental Line. She carried a crew of 118 and 254 passengers. The accident happened in thick fog at 10 p.m. on 7 May. The last opportunity to take sights had been on 4 May, when she was 930 miles south-south-west of the Scillies. Thereafter the Captain relied purely on dead reckoning, sailing at fourteen knots through dense fog; in spite of the proximity of land he did not stop to take soundings. An hour before she struck he reduced speed to seven knots and altered course to south-south-west; although he must have passed close to the Bishop's Rock lighthouse, he did not hear the foghorn. He was at least eight miles out in his position. The vessel began to break up in heavy seas; there were appalling scenes of panic, and Captain Thomas attempted to maintain order by firing his revolver over the heads of the passengers. But he was swept overboard when the bridge carried away; he called to the second officer: 'Good-bye, old fellow. Remember me to my friends.'

No rescue came until the fog lifted next morning; only one boat was successfully launched. There were 331 lives lost, and the fifty-one saved included the first, second, and fourth mates and the bosun. There were the usual recriminations. At the Board of Trade inquiry by James H. Patteson, a stipendiary magistrate, the German government participated by nominating an assessor.[72] The conclusion was that the disaster was caused by Captain Thomas's failure to take soundings and thereby check his dead reckoning position. In due course there was a ceremony in the Guildhall at Penzance at which gifts from the

---

[71] See MT 9/124/M4815/76, on which much of what follows is based. The incident was fully covered in the press, e.g., *The Times* for 10 May and following days.

[72] The Law Officers had in 1860 given an opinion in the case to the *Endymion*, a US vessel burnt in the Mersey, that an inquiry could be held over the loss of a foreign vessel.

German Emperor were presented to those who had given aid to the victims of the disaster.[73]

Next it was the turn of the *Deutschland*, a large transatlantic liner which had put to sea from Bremerhaven on 4 December 1875, carrying emigrants bound for New York.[74] The weather was extremely bad, and navigation in such conditions was, at this time, far from being an exact science. The *Deutschland* blundered about the North Sea, with no very clear notion of her position, until 5 a.m. on Monday, 5 December, when she went aground on the Kentish Knock, a shoal some twenty-five miles off Harwich. A last-minute attempt to go astern failed when the stress of reversing direction fractured the propeller. At the time she was some thirty miles away from the position where her master, Captain Edouard Brickenstein, supposed her to be.

Initially it was a comfortable shipwreck, but the vessel must have been holed; she began to take on water, and as the tide rose she failed to lift. It began to blow a gale, and seas broke over her. It was very cold and snowing. By 10 a.m. on the Tuesday morning she was in such a state that attempts began to be made to abandon her. Discipline soon collapsed as both crew and passengers panicked. Some were washed overboard; characteristic scenes took place amongst those who remained clinging to the decks, and one passenger hanged himself. Rockets were fired and the customary signals of distress made; numerous ships passed by, but for some thirty hours nobody took the least notice. It seemed quite incredible that this should be so. One boat was launched, but it was swamped and the fourth officer and eight others drowned; a second boat, containing the quartermaster, August Bock, and two others, one a sailor, one a passenger, eventually drifted ashore on the Isle of Sheppey on the Wednesday; only Bock remained alive in it. This brought news of the accident, and eventually help came: 135 persons were saved out of 213. Amongst those drowned were five Franciscan nuns from Salzköller, Westphalia: Bartrac Hultenschmidt, Aurea Badzinra, Brigetta Damhorst, Henrica Faessbaender, and Norbeta Reinkaber. They were emigrating to escape the anti-Catholic Falck laws. Their fate inspired Gerard Manley Hopkins to compose *The Wreck of the Deutschland*.

Soon after the disaster became known, the seamen of the coastal towns, particularly those of Harwich and Ramsgate, set about plundering the wreck, which lay exposed and accessible on the shoal; in doing so they were merely following established maritime custom. An artist, employed by the *Illustrated London News*, also arrived on the scene, and the paper published his horrifying drawing of the scene. It shows the wreckers in the saloon, resembling nothing so much as a flock of vultures. The picture shows a corpse being plundered, though this is somewhat discretely presented.[75] *The Times* described the scene, noting that

---

[73] *Cornish Telegraph*, 2 May 1876.

[74] The incident and its aftermath were fully covered in both national and local newspapers on which I have relied. See in particular *The Times* for 8 Dec. and following days.

[75] *ILN*, 18 Dec. 1875, 599–600, 604, 605 has pictures; at 611 is a report.

corpses recovered had been pillaged too, with all rings removed.[76] Stories had, of course, always been told of deliberate wrecking of vessels, for example by showing false lights; inevitably it was suggested that the lost of the *Deutschland* had come about in this way. More plausibly there were allegations of deliberate delay in providing assistance, as well as allegations of wanton negligence. *The Times*, for example, published a strong leader on 10 December, and another on 13 December, in which it was said that for fifteen of the thirty hours the fact of the grounding was known. The tug which first gave assistance was the *Liverpool*, and her master, Captain Carrington, came in for much criticism for acting too slowly. The story gave rise to very strong feelings in Germany; on 13 December one Herr Knapp raised the matter in parliament.[77] He thought that the wreck took place a mere four miles off the shore, a mistake which no doubt further raised the temperature. The German government should investigate the matter.

So far as it was able, the German government tried to cool matters. In due course, on 20 December, the Board of Trade wreck enquiry opened at Poplar, conducted by H. C. Rothery with Captains White RN and Harris RN. It was not usual to hold such an enquiry in the case of a foreign ship becoming a casualty outside the three-mile limit, but it was no doubt done in order to respond to the criticisms which had been made of the failure to give assistance. The German government was asked to nominate an assessor, as had been done in the case of the *Schiller*.[78] Charles P. Butt QC had been briefed by the German government and, no doubt on instructions, made no charges; he also indicated that his clients were quite agreeable to the investigation being in the hands of the British government.[79] But he did point out that 'there had sprung up a feeling abroad and especially in Germany, that it was rather surprising that a large steamer with upwards of 200 persons aboard should have lain on a dangerous sand close to the English coast for thirty hours before any assistance came to her.' He also referred to the picture which had been published of the wreckers. Eventually the enquiry exonerated everyone of blame except Captain Brickerstein, who, it decided, had let his vessel get ahead in its reckoning, and shown 'a very great want of care and judgement'. Captain Brickerstein had indeed seen this coming and was none too pleased at the prospect. He asked Chancellor Bismarck to establish a German official investigation. But the Chancellor explained that under German law no such investigation could be held except in the event of criminal or civil proceedings, and as none were in contemplation the proposal was ruled out. In any event it would have been impracticable to investigate the matter in

[76] Issue of 13 Dec.   [77] *The Times*, 14 Dec.

[78] Recollection of T. H. Farrer in FO 83/732.

[79] Such inquiries were governed by the Merchant Shipping Act 1854, s. 432, and provided for such inquiries where a vessel was 'lost, abandoned or materially damaged on or near the coast of the United Kingdom'. On whether this section applied to a foreign ship see MT 9/195, CO 885/12, Vol. III, No. 262 A.

Germany, where witnesses would not have been available. So, officially, that was the end of the matter. Maritime accident inquiries were not introduced in Germany until 1878; the case of the *Franconia* seems to have been one of the factors which encouraged their establishment.[80]

The effect of the wreck of the *Deutschland* on public opinion was that of inflaming the coastal seafaring community against foreigners, and Germans in particular, just as the wreck of the *Northfleet* had inflamed the public generally against rascally foreigners who sank British ships off the British coast. No doubt these and other tales of the sea played on the deep-seated Victorian fear that civilization, intimately linked to notions of self control and discipline, was under perpetual threat from the animal savagery which lurked in members of all classes and seemed to flourish in the aftermath of disasters at sea, most dramatically perhaps in the maritime custom of killing and eating fellow shipmates when the rations ran out.[81]

Justice for Foreigners

It was against this background that the case of the German Captain Ferdinand Keyn fell to be decided, and there was no doubt what the public wanted—his conviction and punishment. Captain Keyn could not rationally be presented as a hit-and-run captain; he had not disappeared into the night, like the Captain of the *Murillo*. But, as we have seen, both before and after his trial attempts were made to suggest that he had done less than he ought to assist the sinking *Strathclyde*. The atmosphere in which the case was determined was also affected by the fact that this was a period when Britain really did rule the waves; it was not for some years that Germany set out to alter that state of affairs. But the popular British assumption that the high seas belonged to them was not one which went down well with other European States. It is hard to suppose that Captain Keyn could, in the circumstances, receive a fair trial, and had the incident happened a few years earlier he would have been entitled to be tried by a mixed jury of Englishmen and aliens. But this ancient right to trial *per medietatem linquae* had been abolished by the Naturalization Act of 1870.[82]

In the event, Ferdinand Keyn, though he could perhaps expect little mercy from an all-English jury, had nothing to fear from the judiciary; even Sir Robert Phillimore, who had become so emotionally involved in the supposed misconduct of the master of the *Murillo*, voted in favour of quashing his conviction. The solemn legal propriety with which the case was argued and determined by

[80] Letter of 17 Jan. 1985 from Dr B. Meyer-Friese of the Altonaer Museum, Hamburg. MT 9/155/ M13188/78 has the German rules for wreck inquiries.
[81] See M. J. Wiener, *Reconstructing the Criminal. Culture Law, and Policy, 1830–1914* (Cambridge, 1990), 26–8, also my *Cannibalism and the Common Law* (Chicago. Ill., 1984), *passim*.
[82] 33 Vict. c.14. See M. Constable, *The Law of the Other* (Chicago, Ill., 1993), 7.

the Court for Crown Cases Reserved was surely a triumph for the ideal of the rule of law. It was an expression of self-control under the pressure of powerful emotions, and the triumph of the intellect over the passions which, to the Victorian mind, represented the acme of civilization. If all the public really wanted was a scapegoat, a sacrificial victim to appease its wrath, they were not going to get one from the judges of England. To be sure, those judges differed in opinion, and six voted to affirm the conviction; the tone of Cockburn CJ's opinion in favour of Keyn suggests strongly that he thought that they were bowing to popular clamour and usurping the function of the legislature. But although the matter is beyond strict proof, it is, I think, fairer to them to suppose that they, too, set out seriously to determine the case solely by reference to the arcane legal arguments which were acceptable in legal convention. Neither popular clamour nor diplomatic expediency entered into the equation; the decision was a legal decision, not a political one. Today there are those who contend that any distinction between the two is, at least in difficult cases, quite illusory. Victorian judges did not believe that, and perhaps it is this belief which makes a distinction between law and politics possible.

Reversing the Decision

What was the aftermath of the affair? This has been explored in G. Marston's *The Marginal Seabed. United Kingdom Legal Practice*: 'the decision of the Court for Crown Cases Reserved came as a shock to many in Whitehall and Westminster.'[83]

W. Malcolm minuted in the Colonial Office in October 1877 that the case 'seems to have sent people mad'.[84] It was thought by some that the decision was simply wrong. Then it was discovered that an appalling mistake had perhaps been made. Under Customs Acts the Crown, by commission out of the Exchequer, had power to appoint ports and declare their limits; from 1864 this power was transferred to the Lords of the Treasury.[85] On 3 March 1848 in the *Royal Gazette* the port of Dover had been declared to extend to a distance of three miles, so that the accident happened within it. Everyone agreed that English criminal law would apply in a port; ports were not the high seas. But there might be a difference between the *fiscal* port, and what might be called the *homicide* port. It was all very confusing.

Although there was no way for the crown to appeal to a higher criminal court against the quashing of the conviction, a civil action, in which the whole matter

---

[83] (Oxford, 1981), 138; see ch. 6.
[84] CO 23/217 f.448, quoted Marston, *The Marginal Seabed. United Kingdom Legal Practice*, 138.
[85] See 3 & 4 Will. IV c.52 (1833), s. 139; 8 & 9 Vict. c.86, s. 53 (1845); 9 & 10 Vict. c.102, s. 14 (1846).

of jurisdiction could be ventilated anew, could be taken up to the House of Lords. The House might well come to the conclusion that *Regina* v. *Keyn* had been wrongly decided.

A number of civil actions were brought as a consequence of the affair. The vessel itself was arrested in London in one such action, and then released after undertakings had been given by the owners to answer for any damages they might be held liable to pay and for which the vessel would have been security. There was no doubt that there was such liability for property damage, so long as the collision was the fault of the *Franconia*, and in such an action against the ship there was no tricky problem about jurisdiction. The owners conceded fault in the civil litigation, but argued that the *Strathclyde* was also at fault, which would have reduced their liability. It was held in *The Franconia* (1876) by Sir Robert Phillimore, assisted by two Elder Brethren, that the *Franconia* alone was to blame, and this was upheld by the Court of Appeal, though for different reasons.[86] The question of civil liability for causing death and personal injuries was much more tricky. Civil actions were begun over the death of twenty-one passengers and eighteen members of the crew, the solicitors involved being Gellatly and Son and Walton.[87] Because of conflicting authorities it was not clear that the ship could be sued, or, if released on terms, used as security for such actions for loss of life. One of these actions, reported as *The Franconia* (1877),[88] was brought by the widow of James Jeffery, who had drowned, and was started in the Court of Admiralty. Sir Robert Phillimore held that the court had jurisdiction and that such a claim against the ship was good in law.[89] The Court of Appeal split on this, James and Baggaley LJJ agreeing, and Bramwell and Brett LJJ holding the opposite; since the court was evenly divided, the decision of Phillimore stood, but obviously left the situation over other claims quite obscure. Because it was appreciated that the authorities were in conflict, the Privy Council favouring liability and the Queen's Bench, with Blackburn J being unable to make up his mind, taking the other view, Mr Butt, who had won the Privy Council case, advised that an action be brought against the owners, domiciled in Germany, rather than against the *Franconia* itself, which was in England.[90] The suit was brought by Mary A. Harris as adminstrator of James Sullivan, who had drowned. To be on the safe side this was started in the virgin territory of the Common Pleas, peopled by judges on the minority side in *Regina* v. *Keyn*, and an order obtained to serve the writ abroad. But this order was set aside on the ground that the decision in *Regina* v. *Keyn* was binding and applied

---

[86] *The Franconia* (1877) 2 PD 8 (Case B2070. Trial on 9 May, Court of Appeal decision 8 Dec.). A later case, *The Franconia* (1878) 3 PD 164 (Case H347 1877, 19 July) dealt with the limitation of liability by reference to the tonnage of the vessel, over which there was some obscurity.

[87] On what follows, see HO 45/9402/53056. The reported civil cases are *The Franconia* (1876) 2 PD 8, *Harris* v. *The owners of the Franconia* (1877) 2 CPD 173; *The Franconia* (1877) 2 PD 163.

[88] 2 PD 163 (Case J67, 26 Mar., 17 Apr., 2 June).

[89] The action was by consent treated as an *actio in rem*.

[90] They were *The Beta* (1869) LR 2 PC 447, and *Smith* v. *Brown* (1871) 6 QB 729.

to civil liability too, so that the court lacked jurisdiction.[91] A suit would therefore have to be brought in the German courts.

The solicitors wanted to appeal against this up to the House of Lords, which, it was hoped, would overrule *Regina* v. *Keyn*, but their clients were too poor to afford this; they therefore asked for the government to help. But this was refused. The Lord Chancellor was hostile; even if the House said the jurisdiction existed, they would rule that the action ought in the first instance to be begun in Germany. In any event, since the application was by one party only (in legal jargon *ex parte*), the House of Lords would hear argument only on one side. Consequently the Lords, not able to hear both sides of the argument, would refuse to decide on the correctness of the decision in *Regina* v. *Keyn*.

Instead of thus attempting to have the decision overruled, the government response was legislation to reverse it. After one bill was withdrawn, a government Territorial Waters Jurisdiction Bill was introduced. During the debate in August 1878, Sir Hardinge Giffard, who had argued the case for the Crown and lost it, hinted that the decision even gave a licence to foreign rapists; the decision meant that 'the life and honour of any British subject bathing at the sea side— say, of a school girl at Brighton or elsewhere—would be at the mercy of any foreigner on board a foreign ship who choose to take it'.[92] The Act raised a central problem in Dicey's analysis of the British constitution, and one which he never really solved, if indeed it can be solved: how can the ideal of the rule of law be reconciled with the absolute legislative sovereignty of Parliament? If Parliament can change the law at any time, even, if it wishes, retrospectively, and pass any law whatever, however incompatible with the spirit of legality, is not the rule of law a mere empty shell? Since the time of the case of the *Franconia* there have been a number of times when judicial decisions have been promptly reversed by legislation, or even rendered nugatory by executive order, and it is conceivable that the fear of this may have had some chilling effect on judicial independence. Before 1876 it is not easy to think of examples apart from the Thelluson Act of 1800, a non-controversial measure which was not retrospective in operation, and perhaps Fox's Libel Act of 1792.

The problem of collisions between vessels of different nationalities did not, of course, go away; on 25 November 1878 the brand new British sailing barque, *Mole Eilian*[93] (Captain Pritchard), sank the German steamship, *Pomerania* (Captain Schwensen), operated by the Hamburg American Packet Line, off the North Foreland between Folkestone and the Varne sand; out of some 220 persons 172 were saved. After some dithering the Board of Trade abandoned the idea of holding an inquiry.[94] And, in spite of its reversal by legislation, *Regina* v. *Keyn* also refused to go away. It lives on as an important legal authority, as

---

[91] *Harris* v. *The Hamburgh-Amerikanishe-Packetfahrt- Actien-Gessellschaft, Owners of the Franconia* (1877) 2 CPD 173.
[92] 242 Parl. Deb., 3rd. ser., col. 2035.   [93] Her port was Caernarvon.
[94] Papers in FO 83/732.

Mr Geoffrey Marston has shown. It is regularly referred to in analogous disputes to the present day and, with the commercial exploitation of the seabed, its importance has indeed grown rather than diminished in the world of both international and common law legal doctrine.

Keyn on the Beach

As for Ferdinand Keyn himself, the British government rather grudgingly paid his hotel bill, his subsistence, the taxed costs of his defence, which came to the massive sum of £2,533 13s. 3d., and his lost wages of £202 9s. 6d. Before the disaster he is listed in the *Hamburger Seeschiffahrts-Verzeichnis* as *Kapitan* of the *Bavaria* (formerly *Petropolis*) from 1871 to 1873, and of the *Franconia* from 1874 to 1876. The *Franconia* remained a Hamburg ship until 1878, under three captains, but Keyn was not one of them; he was succeeded by a Captain Schmitt, who ran this unhappy vessel aground on a voyage from Curaçao to Cuxhaven in December 1876. In 1878 she was sold to G. C. Transatlantique, and renamed *Oleander Rodrigues*.[95] What eventually became of her I do not know.

After his conviction was quashed, Ferdinand Keyn returned to Hamburg, and there the authorities set about the task of prosecuting him for manslaughter, or at least taking proceedings to investigate the matter. As late as August and September 1879 their efforts continued; the problem was to collect some evidence. There were plans to put interrogatories to Captain John Dodd Eaton. After the loss of the *Strathclyde* he became, in September 1876, master of the *Naples*.[96] This vessel was engaged in the East Indian trade, and he remained with her until late 1878. He then became master of the *Suez*, also in the East Indian trade.[97] He was last heard of in Bombay in 1879, but attempts to trace him thereafter failed. His name has no further entry in Lloyd's Captains' Registers, and either his maritime career ended or he died in India.[98] The problem was typical in the case of crimes supposed to have been committed on the high seas; seamen and passengers who might have served as witnesses became increasingly difficult to locate, and seamen in particular had nothing to gain from co-operation with the prosecuting authorities. So far as I have been able to discover, Captain Keyn never was prosecuted in Germany; it hardly mattered, in view of the fact that his maritime career had been ruined. No doubt in some more humble role he may have gone back to sea, but I have no information as to this possibility.

The Survival of the Legal Spirit

Since 1876 the ideal of the rule of law has taken some nasty knocks from the courts. A familiar example is the conviction of William Joyce for treason in

---

[95] Letter of 25 Mar. 1985 from Dr B. Meyer-Friese.   [96] No. 70728.
[97] No. 70633.   [98] Guildhall MS 18567/32 for 1880-7.

1946.[99] William Joyce, who was an American citizen who had before the Second World War been long resident in England, left the country just before the outbreak of war and became involved in German propaganda broadcasting. He became identified in the popular mind with a composite and partly mythical character, Lord Haw Haw of Zeesen, who possessed a distinctive voice; in reality, Joyce was not the possessor of the voice associated with the broadcasts of Lord Haw Haw. In popular opinion Joyce was thought to be British and ranked as the most notorious traitor of the second war. After the war Joyce was apprehended and put on trial; he had fraudulently obtained an English passport, and it was contended that his possession of this passport entitled him to call on the protection of the Crown. Consequently he owed allegiance during the currency of this passport, and could therefore be guilty of treason when he broadcast from Germany. This legal argument seems to many to be utterly unconvincing; the idea of Joyce being entitled to Crown protection whilst in Germany working for Goebbel's propaganda machine seems ludicrous. It nevertheless was accepted by a majority of the House of Lords and led to his execution. The conviction was also unsatisfactory because there was virtually no evidence that Joyce had broadcast during the currency of the passport, a point not exploited at the trial by his counsel, G. O. Slade KC, either through incompetence, or because his heart was never really in the job of looking after his client, at the time the most hated individual in Britain. Many, at the time and since, have thought that the judges simply bowed to the popular clamour for the execution of the traitor, Lord Haw Haw; in the nature of things, however, the point is incapable of strict proof. Another example is perhaps the decision in the case of *Liversidge* v. *Anderson* in 1941, when the judges washed their hands of responsibility for the protection of civil liberty in the context of wartime detention without trial;[100] again the charge is not capable of strict proof. But whatever may be said of these or of other dubious decisions, the ideal of the rule of law has a lot of life left in it, and there are many judges who, like Cockburn CJ and his colleagues back in 1876, regard it as something which alone gives respectability to the whole enterprise of the law, assuming, of course, that it is possible to do so.

---

[99] *Joyce* v. *Director of Public Prosecutions* [1946] AC 347.
[100] [1942] AC 206. See my *In the Highest Degree Odious*, n. 7 above, for discussion.

Quackery and Contract Law
Carlill v. Carbolic Smoke Ball Company
(1893)

An Object of Mystery

All lawyers, and indeed many non-lawyers, are familiar with the case of *Carlill* v. *Carbolic Smoke Ball Company*,[1] which was before the courts in 1892 and 1893. Continuously studied though it has been by lawyers and law students for close to a century, an air of mystery long surrounded the case; even at the time the very form taken by the celebrated smoke ball was unknown to Lindley LJ, who adjudicated in the case in the Court of Appeal. He is reported to have referred to it as 'a thing they call the "Carbolic Smoke Ball". What that is, I don't know.' Happily, a considerable volume of material survives that makes it possible to recreate at least something of the historical background and significance of this landmark in the history of contract law and its relationship to the seedy world of the late nineteenth-century vendors of patent medical appliances.

The Influenza Epidemic of the 1890s

The story behind the case begins in Central Asia, in the ancient city of Bokhara. Life in Bokhara in the nineteenth century was, even at the best of times, rugged, particularly during the reign of the ferocious Emir Nasrullah, who was, even by the standards of the times, a peculiarly unpleasant piece of work.[2] Although Emir Nasrullah passed on to paradise in 1860, the natural rigours of the place remained, and the winter of 1888–9 was especially grim. According to a contemporary account, by the time spring arrived, as the winter had been so severe the Bokhariots were obliged to spend money on firing, instead of food, so that they were weak from want of nourishment.[3] Being in the main devout followers of

This is a revised version of an article which first appeared in (1985) 14 *JLS* 345.

[1] [1892] 2 QB 484, [1893] 1 QB 256, 8 TLR 680. The fullest reports are in [1892] *The Patent Medicines Journal* at 196, (1892) 40 *Chemist and Druggist* 875 and 41 at 39, 48, 839. The case was, of course, covered by numerous newspapers; there is a leader in the *Daily News* on 5 July 1892 and an article in (1892) 69 *Spectator* 62.

[2] See F. MacLean, *A Person from England and Other Travellers* (London, 1958), ch. 1.

[3] *Report on the Influenza Epidemic of 1889–90* (by Dr F. Parsons) in BPP H.C. 1890–1, XXXIV (Cmnd. 6387 (1891)) 375.

the faith of Islam, they nevertheless persisted in a resolute observance of the fast of Ramadan. This enfeebled them still further. So, when a severe epidemic broke out in the city during the month of May 1889, they died in large numbers. Since 1868 Bokhara had been a Russian protectorate, the imperial government maintaining a legation in the city. The Russians in the legation, less adapted to conditions in Bokhara, suffered particularly severely. At one point all were prostrated, no one remaining in a condition to nurse the invalids. As soon as the sufferers became convalescent, they hurried home to mother Russia to enjoy a change of air and good nursing. Their flight was aided by the newly constructed Transcaspian Railway, completed only in 1888 and terminating, to please the Emir (who disliked such godless things) some eight miles from the ancient city. So it came about that, by the end of November, influenza had moved out of Central Asia and become so well established in St Petersburg that half the population had been attacked. This, in all probability, was how the great pandemic of influenza, 'Russian' influenza, began. There were, as ever, rival theories, which Dr Parsons discussed in his report on the subject; one such attributed the epidemic to the bursting of the banks of the Hoang Ho river in China, which spread malodorous mud over a wide area, which, under the miasmic theory, might then be blamed for the epidemic. Fingers were also pointed at Athabasca in Canada.

The outbreak of influenza in Russia, and its movement across Europe, was of course reported in England. *The Times*, for example, on 30 November 1889, carried a story from its correspondent in St Petersburg:

The epidemic called by the doctors influenza, for want of a better name, continues to rage in St Petersburg. Several Grand Dukes are affected or are just recovering, and the British Ambassador and members of his staff are nearly all ill. The writer has also just recovered from an attack.

The disease spread inexorably across Europe. Britain had last suffered from epidemic influenza in 1847–8, when, in London alone, 1,739 deaths had been attributed to the disease.[4] Since then there had been only isolated cases and a diminishing record of deaths; the figures reached a record low in 1889. But during late October of that year a new wave of infection was quietly establishing itself. By December the disease had become common, though at first this was not generally appreciated. *The Times* published a leading article on the subject on 3 December, speculating belatedly on the possibility that the disease might indeed have then reached England, and offering sage advice on the precautions to be taken by its readers. The writer favoured warm underclothes, well-ventilated rooms, and breathing through the nostrils. He concluded:

---

[4] See T. Thompson, *Annals of Influenza or Epidemic Catarrhal Fever in Great Britain from 1510–1837* (London, 1852). There is an excellent art. in the *Encyclopaedia Britannica* (11th ed., 1910–11). See also *Further Reports and Papers on Epidemic Influenza, 1889–2*, BPP H.C. 189394 (Cmnd. 7051 (1893)), 529.

If people will lead rational lives, they may not indeed be able to bid defiance to an epidemic, the channels of diffusion of which are as yet unknown to us, but they will certainly keep themselves in the best position for resisting its onslaught, or for minimizing the consequences of its occurrence.

But by 13 December even *The Times* had caught up with reality, and rumours of influenza in London were then reported. Soon it became common knowledge that 'Russian' influenza had reached the capital, and by January the disease had reached epidemic proportions. In the city, during the first quarter of 1890, 558 deaths were attributed to it. Though depressing and debilitating, influenza, at least in the form it then took, was not a disease with a high mortality rate. In the absence of complications, such as pneumonia, most recovered, and such deaths as did occur mainly came about as an indirect consequence. But a large portion of the population was temporarily incapacitated.

At this time the nature of influenza was not, of course, understood. A widely held view, and one strenuously argued by Dr Franklin Parsons in the official reports on this and later epidemics, was that microbes, transmitted from person to person, were to blame. But though claims were made from time to time, as by one Dr Richard Pfeiffer,[5] these had not yet been identified microscopically, nor, as we now know, could they have been. Orthodox medicine of the period favoured good nursing as beneficial, but in general offered no certain cure, though there was some support for the use of quinine as a prophylactic. Quinine, it must be noted, was at the time one of the very few drugs available that actually did cure a disease, but that disease, of course, was not influenza. The absence of a certain cure, however, in no way inhibited doctors from prescribing a wide variety of drugs to their unfortunate patients; they came to doctors for treatment, and treatment they duly received. A leader in the *Lancet*, published somewhat later in 1892, cautiously concentrated attention merely on the management of the disease, rather than its cure, remarking gloomily that 'there is no disease in which it is so easy to satisfy oneself of the efficacy of a pet remedy and the truth of a plausible theory as influenza'.[6] The less reputable providers of medical care were not so inhibited, and, during the first epidemic of 1889–90 and later, a wide variety of supposed cures and prophylactics were placed on the market and widely advertised. Thus, in the *Illustrated London News* for 28 December 1889, Brown's Bronchial Troches, formerly advertised for other ailments, were offered as a cure, as were R. Huggins's Ozone Papers; on 4 January Salt Regal featured as a prophylactic under the headline 'The Coming Epidemic! The Coming Epidemic!' and on 25 January Beechams, better known for their liver pills, took a full page of the journal to advertise Beecham's Cough Pills as a specific remedy.

[5] *The Times* 5, 8, 9 Jan. 1892.   [6] [1892] *The Lancet* 320.

The Patenting of the Smoke Ball

On 30 October 1889 one Frederick Augustus Roe, 'of 202 Regent St in the County of Middlesex, Gentleman', submitted an application to patent what he described as 'an Improved Device for Facilitating the Distribution, Inhalation and Application of Medicated and Other Powder'. The application was handled by the patent agents, Haseltine Lake and Company, from 45 Southampton Buildings, conveniently adjacent to the London Patent Office. As described in the specification, the improved device:

comprises a compressible hollow ball or receptacle of India Rubber or other suitable elastic material, having an orifice or nozzle provided with a porous or perforated disc or diaphragm consisting of muslin, silk, wire or gauze, perforated sheet metal or the like, through which, when the ball or receptacle is compressed, the powder will be forced *in a cloud of infinitesimally small particles resembling smoke*.[7]

Accompanying drawings showed two variant forms of this elegant medical appliance, the beauty of which, so its inventor claimed, lay in the fact that the inrush of air when the ball filled prevented the screen from clogging, thus enabling the user to discharge 'a cloud or diffused stream of powder resulting from each compression of the said receptacle'. When exhausted the receptacle could, of course, be refilled. Æsthetic claims were also made; the fact that the powder was both put in and puffed out through a single orifice, so Roe argued, greatly improved the appearance of the appliance. The invention also possessed considerable development potential. It could, for example, be modified so as to have two nozzles, or two oval outlets 'to enable the apparatus to be applied to both nostrils at once' in a swift and concerted assault on the seat of infection. Although surviving examples are rare, one supposed example may be seen in the Country Life Museum at Tresilian Barton, but it does not appear to be the genuine article. A photograph of one which certainly is was published in the *Observer Colour Supplement* for 2 July 1889, and apparently this was sold in the tea rooms of Fortnum and Mason in July 1890.[8] Directions for use of the ball survive in the *Inventor*:

Hold the ball by the loose end below the silk floss, with the thumb and forefinger in front of the mouth. Snap or flip rapidly on the side of the ball, on the place marked 'S' and a fine powder resembling smoke will arise. Inhale this smoke or powder as it arises, as shown in the above illustration. This will cause sneezing, and for a few moments you will feel as if you were taking cold. This feeling will soon pass away and the cure has commenced. If you do not feel the effects at the first inhalation by it making you sneeze, take a second in the same manner.[9]

---

[7] Patent No. 17,220 of 1889. My italics.

[8] It was owned by one W. A. Jackson, who purchased it in Bath in about 1980. He published an art. on the ball in *The Pharmaceutical Historian* 14 (1), 1984, 9–10. The present ownership of the ball is not known to me.

[9] (1890) 6 *The Inventor*: 189.

Other instructions, the product of experience, and associated with the ball sold in 1890, read:

Press the Carbolic Smoke Ball lightly and quickly, and a fine powder resembling smoke will arise. Inhale the smoke or powder vigorously as it arises, from three to five minutes at a time, as shown in the above illustration, for all the undermentioned ailments. This will cause sneezing, and for a few moments the patient will feel as if he had a cold. This feeling will soon pass away, and the cure commences.

IMPORTANT! When inhaling care should be taken to remove the Smoke Ball between each inhalation, so that the moisture from the breath will not affect the covering through which the fine powder, resembling smoke, arises.

This was not Roe's first invention. He had previously devoted his talents to improving the lot of horses, patenting improvements to a form of horseshoe incorporating springs in 1882, 1885, and 1886, as well as improvements to machines for sharpening calks on horseshoes, and for grooming horses.[10] Horses attracted considerable mechanical ingenuity at this time—patent 3,644 of 1892 was a device to prevent self-abuse in stallions—and Roe's contraptions were related to a patent taken out in 1879 for Messrs Dewey of San Francisco, a business with which Roe appears to have been involved.[11] It could be that his 'Improved Device', which was granted patent number 17,220 on 7 December 1889, was initially conceived in order to reduce the hazards and increase the effectiveness of the established practice of medicating horses by puffing powders through tubes down their throats, a technique fraught with the ever-present danger that the horse would retaliate by blowing back.[12] But in the form in which the device was patented, human application was plainly envisaged, though Roe did by 1993 develop a special version for dogs, the 'Dog' Smoke Ball, which was sold with a grave warning: 'CAUTION. The "Dog" Smoke Ball must not be used by Human Beings, being too powerful in its action.' Though, no doubt, other powders could have been used to fill the receptacle (and the patent does not specify), Frederick Roe seems always to have confined himself to using carbolic acid or phenol in powder form, this being the standard germ killer of the time. Patent records also show that Roe was from New York; he is thus described in 1882 and 1885, though in 1885 he was living at 42 Fairholme Road, West Kensington, London, and in 1886 at 10 Duchess Street, off Regents Street. The American origin of the smoke ball is confirmed by an advertising leaflet in the Oxford Museum for the History of Science, which describes it as the 'New American Remedy' and the 'Standard Remedy of America'.

---

[10] Patents 3177 and 4728 of 1882, 8001 of 1885, 8187 of 1886.   [11] No. 4424 of 1879.

[12] Mr Jackson in the art. cited in n. 9 suggests a connection with Patent 5430 of 1887 for a cruder contraption, a cloth puffer of a mixture of carbolic acid and slippery elm or liquorice root.

The Marketing of the Ball

Whether the ball was in fact marketed in America, perhaps as 'the Pulverator', is unknown, but late in 1889 or early in 1890 Roe began to market his Carbolic Smoke Ball in England, moving his premises to 27 Princes Street, Hanover Square, at about this time. The ball was actually manufactured by Messrs Ingrams of Hackney Wick. The influenza epidemic which had begun, as we have seen, in December of 1889, must have come as a godsend to his new enterprise, but the utility of the ball was by no means restricted to this single ailment. The earliest of his advertisements that I have located appeared in the *Illustrated London News* on 11 January 1890. He claimed that the ball, to be had from the Carbolic Smoke Ball Company at their new premises for a price of ten shillings, 'Will positively cure Influenza, Catarrh, Asthma, Bronchitis, Hay Fever, Neuralgia, Throat Deafness, Hoarseness, Loss of Voice, Whooping Cough, Croup, Coughs, Colds, and all other ailments caused by Taking Cold'. Behind this optimism lay a theory, more fully articulated in some of his later advertisements. It was that all these ailments arose from a single cause, taking cold, and were therefore all amenable to the same remedy. He exhibited a note of caution in insisting that the ball was to be used for inhalation only. Carbolic acid, though not at the time a scheduled poison, could be fatal if taken internally in more than small amounts. Inhaling the powder through the nostrils must certainly have produced a numbing and astringent effect and been somewhat disagreeable and, as the directions for use indicate, caused sneezing. Messrs Wilcox and Company, a firm of druggists in business at 239 Oxford Street, seem to have been closely associated with Roe in the promotion of the ball. In late 1889 and early 1890 they offered especially favourable sale or return terms to those who would stock it, and a set of twelve free dummies; this, so the *Chemist and Druggist* later reported, was highly successful.[13]

Frederick Roe was only one of many advertisers who made claims to cure or ward off influenza. It was the practice of the patent medicine vendors to adapt their claims, rather than their products, to the current needs of the market, and Roe was merely doing what was normal in the trade. The product remained the same; its function changed.

According to his later claims, the ball was widely sold during this epidemic, and gave great satisfaction. There is no particular reason to doubt this. In the catalogue of Barclay and Sons Ltd., published for the trade in 1890,[14] it appears in two obscurely different forms, 'the Carbolic Smoke Ball' and 'the Carbolic Smoke (India Rubber) Ball'. The wholesale prices were 88*s*. and 94*s*. a dozen, respectively, with a retail price of 10*s*. During 1890 the appliance does not seem to have been heavily advertised, though a more exhaustive search through the newspapers and journals of the period might reveal advertising that I have missed.

---

[13] 40 *Chemist and Druggist* 142 and 273.   [14] Original in the Science Museum, Kensington.

During 1891, however, the ball was heavily and imaginatively advertised in the *Illustrated London News* at what must have been considerable expense; a full page at this time cost £100 for one issue. Thus on 24 January a series of very specific claims was made: the ball would cure a cold in the head or chest in twelve hours, catarrh in three months, asthma 'in every case' with relief in ten minutes, hoarseness in twelve hours, influenza in twenty-four hours, the bizarre ailment called throat deafness in three weeks, and so on. If used before retiring, the ball would also prevent snoring. After running this advertising for three months, new copy was inserted on 4 April. The list of diseases remained the same, but the theory of the smoke ball was made explicit: 'as all these diseases mentioned above proceed from the same cause—viz. taking cold, they may all be cured by one remedy—viz. the Carbolic Smoke Ball.' An appeal was also made to the snobbery of the readers by providing a list of distinguished people who, it was claimed, used the ball; the use of such testimonials, which could be fraudulent, was standard practice in the quack medicine world. This list included the Duchess of Sutherland; the Earls of Wharncliffe, Westmoreland, Cadogan, and Leitrim; the Countesses Dudley, Pembroke, and Aberdeen; the Marchionesses of Bath and Conyngham; a continental count, Count Gleichen; and a brace of run-of-the-mill lords, Rossmore and Norton. Further lists of satisfied customers appeared on 18 April, 2 May, and 16 May. In addition to aristocrats—nine dukes—doctors now began to appear, including the distinguished Sir Henry Acland KCB, a particularly important client; he was at the time Regius Professor of Medicine at Oxford and physician to the Prince of Wales. Other eminent doctors included Sir James Paget, sergeant surgeon to Queen Victoria, surgeon to the Prince of Wales and Vice-Chancellor of London University. The attractiveness of the advertisements was enhanced by a picture of a young lady using the ball; she was apparently employed in the packing department of Messrs Ingrams, the manufacturers.

With the coming of spring, Roe's advertising changed again; on 30 May the ball was offered as a cure for hay fever, indeed as the only cure for 'a disease that has hitherto baffled the skill of the most eminent physicians'. The approach of winter brought a new advertisement on 14 November, with testimonials from, for example, the Revd Dr Reade of Banstead Downs, Surrey, and Dr Colbourne MD of 60 Maddox Street in London. I have not traced Dr Reade, but a W. W. Colborne does feature in the Medical Directory for 1892, with no address given. Testimonials from clerics and doctors were much favoured in quack medicine advertisements, both professions combining respectability and status with a close association with death, and Roe used the names of very eminent doctors indeed. Whether he had their permission it is not possible to be sure, though I suspect that most of the testimonials were genuine enough, being traded for free samples and, in the case of doctors, free advertising. On 5 December he inserted a much larger advertisement, showing not merely an adult lady using the ball but a child as well; the undated advertising leaflet preserved in Oxford also directed attention to children, who could, it pointed out, be medicated when asleep, thus preserving them from illnesses which, it grimly pointed out, 'usually led to fatal results'. The new advertisement embodied further illustrious testimonials: 'as prescribed by Sir Morell Mackenzie, M. D.'. The Duke of Portland was also quoted as writing 'I am much obliged for the Carbolic Smoke Ball which you sent me, and which I find most efficacious'. And no less than His Grace the Bishop of London confessed that 'the Carbolic Smoke Ball has helped me greatly'. The advertisement in the special Christmas supplement went even further by reproducing the Royal Arms—'By Royal Letters Patent'—with the obvious intention of suggesting that Her Majesty herself had in some way approved the ball. This form of deception was then common in the trade. In the later advertising of the Dog Smoke Ball there was both a picture of the Queen's favourite dog, Windsor Marco, and a testimonial from her canine surgeon, O. Rotheram.

The Recurrence of Influenza 1891–2

Influenza again became established in London during 1891, first in June and July and again during the winter of 1891–2. According to Dr Parsons' meticulous report, the winter epidemic started in November and reached its peak in the week ending 23 January 1892, when 506 deaths were attributed to it, as a primary cause, in London alone, and a further eighty-six as a secondary cause. The dangers of the disease were dramatically illustrated by the death on 14 January of 'Eddie', the Duke of Clarence and Avondale, son of the Prince of Wales, and potentially the future King of England. He was to have married Princess May or Mary of Teck (later Queen Mary by marriage to his brother) on 27 February; she attended his extremely well-populated death-bed. The death provoked Alfred Austin, later in 1896 to become the poet laureate, to pen these appalling lines:

> O, If she could exchange her lot,
> And now were free to choose,
> With one who in some whitewashed cot,
> Over her baby coos,
> And tend the humblest heart that burns,
> To whose awaiting smile the cherished one returns.[15]

It was a demise which must have produced sighs of relief among the *cognoscenti*, for Eddie was not a satisfactory person; indeed it has even been suggested that he was in some way connected with the affair of Jack the Ripper; the original closure date on the much laundered Home Office file is a century from the date

---

[15] *Pall Mall Gazette*, 15 Jan. 1892.

of his death.[16] So far as the general public was concerned, his death made it clear that even the highest in the land were not immune. The epidemic died out in February of 1892.

At this time Frederick Roe was, as we have seen, advertising heavily. The London post office directory for that year lists him at 27 Princes Street, Hanover Square, described, no doubt by himself, as 'maker of carbolic smoke ball'. He had become a specialist. His premises lay next door to those of Sargent and Smith, hair restorers, and the Misses Annie and Selina Marling, ostrich feather manufacturers; it appears a very suitable location. And though no such company had in fact been formally incorporated, Roe, probably with a partner, Henry Teasdale Turner, was trading as the Carbolic Smoke Ball Company, in some association with Messrs Wilcox and Company.

The advertisement which gave rise to the litigation first appeared not in the *Illustrated London News* but in the *Pall Mall Gazette* on 13 November 1891, and again on 24 November and 8 December; it also appeared in substantially the same form in other newspapers, not all of which I have identified. One such was the *Illustrated London News*, which carried the advertisement in substantially the same form on 30 January with a facsimile reproduction of the Duke of Portland's handwritten testimonial, dated 1 March 1891, from 2 Grosvenor Square. The *Pall Mall Gazette*, despite its high moral tone, carried at this period many advertisements for dubious remedies. Thus, readers on 11 November were exhorted to buy Clarke's World Famous Blood Mixture, 'warranted to cleanse the blood of all impurities, from whatever cause arising. For Scrofula, Scurvy, Eczema, Skin and Blood Diseases, Pimples and Sores of all kinds, its effects are marvellous.' On 19 November Beecham's Pills, 'for regulating the system and for all Bilious and Nervous Disorders such as Headaches, Constipation, Weak Stomach, Impaired Digestion, Disordered Livers etc.', were advertised together with Towle's Pennyroyal and Steel Pills for Females, a thinly disguised and no doubt wholly ineffective abortifacient ('quickly corrects all Irregularities and Relieves the Distressing Symptoms so Prevalent with the Sex'). Pepsolic, advertised on 15 December, was even claimed to prevent divorce, which the copywriter attributed to indigestion: 'Causes Bad Temper, Irritability, Peppery Disposition, Domestic Quarrels, Separation and—The Divorce Court'. Issues of 8 and 9 January 1892 published advertisements for Holloway's celebrated ointment, Dr Henry Paterson's Electrolytic Pill, Sequah's Prairie Flower, Dr Dunbar's Alkaram Inhalant, and Epp's Glycerine Jube-Jubes. Between them, they cured more or less everything.

But if Frederick Roe was typical in his extravagant claims, he was early off the mark in directing his advertising specifically to influenza, and none of his

---

[16] For discussion, see H. Montgomery Hyde, *The Cleveland Street Scandal* (London, 1976), 55–105.

competitors seems to have gone so far as to offer a substantial sum of money to purchasers of the ball if it failed to protect them. The text of the relevant advertisement (a particularly dull example of Roe's advertising) read:

£100 REWARD

WILL BE PAID BY THE

CARBOLIC SMOKE BALL CO.

To any person who contracts the increasing Epidemic,

INFLUENZA,

colds or any diseases caused by taking cold, AFTER HAVING USED the BALL 3 times daily for two weeks according to the printed directions supplied with each Ball.

£1,000

Is deposited with the ALLIANCE BANK, REGENT STREET, showing our sincerity in the matter. During the last epidemic of Influenza many thousand CARBOLIC SMOKE BALLS were sold as Preventives against this Disease, and in no ascertained case was the disease contracted by those using the CARBOLIC SMOKE BALL.

One CARBOLIC SMOKE BALL will last a family several months, making it the cheapest remedy in the world at the price—10s. post free. the BALL can be RE-FILLED at a cost of 5s. Address

CARBOLIC SMOKE BALL CO,

27, Princes-street, Hanover Square, London W.

Mrs Carlill and her Family

To the lasting benefit of the law of contract, Mrs Carlill saw this advertisement on the evening of 13 November 1891.

Her full name was Louisa Elizabeth Carlill.[17] She used the name Elizabeth. Her maiden name was Flamank, and she was born at 10. 15 a.m. on 22 October 1845, at West Street, Tavistock, in Devon. Her father was John Walkom Flamank, originally a draper and later a shipping agent, and her mother was Mary (Willcock). She was the third of ten children. On 17 December 1873, at All Saints Church, Clapton Park, she married James Briggs Carlill, the son of an accountant, James Green Carlill.[18] He sometimes dropped the name James, becoming simply Briggs Carlill, and according to family tradition he was an actuary. But he was not a member of the Institute of Actuaries, though the family certainly had connections with insurance. Whatever he eventually became, he was originally a solicitor. He was admitted to the roll in 1870, and practised in Hull until 1882. The Carlill family indeed came from Hull, its prosperity going back to one Briggs Carlill, James Briggs's grandfather, who was a tallow chandler,

---

[17] J 54/740; *Daily Graphic*, 17 June 1892; Tavistock IX 468 Dec. 1845.
[18] 24 May 1848–6 Oct. 1930, Greenwich 1d 966, Dec. (birth), Hackney 1b 661 Dec. 1873 (marriage), 1930 (death). The Carlills were a prosperous family from Hull, and much information can be derived from family wills; they also appear in numerous directories. I have also been assisted by members of the family.

insurance broker, and general commission merchant in Kingston upon Hull. James Briggs moved to London in about 1882 and established a legal practice at 173 Fenchurch Street in partnership with William Crook, under the unpropitious style of Crook and Carlill. This partnership came to an end by 1885, when he was back in Hull in partnership with one Simon Crawshaw; this does not seem to have continued long, as he is not in later law lists. At the time of the action the Carlills were living in West Dulwich; what occupation James Briggs then followed is uncertain. There is a tradition in the family that James Briggs was at some point in his life in trouble with the Law Society for making use of money in his clients' account, and that he even spent some time in Maidstone Prison, but I have been unable to confirm this. Perhaps this ended his legal career.

There were three children of the marriage, a son and two daughters. The son was Harold Flamank Carlill.[19] A graduate of Trinity College, Cambridge, he became a distinguished civil servant in the Board of Trade and a writer on the classics. Of the daughters, one was called Dorothy; as Mrs Brousson she cared for her mother in old age. The family had medical as well as legal connections. John Burford Carlill,[20] our man's uncle, was a London doctor; the Westminster Hospital has, or at least had, a laboratory named after him, endowed by Arthur J. B. Carlill, a Shanghai merchant and director of Dodwell and Company, who was a colourful character who left his considerable estate to his mistress, Beatrice Legge. Hildred Bertram Carlill (1880–1942), father of my informant and cousin to James Briggs, was a very distinguished doctor. As for Elizabeth Carlill herself, she was described by counsel in the legal proceedings as 'a literary lady'. This was a slightly mocking expression, but it is clear that she had, as a writer, an income of her own. I have been unable to trace any writings by her either under her own names, Carlill or Flamank, or under a pseudonym, unless she published under her husband's name. A James Briggs Carlill contributed to a number of Victorian periodicals.[21]

Mrs Carlill saw the advertisement, and on 20 November she purchased a smoke ball from Messrs Wilcox and Company, who operated a druggist's shop at 239 Oxford Street.[22] She paid for the ball out of her literary earnings. The vendors, as we have seen, were actively promoting the ball at the time. According to her account of the matter, which was given in evidence at the trial and not disputed, she assiduously used the ball three times daily for two weeks, in accordance with the already quoted printed instructions supplied with it: 'In the morning before breakfast, at about 2 o'clock, and again when I went to bed'.

---

[19] 1875–1959.   [20] 1814–74.

[21] *Macmillan's Magazine* for Apr. 1893, the *Cornhill Magazine* for Jan. 1869, the *Nineteenth Century* for Aug. 1886 and June 1887.

[22] My account is based upon law reports, newspapers (see n. 2 above), and on PRO J 54/740 (pleadings), J 54/748 (change of solicitor), and KB 25/10 (CA Order Book). The text of the letters comes from the professional journals.

Whether she continued to use the ball thereafter does not appear. On 27 January, that is, at the height of the epidemic, she contracted influenza. She remained ill for two weeks under the care of a Dr Robertson.

On 20 January her husband, James Briggs Carlill, wrote to the Carbolic Smoke Ball Company informing them of what had occurred; possibly her letter was only one of many received at this time:

Dear Sir,
Seeing your offer of a reward, dated July 20, in the 'Pall Mall Gazette' of November 13, my wife purchased one of your smoke balls, and has used it three times a day since the beginning of December. She was, however, attacked by influenza. Dr Robertson, of West Dulwich, attended, and will no doubt be able to certify in the matter. I think it right to give you notice of this, and shall be prepared to answer any inquiry or furnish any evidence you require. I am, yours obediently, J. B. Carlill.

This was ignored. He wrote again, threatening to place the matter in the hands of his solicitors, and received in reply a postcard saying the matter would receive attention. He wrote a third time, and received in reply a printed circular, undated, endorsed 'in answer to your letter of January 20'. This remarkable document read:

Re reward of £200—The Carbolic Smoke Ball Company, seeing that claims for the above reward have been made by persons who have either not purchased the smoke ball at all, or else have failed to use it as directed, consider it necessary that they should state the conditions in which alone such reward would be paid. They have such confidence in the efficacy of the carbolic smoke ball, if used according to the printed directions supplied to each person, that they made the aforesaid offer in entire good faith, believing it impossible for the influenza to be taken during the daily inhalation of the smoke ball as prescribed. In order to protect themselves against all fraudulent claims, the Carbolic Smoke Ball Company require that the smoke ball be administered, free of charge, at their office, to those who have already purchased it. Intending claimants must attend three times daily for three weeks, and inhale the smoke ball under the directions of the Smoke Ball Company. These visits will be specially recorded by the secretary in a book. 27 Princes St Hanover Square, London.

Why this gem was not quoted in the law reports must forever remain a mystery, for it goes a long way toward explaining the hostile judicial attitude to the company.

The letter certainly irritated James Briggs Carlill, who replied, insisting his claim was perfectly honest. To this Roe replied that 'the company considered his letter impertinent and gave him the names of his solicitors'. And so it was that on 15 February an action was commenced to claim the £100 promised. It was not, apparently, the only such action envisaged. The *Chemist and Druggist* for 30 April 1892 records that an application had been made in the previous week in the Chester County Court for an order to compel the company to give the names of the partners trading under the company style; an action to claim the reward was being taken in the High Court. There may have been other actions begun or threatened.

The legal proceedings were handled by Messrs Field Roscoe of 36 Lincoln's Inn Fields, acting as agents for J. E. Foster of 10 Trinity Street, Cambridge. The use of a Cambridge firm is curious. The family lived at the time in West Dulwich, and their son did not matriculate at Cambridge until 1894. There is no direct evidence that the Carlills lived in or near Cambridge at any time. Possibly James Briggs's legal career had crossed with one or other of the partners in the Cambridge firm. Nor is there any documentary evidence as to why the suit was brought at all. But the family tradition is that Mrs Carlill was encouraged to sue by her husband; he was so exasperated by the absurdity of current advertisements that he encouraged the challenging of the company. There is another possibility. On 1 July 1903 Mrs Carlill's daughter, Dorothy (or Dorothea), married Herbert Louis Brousson, son of Louis Maurice Brousson, a well-known journalist of Huguenot decent. Among other papers, he edited the *Inventor* from 1883 to 1892. In April 1890 this published, as an advertisement, Roe's instructions for the use of the ball. The form of the advertisement is odd, and suggests the use of the block simply to fill space in a struggling journal. The ball was not subsequently advertised there. It could be that there was some earlier connection between the families, and that the Broussons had some hand in the matter. The plaintiff's formal statement of claim was delivered on 24 February to the defendant's solicitors, Messrs Rowcliffe, Rawle Johnstone, and Gregory of 1 Bedford Row, London. It was drafted by W. Baugh Allen, junior counsel. A reply, drafted by Herman W. Loehnis, was delivered on 24 March. It was an elaborate document, which set out nine distinct and ingenious objections to the statement of claim. First, it said, the terms of the advertisement had not been accurately stated. Secondly, the plaintiff had not acted in reliance on the advertisement, used the ball as directed, or even caught influenza. Thirdly, the defendants had received no notice of her having purchased the ball, used it, or caught influenza until after she had succumbed to the disease (which in any event they denied). Fourthly, in a more conciliatory way, they conceded that they had indeed published an advertisement in the following terms:

£100 Reward will be paid by the Carbolic Smoke Ball Co. to any person who contracts the increasing epidemic influenza, colds or any disease caught by taking cold after having used the Carbolic Smoke Ball three times a day for two weeks according to the printed directions supplied with each ball . . . One Carbolic Smoke Ball will last a family several months making it the cheapest remedy in the world at the price 10/- post free.

This was, of course, not the complete text of the advertisement, as the pleadings indicated. In particular it left out the claim that £1,000 had been deposited with the Alliance Bank as a sign of sincerity; whether this was true or not was never established at the trial. Fifthly, they repeated that they had had no communication with the plaintiff until 20 January, after, as she claimed, she had contracted

influenza on 17 January. Sixthly, they denied that any valid contract had been
made by them to pay the £100 to the plaintiff, and, if there was such a contract,
it was a gaming contract or bet, and thus legally unenforceable. Seventhly and
eighthly, they said that if the advertisement was to be regarded as a contractual
offer it constituted an offer of an insurance contract, which was never accepted,
and in any event did not satisfy the statutory requirements for a valid insurance
contract.[23] Finally, the ingenious Loehnis said that, if indeed there were a contract, it was void as contrary to public policy. He did not explain why. Probably
what he had in mind was the legal doctrine which forbade the recovery of
contractual penalties, as contrasted with genuine pre-estimates of loss; he would
have argued that £100 was a penal sum.

Confronted with this barrage of defences, Allen contented himself with the
laconic reply, on behalf of his client, that 'except in so far as the defence
consists of admissions she joins issue thereon'.

So it was that *Carlill* v. *Carbolic Smoke Ball Company* came on for trial, on
16 June 1892, in court number five at the Royal Courts of Justice in the Strand,
built, ironically enough, on the site of the premises of a celebrated maker and
advertiser of patent medicines, Thomas Holloway. The judge was Sir Henry
Hawkins, assisted by his fox terrier Jack, which always sat on the bench with
him, together with a special jury.

Neither side appears to have been parsimonious in securing the very best legal
representation. Indeed, the plaintiff's expenditure on counsel suggests that
principle, not money, was at issue. Briefed for her was John Patrick Murphy
QC, assisted by both William Graham and, so the law reports record, one Bonner,
in reality W. Baugh Allen. The defence was led by no less than Herbert Henry
Asquith QC, future Prime Minister, assisted by Herman W. Loehnis. The cost
of this array of legal talent must have been very considerable indeed.

Elizabeth Carlill went into the witness box, and the judge inspected the letters
and the document setting out the instructions for use, and showing a lady using
the ball—the picture appears in many of Roe's advertisements and in the *Inventor*.
Asquith asked her when she used the ball, but did not cross-examine, as the facts
were not really disputed. A full trial before the special jury would have inflated
the costs, and counsel agreed to leave the decision to the judge, giving him
power to enter whatever verdict the jurymen, in his view, ought to have found;
the jury was discharged. The case was then adjourned until Saturday, 18 June,
when the judge heard counsel's argument on the points of law involved. He then
reserved judgment until 4 July, when he entered a verdict in favour of Mrs
Carlill for the £100 claimed, together with costs. He refused an application for
a stay of execution of the judgment pending an appeal. The form of procedure
adopted, which bypassed the jury, was a significant factor in the conversion of
the dispute into a leading case, for the judge gave reasons for his decision in a

[23] 14 Geo. III, c.48.

complex written opinion. Had the matter gone to a jury, the case would have terminated in a laconic jury verdict, and although there could have been an appeal based on the judge's directions to the jury, it is unlikely that the legal elaboration of the case would have proceeded as far as it did.

Frederick Roe was not prepared to accept the judge's decision. Notice of appeal was at once given, and on 5 July another Queen's Counsel, Arthur Cohen, appealed against the trial judge's refusal of a stay of execution, so long as the money was paid into court. The reason for the attempt to stay execution was principally sexist. Being a married woman, Mrs Carlill might be unable to refund the money if she lost the appeal. The judges rejected this; as a 'literary lady' she had her own earnings, and might indeed make as much as £1,000 a year, so Kay J, no doubt slightly frivolously, suggested. Arthur Cohen was one of the leading barristers of the period, particularly in demand for appellate work; his entry into the case must indicate yet again a willingness to pay for the best man available, but not necessarily any dissatisfaction with Asquith. For it was the day of the general election, and Asquith was no doubt busy in his constituency of Fifeshire East. But Roe must have been dissatisfied with his solicitors; they were sacked and replaced by James Banks Pittman of Basin's House, Basinghall Street.

For the appeal itself, Cohen was replaced by Robert B. Finlay, a future Lord Chancellor, and Loehnis by Thomas Terrell. Asquith would not in any event have been available, for he had become Home Secretary on 18 August. Mrs Carlill retained her original solicitors, but leading counsel was also replaced, by Henry Dickens QC, the son of the novelist and future Common Serjeant of London. A second junior counsel was briefed, George John Talbot, an Oxford double first and future judge and Privy Councillor. By this time the legal costs must surely have well exceeded the £100 in dispute between the parties.

The appeal was heard by Lindley, Bowen, and A. L. Smith LJJ on 7 December, and the court, without reserving judgment, unanimously upheld the verdict in favour of Mrs Carlill. For the moment, at least, Frederick Roe accepted defeat, and no attempt was made to carry an appeal to the ultimate tribunal, the House of Lords.

Comical though the facts appear to us today, the decision in favour of Mrs Carlill excited only limited comment in the press of the time. The *Pall Mall Gazette*, however, published a deeply hypocritical leader on 8 December, for the paper carried much quack advertising:

As Mr Justice Lindley pointed out, for once advertisers have counted too much on the gullibility of the public . . . The plaintiff bought the ball and carried out the instructions. Three times a day for two weeks she did it, with faith and with instructions. Three times a day for two weeks she did it, with faith and with industry, and yet the foul fiend gripped her. In vain the ball was smoked in the sight of any germ. Carbolic smoke positively braced the bacilli. But convalescence came, and the plaintiff rose in wrath and smote the company. Mr Justice Hawkins backed her case, and the Court of Appeal has backed Mr

Justice Hawkins. Smoke is good, but the carbolic smoke, we fear, will have lost its
savour.

The *Spectator*'s leader writer, in a piece entitled 'A Novel Breach of Contract',
revealed that he had personally sampled the ball:

To judge from our own experiences, twenty-five violent sneezes is the least result that
can be expected from a single application. Therefore, we may supposed that in the course
of these two weeks, this heroic lady suffered forty-two applications of the ball, and
sneezed violently more than a thousand times.

He argued that no *man* would have pressed the claim to its conclusion; Mrs
Carlill showed 'all that patient determination and persistent importunity of which
only a woman is capable'. The *Chemist and Druggist* welcomed the decision
and took the opportunity to voice disgust at the cynicism of lawyers, in particular Asquith, quoting him as saying: 'We are not discussing the honourable
obligation to pay.' Sir Henry Hawkins's decision was welcomed on 9 July in a
leader in the *Lancet*, then (and now) one of the leading organs of the legitimate
medical profession:

To those amongst our readers who are familiar with the way of the quack medicine
vendor the facts proved the other day by Mrs Carlill in the action she has brought against
the Carbolic Smoke Ball Company will occasion no surprise . . . We are glad to learn that
in spite of the ingenuity of their legal advisers the defendants have been held liable to
make good their promise. People who are silly enough to adopt a medicine simply
because a tradesman is reckless enough to make extravagant promises and wild representations as to its efficiency may thank themselves chiefly for any disappointment that
ensues. Still for this folly, which is only foolish and nothing worse, it is possible to feel
sympathy when the disappointment comes. It is a pleasant alternative to learn that the
dupe has been able, in the present instance, to enforce a sharp penalty.

The *British Medical Journal* simply reported the case without comment. The
doctors at this time were fighting a continuous and not very successful battle
against various forms of quack medicine; in particular, they took strong exception to the extravagant claims made by advertisers.[24]

Yet no doubt there were at the time genuinely satisfied users of the Carbolic
Smoke Ball; indeed, initially Mrs Carlill was one, for in the witness box she
explained how she had recommended the ball to her friends. Although the claims
made for its efficacy were ludicrously optimistic, the puffing of carbolic powder
up the nostrils as a mode of treatment was not in itself any odder than many of
the procedures employed at the time by orthodox medicine. For in the Victorian
world the distinction between quackery and legitimate scientific medicine was
by no means clear. It depended, at least in part, purely on who was prescribing

---

[24] In what follows I have used material both in medical journals and in the Report of the Select
Committee on Patent Medicines (1912–14), BPP 1912–13 (508) IX 99, 1913 IX.1, 1914 414 IX 1,
hereafter called the Norman Report.

the treatment. Much of what the doctors did was either useless or positively harmful, except in so far as it may have improved the morale of the patient. Quack medicine was not obviously any worse as a morale booster and could, especially if available on mail order, be considerably cheaper. As an appliance, the ball was not unorthodox. It was what was, and indeed still is, known as an insufflator, close cousin to an inhaler. Frederick Roe indeed used 'Inhalations London' as his telegraphic address; one sheet of his notepaper survives in the Public Record Office.[25] The medical press of the period regularly reported on new medical appliances, so long as a regular doctor had invented or approved of them, describing and depicting, for example, contraptions such as Dr Blenkarne's Improved Insufflator with Adjustable Tongue Depressor, which, it claimed, surpassed the old established insufflator associated with the name of Dr Osborne. Also advertised in this way in the *British Medical Journal* for 1890 was the more alarming New Vaginal Insufflator. For no human orifice was safe from the assaults of Victorian medical science, and vast ingenuity was expended in perfecting suitable instruments, or even mechanisms for storing them in serried ranks, ready for instant use, such as Reynold's Enema Rack, whose virtues were extolled in the *Lancet* in 1892. The availability of suitable materials encouraged this hideous trade. It was the age of rubber, gutta percha, and vulcanite, and thereby the golden age of the enema, which reached the summit of its development in America with the invention of the J. B. L. Cascade, the initials standing for Joy, Beauty, and Life. This contraption, invented by Henry Child, was promoted by Dr Charles A. Tyrrell, author of *The Royal Road to Health*, a horrendous and obscene work on the mythical condition of auto-intoxication, which reached, so its author claimed, its thirty-seventh edition in 1901.[26] For those in pursuit merely of the more restrained practice of insufflation, Roe's device was one among many, and, for those desiring elegance, there was an abundance of ivory, which Frederick Roe mentioned in his patent specification as a possible material for the orifice.

Nor, of course, were the external surfaces of the body in any way immune from the products of the mechanical ingenuity of the time; one might, if suffering from hysteria, be set upon with Dr Andrew Smart's Dermic Punctator, announced in the *British Medical Journal* in 1889, which enabled the medical man to puncture one's skin simultaneously with large numbers of needles to produce what was euphemistically called counter-irritation. If need be, dilute acid could then be applied to the skin to enhance and sharpen the effect. But Frederick Roe never widened his activities to become involved with either the external surfaces or the more intimate parts of the Victorian anatomy. He concentrated solely upon the nostrils.

The smoke ball's active ingredient, carbolic acid, is a poison, and from 1882

[25] BT 34/895.
[26] See *Nostrums and Quackery*, 311; this was published by the American Medical Society in its campaign against the quacks.

onwards the Pharmaceutical Society had waged a campaign to persuade the Privy Council to add it to the list of scheduled poisons, a campaign which was eventually partially successful in 1900. Earlier it had been freely available, and an article by Dr Robert Lee in the *Lancet* for 1892 indicates that inhaling carbolic acid fumes was a recognized form of treatment for some conditions. We may be fairly confident that it did little more good to his patients than inhaling carbolic dust did for the purchasers of the Carbolic Smoke Ball, but we must not judge Frederick Roe too harshly for his optimism. And, so far as influenza is concerned, the use of the ball compares favourably with the heroic measures adopted for the same condition by Dr J. C. Voight, a product of the medical school at Edinburgh, and described in the *Lancet* in 1892: rectal injections of eucalyptus oil, or the milder methods of Dr John Crerar, who relied on large and repeated doses of potassium bicarbonate. These were inventive spirits; more typical perhaps was the scatter-gun system followed in 1890 by Dr E. C. Barnes, divisional surgeon to the Metropolitan Police:

I gave all cases carbonate of ammonia early, with citrate of potass. and Liq. Ammon. Acetatis, followed quickly or even accompanied with quinine pills in one grain doses three times a day. For the bilious cases two grains calomel, one grain opium followed in two hours with haust. rhei and a mixture containing sodae bicarb. ammonia and chlorodyne. I also found liniment of chloroform and belladonna very valuable.

To be fair to the good doctor, his patients did also receive gruel, beef tea, and brandy, which they surely deserved and needed. But it is perhaps not too surprising that some sufferers preferred the regular use of the Carbolic Smoke Ball.

Roe's Reaction to Losing the Action

The litigation with Mrs Carlill took from 15 February to 7 December 1892 to wend its way through the courts. A less optimistic man than Frederick Roe might have thought it prudent to lie low during this period or even to flee. The scale of his advertising suggests that many balls had indeed been sold during 1891–2, and the reward had been offered over a period of just under three months, through the peak of the epidemic. Initially at least, he must have feared that there would be very many claimants; but perhaps it was this very fear that impelled him to continue his operations boldly during the period when the litigation was being conducted. On 27 February 1892, he was once again advertising the ball from his base at 28 Princes Street: 'SNORING Cured in 24 hours. HAYFEVER Cured in every case. CROUP Relieved in five minutes. WHOOPING COUGH Relieved by first application', and so on. He quoted numerous testimonials: 'Lady Baker writes from Ranston, Blandford, Jan. 19, 1892 "Please send me another Smoke Ball. I and the children have hitherto escaped influenza, though in the thick of it, owing entirely, I believe, to its good effects, I am recommending it to everyone".' Another satisfied customer, quoted in the same advertisement, was Madame Adelina Patti (also Baroness Rolf Cederstrom), who wrote from Craig-y-Nos Castle; she was a celebrated prima donna of the period. There was the Duke of Portland, the Bishop of London, and Sir Frederick Milner, Bart. So far as I have been able to check, all the names given by Roe were of real people, and his testimonials may have been quite genuine.

Though prudently avoiding any further promises of reward, he continued to advertise in the *Illustrated London News* during 1892, again directing his copy toward hay fever once the season started. Thus on 28 May he claimed;

THE CARBOLIC SMOKE BALL will positively cure, and is the only remedy ever discovered which has permanently cured HAY FEVER, a disease which has hitherto baffled the most eminent physicians, who have sought in vain to cure or prevent its annual return.

Testimonials include this touching one from Major Roland Webster: 'The Carbolic Smoke Ball gave me entire satisfaction last summer. I unintentionally got into a field where hay making was going on, and I was not inconvenienced by it. I have not been able to do such a thing for the last twenty years without suffering frightfully.' As for throat deafness, J. Hargreaves wrote to inform the company that 'I can hear my watch tick three or four inches away, which I have not done for months.'

On 12 November Roe redirected his advertising towards winter ailments, with testimonials from such illustrious figures as the Hon. Chandos Leigh, counsel to the Speaker of the House of Commons; the Revd Canon Fleming, canon residentiary at York Minster; and Generals A. L. Playfair and E. T. Hasken. This advertisement further reveals that the smoke balls, originally, as we have seen, an American invention, were being exported, for it provided the addresses of depots in Paris, New York, and Toronto.

This was not the only development in 1892. On 16 December, shortly after the decision had gone against him in the Court of Appeal, Frederick Roe, together with one Henry Edwin Teasdale Turner, agreed to form a limited company to market the ball and another product, a tonic known as Sunilla.[27] Henry Turner was a manufacturing chemist and may previously have been in the business either as a partner or as maker of the ball. The Carbolic Smoke Ball Company Ltd. was incorporated on 19 December with a nominal capital of £5,000 in £1 shares. The objects of the company were 'to purchase and carry on the business heretofore carried on under the style or firm of The Carbolic Smoke Ball Company in London, Paris, New York, and Toronto, and to carry out the agreement of December 16 to manufacture and sell both the ball and "Sunilla"'. Frederick Roe was appointed managing director for a term of five years at a salary of one-fifth of the net profits. The assets of the earlier unincorporated firm were sold for a price of £4,400, £2,000 being paid to Roe in cash and the balance in fully

[27] See BT 31/5463/37795 and BT 34/895/37795.

paid-up shares. In addition to Roe and Turner, the original subscribers, to the extent of one share each, were five clerks, no doubt clerks in the solicitor's office. No list of other shareholders of this company exists in the public records, and in all probability there never were any. The object of the incorporation was presumably to secure the benefits of limited liability and to give Turner a larger share in the business, not to raise capital from the public.

Now it might be supposed that December 1892, just after the loss of the action, was hardly the moment for forming the new company. A flood of claims ought surely to have arrived to drive Roe into the bankruptcy court, for his personal liability for the payment of the £100 rewards would in no way be affected by the later acquisition of limited liability. Counsel in the argument before Hawkins indicated that there had been other claims, and the *Chemist and Druggist* noted one such, from the Chester area, and the *Patent Medicines Journal* also mentions other claims. In the Court of Appeal much was made of this by his counsel, Finlay:

At the present there might be 10,000 people watching for the result of this appeal. There might be a swarm of impostures in the industry of smelling smoke-balls who might continue to march in as long as there was anything to be squeezed out of this unfortunate company.

But no flood of claims seems to have occurred. On 25 February we find the managing director of the new company boldly publishing in the *Illustrated London News* a new advertisement, cunningly framed in order to turn the whole affair to his advantage. In it he pointed out that a reward of £100 had recently been promised to anyone who contracted influenza, or eleven other diseases 'caused by taking cold', after using the ball according to the instructions. The text continues:

Many thousand Carbolic Smoke Balls were sold on these advertisements, but only three persons claimed the reward of £100, thus proving conclusively that this invaluable remedy will prevent and cure the above mentioned diseases. THE CARBOLIC SMOKE BALL COMPANY LTD. now offer £200 REWARD to the person who purchases a Carbolic Smoke Ball and afterwards contracts any of the following diseases.

There followed a list of nineteen ailments: influenza, coughs, cold in the head, cold in the chest, catarrh, asthma, bronchitis, sore throat, hoarseness, throat deafness, loss of voice, laryngitis, snoring, sore eyes, diphtheria, croup, whooping cough, neuralgia, and headache. It will be noted that this offer appears to envisage only a single prize, and the small print went on:

This offer is made to those who have purchased a Carbolic Smoke Ball since January 1, 1893, and is subject to conditions to be obtained on application, a duplicate of which must be signed and deposited with the Company in London by the applicant before commencing the treatment specified in the conditions. This offer will remain open only till March 31, 1893.

What these conditions were, or whether anyone succeeded in claiming the reward, does not appear. But no similar offer appears to have been made in later advertisements, so perhaps the experiment proved costly. The ball continued to be advertised enthusiastically in the early part of 1893, and the summer number of the *Illustrated London News* for that year carried one, typically directed towards hay fever. In June 1893, however, there took place a curious reorganization of the business, which involved the formation of a second limited liability company and a transfer of control.

The new company, called the Carbolic Smoke Ball Company (1893), Ltd., was incorporated on 10 June 1893, with a nominal capital of £35,000 in £1 shares.[28] The objects were:

(A) To purchase and carry on the business heretofore carried on by the Carbolic Smoke Ball Company Limited in London and elsewhere,
(B) To adopt and carry into effect, with or without modification, an agreement expressed to be made between the Carbolic Smoke Ball Company Limited of the first part, Frederick Augustus Roe of the second part, the Bankers' Guarantee Society of the third part, and the Company of the fourth part.

The text of this agreement, which had been signed on 12 June is not in the Board of Trade file, but a later agreement of 12 July, which is, reproduced its terms. The assets of the first company, excluding stock in trade, were to be acquired for £30,000, of which £3,500 was payable in cash and the balance in fully paid-up shares. These shares were to be allotted on the written request of the old company. The agreement was signed by Alfred Grange Shoolbred and W. Martingale, directors of the new company, and Charles W. Kirk, the new company secretary, and by Frederick Roe and Henry Teasdale Turner, directors of the old company. Martingale was the inventor of the New Ozone Inhaler, approved by legitimate medicine in the *Lancet* in 1890.

A summary of the capital and shareholding in the new company was later submitted to the Board of Trade, dated 23 October 1893. At that date, 31,020 shares had been taken up; on 4,520 shares calls had been made of £1 each, of which £4,444 2*s.* had been paid. This represented new capital actually raised. The total amount agreed to be considered as having been paid on 26,500 shares was £1 each, nothing in fact having been paid. This block of shares appears to have been made up from Frederick Roe's own holding in the new company, amounting to 15,500 shares, together with 11,500 shares owned by Maurice Grant and 500 owned by his wife, Frances; Grant was the managing director of the Bankers' Guarantee Company. As for the block of 4,520 shares that were not issued free, Grant's company held 1,583. The largest private shareholder (1,713 shares) was Michael Joseph Connolly, described as a professor of St Edmund College, Ware. Next came one Charles Alfred Stanley Cox with 500. The cloth was well represented by the Revd Gilbert F. Smith Rewse, Rector of St Margaret's

---

[28] BT 31/5604/39021 and BT 34/929/39021.

with St Peter's in Harleston, Norfolk (250 shares), Canon James Fleming (50 shares), and several others. There was one surgeon, John Orton, and even an Indian merchant from Bombay, Devidas Vandravundas. Many holdings were extremely small, such as the shares owned by a Quartermaster Sergeant Samuel Patterson of Gibraltar.

This placed the company under new management and raised a considerable capital sum from the public. Roe retained a stake in the business, but not control, while Henry Turner disappears from the story. How Maurice Grant became involved is obscure. Roe continued to have some connection with the business, for a surviving letter of his, dated 22 June 1895, is written on company writing paper from its premises at 219 Oxford Street, to which the business moved on 2 May 1894. The smoke ball continued to be advertised in the later part of 1893, though under the new management the scale and flamboyance of the advertisements declined. A report to the Board of Trade dated 15 October 1894 notes that no shares had been traded by them. The business seems to have fallen on hard times, for on 19 June 1895 a resolution was passed to wind the company up since it could not, because of its liabilities, remain in business. The then secretary, John Fyvie, was appointed liquidator, and the job was completed by 14 July 1896. Why the company failed is obscure. A decline in the prevalence of influenza does not explain the matter; there were nearly 13,000 deaths from the disease in 1895, and nearly 4,000 in the following year. In any event, the other ailments for which the ball was sold remained common. It may be that the new management had failed to grasp the fact that extensive advertising was essential to success in the quack medicine field.

The earlier of the two companies continued to enjoy a ghostly existence for some further years. On 1 November 1893, at a symbolic meeting held at 99 Newgate Street, a resolution was passed (and later confirmed) to liquidate the company, Frederick Roe being appointed liquidator. It was not a role in which he excelled, and some friction developed between him and the officials of the Board of Trade. The required return for 1893 was not submitted, and the officials complained to Messrs Morton Cutler, who replied that only Roe could help. He failed to do so, and a note in the file indicates that he was spoken to on 17 December 1893, and it was explained that the takeover by the new company did not absolve him from the duty to continue to make returns as required by the Companies Act. Nothing was done in 1894, but on 11 May 1895 Roe, from 219 Oxford Street, wrote to the Board to explain that he did not think that any returns were now needed, since the old company had been swallowed by the new. This did not impress the officials, and, under pressure, he swore an affidavit on 22 June 1895 that, from 17 November 1892 to 16 May 1895, no assets had been received on account of the company. A similar affidavit was sworn on 29 January 1897 at 23 Great Marlborough Street; the address may signify that he was under threat of prosecution. Yet another was submitted on 9 May 1898; Roe was then back in Princes Street at a new address, number 3. No further returns were made, and on 21 June 1907 the Board served formal notice of an intention to strike the company off the register as dissolved. This notice, sent to the registered office at 27 Princes Street, was returned marked 'gone away years ago. Address not known'. Thus, so far as can be told from the material in the Public Record Office, did the carbolic smoke ball and its inventor vanish from recorded history. Records in St Catherine's House show that Roe had died of tuberculosis and valvular heart disease on 3 June 1899, at his premises, 3 Princes Street; he was 57, and his occupation of 'patent medicine proprietor' failed to protect him. He left a widow, but no will.

The Smoke Ball and Contractual Theory

For lawyers, and particularly for law students, *Carlill* v. *Carbolic Smoke Ball Company* rapidly achieved the status of a leading case, a status which it has retained perhaps more securely in England than in the United States. Part of its success derived from the comic and slightly mysterious object involved, but there were two reasons of a legal character that suggest that it deserves its place in the firmament. The first, which is not always fully appreciated, is historical; it was the vehicle whereby a new legal doctrine was introduced into the law of contract. The second is that the decision could be used by expositors of the law of contract to illustrate the arcane mysteries surrounding the conception of a unilateral or one-sided contract.

So far as the first point is concerned, the so-called will theory of contract supposed that all contractual obligations were the product of the joint wills of the contracting parties, embodied in their agreement. The function of law courts, according to this theory, was merely that of faithfully carrying into effect the wishes of the parties to the contract. Further reflection on the implications of this theory, which had powerful support in nineteenth-century thought, suggested that it must necessarily follow that a court should not enforce an agreement unless it was the will of the parties that it should be legally enforced. They might indeed have agreed to do something, for example, go on a picnic, but be unwilling to have this agreement legally enforced. There must, it was said, be a joint intention to create legal relations before an agreement should have any legal consequences. The principal exponent of this dogma was the German jurist, Friedrich Karl von Savigny, and some English contract writers, in particular Sir Frederick Pollock, had incorporated this notion into their accounts of the law: 'If people make an arrangement to go for a walk or read a book together, there is no agreement in a legal senses. Why not? Because their intention is not directed to legal consequences, but to extra-legal ones.' But they were not able to cite any case in which the doctrine had actually been mentioned. Yet it could be used to make sense of certain old cases, such as *Weeks* v. *Tybald* (1605),[29]

[29] (1605) Nov 11, 74 ER 982.

in which the courts had held there to be no contract, cases in reality decided in sublime ignorance of the theories of von Savigny or anyone else, and some long predating his birth. But in legal dogmatics this retrospective reinterpretation is a normal practice, as it is in the reasoning of theologians. Until Mrs Carlill brought her action there was no case which had clearly recognized the requirement of an intention to create legal relations; her case did. It was indeed explicitly argued by Asquith that 'the advertisement was a mere representation of what the advertisers intended to do in certain event. The defendants did not by issuing it mean to impose upon themselves any obligations enforceable by law.' In all probability Asquith took the idea from one of the text writers. His argument was firmly rejected by Hawkins J, who pointed out that the advertisement had stated that £1,000 had been deposited in the Alliance Bank 'showing our sincerity in the matter'. This, he argued, 'could only have been inserted with the object of leading those who read it to believe that the defendants were serious in their proposal'. In the Court of Appeal Lindley LJ related the argument to the law governing 'puffs', on which there was the leading case of *Dimmoch* v. *Hallett* (1862).[30] He said:

We must first consider whether this was intended to be a promise at all, or whether it was a mere puff which meant nothing. Was it a mere puff? My answer to that question is No, and I base my answer on this passage: '£1,000 is deposited with the Alliance Bank, showing our sincerity in the matter.'

The fact that the judges found it necessary to make this point entailed their acceptance of the idea that, without an intention to create legal relations, there could be no actionable contract. Before the Court of Appeal little was made of the point, though Mr Terrell did argue that the promise was too *vague* to be actionable, adding 'It is like the case in which the man intended to induce a person to marry his daughter.' This is a reference to *Weeks* v. *Tybald*. But Lindley's opinion was so framed as to enable the case to be used as an authority for the view that von Savigny's doctrine was part of English law.

As for the second point, most contracts that concern the courts involve two-sided agreements, two-sided in the sense that the parties enter into reciprocal obligations to each other. A typical example is a sale of goods, where the seller has to deliver the goods and the buyer to pay for them. The doctrines of nineteenth-century contract law were adapted to such bilateral contracts, but the law also somewhat uneasily recognized that there could be contracts in which only one party was ever under any obligation to the other. The standard example was a published promise to pay a reward for information on the recovery of lost property: £10 to anyone who finds and returns my dog. In such a case obviously nobody has to search for the dog, but if they do so successfully, they are entitled to the reward. Such contracts seem odd in another way; there is a promise, but

[30] 2 Ch. App. 21.

no agreement, for the parties never even meet until the reward is claimed. Classified as 'unilateral' contracts, such arrangements presented special problems of analysis to contract theorists, whose standard doctrines had not been evolved to fit them. Thus it was by 1892 orthodox to say that all contracts were formed by the exchange of an offer and an acceptance, but it was by no means easy to see how this could be true of unilateral contracts, where there was, to the eyes of common sense, no acceptance needed.

The analytical problems arose in a particularly acute form in the smoke ball case. Thus it seemed very peculiar to say there had been any sort of agreement between Mrs Carlill and the company, which did not even know of her existence until 20 January, when her husband wrote to them to complain. There were, indeed, earlier cases permitting the recovery of advertised rewards; the leading case here was *Williams* v. *Cawardine*, where a reward of £20 had been promised by handbill for information leading to the conviction of the murderer of Walter Cawardine, and Williams, who gave such information, successfully sued to recover the reward.[31] But this was long before the doctrines which made unilateral contracts problematic had become established, and in any event the case was distinguishable. It concerned a reward, whereas Mrs Carlill was seeking compensation. Furthermore, the Carbolic Smoke Ball Company had no chance of checking the validity of claims, of which there could be an indefinite number; much was made of this point in the argument. But the judges were not impressed; their attitude was no doubt influenced by the view that the defendants were rogues. They fitted their decision into the structure of the law by boldly declaring that the performance of the condition—using the ball and getting ill— was the acceptance, thus fictitiously extending the concept of acceptance to cover the facts. And, since 1893, law students have been introduced to the mysteries of the unilateral contract through the vehicle of *Carlill* v. *Carbolic Smoke Ball Company* and taught to repeat, as a sort of magical incantation of contract law, that in the case of unilateral contracts performance of the act specified in the offer constitutes acceptance, and need not be communicated to the offeror.

Bowen LJ's analysis of the facts places the moment of acceptance as the moment when Mrs Carlill completed the three-week period of use stipulated by the directions for use. This was not the only possible view. In argument Finlay attributed a one-sniff theory to his opponents: 'according to the plaintiff, having taken one sniff at the ball, the defendant would not be at liberty to withdraw from the contract—[*laughter*]—because she had altered her position by sniffing.' But Dickens did not agree that this was his view, though he is indeed reported as saying: 'Here the contract arose when the plaintiff began to sniff the ball.' He seems to have thought that the contract only became binding on the defendants on completion of the course. A difficulty with Bowen's and Dickens's view is that it leads to the conclusion that the offer could be withdrawn up to the

[31] (1833) 5 C & P 566, 172 ER 1101.

moment of the last sniff, although the act of reliance by Mrs Carlill took place
earlier than this, either when she bought the ball, or when she started to use it.
The conclusion seems unjust; hence it has been argued that the best analysis is
to suppose there to be two contracts involved, a contract to pay the £100 if the
complete course fails, and a second contract not to revoke the promise to pay
the £100 once the purchaser of the ball starts the course of treatment. Other
complexities, somewhat inadequately dealt with in the case, centred on the scope
of the promise. Did it cover influenza contracted at any date in the future, or
within the period of the epidemic, or while the ball was being used, or within
a reasonable time thereafter? The court settled for the last possibility. And did
the offer apply to any user, a borrower, for example, or someone who had stolen
the ball? But the judges were clearly not impressed with these problems. The
defendants had not behaved as gentlemen, and that, essentially, was that.

Advertising and Quack Medicine

Carlill v. *Carbolic Smoke Ball Company* can, however, be looked at in a
completely different way, not as an incident in the doctrinal history of contract
law, but rather as an incident in the shocking history of advertising and quack
medicine. For, as Eric Jameson puts it: 'Her case made history in the advertising
world and it is said that every patent medicine copywriter has the words *Carlill*
v. *Carbolic Smoke Ball Company* tattooed across his chest.'[32] Purveyors of quack
medicines, appliances, and cures early learned the value of aggressive advertising. Since virtually all their wares were indistinguishably useless, success depended solely on promotion, and in the nineteenth century quackery was advertised
on a massive scale. In the early part of the century the giants were James
Morrison, inventor of the Universal Pill, Herbert Ingram, purveyor of Parr's Life
Pills, and Thomas Holloway, though no list would be complete without a mention
of Cockle's Anti Bilious Pills, which sustained the enormous Fred Burnaby on
his *Ride to Khiva*:

And for physic—with which it is as well to be supplied when travelling in out of the way
places—some quinine, and Cockle's pills, the latter a most invaluable medicine, and one
which I have used on the natives of Central Africa with the greatest possible success. In
fact the marvellous effects produced upon the mind and body of an Arab Sheik, who was
impervious to all native medicines, when I administered to him five Cockle's pills, will
never fade from my memory.

James Morrison, oddly self-styled 'the Hygeist', specialized in vegetable universal
medicines, and published extensively on the merits of his system; a common

---

[32] E. Jameson, *The Natural History of Quackery* (London, 1961), 62. In what follows I have used
H. Sampson, *A History of Advertising from the Earliest Times* (London, 1874); E. S. Turner, *The
Shocking History of Advertising* (London, 1952); the Norman Report; *Secret Remedies* (1909) by the
British Medical Association; and on individuals' entries in the DNB and in Boase. For Beecham I
have used Barker and Harris 378.

feature of quackery is the claim to cure all illness, or an extended list of ill-nesses, by a single remedy, a claim typically made for the smoke ball itself. Herbert Ingram purchased the secret recipe of Parr's Life Pills from one T. Roberts and in 1842 founded the *Illustrated London News*, so it is said, in order to promote their sale. The secret was said to have been passed down through the descendants of the celebrated Old Thomas Parr himself, (?1483–1635). Thomas Holloway, who founded both Holloway College and a large sanatorium for mentally deranged but curable members of the middle classes, sold his pills and ointment from premises at 244 The Strand, where the Royal Courts of Justice now stand. By the time of his death he was annually spending £50,000 on advertising, and had amassed a fortune estimated at £5 million, though much of this had been given away before his death. An archetypal entrepreneur, his death inspired a long editorial in *The Times* for 28 December 1883 on the character of such a man:

> The secret is with the man himself—in his fixed, steady, unwavering purpose of making money and allowing no obstacles to come in the way of this . . . Every action must be looked at from the one single point of view of the money value that may be found in it, or which it may somehow be made to bear . . . Mr Holloway was a master in the art of advertising. The praises of his medicines have been sounded in all lands, and in all known languages. Every available place, from a London hoarding to the Great Pyramid, has been pressed into the service, and has been forced to bear testimony to their merits. Every sufferer from every conceivable disease or failing has thus been duly informed to what quarter he might look for restoration to health and strength.

Later giants in the field included Joseph Beecham (1848–1916) of St Helen's, whose liver pills, 'worth a guinea a box', and less well remembered cough medicine were advertised in the late nineteenth century on a scale rivalled only by Pear's soap and Lipton's tea. In 1889 alone, Beecham spent £95,000 on advertising. The pills were made up to a secret and elaborate recipe handed down from Joseph Beecham's father, Thomas Beecham (1820–1907), who had started his productive life at the age of 8 as a shepherd's boy in Oxfordshire, and who founded the business. Professional analysis suggested that they contained merely aloes, ginger, and soap. By 1913 Beecham was selling fifty tons of pills a year and his business turnover was £340,000. A typical quack, Beecham at various times claimed that his pills, which were essentially laxatives, would cure Bright's disease and syphilis and procure abortions, as well as acting as a rem-edy for numerous less grave conditions. He received a knighthood in 1911 and a baronetcy in 1915, both presumably purchased.

Quackery and the Law

From time to time quacks came into conflict with the law. The most notable nineteenth-century incident involved one John St John Long. He specialized in the treatment of tuberculosis, a disease he confronted with a secret liniment, inhalations, and cabbage leaves, conducting his thriving practice from 41 Harley Street. In 1830 Long stood trial before Park J at the Old Bailey for the manslaughter of one of his patients, Catherine Cashin.[33] She was an Irish girl from Limerick, and her younger sister, Ellen, had been treated by Long without any disastrous results. Catherine, however, died on 17 September, after treatment by blistering, inhalations, liniment, and, of course, cabbage leaves. Although some thirty of Long's patients gave evidence in his favour at the trial, Long was nevertheless convicted; the judge imposed the light sentence of a fine of £250, no doubt a substantial sum, but one which Long had no problem in paying on the spot. During the trial Long acquired a new patient, a Mrs Colin Campbell Lloyd, wife of Edward Lloyd, a Royal Naval post captain. She, in her turn, died, and the coroner's inquest brought in a verdict of manslaughter against him. So Long again stood trial, this time before Bailey B, at the Old Bailey sessions on Saturday, 19 February 1831; the case was considered sufficiently important for the Attorney-General to conduct the prosecution.[34] Long again produced many satisfied clients, and was acquitted. The hostility of orthodox doctors towards Long was intensified by his own attacks on the profession, which, in his view, principally consisted of quacks. Long resumed his practice, but died young three years later, ironically enough of tuberculosis. Controversy over his system provoked a minor pamphlet war, and the founder of the *Lancet*, Thomas Wakley, was a strong critic of his.[35]

Such prosecutions were rare incidents, and had no perceptible effect on quackery. In the later nineteenth century, with the increase in flamboyant advertising, the principal criticism levelled against quackery concentrated on the extravagant claims made for medicines and appliances. A notable example of an extravagantly advertised product was Harness's Electropathic Belt, the brain child of a Cornelius Bennett Harness, President of the Electropathic and Zander Institute. As advertised, for example, in the *Illustrated London News* on 20 February 1892, this not only prevented influenza 'and all weak and languid feelings' but also cured rheumatism, gout, sciatica, lumbago, nervous exhaustion, impaired vitality, brain fag, sleeplessness, ladies' ailments, hysteria, indigestion, constipation, loss of appetite, and kidney troubles. Recommended both for weak men and delicate women as imparting new life and vigour, this appliance could be purchased from the Medical Battery Company, Ltd.[36] at 52 Oxford Street, where Harness and his colleagues maintained a considerable consulting business and engaged in alarming forms of treatment for virtually any form of disability. He also sold an electropathic corset for such women as did not feel attracted to the unisex model. In November 1893 an attempt was made to bring Harness to trial for conspiracy to defraud, together with two of his colleagues. One was a deviant medical man, James Montgomery M'Cully, struck off the medical register

---

[33] (1830) OBSP 856.   [34] (1831) OBSP at 283.

[35] See S. S. Sprigge, *Life and Times of Thos. Wakley* (London, 1897).

[36] BT 31/3457/20909, 4432/28851, 8155/58940, 9144/67755.

in November 1887; the other a salesman. The prosecutor was an aged and somewhat decrepit military man, Colonel Jeremiah Brayser, a veteran of the siege of Lucknow during the Indian Mutiny. He had retired to live in Margate, where he suffered, so he said, from weakness of the loins; there was some ribald suggestion by counsel that he had been contemplating matrimony and had purchased the belt by way of preparation. The prosecution was handled by Thomas Terrell, who had represented Frederick Roe; Horace Avory appeared for Harness. This prosecution failed at a slapstick comedy preliminary hearing before the Metropolitan Police magistrate, James Hannah. On Wednesday, 31 January, he refused to commit for trial, since no jury would have been likely to convict.[37] Although it was possible to call medical and technical evidence to show that the belt was perfectly useless and its inventor a charlatan, the defence was able to reply with abundant evidence from satisfied customers, who were delighted with the results achieved by wearing the appliance. As Mr Hannah commented, when dismissing the case:

It was remarkable that although they daily saw some advertisements of quack medicines supposed to cure all sorts of diseases, no action had been taken by the Director of Public Prosecutions against the persons who issued such advertisements. He thought that if he had seen his way clear to get a conviction, the D.P.P. would undoubtedly have intervened in such cases.

Hence he felt justified in refusing to commit for trial. The *Lancet*, in a leader published on 3 February under the headline 'The Immunity of Quackery', gloomily accepted the correctness of the decision, while deploring the state of the law that brought it about. In fact there was a successful prosecution in the same year; one Francis McConville, alias Thomas Kelly, alias King and Company, alias Hamilton, and alias Professor Hamilton, was convicted on 22 March at Liverpool Assizes before the ferocious Day J of obtaining money by false pretences. He was sentenced to five years' penal servitude, and no doubt Day would have had him flogged if the law had permitted this. He ran the Medical Institute, posing falsely as a qualified doctor, and sold an electric belt as a cure for venereal diseases; he had previously been involved in distributing obscene literature.[38] But this case was the exception, and had there been no pretence to medical qualifications it is unlikely that a conviction could have been achieved.

The *Harness* case, besides serving to discourage further attempts to prosecute, also served to illustrate the uneasy line which then separated the world of the quack from that of the legitimate profession, whose members also employed various more or less absurd contraptions, including some designed to administer electrical treatment. A glance through the regular medical press of the period— the *Lancet* and the *British Medical Journal*—reveals a profession much given to the use of ludicrous appliances, such as the Vitalite Sock, the New Flannel

[37] *The Times*, Nov., Dec. 1893, and Jan. 1894.   [38] See (1894) I *The Lancet* 826.

Squeezer, a contraption resembling a large garlic press, the Invigorator Corset, as well as numerous electrical devices, such as The Automatic Medical Battery made by the H. B. Cox Electrical Company, which could be used to apply, at the physician's choice, three levels of shock to the patient. And, as we have seen, one of the directors of the Carbolic Smoke Ball Company (1893) had his New Ozonic Inhaler described and by implication recommended in the *Lancet* in 1890.

But the very narrowness of the dividing line may have served to intensify the vigour with which the struggle against the quacks was pursued, and the orthodox doctors had certain substantial points to make. They, at least as a rule, abstained from making ludicrously inflated claims as to what they could achieve, and for some ailments they did provide either remedies or at least treatment which alleviated the symptoms. They could also argue that some quack medicines were actively harmful, and that resort to quacks could discourage those who could have benefited from scientific medicine from consulting a qualified doctor. During the early years of this century the battle against the quacks intensified, both in America and in Britain. American quacks exhibited a creative genius that could hardly be matched in England. In addition to the smoke ball itself, there were such products as Tiger Fat, Blessed Handkerchiefs, Hamlin's Wizard Oil, and Cram's Fluid Lightning, and the appliances sold included Dr Hercules Sanche's Oxydeno, Electropoise, Oxygenor, Oxypathos, Oxytonor, and Oxybon, alleged to work by the force of diaduction.[39] The generic expression in America for such products is snake oil, but I have not traced a specific reference to such a product. Public criticism of fraudulent claims was heightened by articles published by Edward Bok in the *Ladies Home Journal* in May and July of 1904, and by Samuel H. Adams in *Collier's Weekly* in 1905 and 1906.

The Regulation of the Trade

All this agitation led in the United States to legislation in the form of the Pure Food and Drugs Act of 1906. In Britain similar agitation was expressed in two publications of the British Medical Association, *Secret Remedies* in 1909, and *More Secret Remedies* in 1912. In 1912 the House of Commons appointed a Select Committee, under the chairmanship of Sir Henry Norman. It reported on 4 August 1914, and came out strongly for new legal regulation of the patent medicine industry, which it viewed as little more than licensed fraud. The Norman Committee investigated the existing state of the law, and the conclusion reached was hardly flattering to English jurisprudence:

[39] See S. H. Holbrook, *The Golden Age of Quackery* (New York, 1959); L. Filler, *The Muckrakers: Crusaders for American Liberalism* (Chicago, 1968); J. H. Young, *The Medical Messiahs* (Princeton, 1967); S. H. Adams, *The Great American Fraud* (Boston, 1906).

The situation, therefore, as regards the sale and advertisement of patent and proprietary medicines and articles may be summarized in one sentence as follows. For all practical purposes British law is powerless to prevent any person from procuring any drug, or making any mixture, whether potent or without any therapeutical activity whatever (so long as it does not contain a scheduled poison), advertise it in any decent terms as a cure for any disease or ailment, recommending it by bogus testimonials and the invented opinions and facsimile signatures of fictitious physicians, and selling it under any name he chooses, on the payment of a small stamp duty, for any price he can persuade a credulous public to pay.

The report was a severe judgement on an industry which at the time was spending around £2,000,000 each year on advertising. It was also a severe judgement on the judge-made law, both criminal and civil, and one which led to the conclusion that more direct regulation was the solution. Underlying the report was a belief, not expressly articulated, that state regulation was the only appropriate reaction to the phenomenon in question: the fact that a fool and his money are easily parted. So far as criminal proceedings were concerned, the impotence of the law was explained by the need to prove 'guilty knowledge' and by the fact (which, of course, cut both ways) that quacks could always produce satisfied customers to give evidence on their behalf. As for civil law, it seemed hardly worth discussing, for it was settled that mere advertising puffs could not be treated as actionable warranties. But Cyril Herbert Kirby, a solicitor employed by the Chemists' Defence Union, seemed to think that there could, in theory at least, be civil liability under section 14(1) of the Sale of Goods Act of 1893, though he could recall only one case which had come to court. The risk of the occasional civil action, normally limited to the recovery of the price paid, could not, of course, have any substantial influence upon the conduct of a trade which could readily discount the risks involved. Kirby did, however, sing the praises of *Carlill* v. *Carbolic Smoke Ball Company*: 'this decision might be useful in the case of medicines advertised as definite cures for certain ailments: it would only apply to a suit by the person injured.' The chairman, surely sceptically, asked: 'are there any other cases to illustrate that point?' And Kirby replied: 'no, I do not know of any case parallel to that, but that has always been treated as a good binding authority.'

That, so far as the Beechams of the world were concerned, was about all it was, and a good binding authority it has remained to this day. Occasionally thereafter an advertiser did, like Frederick Roe, make a specific promise of a reward, as did Elmer Shirley of 6 St James Street in the *Daily Mail* for 5 July 1912. He claimed to be able to cure catarrh and deafness and offered to pay £500 if he failed. Shirley was, in fact, an alias for an individual whose real name was Marr; he was also known as Professor Keith Harvey, and Erasmus Coleman. At one time he had the distinction of employing the celebrated murderer, Hawley Harvey Crippen, alias M. Frankel, whom the English like to claim as one of us, though in reality he was an American. He is the only murderer, so far as I know, who on arrest replied with a metrical line: 'My name is Hawley Harvey Crippen and I come from Coldwater, Michigan, USA.'. Beverley Cross exploited this in writing the lyrics for the short-lived musical comedy *Belle*, in which a song continues:

> And I wish that I was on my way,
> To Coldwater, Michigan,
> USA.

Crippen was one of the few quacks who did lose out in a conflict with the law, for reasons not directly related to his trade, though one theory explains the death of his wife, Belle, as the result of an accidental over-use of hyoscine as a sexual depressant, intended to enable Hawley to concentrate his flagging energies on Miss Ethel Le Neve.

As for the Norman Report, the outbreak of the First World War overtook it, and, as has so often happened to such reports, it accumulated dust for many years. Apart from legislation in 1917 to curb advertisements of cures for venereal diseases, it was not until the later 1930s that any further action took place to curb the trade. Occasionally, however, an advertiser did burn his fingers by forgetting the case of the smoke ball. Thus, in 1932, in *Wood* v. *Letrick Ltd.* the plaintiff recovered £500 against the manufacturers of the Letrik electric comb on facts very similar to the earlier case. Through an advertising agency the combs, of which some 100,000 had been sold at a price of 3*s*. 6*d*., had been advertised in a periodical in the following terms:

New Hair in 72 hours. 'Letrik' Electric Comb.
Great News for Hair Sufferers. What is *your* trouble?
Is it grey hair? In 10 days not a grey hair left. £500 guarantee.
Is it a bald patch? Covered with new hair in 72 hours. £500 guarantee.

The advertisement continued in similar vein to deal with falling hair, dandruff, and straight and lifeless hair, and claimed that 661,000 combs had been sold to all grades in society from royalty downward. The defendant's counsel attempted to argue that the promises were impossible and therefore void at law, but Rowlatt J was unimpressed and awarded the sum claimed, relying upon the smoke ball case. Five other claims were then pending and were presumably paid. But this was an isolated incident, and prudent copywriters could easily continue to deceive the public while keeping clear of the law. So, although Mrs Carlill's action has undoubtedly made a permanent contribution to legal dogmatics, it has caused only an insignificant amount of inconvenience to the likes of Frederick Augustus Roe.

Epilogue

And as for Louisa Elizabeth Carlill herself, she long survived her adventure with the law. After her husband died on 6 October 1930, she lived in a flat in Blackheath, but by 1939 she was established in a hotel on the south coast, probably in Hastings, where she was renowned for her punctuality and her settled practice of drinking one glass of claret with her lunch. She then went to live with her daughter, Dorothy Brousson, at Swan House, in the village of Sellindge, near Folkestone, a lively spot to choose at the time of the Battle of Britain. There she died on 10 March 1942, at the age of 96, principally, as her death certificate records, of old age.

The other cause noted by her medical man, Dr Joseph M. Yarman, was influenza.

Bibliography

ACKERMAN, R., *Repository of Arts, Literature, Commerce, Manufactures Fashions and Politics*, London, 1809–28.

ADAMS, S. H., *The Great American Fraud*, Boston, 1906.

ALLEN, T., *The History of the County of Lincoln from the Earliest Period to the Present Time* (2 vols.), London, 1834.

AMERICAN MEDICAL ASSOCIATION, *Nostrums and Quackery. Articles on the Nostrum Evil and Quackery reprinted with additions and modifications from the Journal of the American Medical Association* (2nd ed.), Chicago, 1912.

AMES, J. B., *A Selection of Cases on the Law of Torts* (Vol. I), Cambridge, Mass., 1893.

—— 'Law and Morals' (1908) 22 *HLR* 97.

AMEY, G., *The Collapse of the Dale Dyke Dam, 1864*, London, 1974.

ANON, *News from Doctors Commons: or, a true account of Mr Hickeringill's appearance there, June 8 1681 Upon a Citation for Marrying People without Bannes of License*, London, 1681.

—— (probably J. Worrall), *The Reports of Sir Edward Coke, knt., in Verse etc.*, London, 1742.

ANSON, W., *Principles of the English Law of Contract*, Oxford, 1879.

ARNDT, H. W., 'The Origins of Dicey's Concept of the "Rule of Law"' (1957) 31 *Australian LJ* 117.

ARNOLD, R. A., *The History of the Cotton Famine*, London, 1864 and 1865.

ATIYAH, P. S., *The Rise and Fall of Freedom of Contract*, Oxford, 1979.

ATKINSON, S., *Theory and Practice of Conveyancing, Comprising the Law of Real Property* (2 vols.), London, 1829.

BAINES, E., *History, Directory and Gazatteer of the County Palatine of Lancaster* (2 vols.), Liverpool, 1824–25, facsimile edition Newton Abbott, 1968.

—— *The History of the County Palatine and Duchy of Lancaster*, ed. J. Croston (5 vols.), Manchester, 1888–93.

BAKER, J. H., *The Reports of Sir John Spelman*, Publications of the Selden Society, Vol. 93, London, 1977.

—— *An Introduction to English Legal History* (3rd ed.), London, 1990.

—— and MILSOM, S. F. C., *Sources of English Legal History. Private Law to 1750*, London, 1986.

BARKER, T. C. and HARRIS, J. R., *A Merseyside Town in the Industrial Revolution. St Helen's, 1750–1900*, London, 1959.

BARTRIP, P. W. J. and BURMAN, S. B., *The Wounded Soldiers of Industry. Industrial Compensation Policy 1833–1897*, Oxford, 1983.

BECKER, D., *Perpetuities and Estate Planning*, Boston, 1992.

BEER, E. S. DE (ed.), *The Diary of John Evelyn* (2 vols.), Oxford, 1955.

BELCHER, W. D., *Kentish Brasses* (2 vols.), London, 1888.

BELL, H. E., *An Introduction to the History and Records of the Court of Wards and Liveries*, Cambridge, 1953.

BENJAMIN, J. P., *A Treatise on the Law of Sale of Personal Property. With Reference to the American Decisions and to the French Code and Civil Law*, London, 1868 (1st American edition by J. Perkins, 1875).

BERESFORD, W. (ed.), *Memorials of Old Staffordshire*, London, 1909.

BERESFORD, R. C., 'The Sprightly Septuagenerian', in W. Barton Leach, *Cases and Texts on Future Interests and Estate Planning*, Brooklyn, 1961.

BERRY, W., *County Genealogies. Pedigrees of the County of Sussex*, London, 1830.

BEWICK, T., *A History of British Birds* (2 vols.), London, 1797 and 1804.

BINNIE, G. M., *Early Victorian Water Engineers*, London, 1981.

BIRD, J. B., *The Laws Respecting Masters and Servants: Articled Clerks, Apprentices, Journeymen and Manufacturers*, London, 1795.

BLACKSTONE, W., *Commentaries on the Laws of England* (4 vols.), London, 1765–9.

BLOME, R., *The Gentleman's Recreation*, London, 1686.

BOASE, F., *Modern English Biography* (6 vols.), Truro, 1892–1921.

BOHLEN, F. H., 'The Rule in *Rylands* v. *Fletcher*' (1910–11) 59 *U Pa. LR.* 298, 373, 423, reprinted in his *Studies in the Law of Torts*.

—— *Studies in the Law of Torts*, Indianapolis, 1926.

BOTT, E., *A Collection of Decisions of the Court of King's Bench Upon the Poor's Laws Down to the Present Time* (2nd ed.), London, 1773.

BOWLEY, M. E. A., *Nassau Senior and Classical Economics*, London, 1937.

BOWRING, E. A., and LORD HOBART, *Free Trade and its so called Sophisms; a reply to 'Sophisms of Free Trade etc. examined by a barrister'* (2nd ed.), London, 1850.

BRADLEY, R., *A General Treatise of Husbandry and Gardening* (2 vols.), London, 1726.

BRAMWELL, G. W., *Self-Help v. State-Help. The Liberty and Property Defence League. Its Origin, Objects and Inaugural Meeting*, Pamphlet, London, 1882.

—— *Lord Bramwell on Liberty and Other Speeches Delivered at the General Meeting of the Liberty and Property Defence League 1882*, Pamphlet, London, 1883.

—— *Laisser Faire*, Pamphlet, London, 1884.

—— *Letter from Lord Justice Bramwell to Sir Henry Jackson Bart. Q.C. M.P.*, Pamphlet, no date.

BRENNER, J. F., 'Nuisance Law and the Industrial Revolution' (1974) 3 *JLS* 403.

BRERETON, W., *Travels in Holland The United Provinces England Scotland and Ireland*, ed. E. Hawkins for the Chetham Society, London, 1844.

BRITISH PARLIAMENTARY PAPERS, *Eighth Report of Poor Law Commissioners*, BPP [389] XIX, 1, 1842.

—— *Third Report of Select Committee on Medical Relief* (531) IX, 93, 1844.

—— *Second Report of the Poor Law Commission*, BPP (595) XXIX, Pt. I.I, 376.

BROOKE, R., *La Graunde Abridgement* (2nd ed.), London, 1576.

BRUNDAGE, A., *The Making of the New Poor Law: The Politics of Inquiry, Enactment and Implementation, 1832–39*, London, 1978.

BULLER, F., *An Introduction to the Law relating to Trials at Nisi Prius*, London, 1790.

BURDICK, F. M., 'Is Law the Expression of Class Selfishness' (1911) 25 *HLR* 349.

BURKE, J. B., *A Visitation of Seats and Arms of the Noblemen and Gentlemen of Great Britain*, London, 1852.

—— *A Genealogical and Heraldic History of the Peerage and Baronetage etc.*, London, 1861 (and numerous other editions, titles varying).

BURKE, B., *The General Armory of England, Scotland and Ireland*, London, 1884.

BURN, R. (ed. G. Chetwynd), *The Justice of the Peace and Parish Officer* (5 vols.), London, 1830.

BURNABY, F. G., *A Ride to Khiva*, London, 1972.

BURROW, J., *A Series of the Decisions of the Court of King's Bench upon Settlement-Cases* (3 vols.), London, 1768–76.

BURTON, W. H., *Elementary Compendium of the Law of Real Property*, London, 1828.

BUTLER, P., *Judah P. Benjamin*, Philadelphia, 1907.

BYLES, J. B., *Observations on the Usury Laws and on the Effect of the Recent Alterations etc.*, London, 1845.

—— ('A Barrister'), *Sophisms of Free Trade and Popular Political Economy Examined*, London, 1849.

—— *Foundations of Religion in the Heart and Mind of Man*, London, 1875.

CALDECOTT, T., *Reports of Cases [of Settlement] Relative to the Duty and Office of a Justice of the Peace 1776–1785* (3 parts in one vol.), London, 1786.

CANE, P., and STAPLETON, J. (eds.), *Essays for Patrick Atiyah*, Oxford, 1991.

CARTWRIGHT, E., *The Parochial Topography of the Rape of Bramber in the Western Division of Sussex*, London, 1830.

CHALLONER, R. (ed. J. H. Pollen), *Memoirs of Missionary Priests*, London, 1924.

CHANDLER, G., *Liverpool*, London, 1957.

CHECKLAND, S. G., and E. O. A. (eds.), *Poor Law Report 1834*, London, 1974.

CLIFFORD, F., *A History of Private Bill Legislation* (2 vols.), London, 1885 and 1887.

COASE, R. H., *The Firm, the Market and the Law*, Chicago, 1988.

—— 'The Nature of the Firm', *Economica* NS 4 (November 1937), reprinted in *The Firm, the Market and the Law*, Ch. 2.

—— 'The Problem of Social Cost' (1960) 3 *The Journal of Law and Economics* 1, reprinted in *The Firm, the Market and the Law*, Ch. 5.

COCKBURN, J. S., *Calendar of Assize Records. Sussex Indictments Elizabeth*, London, 1975.

—— *Calendar of Assize Records. Essex Indictments Elizabeth*, London, 1978.

—— *Calendar of Assize Records. Kent Indictments Elizabeth*, London, 1979.

COCKS, R., *Foundations of the Modern Bar*, London, 1983.

COHEN, M. (ed.), *Ronald Dworkin and Contemporary Jurisprudence*, London, 1984.

COKE, E., *The First Part of the Institutes of the Laws of England, or, a Commentary upon Littleton etc.* (15th ed.) 1794 (normally cited as *Co. Litt.*, numerous editions, pagination standardized).

CONSTABLE, M., *The Law of the Other*, Chicago, 1993.

COOK, T., and PILCHER, R. E. M., *The History of the Borough Fen Decoy*, Ely, 1982.

COSTELLO, J., *Mask of Treachery*, London, 1988.

COWARD, T. A., and OLDHAM, C., *Birds of Cheshire*, Manchester, 1900.

COX, J., 'Sources for Maritime History', 2 *Maritime History* 168.

CRUISE, W., *Digest of the Laws of England Respecting Real Property* (7 vols.), London, 1818.

DALLAWAY, J., *A History of the Western Division of the County of Sussex etc.* (2 vols.), London, 1815–32.

DALTON, M., *The Countrey Justice. The Practice of the Justices of the Peace out of the Sessions* (5th ed.), London, 1635.

DANIEL, W. B., *Rural Sports* (2 vols.), London, 1802.

DAWES, M., *Law on Real Estates, and of Remainders Therein Expressed, Implied and Contingent*, London, 1814.

DEFOE, D., *A Tour thro' the Whole Island of Great Britain: Divided into Circuits or Journeys* (4 vols., 3rd ed.), London, 1742.

DICEY, A. V., *Law of the Constitution*, London, 1885 (1952 ed. by E. C. S. Wade).

Dictionary of National Biography, (current), Oxford, 1917.

DIGGLE, G. E., *A History of Widnes*, Widnes, 1961.

DONNELL, E. J., *Chronological and Statistical History of Cotton*, New York, 1872.

DOWNES, K. (ed.), *The Architectural Outsiders*, London, 1985.

DUCKHAM, H., and DUCKHAM, B., *Great Pit Disasters*, Newton Abbott, 1973.

DUTTON, G., *The Hero as Murderer: The Life of Edward John Eyre*, London, 1986.

DWORKIN, R., *A Matter of Principle*, Cambridge, Mass., 1985.

—— *Law's Empire*, London, 1986.

DYKHUINEN, S., *Endenkooien*, Terra, Lutfen, 1980.

EARWAKER, J. P., *East Cheshire Past and Present, or, a History of the Hundred of Macclesfield in the County Palatine of Chester* (2 vols.), London, 1877 and 1880.

EDEN, F. M., *The State of the Poor, or, A History of the Labouring Classes in England from the Conquest to the Present Period* (3 vols.), London, 1797.

ELLISON, T., *The Cotton Trade of Great Britain, including a History of the Liverpool Cotton Market*, Liverpool, 1886.

ELWES, D. G. C., *A History of the Castles, Mansions and Manors of Western Sussex*, London, 1876.

Encyclopaedia Brittanica; a Dictionary of Arts, Sciences etc. (11th ed.), New York, 1910–11.

EPSTEIN, R. A., 'The Historical Origins and Economic Structure of Workers' Compensation Law' (1982) 16 *Georgia LR* 775.

EVANS, E., *Judah Benjamin. The Jewish Confederate*, New York, 1988.

Extracts from the Information Received by Her Majesty's Commissioners as to the Administration and Operation of the Poor Law, London, 1833.

FAIRFIELD, C., *Some Account of George William Wilshere, Baron Bramwell of Hever, and his Opinions*, London, 1898.

FARNIE, D. A., *The English Cotton Industry and the World Market 1815–1896*, Oxford, 1979.

—— *John Rylands of Manchester*, Manchester, 1993.

FEARNE, C., *An Essay on the Learning of Contingent Remainders*, London, 1772.

FIFOOT, C. H. S., *Judge and Jurist in the Reign of Victoria*, London, 1959.

FILLER, L., *The Muckrakers: Crusaders for American Liberalism*, Chicago, 1968.

FINCH, G. B., *A Selection of Cases on the English Law of Contract*, Cambridge, 1886 (2nd ed. by R. T. Wright and W. W. Buckland, 1896).

FINER, S. E., *The Life and Times of Sir Edwin Chadwick*, London, 1980.

FITZHERBERT, A., *The New Natura Brevium of the Most Reverend Judge Mr Anthony Fitzherbert*, London, 1677 (many other editions, method of reference standardized).

FOLKARD, H. C., *The Wildfowler. A Treatise on Fowling, Ancient and Modern. Descriptive Also of Decoys and Flight Ponds* (4th ed.), London, 1897.

FULTON, T. W., *The Sovereignty of the Sea; an Historical Account of the Claims of the English to the Dominion of the British Seas, and of the evolution of Territorial Waters; with Special Reference to the Right of Fishing and the Naval Salute*, Edinburgh, 1911.

FRIDMAN, G. H. L., 'The Rise and Fall of *Rylands* v. *Fletcher*' (1956) 34 *Can. Bar Rev.* 810, with correspondence at 1225.

GALE, C. J., and WHATELY, T. D., *A Treatise on the Law of Easements*, London, 1839.

GIBBS, V. (ed. G. E. Cockayne), *The Complete Peerage of England, Scotland, Ireland, Great Britain and the United Kingdom* (8 vols.), London, 1887–98.

GILBERT, M., *The Oxford Book of Legal Anecdotes*, Oxford, 1986.

GOLD, J., 'Common Employment' (1937) 1 *MLR* 224.

GOLDSMID, F. J., *Telegraph and Travel: A Narrative of the Formation and Development of Telegraphic Communication between England and India*, London, 1874.

GOLDSMITH, O., *A History of the Earth and Animated Nature* (2 vols.), Edinburgh, 1840.

GOSDEN, P. H. J. H., *The Friendly Societies in England, 1815–1875*, Manchester, 1961.

GRAY, J. C., *The Rule Against Perpetuities*, Boston, Mass., 1886.

GRIFFITH, J. A. G., *The Politics of the Judiciary* (4th ed.), London, 1991.

HARE, J. I. C. CLARK, and WALLACE, H. B., *American Leading Cases*, Philadelphia, 1847.

HARRISON, S., *A Complete History of the Great Flood at Sheffield*, Sheffield, 1864.

HEARN, W. E., *The Government of England, Its Structure and Its Development*, London, 1867.

HEIDE, G. D., VAN DER, and LEBRET, T., *Achter de Schermen* [*Behind the Screens*], Kinheim-Uitgeverij, Heiloo, 1944.

HENDERSON, W. O., *The Lancashire Cotton Famine*, Manchester, 1934.

HEUSTON, R. F. V., 'Who Was the Third Lord in *Rylands* v. *Fletcher?*' (1970) 86 *LQR* 160.

HICKERINGILL, E., *Jamaica Viewed: with all the Ports, Harbours, and their several soundings, Towns . . . etc.*, London, 1661.

—— *Curse ye Meroz, or the Fatal Doom. In a Sermon preached . . . before the Lord Mayor etc.* London, 1680.

—— *The Late Famous Tryal of Mr Hickeringill . . . Author of the Naked Truth*, London, 1681.

—— *Scandalum Magnatum: or, the Great Trial at Chelmsford Assizes. Held March 6, for the County of Essex. Betwixt Henry Bishop of London, Plaintiff, and Edm. Hickeringill, Rector of the Rectory of All Saints Colchester defendant . . . To-gether with the note of the Writ called Supplicavit etc . . .* , London, 1682.

—— *The Ceremony Monger. His Character in Five Chapters. With some Remarks upon the New Star-Chamber, or late Course of the Court of King's Bench*, London, 1689.

—— *A Burlesque Poem in Praise of Ignorance*, London, 1708.

HODDER, E., *The Life and Times of the Seventh Earl of Shaftesbury K.G.* (3 vols.), London, 1886.

HOLBROOK, S. H., *The Golden Age of Quackery*, New York, 1959.

HOLDSWORTH, W. S., *A History of English Law* (16 vols.), London, 1922–66.

HOLLAND, T. E., *The Elements of Jurisprudence*, Oxford, 1880 (2nd ed., 1882; 3rd ed. 1886; 4th ed. 1887).

HOLMES, O. W., *The Common Law*, Boston, Mass., 1881.

—— *Collected Legal Papers*, New York, 1920.

HOPKINS, G. M., 'The Wreck of the Deutschland', *The Poems of Gerard Manley Hopkins* (ed. W. H. Gardiner and N. H. Mackenzie), London, 1967.

HORSFIELD, T. W., *The History, Antiquities and Topography of the County of Sussex* (2 vols.), Lewes, 1835.

298 *Bibliography*

HOWE, M. DE W., *Justice Oliver Holmes: The Proving Years 1870–1882*, Cambridge, Mass., 1963.

HOWELLS, R. J., '*Priestley* v. *Fowler* and the Factory Acts' (1963) 26 *MLR* 367.

HUGHES, T., *Tom Brown's Schooldays*, London, 1857.

HUGILL, S., *Shanties of the Seven Seas*, Oxford, 1966.

HURSTFIELD, J., *The Queen's Wards. Wardship and Marriage under Elizabeth I*, London, 1973.

HYDE, H. MONTGOMERY, *The Cleveland Street Scandal*, London, 1976.

HYLAND, ST G. K., *A Century of Persecution Under Tudor and Stuart Sovereigns from Contemporary Records*, London, 1920.

INGHAM, T., 'The Rise and Fall of the Doctrine of Common Employment' [1978] *Juridical Review* 106.

JAMESON, E., *The Natural History of Quackery*, London, 1961.

JOHNSON, P., *The Oxford Book of British Political Anecdotes*, Oxford, 1989.

JONSEN, A. R., and TOULMIN, S., *The Abuse of Casuistry: A History of Moral Reasoning*, Cambridge, 1988.

KENNY, C. S., *A Selection of Cases Illustrative of the Law of Contract*, Cambridge, 1922.

KIEVE, J., *The Electric Telegraph: A Social and Economic History*, Newton Abbott, 1973.

KINNEY, A. F., *Elizabethan Backgrounds*, Hampden, Conn., 1975.

KITCH, E. W., 'The Fire of Truth: A Reminiscence of Law and Economics at Chicago 1932–1970', XXVI *JLE* 163.

KOSTAL, R. W., *Law and English Railway Capitalism 1825–1875*, Oxford, 1994.

KUSSMAUL, A., *Servants in Husbandry in Early Modern England*, Cambridge, 1981.

LANGDELL, C. C., *A Selection of Cases on the Law of Contracts*, Boston, 1871 (2nd ed., including a summary of the Law of Contract, 1879).

LEACH, W. B., 'The Rule against Perpetuities and Gifts to Classes' (1938) 51 *HLR* 1329.

—— *Cases and Materials on the Law of Future Interests*, Chicago, 1935 (2nd ed., 1940).

—— *Cases and Text on the Law of Wills*, Boston, Mass., 1947.

—— and LOGAN, J. K., *Cases and Text on Future Interests and Estate Planning*, Brooklyn, 1961.

LEITES, E. (ed.), *Conscience and Casuistry in Early Modern Europe*, Cambridge, 1988.

LEONI, G., *The Architecture of A. Palladio, Revis'd, Design'd and Publish'd by Giacomo Leoni, A Venetian, Architect to His Most Serene Highness the Elector Palatine* (2 vols.), London, 1716, 1720.

LEWIN, G., *A Summary of the Laws Relating to the Government and Maintenance of the Poor*, London, 1828.

LEWIS, W. D., *A Practical Treatise on the Law of Perpetuities*, London, 1843.

LEWIS, G., *Lord Atkin*, London, 1983.

LITTLETON, T., *Tenures*, London, 1481 (many later editions).

LOWER, M. A., *The Worthies of Sussex: Biographical Sketches of the Most Eminent Natives or Inhabitants of the County . . . etc.*, Lewes, 1865.

—— *A Compendious History of Sussex Topographical, Archaeological and Anecdotal* (2 vols.), Lewes, 1870.

LUBBOCK, R., *Fauna of Norfolk*, London, 1879.

McCULLOCH, J. R., *Principles of Political Economy with Some Inquiries Respecting their Application and a Sketch of the Rise and Progress of that Science*, Edinburgh, 1849.

McCULLOUGH, D. G., *The Johnstown Flood*, London, 1968.

McLAREN, J. P. S., 'Nuisance Law and the Industrial Revolution—Some Lessons from Social History' (1983) 3 *OJLS* 155.

MACLEAN, F., *A Person from England and Other Travellers*, London, 1958.

McLEOD, R. M., 'The Alkali Acts Administration 1863–4: the Emergence of the Civil Scientist' (1965) 9 *Victorian Studies* 85.

MARKHAM, S., *John Loveday of Caversham 1711–1789. The Life and Tours of an Eighteenth Century Onlooker*, Salisbury, 1984.

MARSHALL, D., *The English Poor in the Eighteenth Century*, London, 1926.

MARSTON, G., 'The Centenary of the *Franconia* Case—the Prosecution of Ferdinand Keyn' (1976) 92 *LQR* 93.

—— *The Marginal Seabed. United Kingdom Legal Practice*, Oxford, 1981.

MAST, G., 'Endenkooien op de waddeneilanden' [Duck Decoys of the West Frisian Islands], (1992) *Wadden Bulletin* 132.

MEADE R. D., *Judah P. Benjamin, Confederate Statesman*, New York, 1943.

MOLLOY, R. T., '*Fletcher* v. *Rylands*—A Reexamination of Juristic Origins', (1942) 9 *U Chi. LR* 266.

MONTAGNE, P. (ed. R. J. Courtine), *Nouveau Larousse Gastronomique*, Paris, 1967.

MORANT, P., *The History and Antiquities of the . . . Town and Borough of Colchester in the County of Essex*, London, 1748.

—— *History and Antiquities of the County of Essex* (2 vols.), London, 1768.

MORRIS, J. H. C., and LEACH, W. B., *The Rule against Perpetuities* (2nd ed.), London, 1962.

MOSS, H. R., *The Monumental Effigies of Sussex*, Hove, 1933.

MOUSLEY, J. E., *Sussex Country Gentry in the Reign of Elizabeth* (London Ph.D thesis 1955).

Muniments of the Corporation of the City of Salisbury, Historical Manuscripts Commission, Dublin, 1907.

NEALE, J. P., *Views of the Seats of Noblemen and Gentlemen* (2nd. Ser., 5 vols.), London, 1824–9.

NEWARK, F. H., 'Non-natural User and *Rylands* v. *Fletcher*' (1961) 24 *MLR* 557.

NIMROD (pseudonym for Charles James Apperley), *Memoirs of the Life of the late John Mytton Esq. of Halston, Shropshire etc.*, London, 1835.

NOLAN, M., *A Treatise on the Laws of Relief and Settlement of the Poor* (2 vols.), London, 1805.

OGILBY, J., *The Fables of Aesop Paraphras'd in Verse*, London, 1665.

OLDHAM, J., *The Mansfield Manuscripts and the Growth of English Law in the Eighteenth Century*, London, 1992.

ORMEROD, G., *The History of the County Palatime and City of Chester* (2 vols., 2nd ed.), London, 1882.

PALMER, R., *The Oxford Book of Sea Songs*, Oxford, 1986.

PALMER, R. C., *English Law in the Age of the Black Death 1348–1381; a Transformation of Governance and Law*, Chapel Hill, N. Carolina, 1993.

PARKHURST, P. G., *Ships of Peace: A Record of Some of the Problems which came before the Board of Trade in connection with the British Mercantile Marine, from early days to the year 1885 compiled from official records*, Vol. I, New Malden, 1962 (Vol. II was never published).

PAYNE-GALLWEY, R. W. F., *The Fowler in Ireland, or Notes on the Haunts and Habits of wildfowl and seafowl including Instructions in the Art of Shooting and Capturing them*, London, 1882.

—— *The Book of Duck Decoys. Their Construction, Management and History*, London, 1886.

—— *Letters to Young Shooters*, 1st series, London, 1890; 2nd Series, London, 1894; 3rd Series, London, 1896.

—— *Crossbows, Medieval and Modern, Military and Sporting . . . with a Treatise on the Balista and Catapult of the Ancients*, London, 1903.

—— *The Mystery of Maria Stella, Lady Newborough*, London, 1907.

—— *A Summary of the History, Construction and Effects of the Projectile Throwing Engines of the Ancients with a Treatise . . . etc.*, London, 1907.

—— *The History of the George worn on the Scaffold by Charles I*, London, 1908.

—— *The Pedigree of Frankland of Thirkelby*, London, 1910.

—— *High Pheasants in Theory and Practice*, London, 1913.

—— *The War: a Criticism*, London, 1915.

PELLEW, J., 'The Home Office and the Explosives Act of 1875', (1974) 18 *Victorian Studies* 175–94.

—— *The Home Office 1848–1914: From Clerks to Bureaucrats*, London, 1982.

PENNANT, T., *British Zoology*, London, 1812.

PEVSNER, N., *The Buildings of England. Staffordshire*, London, 1974.

PIGOU, A. C., *Wealth and Welfare*, London, 1912.

—— *The Economics of Welfare*, London, 1920, 1924, 1929, 1952.

—— *Economics in Practice. Six Lectures on Current Issues*, London, 1935.

Political Economy Club. Minutes of Proceedings 1899–1920, Roll of Members and Questions Discussed, London, 1921.

POLLOCK, F., *Principles of Contract at Law and in Equity*, London, 1876.

—— *The Law of Torts*, London, 1887.

POUND, R., 'The Economic Interpretation and the Law of Torts' (1940) 53 *HLR* 365.

—— *Interpretations of Legal History*, Cambridge, Mass., 1946.

POWELL, G. M., *Guide to St Mary's Church Thakeham*, Pamphlet, Brighton, no date.

PRICHARD, M. J., 'Nonsuit: A Premature Obituary' [1960] *CLJ* 88.

Publications of the Catholic Record Society, Vol. 1 (current), London, 1905– .

RANDELL, H., *An Essay on the Law of Perpetuities and on Trusts of Accumulation*, London, 1822.

READE, C., *Put Yourself in His Place*, London, 1870.

—— *Mr Secretary Walsyngham and the Policy of Queen Elizabeth* (3 vols.), Oxford, 1925.

READE, A. L., *The Audley Pedigrees*, privately printed, London, 1929–36.

REPTON, H. (ed. J. C. Loudon), *The Landscape Gardening and the Landscape Architecture of the late Humphrey Repton Esq.*, London, 1840.

ROBERTSON, J. M., *A Guide to the Country Houses of the North West*, London, 1991.

RYDZ, D. L., *The Parliamentary Agents: A History*, London, 1979.

RYE, W., *Norfolk Families*, Norwich, 1913.

SAMPSON, H., *A History of Advertising from the Earliest Times*, London, 1874.

SAVIGNY, F. K., VON, *System des Heutigen Romischen Rechts*, Berlin, 1840–9.

SEMMEL, B., *Jamaican Blood and the Victorian Conscience: the Governor Eyre Controversy*, Boston, 1963.

SIMPSON, A. W. B., 'Legal Liability for Bursting Reservoirs: The Historical Context of *Rylands* v. *Fletcher*' (1984) 13 *JLS* 209.

—— *A History of the Land Law*, Oxford, 1986.

—— *A History of the Common Law of Contract. The Rise of the Action of Assumpsit*, Oxford, 1987.

—— *Legal Theory and Legal History. Essays on the Common Law*, London, 1987.

—— 'Contracts for Cotton to Arrive: The Case of the Two Ships *Peerless*', (1989) 11 *Cardozo LR* 287.

—— 'Legal Iconoclasts and Legal Ideals' (1990) 58 *Univ. Cincinnati LR* 819.

—— *In the Highest Degree Odious. Detention without Trial in Wartime Britain*, Oxford, 1992, revised ed. 1994.

—— *Cannibalism and the Common Law. A Victorian Yachting Tragedy*, London, 1994.

SMITH, J. W., *A Compendium of Mercantile Law*, London, 1834.

—— *Leading Cases in Various Branches of the Law* (2 vols.), London, 1835 and 1840.

SMITH, N., *A History of Dams*, London, 1971.

SMITH, R., *Trial by Medicine: Insanity and Responsibility in Victorian Trials*, Edinburgh, 1981.

SOUTHWELL, T., 'Norfolk Decoys', *Transactions of the Norwich and Norfolk Naturalists Society*, Vol. II (1874–9), 538.

SOUTHWELL, T., 'Wild-Fowl Driving in the Sixteenth Century', *Transactions of the Norwich and Norfolk Naturalists Society*, Vol. VII (1899–1904), 90.

SPEED, J., *The Theatre of the Empire of Great Britaine*, London, 1611.

SPELMAN, H., *The English Works of Sir Henry Spelman . . . etc.*, London, 1723 (this includes *Icenia sive Norfolciae Descriptio Topographia*).

SPIKE, E., *The Law of Master and Servant As Established by Decisions of the Courts at Westminster In Regard to Domestic Servants and Clerks*, London, 1839.

SPRIGGE, S. S., *Life and Times of Thos. Wakley*, London, 1897.

SPRING, E., *Law, Land and Family*, London, 1994.

STEER, F. W., *Guide to the Church of the Holy Sepulchre Warminghurst. Sussex Churches No. 22*, pamphlet, Chichester, 1960.

STEPHEN, H. J., *A Treatise on the Principles of Pleading in Civil Actions*, London, 1866.

STUKELEY, W., *Itinerarium Curiosum or, an Account of the Antiquitys . . . etc.*, London, 1724.

SUGDEN, E. B., *A Practical Treatise of Powers*, London, 1821.

TAYLOR, W., *Analysis of Evidence before the Sheffield Jury on the Cause of the Failure of the Bradfield Reservoir*, Sheffield, 1864.

THOMPSON, E. P., *Whigs and Hunters. The Origin of the Black Act*, New York, 1975.

THOMPSON, T., *Annals of Influenza or Epidemic Catarrhal Fever in Great Britain from 1510–1837*, London, 1852.

THURSTON, G., *The Great Thames Disaster*, London, 1965.

TODD, J., *The Marketing of Cotton*, London, 1934.

TRIMBLE, W. R., *The Catholic Laity in Elizabethan England 1558–1603*, Cambridge, Mass., 1964.

TURNER, E. S., *The Shocking History of Advertising*, London, 1952.

TURNER, J., *The Dolphin's Skin*, London, 1956.

TWYCROSS, E., *The Mansions of England and Wales* (6 vols.), London, 1848–50.

TYRRELL, J., *Suggestions Sent to the Commissioners Appointed to Inquire into the Laws of Real Property*, London, 1829.

VINER, C., *General Abridgement of Law and Equity* (23 vols.), London, 1741–53.

WALKER, N., *Crime and Insanity in England*, Vol. I, Edinburgh, 1968.

WARREN, S., *A Popular and Practical Introduction to Law Studies*, London, 1835.

WARREN, S., *Miscellaneous Critical, Imaginative and Juridical Contributions to Blackwood's Magazine* (2 vols.), London, 1855.

WATTS, J., *The Facts of the Cotton Famine*, Manchester, 1866.

WATTS, C. and M., 'Unravelling Merchant Seamens' Records' (1979) 19 *Genealogists Magazine* 313.

WEBB, E. A., MILLER, G. W., and BECKWITH, J., *The History of Chislehurst, its Church, Manors and Parish*, London, 1899.

WENTWORTH DAY, J., *Coastal Adventure*, London, 1949.

—— *A History of the Fens*, London, 1954.

WHEATLEY, H. B., *The Diary of John Evelyn*, London, 1906.

WHITAKER, J., *British Duck Decoys of To-day*, London, 1918.

WHITE, W., *Directory of Lincolnshire and Hull*, Sheffield, 1826.

—— *The History and Directory of . . . the County of Lincolnshire*, Sheffield, 1842 and 1856; facsmimile ed. of the 1856 ed., Newton Abbott, 1969.

WHITE, F. T., and TUDOR, O. D., *A Selection of Leading Cases in Equity*, London, 1847.

WIENER, M. J., *Reconstructing the Criminal. Culture Law, and Policy, 1830–1914*, Cambridge, 1990.

WILLIAMS, M., *Seven Years History of the Cotton Trade*, Liverpool, 1868.

WILLIAMS, O., *The Historical Development of Private Bill Procedure and Standing Orders in the House of Commons* (1948), 107–11.

WILLIAMSON, O. E., and WINTER, S. G. (eds.), *The Nature of the Firm. Origins, Evolution and Development*, Oxford, 1993.

WILLUGHBY, F. (trans. J. Ray), *The Ornithology of Francis Willughby of Middlelton in the County of Warwick Esquire . . . etc.*, London, 1678.

WRIGHT, T., *History and Topography of the County of Essex comprising its Ancient and Modern History . . . etc.* (2 vols.), London, 1831 and 1835.

WYATT, H. R. P., *Fragments of Findon*, Worthing, 1926.

YOUNG, J. H., *The Medical Messiahs*, Princeton, 1967.

Index